PERSPECTIVES ON INSTRUCTIONAL TIME

Research on Teaching Monograph Series

PUBLISHED TITLES

JERE E. BROPHY AND CAROLYN M. EVERTSON,
    Student Characteristics and Teaching
SUSAN URMSTON PHILIPS, *The Invisible Culture:*
    Communication in Classroom and Community on
    the Warm Springs Indian Reservation
HARRIS M. COOPER AND THOMAS L. GOOD *Pygmalion Grows*
    Up: Studies in the Expectation Communication Process
THOMAS L. GOOD, DOUGLAS GROUWS, AND HOWARD
    EBMEIER, *Active Mathematics Teaching*
ROBERT E. SLAVIN, *Cooperative Learning*
LEONARD S. CAHEN, NIKOLA FILBY, GAIL McCUTHEON,
    AND DIANE W. KYLE, *Class Size and Instruction*
PHILIP A. CUSICK, *The Egalitarian Ideal and the*
    American High School
LARRY CUBAN, *How Teachers Taught: Constancy and Change*
    in American Classrooms: 1890–1980
GARY NATRIELLO AND SANFORD M. DORNBUSCH,
    Teacher Evaluative Standards and Student Efforts
CHARLES W. FISHER AND DAVID C. BERLINER,
    Perspectives on Instructional Time

(continued on p. 359)

PERSPECTIVES ON INSTRUCTIONAL TIME

Editors

Charles W. Fisher

FAR WEST LABORATORY
FOR EDUCATIONAL
RESEARCH AND DEVELOPMENT

David C. Berliner

UNIVERSITY OF ARIZONA

Longman

New York & London

Citations to materials reprinted from other sources appear in an acknowledgments section on p. xix, which constitutes a continuation of the copyright page.

Perspectives on Instructional Time

Longman Inc., 95 Church Street, White Plains, N.Y. 10601
Associated companies, branches, and representatives throughough the world.

Developmental Editor: Lane Akers
Editorial and Design Supervisor: Naomi Silverman
Production Supervisor: Diane Kleiner
Composition: Graphicraft Typesetters Ltd.
Printing and Binding: Malloy Lithographing, Inc.

Library of Congress Cataloging in Publication Data

Main entry under title:

Perspectives on instructional time.

   Bibliography: p.
   Includes index.
   1. School day—United States—Addresses, essay, lectures. 2. School week—United States—Addresses, essays, lectures. 3. School year—United States—Addresses, essays, lectures. 4. Time management—Addresses, essays, lectures. 5. Curriculum planning—United States—Addresses, essays, lectures. I. Fisher, Charles W. II. Berliner, David C.
LB3033.P47 1985 371.2′4   84-15398
ISBN 0-582-28414-7

Manufactured in the United States of America
Printing: 9 8 7 6 5 4 3 2 1   Year: 93 92 91 90 89 88 87 86 85

This book is dedicated to the memory of
our colleague and friend

Leonard S. Cahen
(1930–1983)

Contents

PART II: INSTRUCTIONAL TIME: VIEWS FROM THREE DISCIPLINES

PART III: INSTRUCTIONAL TIME: CONTEMPORARY CONCEPTIONS

PART IV: INSTRUCTIONAL TIME: CLASSROOM RESEARCH

Contributors

LINDA M. ANDERSON, Department of Teacher Education, Michigan State University, East Lansing, Michigan

LORIN W. ANDERSON, College of Education, University of South Carolina, Columbia, South Carolina

REBECCA BARR, Department of Education, University of Chicago, Chicago, Illinois

DAVID C. BERLINER, Department of Educational Psychology, University of Arizona, Tucson, Arizona

BENJAMIN S. BLOOM, Department of Education, University of Chicago, Chicago, Illinois and School of Education, Northwestern University, Evanston, Illinois

BYRON W. BROWN, Department of Economics, Michigan State University, East Lansing, Michigan

LEONARD S. CAHEN (deceased), College of Education, Arizona State University, Tempe, Arizona

JOHN B. CARROLL, Psychology Department, University of North Carolina, Chapel Hill, North Carolina

ROBERT DREEBEN, Department of Education, University of Chicago, Chicago, Illinois

GARY D FENSTERMACHER, Northern Virginia Graduate Center, Virginia Polytechnic Institute and State University, Falls Church, Virginia

NIKOLA N. FILBY, Research and Development Division, Far West Laboratory for Educational Research and Development, San Francisco, California

CHARLES W. FISHER, Research and Development Division, Far West Laboratory for Educational Research and Development, San Francisco, California

ANNEGRET HARNISCHFEGER, School of Education, Northwestern University, Evanston, Illinois

PHILIP W. JACKSON, Department of Education, University of Chicago, Chicago, Illinois

NANCY KARWEIT, Center for Social Organization of Schools, The Johns Hopkins University, Baltimore, Maryland

GAEA LEINHARDT, Learning Research and Development Center, University of Pittsburgh, Pittsburgh, Pennsylvania

RICHARD MARLIAVE, formerly with Research and Development Division, Far West Laboratory for Educational Research and Development, San Francisco, California

DENIS C. PHILLIPS, School of Education, Stanford University, Stanford, California

DANIEL H. SAKS, Department of Educational Leadership, Vanderbilt University, Nashville, Tennessee

MICHAEL SCRIVEN, Department of Education, The University of Western Australia, Nedlands, Western Australia, Australia

W. JOHN SMYTH, Department of Education, Deakin University, Geelong, Victoria, Australia

JANE A. STALLINGS, Department of Teaching and Learning, Vanderbilt University, Nashville, Tennessee

MARGARET C. WANG, Learning Research and Development Center, University of Pittsburgh, Pittsburgh, Pennsylvania

DAVID E. WILEY, School of Education, Northwestern University, Evanston, Illinois

Preface

Every decade or two since the turn of the century, the research community has reminded the community of practitioners that time is a fundamental variable to consider when studying curriculum, instruction, and student learning in schools. In the last few years we have seen a renewed interest in instructional-time usage, in part, because schools have been perceived to have many shortcomings. Legislators, state regents, school board members, administrators, and a broad spectrum of the American public have been seeking solutions to the problems they have identified. And virtually all these concerned citizens recognize that the use of school time is an issue deserving of serious discussion.

The papers in this collection were written by empirical researchers and other scholars for a conference that took place at Northwestern University in 1981. At that time, the research community was engaging in extensive conceptual and empirical work on time-based instructional variables. This period of work on time-based variables was closely associated with work on instructional effectiveness. These research areas provided a reasonably coherent set of results on effective instruction in elementary schools. As a result, the work on time-based variables not only increases our knowledge about instruction in school settings, but also contributes to the design and implementation of practical school-improvement efforts. The thrust for school reform in the mid-1980s is drawing heavily on both the concepts and findings from this area of educational research. Much attention is focused on the way in which time is used in schools. The many recent reports expressing concern about our educational system demonstrate this point. For example, in the spring of 1983, the National Commission on Excellence in Education released their report *A Nation at Risk*. Among the commission's recommendations were some about the duration of school days and the school year, classroom time-on-task, and home time spent on academic pursuits. The Carnegie Foundation for the Advancement of Teaching supported and released in the same year a study of the American high school. Their report also had recommendations about how school time should be spent. Another study of high schools, conducted by Theodore Sizer, former dean of the Harvard Graduate School of Education and head-master of a prestigious preparatory school, was recently released and time issues were once again salient. John Goodlad, former dean of the Graduate School of Education at the University of California at Los Angeles recently published *A Place Called School*. That book describes educational pro-grams in hundreds of contemporary classrooms and schools. It features an examination of how school time is used. Reports by The Twentieth Cen-tury Fund, the Educational Commission of the States, and even Mortimer Adler's *Paidea Proposal* highlight issues pertaining to instructional-time usage. From all quarters—from researchers, critics, policymakers, and the public—comes concern for how time is used. The contribution of this volume to the discussions of schooling in the mid-1980s is to provide re-search perspectives on instructional time. We hope that the various per-spectives presented by these authors will illuminate the ongoing discussions of those who describe and analyze the status of schooling in contemporary America, and of those who propose alternative paths for school improvement.

Partial support for the conference at Northwestern University was pro-vided by the National Institute of Education, United States Department of Education. The conference was hosted by the Far West Laboratory for Ed-ucational Research and Development, San Francisco, California (Charles Fisher and David Berliner), and by the *Mer Licht* research group (Annegret Harnischfeger and David Wiley) of Northwestern University.

The presentations made at the conference have been edited and some additional important papers have been added to the collection. The papers are presented in five parts. Part I begins with a review of research about instructional time, and continues with an analysis of the impact of John B. Carroll's Model of School Learning in the 22 years since its appearance in 1963. Carroll's model launched a good deal of the contemporary interest in research on instructional time and we are fortunate that the analysis of the events subsequent to the publication of this influential paper is provided by Professor Carroll. This part also includes the original paper by John B. Carroll on his Model of School Learning, and the original paper by Benja-min Bloom on mastery learning describing that system of instruction based, in part, on the Carroll model.

Part II of this volume contains views of instructional time from three disciplines—philosophy, sociology, and economics. Part III consists of three papers offering contemporary conceptions of instructional time. In Part IV, six papers describing empirical research on various aspects of in-structional time are featured. Finally, Part V consists of critiques on other papers in this volume and more general issues of research on instructinal time. We have provided a short descriptive introduction at the beginning of each chapter.

Charles W. Fisher
David C. Berliner

Acknowledgments

Quotation, Ch. 1, p.4 and Ch. 16. p. 284, from Philip W. Jackson, Looking into education's crystal ball. Reprinted from *Instructor* August 1977, © 1977 by The Instructor Publications, Inc. Abbreviated version used by permission.

Quotation, ch. 1, p. 8, from David C. Berliner, (1976). Impediments to the study of teacher affectiveness, *Journal of Teacher Education, 21* (1). Reprinted by permission of the American Association of Colleges of Teacher Education.

Quotation, Ch. 1, p. 5; quotation, Ch. 1, p.6 and Ch. 8, p. 135; quotation, Ch. 8, p. 139. From Harnischfeger, A., & Wiley, D. E. (1975), Teaching–learning prcesses in elementary school: A synoptic view, *Studies of Educative Processes,* (No. 9), Chicago: University of Chicago. Also as Hernischfeger, A., & Wiley, D. E.1 (1976). The teaching–learning process in elementary schools: A synoptic view, *Curriculum Inquiry, 6* (reprinted by permission of John Wiley & Sons), and in D. A. Erickson (E). (1976). *Readings in educational research: Educational organization and administration* (pp. 195–236), San Francisco: McCutchan; copyright American Educational Research Association.

Quotation, Ch. 8, p. 135, and Figure 8.1, Ch. 8, p. 137. From Harnischfeger, A., & Wiley, D.E. (1978), Conceptual issues in models of school learning, *Studies of Educative Processes* (No. 10) Chicago: University of Chicago (ML-GROUP,CEMEREL) Also in *Journal of Curriculum Studies, 10*(3), 1978 (reprinted by permission of Taylor & Frances, Ltd.)

Extract, Ch. 20, pp. 334–337. From N. Gage & D. Berliner (1975), *Educational Psychology* (1st ed.), Chicago: Rand–McNally. Reprinted by permission of Houghton Mifflin Company.

Ch. 17. p. 302, "Time held me green and dying/Though I sang in my chains like the sea." From Dylan Thomas, "Fern Hill," *The Collected Poems of Dylan Thomas,* 1953 by Dylan Thomas. Reprinted by permission of New Directions Publishing Corp.

Part I

Instructional Time:
Background

1

A Context for the Study of Time and Instruction

W. John Smyth
Deakin University

EDITORS' INTRODUCTION

Dr. Smyth studied instructional-time variables as part of his doctoral work in educational administration. He saw clearly the importance of the decisions made about time by administrators and teachers. He has written and lectured extensively throughout Australia on instructional-time variables, focusing on student-engaged time, in particular.

In this chapter Dr. Smyth first provides a background on teacher-effectiveness research. He points out that only when researchers begin looking at what students actually do in classrooms will it be possible to develop adequate theories relating teacher behavior to student achievement. Among the most important student classroom behaviors intervening between the teachers' actions and measures of student achievement is student-engaged learning time. Smyth sees student-engaged learning time as a necessary, though by no means sufficient, mediating process in classroom research on learning.

Time and the schooling process are discussed next. Smyth concludes that although allocated time has its usefulness as a metric, and as a variable when examining the time spent in different subject matters, it is student-engaged time with subject matter that is the more crucial and fruitful variable to study. Smyth then reviews this literature. He does not provide an exhaustive review, but does highlight the findings and methods used in research on engaged time during the early part of the century, during the more modern era, and during the most recent era of studies of time-on-task, attention, or engagement.

After reviewing some of the important research work in the three stages he identified, Smyth discusses the implications of this research for practice and for future researchers. The entire chapter is one of context setting for the many and diverse chapters that follow. The diversity of the chapters in this volume make it abundantly clear that research on instructional time is no longer narrowly focused on only allocated-time or engaged-time variables.

3

INTRODUCTION

Let us begin, at the outset, by emphasizing that time is not viewed as having any kind of magical qualities. As Harris and Yinger (1977) have noted, "Researching the role that time plays in teaching and learning will not be a panacea for understanding classroom processes, but it should provide at least some understanding of an influential mechanism affecting classroom life" (p. 12).

Time is, therefore, one of a number of useful variables for analyzing classrooms. The way in which teachers choose to allocate time and the way in which pupils are allowed to spend that time provide us with valuable insights into the values teachers hold with respect to learning. We might all be guided by the wise words of Philip Jackson (1977):

> There has been a lot of talk about the importance of time in the determination of educational outcomes.... Certainly, we should take a look at how time is being used or misused in our schools. It may indeed turn out to be the culprit that critics claim it is. As we test this possibility, however, we must keep in mind that time itself is valueless. It acquires value chiefly because it marks the expenditure of a precious commodity—human life ... let us not seize too quickly at remedies for our educational ailments that call for little more than adding days or hours to our present efforts. The real key lies in making better use of the time we already have. (p. 38)

In this chapter I shall, first, place the research on pupil-engaged learning time in the context of research on teacher effectiveness; second, I shall survey the actual research on pupil-engaged learning time; third, I shall look at some of the more promising possibilities as far as the practical implications of this strand of research are concerned; finally, I shall comment on the research that I think is needed in the future.

RESEARCH ON TEACHER EFFECTIVENESS: BACKGROUND TO STUDIES ON PUPIL-ENGAGED LEARNING TIME

In an attempt to identify the correlates of effective teaching, research in the past 20 years has focused heavily on trying to isolate and identify teacher characteristics and behaviors that correlate with measured student cognitive achievement gains. As well as concentrating on a narrow range of teacher-behavior variables, and often lacking a rationale or framework to guide them in the selection of appropriate variables (Borich & Madden, 1977; Cruickshank, 1976), the majority of these studies related instructional processes *directly* to student-achievement test scores. The outcome of this process–product research in the 1960s and early 1970s was a spate of "teacher should" statements that largely ignored the nature of the learning process itself (Rosenshine, 1977a). Since these initial attempts to isolate the prescriptive universals for effective teaching, the research emphasis has shifted from a primary concern with teaching behaviors per se, to a number of other instructional variables.

While not dismissing the importance of teacher behavior in generating pupil effects, a promising line of research has emerged based on the student variables expressed in the work of Carroll (1963) and Bloom (1974). Of particular note was the realization that teacher behavior, as such, does not influence student achievement directly (Berliner, 1976, 1978; 1979; Harnischfeger & Wiley, 1976, 1978; Rosenshine, 1977a). Research of this kind, therefore, begins by looking first at what pupils do in order to learn and, second, at what teachers do that is associated with that learning. Insertion of the concept of "pupil pursuits" between teacher behavior and student learning, and its subsequent scrutiny by researchers, conforms with what Doyle (1978) describes as the mediating-process paradigm. This is to be contrasted to the process–product paradigm referred to above where the focus was upon measured teacher-classroom behaviors (processes) and measures of pupil-learning outcomes (products).

Impetus for the recent shift in research emphasis toward, the mediating-process paradigm has been provided by Harnischfeger and Wiley (1976), who stated that "a fruitful theory of teaching and learning must treat the pupil's activity as causally intermediate between the teacher's implementation of the curriculum and the pupil's learning. Pupil pursuits are therefore the focus of our conception of teaching-learning processes" (p. 10).

Incorporation of the activities and pursuits of pupils in studies ostensibly directed at isolating teacher effects is in accord with the need expressed by Dunkin and Biddle (1974) and Borich and Madden (1977) to depart from single-criterion studies and move toward the development of conceptual and research strategies that are more in tune with the complex realities of classroom settings.

Discussing recent research in the study of teaching, Cruickshank (1976) noted an unfortunate absence of knowledge among researchers as to how or why independent variables had been chosen. Part of the reason he attributed to a "lack of rich theoretical bases to assist us in the selection of meaningful variables to guide our research efforts" (p. 58).

Although abundant process–product research has related the observed behaviors of teachers to student-outcome measures, little research has explored the possibility of pupil pursuits as a mediating variable between teacher behavior or setting variables, on the one hand, and pupil achievement, on the other. Commenting on the state of knowledge of research on teaching, Flanders (1977) indicated the beginning of a change in research thinking from the exclusive concern with the teacher as the object of concern, when he said, "As the science (and art) of research on the effects of teaching progresses, it is very unlikely that researchers will remain satisfied with this rigid prescription. Defensible designs in which the unit of sampling is a student, or an encounter, or a single act, or a pattern of acts can and no doubt will be developed'' (p. 14). Further indication of the need to focus on pupil pursuits in research on teaching, rather than teacher behavior and classroom achievement means, was provided by Rothkopf (1970) when he stated, ''In most instructional situations, what is learned depends largely on the activities of the student. It therefore behooves those interested in the scientific study of instruction to examine these learning activities'' (p. 325). In a similar stance, Anderson (1970) stated that ''the activities the student engages in when confronted with instructional tasks are of crucial importance in determining what he will learn'' (p. 349).

Commenting on the narrowness of traditional research designs that emphasized the ''how'' of teaching, Harnischfeger and Wiley (1976) noted that this research ''attends to teacher behavior, but disregards the pupils' activities and the joint action of teacher and pupil'' (p. 11). The focal position of pupil pursuits or activities, as the missing mediating linkage in the chain of influences affecting pupil acquisition, was stated by Harnischfeger and Wiley (1976), when they said,

> All influences on pupil achievement must be mediated through pupil pursuits. No one can gain knowledge or take up new ways of thinking, believing, acting or feeling except through seeing, looking and watching, hearing and listening, feeling and touching. These control what and how one learns. Less proximal influences, whether as general as the district curricula and the school organization or as idiosyncratic as a given teacher's education, personality, planning and activities, directly control and condition these pursuits, and not the pupil's ultimate achievement. The focus on this particular causal linkage is the central uniqueness of our model; most earlier studies, by contrast, have regarded teacher behavior as directly, if mysteriously, influencing achievement. (p. 11)

Berliner (1976) dismissed simplistic models of the teaching-learning process which failed to recognize pupil and teacher pursuits as important intermediate variables. Berliner proposed research that involved the investigator in working intensively, with a small number of students in natural classroom settings with a view to gaining insights into the mechanisms by which individual students attended to the task of learning.

My own research (Smyth, 1979), and that of other contemporary investigators, emerges, therefore, from an expressed need to examine the teaching process via the intermediate variable of pupil in-class activities or pursuits. In so doing, it is important to avoid what Harnischfeger and Wiley (1978) described as ''the fragmentation of the triad of pupil, teacher and curriculum'' (p. 46). At the same time, there is a need to acknowledge mediating effects of the much broader aspects of classroom task and activity structures, and the environmental demands imposed by the nature of the classroom itself, as suggested by Doyle (1978) in his classroom ecology paradigm. Contemporary research, therefore, is much more complex than research done in earlier times.

TIME AS A VARIABLE IN STUDYING TEACHING

The notion of time is prominent in contemporary studies of teaching and learning. There are two major ways in which the concept of time has been used in research in schools. The economic perspective on time conceptualizes time as a resource or input into the educational process (Thomas, 1971) and is concerned primarily with productivity. Time is emphasized as a resource having alternative uses, which, when combined with other educational resources, optimizes the output of specified school objectives. According to Karweit (1978), the impact of allocating time in alternative ways is important for school personnel because it is one of the few variables over which they can exercise discretionary control. Bloom (1974), Garner (1976, 1978), Kiesling (1978), and Winkler (1975) have indicated the potential of time-related variables as indices of classroom efficiency for different instructional techniques. The economic perspective on time is discussed in Chapter 7 and is not of further concern in this chapter.

A psychological perspective considers time as a prominent determinant of learning. Bloom (1974) noted that although time has been a variable in the laboratory study of animal and human learning since the turn of the century, it has only recently emerged as important in classroom studies. Current research interest in time as a classroom variable is traceable to Carroll's (1963) "Model of School Learning." The development of that model is discussed, by Carroll, in Chapter 2; the original Model of School Learning is reprinted in Chapter 3. Carroll's model has five elements, three of which are time related—time needed, time allowed, and time spent on learning. According to Bloom (1974), by placing time as a central variable in school learning, Carroll generated a major shift in emphasis in research on teaching and learning.

Bloom (1974) claims among the advantages of time as a classroom research variable: (1) time can be measured with the kind of macro (years, months) or micro (minutes, seconds) precision desired by researchers, and (2) time-related measurements have qualities absent in other conventional forms of measurement, namely equality of units, an absolute zero, and comparability between individuals. Denham (1978) claims that academic learning time, as conceived in recent research efforts, provides "a vocabulary and a way of seeing what is occurring in the classroom" (p. 5). The use of time-related variables alters the tendency of past research on teaching which considered "the method and manners of the teacher, forgetting to notice whether the students are working" (Denham, 1978, p. 5). Looking at what the student does in his or her daily activities is not a startling revelation.

Research over a number of years (Block & Burns, 1977; Cobb, 1972; Edminston & Rhoades, 1959; Fisher, Filby, & Marliave, 1977; Lahaderne, 1968; Marliave, Fisher, & Dishaw, 1977; McDonald, 1975; Morsh, 1956; Olson, 1931; Samuels & Turnure, 1974; Stallings & Kaskowitz, 1974;

Weber, 1976) has consistently shown the proportion of study time students spend actively engaged in learning to be positively related to academic achievement.

Even after acknowledging that pupil-engaged time in classrooms is not a perfect proxy for school learning because of the obvious omission of learning that takes place outside of the classroom, as well as the technical difficulty of ascertaining pupil engagement, it still appears reasonable to claim, as Harris and Yinger (1976) do, that "time is a useful, measurable, and sensible proxy variable for student learning" (p. 8). Referring to the potential for isolating effective teaching practices from such research, Harris and Yinger (1976) claim that although time-based variables in schooling are not learning per se, research has established such a high correlation with pupil learning that effective teaching could be discriminated with the use of time variables. Whether it is possible to say, as they do, that engaged pupil time is more than a proxy for learning, and that "student behavior that is classified as 'engaged' is the visible evidence of learning taking place," is likely to be open to lively debate. Although we cannot directly observe the psychological process of learning as it occurs, it is feasible to observe *one* of the physical manifestations of it. On these grounds, time-on-task, pupil engagement, and content covered seem to be potent variables in the attempt to assess effective teaching and learning.

Time, in its various dimensions, is nevertheless a complex variable. As Berliner (1977) stated, "Our faith in the potency of the variable remains strong. But our belief that the relationship between time and outcomes is very complex is also becoming very strong" (p. 5).

Despite the difficulties inherent in this line of research, the need to pursue the possibilities further has been expressed by Berliner (1976): "Very little data are available describing the nature of the instructional activities and episodes a child engages in each day. Since instructional time appears to be an important variable in the learning process, accurate records of how time has been allocated to the various instructional activities and episodes is needed" (p. 7).

Rosenshine (1977a) was even more precise as to the nature of needed research, when he stated, "There is a great need for descriptive data on the percentage of engaged time which are obtained in different settings, as well as on the setting variables which may contribute to engaged time" (p. 25).

Ryan and Cooper (1975) noted that anthropologists had an important message for social science researchers, namely, that the humdrum aspects of human existence have cultural significance. As applied to education, Jackson (1968) maintained that if we are to understand what happens in elementary school classrooms, we must look closely at routine events. Given that the average American school year is approximately 180 days, of roughly 5 hours in length, it would not seem unreasonable to ask how students spend the 6300 hours they are in attendance during their elementary schooling, especially those aspects which are ostensibly spent in academic learning pursuits.

Tabulation of the number of hours officially prescribed by school authorities and the number of hours teachers claim to allocate per class to mathematics, science, reading, language arts, social studies, music, art, and so on, is an easy task. Of questionable validity, however, is the inference that these statistics represent time productively spent by individual students in learning.

STUDIES OF PUPIL-ENGAGED LEARNING TIME

Research on "pupil attention," "pupil time-on-task," or "pupil engagement" has an extensive history that reflects a continuing concern with the phenomenon by both researchers and classroom practitioners. Jackson (1968) summarized the pragmatic view of many teachers when he said of the importance of this topic,

> From a logical point of view few topics would seem to have greater relevance for the teacher's work. Certainly no educational goals are more immediate than those that concern the establishment and maintenance of the student's absorption in the task at hand. Almost all other objectives are dependent for their accomplishment upon the attainment of this basic condition. (p. 85)

With findings extending back to the beginning of this century, researchers have found this to be a fertile area for inquiry. Indeed, why has concern with this topic lingered on when educational fads are traditionally short-lived? My own survey of research (Smyth, 1980a) in this area led to the identification of three recognizable phases or eras.

1. An *early* era, in which both the problem and the approach were mechanistic and concerned with issues of efficiency and effectiveness as it related to teaching;
2. A *modern* era, that was preoccupied with establishing a correlational association with pupil achievement, and where the methodology reflected the need to verify data collected by observational means;
3. A *recent* era, where the nexus with achievement has been established, and where current efforts are being directed at isolating associated teaching and classroom-related variables.

These developmental phases in research on pupil-engaged learning time provide us with a heightened sense of awareness about the history of this strand of research. On these grounds, it warrants brief investigation.

Early Studies: A Measure of Teacher Effectiveness

A number of classroom studies in the 1920s and 1930s in the United States, which had pupil attention as their focus, were really designed to obtain an index of teaching effectiveness. Given the prevailing industrial and business ethos of "scientific management" and the general concern with efficiency and cost effectiveness, it is not altogether surprising to find this emphasis spilling over into schools.

French (1924), for example, demonstrated a high correlation between principal ranking of teacher ability and observer judgment of group attention. Median group attention rates were found to exceed 90%. Morrison's (1926) technique of obtaining class "attention scores" by scanning the class row by row each minute and noting inattentive students (as indicated by body position and eye movements) on a score card remained in vogue for 20 years. Studies that followed directly from the initial work of French and Morrison were based on the premise that unless teachers aimed for 100% class involvement they were delinquent in their duties (Bjarnason, 1925; Knudsen, 1930; Olson 1931; Symonds, 1926).

Increased use of Morrison's technique resulted in a number of studies designed to refine, reflect upon, and test the measurement of pupil attention. Blume (1929) concluded that "once the technique has been learned, the attention scores thus obtained have a high degree of reliability" (p. 43). Barr (1926), on the other hand, dropped attention scores altogether as a method of evaluating teacher effectiveness, on the grounds of unreliability. Likewise, Shannon (1936) rejected attention scores as an indicator of teacher effectiveness. Washburne, Vogel, and Gray (1926), while finding attention levels of between 90% and 97.5 %, questioned whether student eyes on the book were necessarily accurate indicators of attention to academic tasks. Morrison's (1926) response to the problem of determining attentiveness in expressionless students was that extended observation of the pupil would give clear evidence, and that the score card could be amended accordingly. Knudsen (1930) dismissed the problem of student "faking" of attention on the grounds that it would be relatively consistent from class to class.

In that it was clearly designed to discredit Morrison's technique of class attention scores, Shannon's (1942) experimental study represented a significant move. His approach was compelling in its logic. If the teacher presented unfamiliar material to pupils, in which a number of identifiable key ideas were contained, it should be possible to observe students for attentiveness at the instant of presentation and to follow up with a test to specifically test for those ideas. Shannon's correlational findings between observed attention and achievement of .67 for boys and .34 for girls were considered sufficiently low for Shannon to discredit the import of pupil attention scores.

Retrospectively examining research findings, although a necessary undertaking, is in many ways analogous to reading the last pages of a thriller before chapter one. Almost by definition, we are bound to regard earlier efforts as naive, unless we are sensitive to the context and milieu from which they emerged. This is particularly true of this line of research, which must be interpreted against the history of contemporary prejudices as to classroom management strategies. If these early studies were different from their more recent counterparts, it was in respect to the following:

1. They were *mechanistic*. That is to say, their focus was upon overt pupil behavior with no attempt to examine pupil attention in the light of teacher intentions. They were based on the explicit and unrealistic assumption that all pupils should be totally attentive all of the time.
2. They were *group oriented*. The unit of analysis was the total class. Hence the repeated reference throughout these studies to "class attention scores." Aggregations of this kind suffer from the defect of concealing more than they disclose about the nature of classroom processes.
3. They were *superficial*. No attempt was made to incorporate pupil attention into any kind of explanatory framework, nor was an endeavor made to analyze the meaning behind and the reasons for pupil involvement and detachment during academic tasks.
4. They were *content free*. Pupil involvement was not distinguished according to the nature of the curriculum content encountered.
5. They were *evaluative*. The primary purpose behind these studies was to obtain an index of teacher effectiveness for purposes of promotion and salary increments. (Smyth, 1979, p. 51–52.)

On the positive side, these studies were cumulatively adding to the knowledge base of what was clearly perceived to be an important classroom teaching/learning variable. Although we may question the absence of a sound guiding theoretical framework or the efficacy of this work as a mechanism of teacher evaluation, what is of singular importance with respect to this early research is the isolation of pupil attention as a central and measurable classroom variable.

Modern Era: Correlational Studies

In the decade from the early 1940s, pupil attention was largely ignored as a researchable topic. Jackson (1968) explains this unpopularity as being due to the implied authoritarian emphasis in pupil-attention studies, during a time when classrooms were being promoted as democratic settings. When the topic did reemerge in the early 1950s, it was with a different emphasis. Bloom (1953) and his graduate students (Gaier, 1953; Schultz, 1951) were concerned with pursuing the underlying or covert mental activity of pupils while ostensibly engaged in academic pursuits. Using a stimulated recall technique of recording classroom dialogue and then replaying it to students and asking them about their thoughts at the time, Bloom found university students' thoughts to be on-task for 64% of the time during lectures and for 55% of the time during class discussions—a marked contrast to Morrison's figures of 90+%. Hudgins (1967) and Taylor (1968), however, both reported negative correlations between observed attention and pupil self-reports of attentiveness.

At approximately the same time, a second group of studies actively pursued the linkage between pupil attention and achievement. Working with Air Force trainees, Morsh (1956) found a negative correlation between off-task behavior and predicted test score, while Edminston and Rhoades (1959) found a positive correlation between time-on-task and standardized test scores for high school students. Lahaderne's (1968) investigations revealed a positive correlation between attention and pupil achievement, whereas Anderson (1976) and Özcelik (1973) found the amount of time pupils actually spend on-task to be highly predictive of student learning. Samuels and Turnure (1974) found increasing degrees of pupil attention to be related to superior word recognition among first-graders, as did McKinney, Mason, Perkerson, and Clifford (1975) with 8-year-olds. With 11-year-olds, Cobb (1972) found attentiveness to be the most consistent in-class predictor of arithmetic achievement. Stallings and Kaskowitz's (1974) study of third-grade low achievers in mathematics found a high positive correlation between time-on-task and mathematics achievement. Reflecting the beginnings of a move toward the analysis of controllable variables, Hess and Takanishi (1973) found a negative relationship between size of pupil groupings and pupil engagement on-task.

The thrust of the research endeavors during the period beginning in 1950 and culminating in the early 1970s was therefore two-pronged. On the one hand, there was the move to substantiate the observational approach to pupil attention by means of introspective psychological techniques; on the other hand, there were the concerted moves toward forging a nexus between pupil attention and subsequent achievement.

Recent Studies: Isolation of Controllable Variables

Unlike previous classroom research, current endeavors have proceeded on the basis of two fundamental, albeit obvious, assumptions: (1) the amount of time an elementary teacher allocates to a learning topic constitutes the maximal in-class exposure of students, and (2) even under the most optimistic conditions it would be unreasonable (indeed, inhumane) to expect pupils to be totally occupied in learning for all of the available time. Based on these presumptions the hypothesis has been advanced that after allowing for the difficulty of the learning material and its impact on the level of pupil success, the amount of time a pupil spends actively learning will provide a realistic indicator of achievement. The corollary is that where pupils are observed to be diligently involved in learning tasks, the "appropriate motivational and attitudinal conditions could account for this involvement" (Marliave, Cahen, & Berliner, 1977, p. 11), and the reverse also applies.

Although credit for rekindling the interest in time-on-task studies and the flurry of empirical research in the 1970s is directly traceable to the work of Bloom and his students at the University of Chicago, it is the theoretical and empirical work of researchers at the Far West Laboratory for Educational Research and Development via the Beginning Teacher Evaluation Study (BTES) that has generated some of the most interesting discussion and the most compelling and persuasive evidence (Berliner, 1978, 1979; Fisher, 1980; Fisher et. al. 1978; Marliave, 1980). Of particular salience is their conceptualization of a group of loosely linked variables they describe as Academic Learning Time (ALT). Simply stated, ALT comprises the time a pupil spends attending to academic learning tasks, under conditions that yield high levels of success. While it is premature at this stage to prescribe optimal or even desirable levels of ALT, it would seem reasonable to suggest that the more ALT a pupil accumulates, the greater the presumption of learning. The consistency of the relationship between ALT and achievement across a number of studies when measured by criterion testing is particularly encouraging (Fisher, Filby, Marliave, Cahen, Dishaw, Moore, & Berliner, 1978; Rosenshine & Berliner, 1978).

The individual elements that collectively constitute ALT are worth closer analysis. Basically, they comprise three: (1) allocated time, (2) engagement rate, (3) success rate (Fisher et al., 1978). *Allocated time* is best described as the amount of time made available by the teacher for learning. Although it is a gross variable, it does represent the outer boundaries of pupils' in-class opportunities to interact with learning materials and ideas. *Engagement rate* represents an attempt to gauge the proportion of allocated time during which pupils appear to be learning, as evidenced by their overt attending to learning tasks. Neither of these concepts makes any claims to impute value or meaningfulness to the learning activities embedded within these time frames. It is quite conceivable that at least some pupils may spend time on learning activities that are so easy, or so hard, as to be of little real educational value. Notwithstanding the need to provide a certain amount of challenging material, pupils in the classrooms of the BTES research learned most when they experienced high levels of success. The effect, however, was clearer with the younger children at grade two than with the older children at grade five. *Success rate*, the third element of ALT, therefore measures the relative proportion of observed instructional time pupils spent on tasks providing high, medium, and low levels of success, respectively.

Thus, elementary school classrooms where teachers allocated more time to basic reading and mathematics skills, where engagement rates were higher, and where pupils experienced high levels of success had relatively high levels of achievement in those areas of learning.

ENGAGED TIME AND TEACHING VARIABLES

The nexus between any group of process variables (such as ALT) and learning outcomes will amount to little more than an academic exercise unless it is possible to relate these findings to teaching behaviors that not only make a difference, but that are also controllable. The BTES research does establish a number of such connections (Fisher et al. 1978). Teacher diagnostic skills, for example, in accurately assessing the entering behavior of individual pupils with respect to the task difficulty of materials, was shown to be a close predictor of pupil ALT, success rate, and achievement. Certain teacher interactive behaviors were directly related to high levels of pupil task engagement. Teachers who emphasized academic goals and who displayed high levels of actual involvement with pupils on learning tasks, in contrast to seatwork or assignment activities, generated higher levels of achievement among their pupils. Similarly, clarity of teacher directions on how to undertake learning tasks, praise, and feedback on correctness of pupil responses were associated with higher levels of pupil learning. Alternatively, where teachers did not predict learning difficulties accurately or responded to pupil learning problems on an ad hoc basis or where teachers frequently criticized or reprimanded pupils, then these teachers had classrooms where ALT and pupil achievement were low.

Other research (McDonald, 1975; Stallings & Kaskowitz, 1974) has generally supported the nature of the above relationship between task-related pursuits of elementary school pupils and the need for the teacher to adopt a structured, academically oriented or "direct" approach to the teaching of basic skills in reading and mathematics (Rosenshine, 1977a, 1977b, 1979). As Berliner (1980) pointed out, there is nothing inherently inconsistent with this approach and classroom settings that are characterized by warmth, friendliness, and high levels of pupil responsibility.

Although we should be cautious about interpretation and generalization, some statistics emerging from descriptive studies of U.S. classrooms are disturbing. These studies have relied entirely on volunteer classrooms, and may not therefore be representative of classrooms generally. McDonald (1976), for example, reported median engaged times in a sample of grade two and grade five California classrooms, in reading and mathematics, of under 90 hours for the school year. Smyth (1979), in a grade six study of a Canadian classroom, found engagement levels of individual pupils varying from as low as 38% of allocated time to as high as 78%. When engagement and success rates were considered, and the figures extrapolated to a school year, interpupil differences could be expected from 46 hours of ALT in reading and mathematics for one student, compared with 280 hours for another. These are dramatic differences between pupils in a single classroom!

IMPLICATIONS FOR PRACTITIONERS

A predictable reaction from a skeptical practitioner regarding the matters raised so far may well be: "So what's new? Teachers have known these things for years!" Novel or not, the findings discussed here do contain substance.

If nothing else, they provide confirmation to "good" teachers that tried and tested practices grounded in teachers' own theories of classroom practice do in fact stand up credibly under close empirical scrutiny. Confirmation of commonsense notions, however, does not necessarily imply widespread or common acceptance. While research and the visions of some practitioners may both point to pupil work involvement as a logical concomitant to learning, let us not delude ourselves into believing that all classroom practitioners possess the necessary skills required for implementation. Many of the requisites can be acquired, but only as a consequence of careful observation and extensive practice.

Berliner (1980) summed up the usefulness of ALT variables to teachers when he described them as "orienteering variables," that is, a group of salient and manipulable concepts of which teachers might be mindful in reflecting upon the likely impact of their teaching on pupils. One of the more disturbing aspects of this research is the considerable variability that can exist between pupils in accumulations of ALT. Even where pupils have the same opportunity to learn, as measured by uniform teacher allocations of time, alarming disparities can exist among pupils both in levels of engagement and in time spent on pursuits regarded as individually meaningful (high success rate).

On one level the message is a relatively simple one—teachers should recognize the long-term potential of their allocations of learning time. Time is more than something to be used up, or a void to be filled; it represents the expenditure of a scarce resource, the allocation of which precludes other alternative uses (opportunity cost). In real terms it represents a reflection of values held to be important. To heighten their own awareness of this dimension, teachers might keep personal logs or diaries of how they allocated class time both across and within subject areas. Mutual disclosure among groups of teachers within a school might usefully serve to uncover gross inequities.

At the more complex level of interactive teaching behaviors that impinge upon ALT variables, the self-monitoring process becomes more difficult. Within limits it is possible for teachers to collect process data on the engagement levels of segments of the class during ongoing activities. Carefully selected target pupils (Smyth, 1979) can provide rich and revealing "windows" on pupils' learning. Such feedback data may or may not constitute a basis for decisions to modify teaching behaviors or classroom organization. Given the complexities of classrooms and the multiplicity of occurrences competing for the teacher's attention, monitoring of this kind is clearly circumscribed. Furthermore, evidence suggests that teachers rarely alter their behavior on the basis of a logical and rational search for data and alternatives (Eggleston, 1979). A more viable alternative, particularly in providing a mirror of teaching behavior as it directly relates to aspects of ALT concerned with teacher monitoring of pupil seatwork, provisions of feedback to pupils, and clarity of instructions, would involve the collabortive assistance of a colleague in selectively collecting the appropriate classroom data (Boehm & Weinberg, 1977; Good & Brophy, 1978; Walker & Adelman, 1975). Collegial and nonthreatening disclosure of these data (Smyth, 1980b) may not only reveal areas of teaching related to ALT requiring attention, but also provide a forum for collective dialogue on ways of modifying teaching behavior.

Debate over exact means by which to effect changes in teacher behavior is probably a topic for another place. What is worth reiterating here are the kinds of teacher-controllable variables that impact on levels of pupil ALT.

Nothing is guaranteed to have quite the disintegrating effect on the lesson as widespread pupil confusion! Moves designed to avoid this will enhance levels of ALT. Teacher structuring of basic-skill lessons in reading and mathematics, so pupils are clear from the beginning as to aims, expected outcomes, desirable work patterns, and activities to do upon completion, are hallmarks of executive teacher action designed to enhance levels of pupil ALT. Teaching time devoted to excessive behavioral reprimands—whether born out of boredom, frustration with the difficulty of the task, or unclear directions—has detrimental effects on the accumulations of ALT for pupils directly involved and the class at large. Careful, flexible, and humane planning of the kind being suggested obviates costly reductions in pupil ALT by avoiding confusion, long wait times, and mindless repetition. It serves the equally important function of conveying to pupils a businesslike sense of the teacher's feeling of importance about academic pursuits.

I would be remiss if I did not also highlight an apparent paradox likely to confront teachers in their quest to maximize class ALT. Class recitation sessions contain the greatest potential for enhancing overall engagement by virtue of the built-in capacity of the setting—the teacher can collectively monitor all pupils at once. But what of task difficulty, the other component of ALT? Individual seatwork, on the other hand, has the ingredients for providing high levels of pupil success, but at the expense of diminished teacher monitoring ability. What of pupil engagement in those settings? Resolution of this problem would seem to reside in the sensible and selective application of whole-class, group, and individualized techniques according to particular circumstances.

FUTURE RESEARCH

Despite an extensive tradition of research, together with the recent intensified interest, the possibilities for further research into aspects of pupil engagement remain numerous. From the vantage point of one primarily concerned with the issue of instructional time (especially engaged time) from a classroom-process and teacher-development perspective, I see the research as proceeding with varying degrees of intensity at four levels.

1. Efforts to further substantiate the engaged time–pupil achievement nexus
2. Endeavors to extend the range of teacher behavior and classroom context variables that relate to enhanced levels of pupil-engaged learning time
3. A concerted thrust in the direction of intervention studies. Researchers would work intensively and collaboratively with teachers in trying a variety of methods for monitoring the implementation of findings from instructional-time research
4. Methodological research that explores definitive design, and observational aspects of research on engaged time.

Let me deal with each of these a little more fully.

Deepening and Broadening the Engaged Time–Achievement Nexus

Not many people seriously dispute the general nature of the association between engaged time and pupil achievement. What is being questioned is the strength of that relationship and its consistency across different types of pupils, content areas, and grade levels (Lomax & Cooley, 1979).

Perhaps we need to look a little more carefully at some of the interacting variables. Larrivee and Vacca (1980), for example, found that student ability level was a potentially confounding source when considered with allotted time, engagement rate, and difficulty level. Rusnock and Brandler (1979) and Smyth (1979) both found quite different patterns of off-task behavior between high- and low-ability students. Whereas low-ability students tended to interrupt academic pursuits with off-task behavior, high-ability students tended to finish an academic task and then engage in off-task behavior. Descriptive studies of individual students over extended periods would enable us to substantiate this observation.

There is also the obvious need to extend the research on engaged time and achievement beyond reading and mathematics in elementary schools. There are encouraging signs of this already happening, for example, in the work of Smith (1979) in elementary social studies. There is still, therefore, a considerable amount of consolidation and replication work that needs to be done to build upon the very productive work already accumulating at the elementary school level. One point that emerges with some clarity is the fact that much of the research at this level has been correlational, involving relatively large numbers of pupils and classrooms.

Indeed, there are sound reasons as to why developments should have proceeded in the direction they have. Perhaps what we need to do now is consider the possibilities of studies of an intensive observational/descriptive kind that focus on small numbers of individual pupils over an extended period. Perhaps the ecological analyses of pupil involvement along the lines suggested by Stodolsky (1979) and the narrative record approaches of Evertson, Emmer, and Clements (1980) and Smyth (1979), hold some promise in this regard. This work will be expensive in terms of effort, but it may be revealing in what it tells us about the day-to-day variability and the contextual aspects of pupil engagement. Keeping in mind Lomax and Cooley's (1979) point that "the ultimate goal of most researchers in education is the development of causal models" (p. 17), to move in the direction suggested is one logical next step. To do it effectively we will have to be prepared to commit ourselves to probing introspective studies (using stimulated recall or some other technique) of both pupils and teachers. The real answers to perplexing questions such as engagement variability probably lie within the minds of individual pupils and their teachers. This does not mean we should eliminate entirely the possibilities of quasi-experimental studies of the kind undertaken by Borg and Ascione (1979) and McKenzie (1979).

The relatively neglected secondary school also comes to mind; with a few notable exceptions (Evertson, Emmer, & Clements, 1980; Frederick, Walberg, & Rasher, 1979; Stallings, 1980), this is virgin soil. The secondary school is a fertile and relatively untapped area in research on pupil engagement. We know lots about student subcultures, alienation, and school-to-work transition, but we are still blissfully ignorant about school-related factors that influence accumulations of pupil-engaged learning time at the secondary level, how this interfaces with achievement, and which teacher-controllable variables impinge on it. With the mounting concern about the student outcomes in secondary schools, we should be looking a lot more carefully at the "process" aspect within secondary schools. We could well replicate and extend to the secondary school much of the research that has been done on engaged time at the elementary level. We may, for example find that allocated time emerges as a much more salient variable here than is the case in elementary schools. If this is the case, then maybe we will be speaking to a different audience for our research findings—principals and others who control scheduling and timetabling—rather than teachers. These are important matters that should be investigated.

Teacher Behavior and Classroom Context Variables

It is my belief that the BTES has not isolated anything like the full range of options comprising teacher-controllable variables related to pupil-engaged learning time. Indeed, one of the more impressive aspects of the BTES research lies in the fact that findings are not encapsulated in the immutable form of "teacher should" statements. As Inglis (1980) has indicated, the model and the findings associated with it provide teachers with a "lens" with which to usefully view their own teaching and what is occurring in their classrooms. There has been no attempt to straitjacket teachers, as some early critics suggested. The idea of in-depth case study analyses of the teacher-as-executive managing pupil involvment during learning (Smyth,

1981a) might prove to be a beneficial way of demonstrating the ways in which successful teachers have developed coping strategies (see Emmer & Evertson, 1981). The work of Stallings (1980), where teachers were observed for three days and then a time usage profile developed of their teaching along with recommendations, appeals to me as being a particularly productive route worth following. Data presented to teachers on their own classrooms, and recommendations derived from that base, have a good deal of credibility and appeal.

As we explore further the full implications of current research findings relating to engaged time across different contexts, the repertoire of teacher-controllable variables will certainly expand beyond the handful initially posited and substantiated in the BTES. As Bell and Davidson (1976) found, there can be little doubt that teacher behaviors are an important intervening variable in the relationship between pupil time-on-task and pupil achievement. What I find exciting is the likely mechanism by which this might occur. Rather than "promising" teacher-behavior variables emanating solely from researchers, I believe that teachers' insights about themselves, their teaching practices, and their classrooms will increasingly provide the source of new ideas worth testing. Based on diary and journal records about what seems to work, teachers' thoughtful observations could provide educational researchers with a rich domain in which to extend. This is not to suggest that practitioner insights would supplant or necessarily replace hypotheses derived by more conventional means—rather, they would complement that process.

Intervention Studies to Monitor Research Implementation

Although I thoroughly endorse the idea of research findings being implemented and monitored at the grass-roots level by those most affected by them, as in the case of the highly successful BTES minigrants program, I also believe that there should be a spillover effect by researchers in the form of monitoring at least some parts of the implementation process. As Fisher (1980) has indicated, "knowing what" (research findings) and "knowing how" (the application of research findings), are two separate entities. If we *really* believe what we preach about the importance of "monitoring" and "feedback," it behooves us to carry this forward into our own learning and research. Accordingly, I would argue strongly for a segment of research on engaged time that has as its focus the actual implementation of extant findings (Smyth, 1981b).

The reality, in all probability, will be an "organic" or adaptive process whereby teachers and researchers collaboratively interpret, negotiate, and modify the findings to suit their own idiosyncratic circumstances. Unless we actually participate in and monitor the findings relating to pupil-engaged learning time at the classroom level, molding and shaping staff development models that fit with the spirit of the findings we are trying to implement, we run the risk of much of our painstaking efforts at the design and fieldwork phase being wasted.

The outcome of this kind of research will be researchers who are better informed about the realities of classroom and school situations, and who are able to communicate with teachers and principals about effective mechanisms of implementation they might try themselves. A range of different implementation options that have been carefully monitored *may* provide classroom practitioners with a benchmark against which to gauge their own efforts. A modest beginning has been made in this direction by Berliner (1978), Stallings (1980), and Smyth (1979).

While a number of possibilities exist along the summative-formative teacher evaluation continuum as far as research on instructional time is concerned, an interesting possibility has been raised by Halpin (1979). Basically his suggestion consists of teachers using allocated and engaged time as a metric for rendering an account of their own classrooms or school practices. He envisages schools, departments within schools, and individual classroom teachers as giving an account of the management of their active learning time. Although there is an element of accountability in this, the intent is to provide a way in which "a school could begin to examine and report (both to itself and to outsiders) what factors in their school settings and classroom behaviors may contribute to learning and learning failure in the total amount of active learning time made available" (p. 212).

He envisages schools as developing case studies of their use of time, possibly including:

1. Documentary evidence of the amounts of time allocated to particular curriculum areas;
2. Documentary evidence that focuses on those structural features of school life (e.g., size of classes, available resources, demands of public examinations) which constrain teachers' efforts to extend time allocations;
3. Documentary evidence (e.g., diaries) of the ways in which a representative sample of teachers use their time in a typical working day;
4. Edited minutes of staff meetings, etc., where issues relating to time allocation, in and between subject areas, have been discussed;
5. Edited policy documents relating to school measures such as curriculum structure and intraschool grouping, and how they affect teachers' use of time;
6. Representations of videotapes or photographic slides of what happens in classrooms;
7. Statements of staff and pupil absences that include predictions on how both affect achievement levels. (pp. 212–213)

In many respects, the suggestions of Halpin are not far removed from the "model of on-going student learning behaviors" posited by Marliave (1980). Here, teachers and others rely on pupil academic learning time as an alternative source of feedback to traditional testing.

Methodological Studies Relating to Engaged Time

Cutting across the three major research areas already outlined is the need to pursue studies designed to refine the methodological aspect of this line of research. I refer to the kind of study recently reported by Karweit and Slavin (1980), which raised questions such as the following as ones that need to be continually under review:

1. The definition of off-task behavior
2. The length of observation visit
3. The number of days of observation
4. The scheduling of observations
5. The sampling of students for observation

Although recognizing that the answers to these questions are partially dependent on the bigger research questions we are pursuing, unless we do have answers to questions such as how best to define off-task behavior, how much continuous time we need to observe our subjects, how frequently we should observe and at what time during the school year, and how many students we should observe simultaneously, then the utility of our eventual research findings will suffer as a consequence.

CONCLUSION

This chapter commenced by discussing research on pupil-engaged learning time as a subset of research on teacher effectiveness. Although classroom teachers have long acknowledged the potency of pupil engagement as a variable in the acquisition of knowledge by pupils, researchers are only just beginning to uncover the complex web of interrelationships.

Although it was the simplistic relationship between engagement and teaching effectiveness that spurred early research, later investigations concentrated on establishing and substantiating the nexus between pupil pursuits during learning tasks and measures of achievement. Conceptualizations of teaching and learning that ignore any of the triad of pupil, teacher, and curriculum run the risk of fragmentation. The latest research has incorporated engagement as one of a package of predictive variables labeled academic learning time. As well as being theoretically sound and practically based, this amalgam appears to be consistently related to levels of pupil achievement, at least in basic skill subjects in reading and mathematics in elementary schools. The extant research has implications for practitioners and for the design of future research studies.

The study of pupil attention, engagement, or use of academic learning time fits well with the view expressed by Jackson (1968) that before we can hope to understand what happens in classrooms, we must first carefully investigate the myriad of events that constitute daily routines. The apparently humdrum occurrences assume added significance when subjected to intense scrutiny. Yet, despite our focus on the routine and the mundane, we should not be deluded into believing that these issues can be dispensed with perfunctorily in a prescriptive fashion. Berliner and Rosenshine (1977) captured the essence of the paradox when they concluded, "The factors relating to knowledge acquisition in the classroom may be viewed as both disarmingly simple, and frightfully complex at the same time" (p. 394).

REFERENCES

Anderson, L. W. (1976). An empirical investigation of individual differences in time to learn. *Journal of Educational Psychology, 68*(2), 226–233.

Anderson, R. C. (1970). Control of student mediating processes during verbal learning and instruction. *Review of Educational Research, 40,* 349–369.

Barr, A. S. (1926). *Characteristic differences in the teaching performance of good and poor teachers of the social studies.* Bloomington, IL: Public School Publishing.

Bell, M. C., & Davidson, C. W. (1976). Relationships between pupil on-task performance and pupil achievement. *Journal of Educational Research, 69,* 172–176.

Berliner, D. C. (1976). Impediments to the study of teacher effectivenes. *Journal of Teacher Education, 21*(1), 5–13.

Berliner, D. C. (1977, April). *Instructional time in research on teaching.* Paper presented at the annual meeting of the American Educational Research Association, New York.

Berliner, D. C. (1978, March). *Changing academic learning time: Clinical interventions in four classrooms.* Paper presented at the annual meeting of the American Educational Research Association, Toronto.

Berliner, D. C. (1979). Tempus educare. In P. L. Peterson & H. J. Walberg (Eds.), *Research on teaching: Concepts, findings and implications.* Berkeley, CA: McCutchan.

Berliner, D. C. (1980, May). *The teacher as an executive administering a learning environment.* Paper presented at the South Pacific Association of Teacher Education.

Berliner, D. C., & Rosenshine, B. V. (1977). The acquisition of knowledge in the classroom. In R. C. Anderson. R. J. Spiro, & W. E. Montague (Eds.), *Schooling and the acquisition of knowledge.* Hillsdale, N.J.: Lawrence Erlbaum.

Bjarnason, L. (1925, September). Relation of class size to control of attention. *Elementary School Journal, 26,* 36–41.

Block, J. H., & Burns, R. B. (1977). Mastery learning. In L. Shulman (Ed.), *Review of research in education, 4.* Itasca, Ill.: Peacock.

Bloom, B. S. (1953, April). Thought processes in lectures and discussion. *Journal of General Education, 7*(3), 160–169.

Bloom, B. S. (1974, September). Time and learning. *American Psychologist, 29,* 682–688.

Bloom, B. S. (1980, February). The new direction in educational research: Alterable variables. *Phi Delta Kappan, 61*(6).

Blume, C. E. (1929). Techniques in the measuring of pupil attention. In J. F. Hosie (Ed.), *The national conference of supervisors and directors of instruction, second yearbook.* New York: Bureau of Publications, Teachers College, Columbia University.

Boehm, A. E., & Weinberg, R. A. (1977). *The classroom observer: A guide for developing observation skills.* New York: Teachers College, Columbia University.

Borg, W., & Ascione, F. (1979). Changing on-task, off-task, and disruptive behavior in elementary mainstreaming classrooms. *Journal of Educational Research, 72*(5), 243–252.

Borich, G. D., & Madden, S. K. (1977). *Evaluating classroom instruction: A sourcebook of instruments.* Reading, Mass.: Addison-Wesley.

Carroll, J. B. (1963). A model of school learning. *Teachers College Record, 64*(8), 723–733.

Cobb, J. A. (1972). Relationship of discrete classroom behaviors to fourth grade academic achievement. *Journal of Educational Psychology, 63*(1), 74–80.

Cruickshank, D. P. (1976, Spring). Synthesis of selected recent research on teacher effects. *Journal of Teacher Education, 27*(1), 57–60.

Denham, C. (1978, March). *Utilizing research: Can we agree on the findings?* Paper presented at the annual meeting of the American Educational Research Association, Toronto.

Doyle, W. (1978). Paradigms for research on teacher effectiveness. In L. W. Shulman (Ed.), *Review of Research in Education, 5.* Itasca, Ill.: Peacock.

Dunkin, M. J., & Biddle, B. J. (1974). *The study of teaching.* New York: Holt, Rinehart and Winston.

Edminston, R. W. & Rhoades, B. J. (1959). Predicting achievement. *Journal of Education Research, 52*, 177–180.

Eggleston, J. (Ed.). (1979). *Teacher decision–making in the classroom: A collection of papers.* London: Routledge & Kegan Paul.

Emmer, E. T., & Evertson, C. M. (1981). Classroom management: A review of recent research. *Educational Leadership, 38*(4), 342–347.

Evertson, C. M., Emmer, E. T., & Clements, B. S. (1980, February). *The junior high classroom organization study: Summary of training procedures.* Research and Development Center for Teacher Education, University of Texas, Austin. Research and Development Report No. 6101.

Fisher, C. W. (1980, April). *Academic learning time as instructional feedback.* Paper presented at the annual meeting of the American Educational Research Association, Boston.

Fisher, C. W., Filby, N. N., & Marliave, R. S. (1977, April). *Instructional time and student achievement in second grade reading and mathematics.* Paper presented at the annual meeting of the American Educational Research Association, New York.

Fisher, C. W., Filby, N. N., Marliave, R. S., Cahen, L. W., Dishaw, M. M., Moore, J. E., & Berliner, D. C. (1978). *Teaching behaviors, academic learning time, and student achievement.* Technical Report V-1, Final Report of Phase III-B, Beginning Teacher Evaluation Study. San Francisco: Far West Laboratory for Educational Research and Development.

Flanders, N. (1977). Knowledge about teacher effectiveness. *British Journal of Teacher Education, 3*(1), 3–26.

Frederick, W., Walberg, H., & Rasher, S. (1979). Time, teacher comments, and achievement in urban high schools. *Journal of Educational Research, 73*(2), 63–65.

French, W. C. (1924). The correlation between teaching ability and thirteen measurable classroom activities. Unpublished masters thesis, University of Chicago. Cited by P. W. Jackson, *Life in Classrooms*. New York: Holt, Rinehart & Winston, 1968.

Gaier, E. L. (1953, October). The relationship between selected personality variables and the thinking of students in discussion classes. *School Review, 60*, 404–411.

Garner, W. (1976, December). Time in learning and schooling. *APSS Know How, 28*(4 & 5), 1–4.

Good, T. L., & Brophy, J. E. (1978). *Looking in classrooms* (2nd ed.). New York: Harper & Row.

Halpin, D. (1979). Accountability, answerability, and the reporting of active learning time. *British Journal of Teacher Education, 5*(3), 199–217.

Harnischfeger, A., & Wiley, D. E. (1976). The teaching-learning process in elementary schools: A synoptic view. *Curriculum Inquiry, 6*(1), 5–43.

Harnischfeger, A., & Wiley, D. E. (1978, May). A perspective for research policy. *Educational Technology, 18*, 46–50.

Harris, T., & Yinger, R. (1976). *Time: Current directions in research on teaching.* Meeting of the Invisible College of Researchers on Teaching, Michigan State University, Ann Arbor.

Hess, R. D., & Takanishi, R. (1973). *Teacher strategies and student engagement in low income area schools.* Research and Development Memorandum No. 105. Stanford: Stanford Center for Research and Development in Teaching. (ERIC Documents Reproduction Service No. ED 087 768)

Hudgins, B. R. (1967). Attending and thinking in the classroom. *Psychology in the Schools, 4*(3), 211–216.

Inglis, S. A. (1980, August). Commentary: Nascency and the BTES. *BTES Newsletter*, No. 7. Sacramento: California Commission for Teacher Preparation and Licensing.

Jackson, P. W. (1968). *Life in Classrooms.* New York: Holt, Rinehart and Winston.

Jackson, P. W. (1977). Looking into education's crystal ball. *Instructor, 87*(38), 38.

Karweit, N. (1978, January). *The organization of time in schools: Time scales and learning.* Paper presented at the National Invitational Conference on School Organization and Effects, San Diego.

Karweit, N., & Slavin, R. E. (1980, April). *Measuring time on-task: Issues of timing, sampling, and definition.* Paper presented at the annual meeting of the American Educational Research Association, Boston.

Kiesling, H. W. (1978). The productivity of instructional time by mode of instruction for students at varying levels of reading skills. *Reading Research Quarterly, 13*(4).

Knudsen, C. W. (1930, May). A program of high school supervision. *Peabody Journal of Education, 7*, 326–327.

Lahaderne, H. M. (1968). Attitudinal and intellectual correlates of attention: A study of four sixth grade classrooms. *Journal of Educational Psychology, 59*(5), 320–324.

Larrivee, B., & Vacca, J. M. (1980, April). *A comparison of ALT for mainstreamed, low, average, and high ability students.* Paper presented at the annual meeting of the American Educational Research Association, Boston.

Lomax, R. G., & Cooley, W. W. (1979, April). *The student achievement–instructional time relationship remains unsubstantiated.* Paper presented at the annual meeting of the American Educational Research Association, San Francisco.

Marliave, R. S. (1980). *Beyond engaged time: Approximations of task appropriateness in terms of on-going student learning behaviors.* Paper presented at the annual meeting of the American Educational Research Assocation, Boston.

Marliave, R. S., Cahen, L. S., & Berliner, D. C. (1977). *Prolegomenon on the concept of the appropriateness of instruction.* Technical Report IV-1, Beginning Teacher Evaluation Study. San Francisco: Far West Laboratory for Educational Research and Development.

Marliave, R. S., Fisher, C. W., & Dishaw, M. M. (1977). *Academic learning time and student achievement in the A-B period.* Technical Note V-1a, Beginning Teacher Evaluation Study. San Francisco: Far West Laboratory for Educational Research and Development.

McDonald, F. J. (1975, November). *Research on teaching and its implications for policy making: Report on Phase II of the Beginning Teacher Evaluation Study.* Paper presented at the Conference on Research on Teacher Effects, University of Texas, Austin.

McDonald, F. J. (1976). *Beginning Teacher Evaluation Study, Phase II 1973–74, Summary report.* Princeton, N. J.: Educational Testing Service. (ERIC Document Reproduction Service No. ED 127 375)

McKenzie, G. R. (1979). Effects of questions and test-like events on achievement and on-task behavior in classroom concept learning presentation. *Journal of Educational Research, 72*(6), 348–351.

McKinney, J. D., Mason, J., Perkerson, K., & Clifford, M. (1975). Relationship between behaviors and academic achievement. *Journal of Educational Psychology, 67*(2), 198–203.

Morsh, J. E. (1956). *Systematic observation of instructor behavior.* Developmental report AF PTRC-TN-56-52. San Antonio: Air Force Personnel and Training Research Center, Lackland Air Force Base.

Morrison, H. C. (1926). *The practice of teaching in the secondary school.* Chicago: University of Chicago Press.

Olson, W. C. (1931). A study of classroom behavior. *Journal of Educational Psychology, 22,* 449–454.

Özcelik, D. A. (1973). Student involvement in the learning process. Unpublished doctoral dissertation, University of Chicago. Cited by B. S. Bloom, Time and learning, *American Psychologist,* September 1974, *29,* 687.

Rosenshine, B. V. (1977a). *Primary grades instruction and student achievement.* Unpublished manuscript. (ERIC Document Reproduction Service No. ED 142 308)

Rosenshine, B. V. (1977b). Review of teaching variables and student achievement.

In G. Borich (Ed.), *The appraisal of teaching: Concepts and process.* Reading, Mass.: Addison-Wesley.

Rosenshine, B. V. (1979). Content, time and direct instruction. In P. L. Peterson & H. J. Walberg (Eds.), *Research on teaching: Concepts, findings, and implications.* Berkeley: McCutchan.

Rosenshine, B. V., & Berliner, D. C. (1978). Academic engaged time. *British Journal of Teacher Education, 4*(1), 3–16.

Rothkopf, E. Z. (1970). The concept of mathmagenic activities. *Review of Educational Research, 40.*

Rusnock, M., & Brandler, N. (1979, April). *Time off-task: Implications for learning.* Paper presented at the annual meeting of the American Educational Research Association, San Francisco.

Ryan, K., & Cooper, J. M. (1975). *Those who can, teach* (2nd ed.). Boston: Houghton Mifflin.

Samuels, S. J., & Turnure, J. E. (1974). Attention and reading achievement in first grade boys and girls. *Journal of Educational Psychology, 66*(1), 29–32.

Schultz, S. B. (1951). A study of relationships between overt verbal behavior in the classroom and conscious mental processes of the students. Unpublished doctoral dissertation, University of Chicago. Cited by P. W. Jackson, *Life in Classrooms.* New York: Holt, Rinehart and Winston, 1968, 98.

Shannon, J. R. (1936, March). A comparison of three means of measuring efficiency in teaching. *Journal of Educational Research, 29*, 501–508.

Shannon, J. R. (1942, April). Measure of the validity of attention scores. *Journal of Educational Research, 35*, 623–631.

Smith, N. M. (1979). Allocation of time and achievement in elementary social studies. *Journal of Educational Research, 72*(4), 231–236.

Smyth, W. J. (1979). *An ecological analysis of pupil use of academic learning time.* Unpublished doctoral dissertation, University of Alberta.

Smyth, W. J. (1980a, January). *Pupil engaged learning time: Concepts, findings, and implications.* Occasional Paper Series. Research Report 79-1-4, Centre for Research in Teaching, University of Alberta.

Smyth, W. J. (1980b). Clinical supervision: A reality centered mode of in-service education. *Educational Technology, 20*(3).

Smyth, W. J. (1981a). Teacher-as-executive: Managing pupil engagement during learning. In L. Lomas et al. (Eds.), *Classroom Processes.* Geelong, Victoria: Deakin University.

Smyth, W. J. (1981b). Research on teaching: What's in it for me? *The Australian Administrator, 2*(1), 1–4.

Smyth, W. J. (1981c, March). *Two for the price of one: Staff development through the utilization of findings from research on teaching.* Paper presented at the annual meeting of the American Educational Research Association, Los Angeles.

Stallings, J. A. (1980). Allocated academic learning time revisited, or beyond time on task. *Educational Researcher, 9*(11), 11–16.

Stallings, J. A., & Kaskowitz, D. (1974). *Follow-through classroom observation evaluation, 1972-73.* Menlo Park, Calif.: Stanford Research Institute.

Stodolsky, S. (1979, April). *Ecological features of fifth grade math and social studies classes and their relation to student involvement.* Paper presented at the annual meeting of the American Educational Research Association, San Francisco.

Symonds, P. M. (1926, April). Study habits of high school pupils shown by close observation of controlled groups. *Teachers College Record, 27,* 713–724.

Taylor, M. (1968). *Intercorrelations among three methods of estimating students' attention.* Report Series 29. Stanford: Stanford Center for Research on Teaching.

Thomas, J. A. (1971). *The productive school: A systems analysis approach to educational administration.* New York: Wiley.

Thomas, J. A. (1977). *Resource allocations in classrooms.* Unpublished research report. Education Finance and Productivity Center, Department of Education, University of Chicago.

Walker, R., & Adelman, C. (1975). *A guide to classroom observation.* London: Methuen.

Washburne, C., Vogel, M., & Gray, W. S. (1926). Results of practical experiments in fitting schools to individuals. *Journal of Educational Research,* Supplementary Issue. Bloomington, IL: Public School Publishing Company.

Weber, M. B. (1976). The effects of environmental congruence on time-on-task, lower mental process achievement, and higher mental process achievement. Unpublished doctoral dissertation, University of Chicago. *Dissertation Abstracts International,* 1977, 713A.

Winkler, D. R. (1975). *Time and learning: An economic analysis.* Unpublished manuscript. Santa Barbara: University of California.

2

The Model of
School Learning:
Progress of an Idea

John B. Carroll
University of North Carolina at Chapel Hill

EDITORS' INTRODUCTION

We are fortunate, indeed, to have the distinguished psychologist J. B. Carroll personally relate the genesis and history of one of the most influential papers in education and psychology. Dr. Carroll was heavily involved with research on foreign language learning in the late 1950s. Like other creative scientists after years of work in an area, he proposed a deceptively simple formulation of the relation among the variables he worked with. The basis of the model of school learning was outlined over a single Sunday morning in 1959. With its publication in 1963 in the *Teachers College Record*, the model gradually became the source of a great deal of thinking, developmental work, and intellectual debate.

The model influenced Professor Bloom, of the University of Chicago, serving as one of the sources for his development of the exciting and controversial instructional system known as learning for mastery. The model of school learning served also as the basis of Wiley and Harnischfeger's interest in the relations between quantity of schooling and achievement (their recent work is included as Chapter 8 in this volume). Carroll's model also served as the basis for the Beginning Teacher Evaluation Study, which is described in a number of chapters in this volume. Through numerous citations Carroll documents how the model has served as an influential guide to educational research and educational evaluation in many nations.

Carroll goes on to examine the research questions about different components of the model—allocated time and time-on-task, perseverance, aptitude, opportunity to learn, ability to understand instruction, degree of learning, and learning rate. Carroll notes that the concept of aptitude appears to be in need of clarification. The concept was not meant to be synonymous with entering ability as suggested by some "such environmentalists," who are often associated with mastery learning approaches. Carroll uses the term *aptitude* as it has been used by differential psychologists. In this chapter it is also pointed out that there are individual differences in learning rates, but that they could be specific to a given task. Moreover, it is assumed that learning rates can be predicted by appropriate measures of aptitude. Opportunity to learn, another key concept in the model, was originally a measure of how much time a student needed to complete a learning task. Carroll points out how this concept has become extended to mean amount of content covered, a consistent positive predictor of student achievement.

Carroll discusses criticisms of the model of school learning, which he classifies as three types: criticisms about the philosophical basis of the model, criticisms about the underlying theory, and criticisms of its efficiency and practicality as a guide to researchers and practitioners. Carroll's insightful handling of these criticisms makes him sound much more reasonable than some of the most passionate of the model's critics.

"A Model of School Learning" was published in the *Teachers College Record* in 1963. The article (Carroll, 1963a) represented an attempt to give a unified perspective on the types of basic variables, and their interrelationships, that were proposed as affecting a student's degree of achievement in school subjects such as reading, mathematics, and others that involve the cumulative acquisition of skills and knowledges. It seems to have been one of my more influential writings, even though I classify it as a "think piece" rather than a solid report of research. I count 168 citations of it listed in the volumes of the *Social Sciences Citation Index* over the years 1969–1980, but many other references to it are to be found. Further, the article has been reprinted and translated a number of times.[1] It has been a matter of some curiosity and interest to me to work through the various citations and subsequent research to see how the ideas set forth in the original article have been used, interpreted, emphasized, supported, not supported, questioned, or criticized over the years since its first publication. In this chapter I take the opportunity to comment on these uses and reactions and to discuss the climate of educational theory and practice over the past several decades that nurtured the continuing interest in the model of school learning (MSL).

It may be of some relevance to relate the circumstances that led to the publication of the article. Over a number of years, my research interests had centered in various problems connected with the teaching and learning of foreign languages (Carroll, 1966), in particular, the prediction of success in learning foreign languages through measurements of "foreign language aptitude" (see Carroll, 1981). Chiefly with the support of the Carnegie Corporation of New York, I had developed a battery of tests (Carroll & Sapon, 1959) that seemed under many circumstances to have high effectiveness in predicting the degree of such success. But they did not always have high validity; in fact, sometimes the validity coefficients were essentially zero. In preparation for a presentation that I had been invited to give at a symposium to be held at the University of Pittsburgh in February 1960 on training research and education (Glaser, 1962), I resolved to survey all my results to try to see what factors, in the light of the varying settings in which my studies had been conducted, seemed to affect the predictiveness of the tests. It seemed that there were many varieties and conditions of foreign language instruction. One variable was the amount of intensiveness—from the highly intensive courses in which individuals were put under considerable pressure to keep up with a fast-moving course in which they had as much as five to eight hours of instruction per day, to the much less intensive, three-hours-per-week courses in liberal arts colleges and universities. Generally, aptitude measures were much more predictive in intensive courses than in nonintensive courses. But there were other variables: Students might be uniformly highly motivated, or there might be wide individual differences in motivation. Instruction could be conducted in a rather "intellectual," formalistic way with much discussion of grammar and language features, or it could be conducted with much active practice, drill, and feedback. Thinking about the way in which all these variables might interact with one another and affect the predictiveness of aptitude measurements, I somehow got the idea of developing a general learning model that could explain my results. I remember that it was one Sunday morning in the summer of 1959 that, in just a couple of hours, I made a rough draft of my model, listing classes of variables and postulating their relationship.

It all seemed so simple and obvious, once one thought about it. A critical variable was time: People took different amounts of time to achieve a given level of proficiency. There were several reasons why they might take different amounts of time. It was certainly conceivable, and much evidence supported the idea, that there were inherent differences among people in their learning rates, and that these inherent differences were reflected in performance on my aptitude battery. But also, people might take different amounts of time because some were well motivated and attended to their learning with much effort, while others gave less attention and effort to their learning during periods when they were nominally engaged in study. Further, some might take more time because they had difficulty understanding what they were to do, or the content of their lessons. When the instruction was relatively formal and "intellectual," this would affect students of relatively lower intellectual ability more than those of high intelligence, who would be able to figure out the instructional content on their own. Finally, when instruction was paced at a higher rate than a student could take it, a student would fall behind.

From all this, I derived a "model for studying the prediction of success in complex learning tasks" (Carroll, 1962a) that specified three basic variables in terms of time: (a) *aptitude*, as reflected in the amount of time that a student would need to learn something to a specified criterion, assuming high motivation (perseverance), ample opportunity to learn, and an optimal quality of instruction; (b) *perseverance*, as reflected in the amount of time that a student would be willing to engage in active learning; and (c) *opportunity to learn*, as reflected in the amount of time that the organization of a course, or other circumstances, would allow for learning. Two other variables were not specified in terms of time, but would interact with the first three in such a way that they might possibly be measured: (d) ability to understand instruction—a variable that might become more critical as the quality of instruction decreased, and (e) quality of instruction—seen as a variable that could affect the amount of time that a student would need to master a task, and thus affect the importance of the student's aptitude, particularly when quality of instruction was low. I did not try at the time to specify exactly how one might evaluate quality of instruction, but I could have reeled off a whole host of variables that might index instructional quality.

The basic variables in the model were defined formally and put into a functional equation in which degree of learning was expressed as a function of the ratio of time actively engaged in learning (as a function of aptitude, perseverance, and opportunity to learn) to the time that the student would need in view of his or her aptitude, ability to understand instruction, and the quality of the instruction offered. This equation, with some ad hoc assumptions, was used in a computer simulation that looked at how the validity of aptitude measurements might vary as a function of different kinds of instructional conditions, and average student motivation (perseverance). The results seemed to explain, in a general way, the variation in actual results that I was getting. Although I never published the actual computer program, the formal statement of the model and detailed results were presented both in the article prepared for the February 1960 Pittsburgh symposium (Carroll, 1962a) and in an article presented at a Harvard symposium (April 1961) on the uses of computers (Carroll, 1962b).

At the time of the Pittsburgh symposium, I looked upon my model as an interesting theoretical exercise. While I felt it might be useful in my further studies of foreign language aptitude, I had no plan to generalize it to types of learning other than foreign language learning. Somehow my work came to the attention of E. Joseph Shoben, Jr., at that time the editor of the *Teachers College Record*. Apparently impressed with the possibilities of applying my model to other types of learning, he communicated with me and encouraged me to write an article for his journal that would develop my ideas for wider dissemination. I did so, introducing my essay as giving "a schematic design or conceptual model of factors affecting success in school learning and of the way they interact" (Carroll, 1963a, p. 723) and adding a few comments about its implications for concepts of underachievement and overachievement. I called the model a model of *school* learning because I desired to distinguish it from models in the general theory of learning, even though, as Garner (1978) notes, "there is nothing about school in it," and it was certainly not intended to be limited to applications in schools. The article was tucked away as the last formal article published in the May 1963 issue; it was not even featured by having its title listed on the front cover of that issue. Apparently the article drew little attention at the time; at least, I am not aware that it directly stirred up any great interest.

There the matter rested for several years, except that I myself used the model in designing and interpreting some of my further research in foreign language education, and referred to it in my teaching and in a number of public appearances, seminars, workshops, and the like. For example, during the summer of 1964, in serving as a group leader at a six-week advanced workshop for young educational researchers, held at Stanford University under the leadership of Lee Cronbach, I featured the MSL and encouraged the participants in my group to think about how it might be further elaborated and studied in educational contexts. At times we thought the model was so general and flexible that it was not really testable as a theory of instruction. Nevertheless, I gave an evening public lecture on it that was eventually published under the titile "School Learning over the Long Haul" (Carroll, 1965). Subsequently, I was also able to promote the model in educational research workshops that took place in Europe—in Sweden in 1968, in France in 1970, and in West Germany in 1971 (Edelstein & Hopf, 1973). As a result, the model was given considerable discussion in the European literature (e.g., Achtenhagen, 1978; Bonsch, 1977; Flammer, 1975; Lundgren, 1972).

Examples of use of the MSL in my research on foreign languages and related topics are my studies of the parameters of foreign language learning in programmed instruction in Mandarin Chinese (Carroll, 1963c), in intensive foreign language instruction in the Peace Corps (1966), and in the interpretation of survey results on language proficiency among seniors majoring in a foreign language in U.S. colleges and universities (1967), and among students of French at elementary and secondary school levels in eight countries (1975). The model has consistently been found useful in guiding foreign language instruction and has often been cited by theorists of foreign language instruction (Bockman, 1972; Carroll, 1974c; Jakobovits, 1970). In an article prepared for a conference on the aptitude-achievement distinction (Carroll, 1974b), I pointed out that foreign language aptitude research offers many examples where a clear distinction between aptitude and achievement can be made, and I offered a special set of criteria for distinguishing these concepts not only in foreign language research but also in other areas of school success prediction.

Prompted by an associate, I helped design and conduct a small experimental study of the MSL (Carroll & Spearritt, 1967). Using a programmed-instruction technique involving the learning of an artificial foreign language, the experiment sought to determine the effect of manipulating quality of instruction, opportunity for learning, and perseverance, in interaction with measures of IQ taken from school records. The results suggested that poor-quality instruction depressed performance of children at all intelligence levels and that it led to reduced perseverance on the part of children of high intelligence. Learning was also shown to be highly inefficient when students had insufficient opportunity for learning. The empirical data thus generally confirmed the trends hypothesized in the model, though not in every detail.

One other paper prepared and presented at the conference on the aptitude-achievement distinction seemed of particular interest and significance (Carroll, 1974a). Through mathematical elaboration of the MSL, it showed that it could be applied to large-sample, cross-sectional data on aptitude and achievement measures to indicate that students are *consistently* and very systematically spread out in achievement according to measured aptitude, at least in school systems using conventional procedures of instruction, and that the degree of dispersion increases systematically from grade 1 to grade 12. The results led me to think that there is no necessary connection between aptitude and achievement, but that the connection arises because of customary modes of placing, teaching, and promoting students. Presumably, if those modes were altered in some way, the connection between aptitude and achievement might not be as strong as it is usually observed to be.

GENESIS OF THE MODEL: SOME MORE INDIRECT INFLUENCES

It would seem that the feature of the MSL that has attracted most attention is its assertion that aptitude is a matter of individual differences in the amount of time that people need to master a task and the implication that nearly anyone can learn any task if given enough time to do so. (In framing this part of the model, I assumed that some students might need an infinity of time to master a task, and thus in practice could not be expected to do so.) Certainly this is not new idea. Cronbach (1972) traced it back to John Locke, and it has been pointed out (Bloom, 1974a) that the idea is implicit in writings of educational philosophers such as Comenius and Herbart. I cannot claim to have been directly influenced by these writers, for I have paid relatively little attention to the philosophy of education. I had been dimly aware that educational experiments in the 1920s had tried manipulating time and opportunity to learn (Morrison, 1926; Washburne, Vogel, & Gray, 1926), but again, I would not claim intellectual ancestry from those sources. Rather, my notions developed more directly from observations of individual differences in time requirements in foreign language learning, programmed instruction, and related settings. Such observations were also the source of my notions about opportunity to learn, perseverance, ability to understand instruction, and quality of instruction. I had also become fascinated with time as a variable from reading research studies on human learning. Time (or its exchange equivalent, number of trials) has always been recognized as a critical value in designing and analyzing experiments on various kinds of human learning. Around the time that I constructed my model, verbal learning theorists were excited by findings of Bugelski (1962) to the effect that total presentation time—however it was divided into separate trials—seemed to be the critical variable in a variety of learning experiments. Also, I had been stimulated by what I regarded as the elegance of Thurstone's (1930) theoretical derivation of a function relating learning time to list length, and a student and I conducted an experiment to verify certain aspects of Thurstone's formulation (Carroll & Burke, 1965). In the back of my mind was the notion that all task and skill learning might ultimately be described more precisely in terms of parameters for task characteristics and individual differences.

EXTENSIONS OF THE MSL

Around 1967 or 1968, in personal contacts with Benjamin Bloom and some of his students, I became aware that Bloom himself had become very much interested in the MSL and was attempting to apply it to promote better and more efficient learning. I understood, in fact, that he was conducting an extensive series of experiments in what he was calling "mastery learning" in Chicago schools and in his own graduate courses. Naturally, I was gratified that someone with the brilliance, creativity, and energy of Bloom was taking an interest in the MSL and putting it to use. I myself was too much occupied with other matters to try to mount practical experiments with it, even in foreign language instuction. For the most part, I preferred to take the role of theorist, with respect to the MSL, rather than active experimenter.

Bloom's first publication on mastery learning appears to have been an essay published in a newsletter of the Center for the Study of Evaluation of Instructional Programs at UCLA (Bloom, 1968). The essay presented the model pretty much as I had originally formulated it, and pointed out how "mastery" of learning tasks might be attained by manipulating variables of time, opportunity, and quality of instruction. Bloom emphasized the possible role of "formative evaluation" (a term that had been promoted by Michael Scriven). He also suggested that various "alternative" learning resources, such as small-group tutorial sessions, feedback, and correction, would promote learning. One of his doctoral students (Kim, 1968) mounted an extensive program of mastery learning in his native country, South Korea, apparently with spanking success.

Over the subsequent years, Bloom's ideas on mastery learning developed and flourished. Principles of mastery learning were an important focus of *Handbook of Formative and Summative Evaluation of Student Learning* (Bloom, Hastings, & Madaus, 1971). Some of Bloom's students were particularly energetic in bringing these principles to the attention of the educational community (Block, 1973, 1974a; Block & Anderson, 1975; Torshen, 1977), and by 1976 enough research evidence had accumulated for Block and Burns (1976) to write an extensive review of this work, pointing out that most of this evidence suggested that mastery learning programs could be highly successful. As research progressed, Bloom and his colleagues came to feel that the original form of the MSL had to be modified to allow for the fact that in the course of continuing programs of mastery learning the time that students needed to master learning tasks seemed to decrease in both central tendency and variance (Bloom, 1974a). A major work (Bloom, 1976) presented a new formulation of mastery learning principles and summarized the research evidence that supported it.

Together with Bloom's work, the MSL inspired still other major lines of development. David Wiley and Annegret Harnischfeger (1974) saw the relevance of the MSL model, with certain revisions and refinements that they developed (Harnischfeger & Wiley, 1976; 1978), to the evaluation of total school programs, particularly when attention was paid to total "quantity of schooling." Similarly, at the Learning Research and Development Center at the University of Pittsburgh, research on its programs of Individually Prescribed Instruction (IPI) developed under the leadership of Robert Glaser made use of the MSL in formulating research evaluations (Wang & Lindvall, 1970; Wang & Yeager, 1971; Yeager & Lindvall, 1967). Wang (1970) confirmed that learning rate was not necessarily a general trait, but could be highly task specific. Cooley and Lohnes (1976) urged use of the MSL in categorizing the variables to be studied in educational evaluation, and these ideas were realized in a number of evaluative studies (Cooley & Emrick, 1974; Cooley & Leinhardt, 1975; Leinhardt, 1977a, 1977b, 1978, 1980). Still other interesting extensions of the MSL have been proposed by Bennett (1978) and Centra and Potter (1980).

Certainly the most extensive and systematic use of the MSL in research on school learning occurred in the Beginning Teacher Evaluation Study in California (Denham & Lieberman, 1980; Fisher, Marliave, & Filby, 1979). The concept of student time-on-task was further reformulated to focus on what has been called academic learning time (ALT) or academic engaged time (Rosenshine & Berliner, 1978), that is, time during which the student is actively engaged in learning tasks that are somewhat challenging but on which a high success rate can be attained. The project discovered that there could be wide variation among classes and among students in the proportions of ALT even with similar amounts of allocated time, and that these proportions were correlated significantly with student achievement. In its dissemination phase, the project directors encouraged teachers to organize their work so as to optimize ALT proportions for all students.

In the meantime, frequent mention and use of the MLS was made in numerous reports of mastery learning programs in a variety of subjects at various levels of schooling. Mastery learning, as based on the MLS, became a guide to the formulation and evaluation of new reading programs (e.g., Fredrick, 1977; Guthrie & Tyler, 1978; Kiesling, 1978; Paradis & Peterson, 1973; Smith & Katims, 1977; Trogdon, 1980). Similar developments occurred in school mathematics (e.g., Burrows & Okey, 1975; Hymel, 1974; Kretschmann & Malburg, 1976), science (Latta, Dolphin, & Grabe, 1978), foreign languages (Bockman, 1972; Nieman & Smith, 1978), educational psychology (Denton & Seymour, 1978; Lee & McLean, 1979; Terrill, Berger, & Mulgrave, 1973), statistics and test theory (Airasian, 1972; Pfaff & Schmidt, 1974), nursing education (Geissler, 1974; Huckabay, 1978; Huckabay & Arndt, 1976; Mentzer & Scuglia, 1975; Wolf & Quiring, 1971), pharmaceutical training (Manasse & Lasker, 1976), and dentistry (Brundo, 1976). Dorsel (1978) suggested applying the model to the learning of athletic skills—golf, football, bowling.

The model has also served as a basis for a number of mathematical models of the learning process, the allocation of instructional time, or causal effects in education (Besel, 1972; Bulcock, Lee, & Luk, 1979; Chant & Luenberger, 1974; Cotton, 1975; Hicklin, 1976; Munck, 1979; Sagiv, 1979).

New concepts and inventions are often arrived at independently at approximately the same time or period in history. Keller's (1968) Personalized System of Instruction (PSI) bears much similarity to Bloom's mastery learning and is founded on many of the same ideas that are fomulated in the MSL, but contrary to what is suggested by some writers (e.g., Rupley & Longnion, 1978), Keller was not influenced by the MSL, as I have confirmed through personal communication with him. Nevertheless, it seems legitimate to consider research on PSI as relevant also to the MSL, as Block and Burns (1976) have done. Also, one need not regard PSI and mastery learning as competing models; they have the same general aims, and entail generally similar procedures and problems. The MSL does, however, lay more stress on aptitude and time variables.

The model of school learning has had, then, a consistent and perhaps increasing influence in many areas of education, not only in the United States but also in a number of both developed and developing countries abroad. It has come to the attention of the public in such prestigious media as the *New York Times* (Fiske, 1980), and has been featured in a number of textbooks and readings in educational psychology (e.g., De Cecco, 1968; Willerman & Turner, 1979). It seems to have been an idea whose time has come and that is here to stay.

THE APPEAL OF THE MODEL

Why, I have mused, during this period in the history of education has the model of school learning and its derivatives so captured the attention of educators that it has had the influence it seems to have had (Guskey, 1980;

Husén, 1979; Ladas, 1980)? Its ideas were oversimplified and in most respects not really new. The idea that learning takes time is so obvious as to be almost trivial: In comments on the BTES project an editorial writer in a recent issue of *Basic Education* (1980) wondered why "so much research is necessary to validate the obvious." (But then, much scientific attention has been devoted to the effects of gravity, also an "obvious" variable.) Of slightly more novelty is the proposition that variations in aptitude can be correlated with variations in the amount of time a student needs to master a task: Teachers have always recognized differences between "fast" and "slow" learners. Yet, the implication of this proposition, that students should be allowed to proceed at their own rate in order to take the amount of time they need, has been the linchpin for all sorts of applications and interpretations of the model. Perhaps the model's appeal to educators in general lies in its suggestion that a radical revision of customary school practices in this regard was needed. Bloom's mastery learning concept added the suggestion that if all the elements of the model were properly orchestrated, all or nearly all students could master almost any task demanded in the school curriculum.

Of course the model did not rely solely on learning time as such. It suggested that only time that the student was actively engaged in learning really counted toward achievement. It recommended also that instructional quality should be adjusted to meet the needs of students of lesser aptitude, particularly when a student might have difficulty understanding what was to be learned and what had to be done to accomplish this learning.

The practical application of these ideas took some years to evolve to its present state (Hyman & Cohen, 1979). Bloom (1976) concentrated on insuring that students had adequate "cognitive entry characteristics" and providing students with necessary "feedback and correction." The BTES project recognized that it was not solely the amount of time devoted to a learning task that counted, but that it was the *kind* of time utilization, or more specifically, the kinds of learning events that took place during this time, that were critical. Academic engaged time was defined in the BTES project as time during which students were mastering new tasks in which they could have a high success rate. Berliner (1979, p. 121) contrasts this "academic focus" of time with situations in which "large amounts of time were spent in telling stories or in art, music, and play activities." (One hopes that this does not mean that telling stories, or art, music, and play activities were to be totally excluded from school programs.)

All this suggests that although it is "obvious" that time is a variable in learning, it is *not* obvious how available learning time can best be used. The history of educational research on teaching demonstrates that with rare exceptions, this was a critical point that was too often neglected. Rosenshine (1979) assigns the MSL and its extensions to a "third cycle" of research on teaching. In a first cycle, beginning in the 1930s, interest focused on finding out whether measurable "teacher characteristics" were related to student achievement; in general the findings were negative or highly unclear. Perhaps these research efforts might have been more productive if they had been concerned with any teacher characteristics that might relate to teachers' use of available learning time. A second cycle of research, occurring in the 1950s and 1960s, focused on classroom interactions; again, despite small victories, no major theory or model of school practice emerged. It may be suggested that classroom interaction research should attend to interactions that result in higher amounts of academic engaged time. The third cycle, then, turned attention on "direct" instructional variables, that is, variables that could be demonstrated both logically and empirically to affect learning outcomes. The virtue of the MSL was that it suggested what these direct instructional variables might be, and how they might be related. In this sense, the MSL became, it seems, a much-needed guide to educational research and educational evaluation (Cooley & Lohnes, 1976; Hambleton, 1974; White & Duker, 1973). Obviously, the model could not have spelled out all the details, but those details are generally being filled in by the many educational researchers who have been guided by it.

COMPONENTS OF THE MODEL: RESEARCH QUESTIONS

What are these details? It is impossible to survey here all the research that has some bearing on the MSL and its extensions; for reviews and general treatments see, for example, Block and Burns (1976) and Peterson and Walberg (1979). Attention will be focused on certain highlights of this research and certain problems arising in connection with the components suggested by the model.

A general comment is in order on whether the model "works" and is scientifically valid. Block and Burns (1976), summarizing research on whether the model "works," came to a generally affirmative conclusion. They continued:

> The approaches have not had as large effects on student learning as their advocates proposed are possible, but they have had consistently positive effects. In quantitative terms, mastery approaches have usually produced greater student learning than nonmastery approaches, and they have usually produced relatively less variability in this learning. In qualitative terms, mastery approaches have typically helped students acquire higher order learning, though there is some question as to whether this higher order learning has been retained. (p. 25)

The reader may be reminded that in some early discussions of the MSL at the 1964 summer seminar mentioned earlier, some of the participants and I tended to feel that the MSL may not be a truly testable model, in the sense that any failures in its working might be attributed to failures to implement the model adequately, either in the design of educational programs, the measurement of relevant variables, or the analysis of data. Certainly there seem to be a number of instances in which apparent failures of mastery learning can be characterized in this way. For example, Smith (1979) obtained results that suggested that "the usefulness of allocated time as a potent variable in planning or evaluation of instruction seemed questionable" (p. 231). In evaluating such a finding, one would have to ask whether "allocated" time was defined in such a way as to limit it to what the BTES project called academic engaged time. (Other problems in Smith's study included the relevance of the instruction to the criterion measure chosen.) Similarly, Kibby's (1979) finding that time was not a significant variable in certain phases of an experiment on teaching "initial word learning" to beginning readers would have to be appraised in terms of the particular instructional conditions used in the study (see also Fredrick & Walberg, 1980).

On the other hand, the model is testable in the sense that it makes predictions concerning the effects of its variables, and if the variables are appropriately manipulated and measured, sound tests can be conducted. Among experiments illustrating this point are those by Anderson (1975), Arlin (1974), Block (1974b, 1975), Carroll and Spearritt (1967), Carver (1970), James (1975), and Lewis (1970). In general, predictions made by the model were confirmed in these experiments; where they were not, possible refinements or modifications of the model could be considered.

Time, Time-on Task

Comments made above have already suggested that sheer quantity of time allocated to learning is not necessarily the critical variable. This has been pointed out by many observers (e.g., Buss & Poley, 1976; Eigler, Macke, Nenniger, Poelchau, & Sraka, 1976; Harnischfeger & Wiley, 1978). The quality of learning that goes on in the allocated time, possibly captured by the BTES project's concept of academic engaged time (Denham & Lieberman, 1980; see also Grannis, 1978), is what is crucial. This principle has suggested to some investigators that time-on-task, interpreted as time accompanied by student involvement, should itself be a modifiable, "alterable" variable (Anderson, 1980; Bloom, 1980; Stuck, 1980). But how can student involvement time be manipulated? Programmed instruction has been proposed as one method, and while programmed instruction generally produces greater student learning on the average, it has not been particularly effective in reducing individual differences in learning (Carroll, 1963d; Flammer, 1973). Increasing the intensiveness of instruction has been considered by other workers (Hefferlin, 1972; Meyen & Lehr, 1980, with particular reference to "mildly handicapped children"). Giving students data on estimated completion time was tried and found wanting (Colton, 1974).

There has been considerable research on the effects of self-pacing versus teacher pacing of mastery learning instruction. While no significant differences were found between these two procedures by Morris, Suber, and Bijou (1978), significant interactions with remediation strategies (Denton & Seymour, 1978) or with student ability levels (Arlin & Westbury, 1976; Latta, Dolphin, & Grabe, 1978) have been found. Nevertheless, the types of interactions with ability found by Arlin and Westbury were quite different from those observed by Latta et al. Sanderson (1976) learned from student interviews that some students disliked mastery learning procedures, and thus spent less time than they needed—less time than under traditional techniques where teachers provided pacing. Apparently the effect of self-pacing under mastery learning procedures depends on many additional variables.

Perseverance

The MSL postulated that time-on-task would be a function of the amount of time the student is "willing" to spend on learning, and that the amount learned would depend on the amount of time actually spent, regardless of whether the student "liked" this learning. Research has not given adequate attention to verifying these predictions, although some of the research on increasing student involvement would have a bearing. Perhaps the original statement of the MSL was unclear on what would be meant by student "willingness" to spend time. Actually it was intended that anything that might motivate students to spend active or engaged learning time would produce "perseverance," but use of the term motivation was avoided because of difficulty in its definition.

An obvious case in which students in "alternative schools" showed reduced perseverance in learning as compared to students in more conventional schools was cited by Skager, Morehouse, Russock, and Schumacher (1973). Clifford (1973) investigated conditions under which liking and learning are positively correlated, finding that such a correlation is a multiplicative function of task commitment on the part of the student and the extent to which the student feels personally accountable for performance outcomes. Possibly mastery learning research should pay more attention to developments in motivational psychology (Atkinson, Lens, & O'Malley, 1976; Atkinson & Raynor, 1974; Weiner, 1974), which indeed are very much concerned with learning-time variables.

Aptitude

In view of the fact that the MSL was developed in the context of research on aptitude (in foreign language learning), it is rather surprising that mastery learning research has paid relatively little attention to this variable, which was postulated to be measurable separately from learning time needed and yet to be a predictor of it. Some mastery learning studies have included measures of general intelligence or general scholastic aptitude in their study designs and analyses (e.g., Carver, 1970; Latta, Dolphin, & Grabe, 1978; Sjogren, 1967), but there have been few attempts to link specific variables of individual differences in aptitude (e.g., those identified by factor analysis) with learning rates or performance outcomes. Bloom (1976, 1980) has continued to take the "arch-environmentalist stance" (Cronbach & Snow, 1977, p. 109) that any initial differences in aptitude are to be identified with relatively modifiable "cognitive entry" characteristics such as possession of specific skills and knowledges that are relevant for a new learning task. This stance seems to be reflected in the Cooley-Lohnes (1976) model for educational evaluation, which converts "aptitude" into a variable of "initial performance" that can be measured at least in part by general ability tests. Studies employing this model do indeed find a major percentage of predictor variance in general-ability tests. For example, Leinhardt (1977a) found 46.6% of outcome variance in a major evaluation study of Follow Through classrooms predicted uniquely from an "input" variable consisting of scores of the Lorge-Thorndike Intelligence Test combined with scores on a "mathematics placement" test. The report on the BTES project (Denham & Lieberman, 1980, particularly W. R. Borg's chapter therein) similarly found high predictiveness for an input variable ("preachievement"); it does not state exactly how this input variable was measured, but one may assume that it was composed of measures of, or at least reflected, general scholastic ability.

In mastery learning research, therefore, there seems to have been a tendency to suppress attention to strictly aptitude variables in favor of vaguely defined "input" or "prior-learning" variables, and further, to suppress or de-emphasize the importance of even these input variables. To be sure, the MSL acknowledges the operation of prior-learning variables as accounting for lessened "time needed" among students who have to some extent profited from prior learning, but it was not intended that such prior-learning variables would account for all the variance in active learning time needed. Even Bloom's (1976) demonstrations of reduced variance in learning time needed in successive phases of mastery learning programs cannot be interpreted as entirely eliminating the effect of aptitude variables, that is, relatively permanent characteristics of individuals that affect learning rates. Flammer (1975, pp. 230–248) has reviewed some of the evidence for the persistent effects of such aptitude variables; indeed, Flammer claims that individual differences tend to increase under programmed instruction. Carroll (1974a) analyzed cross-section data from nationally administered aptitude and achievement tests to show that the variance of aptitude-dependent achievement increases markedly and systematically over grades 1–12, although one might suppose (perhaps unrealistically) that such results might not have been obtained if mastery learning procedures had been applied nationwide over the corresponding time period.

Of particular interest in this connection are results reported by

Gettinger and White (1979), who found that work-sample tests of "time to learn" (TTL) were superior to ordinary IQ tests as predictors of school learning outcomes. The generally strong predictiveness of the Modern Language Aptitude Test (Carroll, 1962a, 1963c, 1966, 1974b) may possibly be explainable in part as due to the fact that many subtests of this battery are in effect work-sample learning tests. Of course, the mere fact that an aptitude test is a work-sample test does not exclude the possibility that it is in part a measure of prior-learned skills and knowledges, but it also leaves open the possibility that basic, relatively permanent individual differences in aptitude are reflected in work-sample tests. This possibility is strengthened by the observation that many aptitude and work-sample measurements are relatively resistant to improvement in scores through practice and training.

In short, the question of aptitude as a determinant of learning time needed remains relatively unexplored in the literature on mastery learning approaches. Because this question must be left open, one must avoid taking the "arch-environmentalist" position taken by many mastery learning advocates. Environment and nurture are important, manipulable variables but it is difficult to believe they are the whole story, much as one might like to believe this.

Opportunity to Learn

Strictly speaking, opportunity to learn was defined in the original MSL as the amount of time allowed for learning a task. The implication was that if this time was less than the time a student needed, learning would be less than complete, and that opportunity to learn in conventional teaching programs would be less than desirable for many students. Research in mastery learning and direct instruction has explicitly considered opportunity to learn in this definition when conventional teaching programs, with limited time allowances, are contrasted with mastery learning programs in which ample time is allowed—perhaps through required homework assignments, tutorial sessions for selected students, and the like. Pratzner (1972) has considered the problem of estimating the amount of time needed, setting boundaries around the "most likely time" as "optimistic time" and "pessimistic time"; he did not, however, propose using aptitude measures to make these estimates, as the MSL would suggest.

In the BTES project (Denham & Lieberman, 1980), opportunity to learn seems to correspond to "allocated time," and the concern was to use this allocated time with with maximal efficiency by making a maximal proportion of it "academic engaged time."

In many writings about mastery learning and direct instructional procedures, however, opportunity to learn has been equated to "content covered." As Walker and Schaffarzick (1974, p. 101) remark, at a minimum a curricular element must be *presented* in order to be learned.

That is, at least *some* time must be devoted to presenting it. Rosenshine (1979, p. 32) takes opportunity to learn in this sense, and after citing a number of studies, concludes that "in all studies but one, significant relations were found between content covered and gains in student achievement." A further study supporting the importance of covering content is by Arehart (1979), who also manipulated amount of emphasis given to different curricular objectives. Such studies and the ideas on which they are based represent a valid and highly useful extension of the MSL, particularly since it seems unfortunately to be the case that school programs do not always give adequate coverage to all instructional objectives.

Quality of Instruction

In the term *quality of instruction* the original MSL attempted to summarize aspects of instruction and instructional material that conveyed a clear presentation of the learning task—its nature, objectives, content, hierarchical structure (if any), etc. It could have mentioned a host of other factors that might contribute to quality of instruction—motivating and inspiring students: teaching in an interesting and vivid manner; giving praise, feedback, and correction; and so forth. Indeed the notion of quality of instruction covers a very broad region of educational psychology. Feldhusen, Hynes, and Ames (1976, p. 14) interpret the MSL as defining quality of instruction "in a circular manner as follows: Instructional quality is adequate if a student learns successfully from it." Such a circular definition was not intended, although it might prove a basis for testing elements of instructional quality. In studies of the MSL, there seem to have been few attempts, other than in a study by Carroll and Spearritt (1967), to manipulate quality of instruction, for example, by deliberately degrading certain elements of it. The assumption seems to be that in all studies of mastery learning, quality of instruction should be maintained at as high a level as possible, while other elements are manipulated. Thus we have little if any evidence to confirm the MSL's proposal that quality of instruction interacts with aptitude and ability to understand instruction in such a way as to increase needed learning time for low-aptitude students.

Ability to Understand Instruction

It was the intent of the original MSL to make a clear distinction between those student characteristics that were directly relevant to learning time needed for the task per se and those that would interact with quality of instruction. As in the case of research on true aptitude variables, as discussed above, there has been little research on ability to understand instruction and its possible interaction with instructional quality. A case where such interaction might be expected would be one where the vocabulary and readability level of instructional material is pitched above a student's ability to comprehend it, but such cases appear not to have been explicitly investigated in the context of the MSL and its extensions. It is possible, however, that studies that have used general-ability measures as input variables (e.g., Carver, 1970; Thompson, 1980) illustrate an effect of the ability to understand instruction. Thompson, for example, found that most outcome variance in a calculus course was accounted for by "aptitude" (as measured by high school GPA and scholastic aptitude tests), and there was no significant interaction of aptitude with treatment (individualized mastery learning versus traditional instruction systems). In practice it may be difficult to distinguish comprehension ability from task-specific aptitudes. Anderson (1979) points out that when one is predicting performance in a diversity of courses and subject matters, general-ability measures are probably of greater use than specific-aptitude measures.

Degree of Learning

The MSL suggested that the degree of learning at any time during the course of learning would be a function of the ratio between the time taken (in active learning) and the time needed; it avoided specifying whether this function would be linear, because the function might depend on the type of learning task. For example, some simple tasks might have all-or-none achievement, in which case the learning curve would be a step function. For incremental learning of complex skills, such as in foreign language learning, the function can be approximately linear (Carroll, 1963c); such a function was also found by Sjogren (1967) with programmed instruction in several different subjects.

Learning Rate

Learning rate is a concept that is different from degree of learning; it pertains to the relative speed with which students complete learning, and would be computed as the ratio between a measure of progress of gain over a certain period (whether or not mastery is attained during that period) and the length of the period. The model assumes that there are individual differences in learning rates, but that these might be specific to a given task. It also assumes that learning rates could be predicted by appropriate measures of aptitude.

Individual differences in learning rates predicted from aptitude measures can be clearly discerned in studies of foreign language learning in adults, whether under programmed instruction (Carroll, 1963c) or in intensive group instruction (Carroll, 1966). It appears to have been more difficult to obtain consistent and reliable measures of learning rate in elementary school subjects such as reading and mathematics. Perhaps this is because children's learning behavior is not as well organized as is that of adults. Working within the framework of Individually Prescribed Instruction, Yeager and Lindvall (1967) found that several measures of rate showed little consistency over separate units of instruction, even in the same subject matter, and generally negligible correlations with IQ. Number of units completed per year did, however, correlate with initial levels of placement. In the same context, Wang (1970) concluded that learning rates are task specific; while some rate measures could be fairly well predicted from measures of IQ and previous achievement, the patterns of predictor correlations were too heterogenenous to support any clear explanations for the relationships. It is possible that these early results in the IPI setting were cloudy because IPI's management system was still under development; also, the concept of academic engaged time had not been evolved. In a later report, Wang (1979) found that task-completion rates could be significantly well predicted from measures of aptitude and quality of instruction. Some of the results from the BTES project (Denham & Lieberman, 1980) are also of relevance. Apparently much further work is needed to clarify the measurement and prediction of learning rates. Although several proposals have been made about this topic (e.g., Packard, 1972) a thorough review and critique of the available evidence is needed before useful investigations can be initiated.

CRITICISMS OF THE MODEL OF SCHOOL LEARNING

In the educational literature one can find sporadic critical comments, either of the Carroll MSL specifically, or of some of its extensions such as Bloom's mastery learning concept. The comments do not always specify which model or concept they refer to. Whatever their targets, these critical comments merit consideration and in many cases responses.

Criticisms can be roughly classified into those of (a) the philosophical basis of the model, (b) its underlying theory, and (c) its efficacy or practicality as applied in the conduct of educational programs.

Philosophical Basis

Those who criticize the philosophical basis of these concepts (e.g., Kepler, 1980; Szilak, 1976) are disturbed with the narrow, rigid, and mechanistic view of the educational process that seems to be assumed by the MSL or its extensions, that is, the view that education can be specified as a series of tasks to be learned, each with clearly defined behavioral objectives and characteristics, and each capable of being taught in the light of a series of learning parameters. As the orginator of the MSL, I would disavow any such narrow view of education. I carefully limited the application of the MSL to those aspects of education that *can* be specified as learning tasks of a certain kind, and I do not believe it can be denied, even by critics, that at least *some* aspects of the school curriculum can and must be specified in this way. Children have to learn to read before they can appreciate literature; musicians have to learn theory and technical skills before they can work with the subtler varieties of style that make for good music; and so forth. The MSL and mastery learning would apply to learning skills in reading or music, not to appreciating literature or fine music. Mueller (1976) claims that use of the MSL and mastery learning does not promote independent learning. But the model is not intended to apply to promoting independent learning; there are other ways of doing this.

Far from criticizing the model for an unduly narrow view of the learning process, Chadwick (1979) is concerned that though the model is a "systematic approach," its adherents fail to adopt a "systems approach," that is, that its potential impact is lessened by failure to perceive how specific learning programs must be implemented within the broader context of the total educational process. This criticism is quite probably fair and deserves serious consideration.

Underlying Theory

Those who criticize the theory underlying the model are, I fear, often guilty of misunderstanding it. The model does not claim that time is the only variable in learning, or even the most important variable, as critics as widely separated as Cronbach and Snow (1977) and Szilak (1976) seem to allege. Although several of the model's variables are expresed in terms of time, what goes on in that time is more important. Critics are confusing necessity and sufficiency: Time is undoubtedly necessary, but not sufficient. The model does not by any means claim, as Satterly and Telfer (1979) allege, that "teaching behavior does not directly influence a child's achievement" (p. 169). Quality of instruction is an important variable in the model, and teachers' decisions also affect other variables, such as the opportunity to learn and student perseverance.

The complaint of Eigler et al. (1976), that the MSL and mastery learning deal with "one-dimensional" objectives is unfounded; these models can apply to multiple goals simultaneously, each with its own characteristics and implications for how learning should proceed. Buss and Poley (1976) reiterate that "time explains little by itself"; and state that they favor an objective of "maximizing potential" rather than the attainment of specific objectives. But the MSL, at least, is not in conflict with the goal of maximizing potential; in fact, it should further the attainment of such a goal. According to the MSL, aptitude is relevant to potential in the sense that it predicts how long a student needs to learn a task; if that time is not so long as to be unreasonable in the light of other circumstances, the other variables in the model can guide efficient attainment of potential.

There has been much discussion (e.g., Buss, 1976; Flammer, 1973, 1975) about Bloom's proposal that individual differences will "vanish" under mastery learning. In my opinion (Carroll, 1976), this hypothesis was more in the nature of a slogan or rallying cry. Under specially contrived conditions, individual differences could be made to "vanish," that is, by prohibiting further learning after a subject has met a certain criterion of performance. This would not be the normal case, however; students are usually allowed to continue learning after reaching a criterion. Bloom apparently meant only to suggest that through mastery learning procedures low-aptitude subjects could be brought to attain objectives that they would not normally attain under traditional procedures. Furthermore, normally objectives are set that are within the reach of all or nearly all students, given appropriate instruction.

The criticism just discussed relates to the "arch-environmentalist stance" that has been attributed to Bloom and his followers (Cronbach & Snow, 1977), that is, the position that seems to propose that all or nearly all students can be brought to attain nearly any objective, no matter how difficult or advanced. Such a stance is obviously unrealistic, and is not necessarily implied by the MSL. In fact, the model explicitly assumes that needed learning time for some tasks would be of infinite length for some students, and thus that in practice such students would not be expected to master such tasks. The MSL makes no attempt to assert that all individual differences are of purely environmental origin. On the other hand, the model focuses on those environmental and temporal variables that can be manipulated to maximize students' learning (and thus their potential).

Efficacy

A fundamental criticism often voiced is that mastery learning procedures guided by the MSL are not universally effective, or that they are not effective for all students (Mueller, 1976). Probably no instructional theory could be devised that would universally and uniformly produce maximal results for all students. Nevertheless, Block and Burns's (1976) conclusion that mastery learning procedures *generally* yield more favorable results than non-mastery procedures suggests that mastery learning, and the MSL on which it is based, has represented an important forward step in the development of more effective instructional procedures. Indeed, I have occasionally been made aware of complaints that mastery learning procedures are *too* effective, because when most students attain all the goals of a course, it becomes problematic to utilize the "grading on the curve" philosophy that underlies much instruction, particularly at secondary and collegial levels.

Mastery learning does, of course, entail problems (Horton, 1979), and many of these remain to be resolved or worked out. For example, Nance (1976) points out that students may be held back unnecessarily when they fail to meet a high performance standard. Block's (1972, 1974b, 1975) experiments in manipulating performance standards suggest, in fact, that such standards need not be set at excessively high levels; requiring 75% performance may be generally better than insisting on 95%. In the context of PSI with student teachers of reading, Miller and Ellsworth (1979) found that a modified mastery approach (MMA), in which students were given only two trials on each unit, was superior to a mastery approach (MA) in which students were given unlimited trials. In the time constraints of an academic semester, the MMA students were able to attempt more units and achieved higher scores on a final examination than MA students, probably because through partial learning of more material they were able to cover more of the course objectives.

Other problems with mastery learning relate to how much extra learning time is needed by low-aptitude students, how best to utilize this extra learning time through "remedial" or "corrective" work (see, for example, O'Connor, Stuck, & Wyne, 1979), and how much such extra study time may interfere with the student's other activities, both curricular and extracurricular. Block and Burns (1976) identify research that suggests, tentatively, that these problems are not as serious as might be thought, and that they can be solved. This a prime area for further research, however.

OVERALL EVALUATION OF THE MODEL

It is hoped that this chapter does not exude the "feigned optimism" about the MSL and mastery learning that disturbed Myers (1974). The MSL was never offered as an educational panacea; it was intended chiefly as a guide to research on direct instruction and to the interpretation of variations in student achievement. For these purposes it seems to have served well, as the many research investigations cited here testify. Its extensions and refinements have enabled educational researchers to perceive and formulate their research problems about instruction more clearly and penetratingly. Still, it is obvious that much work remains to be done to utilize the model and its extensions to the fullest. Many aspects of the MSL have never been adequately investigated—for example, relations between aptitudes and learning rates, and those phases of quality of instruction that relate to assisting low-aptitude students to make their learning more effective.

It is gratifying, nevertheless, to have seen the MSL serve as the basis for the planning and evaluation of new types of educational programs. Programs based on Bloom's mastery learning concept, the University of Pittsburgh's Individual Prescribed Instruction, and the Beginning Teacher Evaluation Study are cases in point, and all appear to have proved themselves to be superior to traditional or conventional programs beyond a mere Hawthorne effect. None of these programs can be expected really to reduce individual differences in learning and achievement to a "vanishing point," but if they are applied "over the long haul" (Carroll, 1965) they hold promise of raising levels of educational achievement to new highs—if, indeed, the many worrisome countervailing trends in contemporary society do not throw sands in the wheels of progress.

NOTES

1. Reprintings and translations of which I am aware are the following:
   In P. E. Johnson (Ed.). (1971). *Learning: Theory and practice* (pp. 326–339). New York: Crowell.
   In H. V. Perkins (Ed.). (1972). *Readings in human development* (p. 66). Belmont, Calif.: Wadsworth.
   In M. Mohan & R. E. Hull (Eds.). (1974). *Individualized instruction and learning* (pp. 33–50). Chicago: Nelson-Hall.
   In L. Willerman & R. G. Turner (Eds.). (1979). *Readings about individual and group differences*(pp. 106–119). San Francisco: Freeman.
   In W. Edelstein & D. Hopf (Eds.). (1973). *Bedingungen des Bildungsprozesses* (pp. 234–250). Stuttgart: Klett.

REFERENCES

Achtenhagen, F. (1978). *Beanspruchung von Schulern: Methodisch-didaktische Aspekte*. Bonn: Bunderminister für Bildung und Wissenschaft.

Airasian, P. W. (1972). An application of a mastery learning strategy. *Psychology in the Schools*, *9*, 130–134.

Anderson, L. W. (1975). Student involvement in learning and school achievement. *California Journal of Education*, *26*, 53–62.

Anderson, L. W. (1979). Considerations for setting performance standards on entrance examinations. *Educational Technology*, *19*(7), 22–25.

Anderson, L. W. (1980). *New directions for research on instruction and time-on-task*. Paper presented at the annual meeting of the American Educational Research Association, Boston.

Arehart, J. E. (1979). Student opportunity to learn related to student achievement of objectives in a probability unit. *Journal of Educational Research*, *72*, 253–259.

Arlin, M. N., Jr. (1974). The effects of formative evaluation on student performance. In H. F. Crombag & D. N. DeGruijter (Eds.), *Contemporary issues in educational testing* (pp. 203–217). The Hague: Mouton.

Arlin, M. & Westbury, I. (1976). The leveling effect of teacher pacing on science content mastery. *Journal of Research in Science Teaching*, *13*, 213–219.

Atkinson, J. W., Lens, W., & O'Malley, P. M. (1976). Motivation and ability: Interactive psychological determinants of intellective performance, educational achievement, and each other. In W. Sewell, R. Hauser, & D. Featherman (Eds.), *Schooling and achievement in American society* (pp. 29–60). New York: Academic Press.

Atkinson, J. W., & Raynor, J. O. (Eds.). (1974). *Motivation and achievement*. Washington, D.C.: V. H. Winston.

Basic Education. (1980). Time on task, and off. *Basic Education*, *24*(10), 13–14.

Bennett, S. N. (1978). Recent research on teaching: A dream, a belief, and a model. *British Journal of Educational Psychology*, *48*, 127–147.

Berliner, D. C. (1979). Tempus educare. In P. Peterson & H. Walberg (Eds.), *Research on teaching: Concepts, findings, and implications* (pp. 120–135). Berkeley, Calif.: McCutchan.

Besel, R. (1972). A linear model for the allocation of instructional resources. *Socio-Economic Planning Sciences, 6,* 501–506.

Block, J. H. (1972). Student learning and the setting of mastery performance standards. *Educational Horizons, 50,* 183–191.

Block, J. H. (1973). Teachers, teaching, and mastery learning. *Today's Education, 62*(7), 30–36.

Block, J. H. (Ed.). (1974a). *Schools, society, and mastery learning.* New York: Holt, Rinehart and Winston.

Block, J. H. (1974b). Student learning and the setting of mastery performance standards. In E. Torrance & W. White (Eds.), *Issues and advances in educational psychology* (rev. ed.). Itasca, Ill.: Peacock.

Block, J. H. (1975). *Mastery performance standards and student learning: A replication.* Santa Barbara, Calif.: University of California.

Block, J. H., & Anderson, L. W. (1975). *Mastery learning in classroom instruction.* New York: Macmillan.

Block, J. H., & Burns, R. B. (1976). Mastery learning. *Review of Research in Education, 4,* 3–49.

Bloom, B. S. (1968). Learning for mastery. *Evaluation Comment, 1*(2).

Bloom, B. S. (1974a). An introduction to mastery learning theory. In J. H. Block (Ed.), *Schools, society, and mastery learning* (pp. 3–14). New York: Holt, Rinehart and Winston.

Bloom, B. S. (1974b). Time and learning. *American Psychologist, 29,* 682–688.

Bloom, B. S. (1976). *Human characteristics and school learning.* New York: McGraw-Hill.

Bloom, B. S. (Ed.). (1980). *The state of research on selected alterable variables in education.* Chicago: Department of Education, University of Chicago.

Bloom, B. S., Hastings, J. T., & Madaus, G. F. (Eds.). (1971). *Handbook of formative and summative evaluation of student learning.* New York: McGraw-Hill.

Bockman, J. F. (1972). An analysis of the learning process: A rationale for the individualization of foreign language instruction. In H. B. Altman (Ed.), *Individualizing the foreign language classroom: Perspectives for teachers* (pp. 33–52). Rowley, Mass.: Newbury House.

Bonsch, M. (1977). Zum gegenwartigen Stand der Begabungsforschung und seiner Berucksichtigung in der Unterrichtspraxis. *Unterrichtswissenschaft, 5,* 66–76.

Brundo, G. C. (1976). In-service teacher training in removable prosthodontics. *Journal of Prosthetic Dentistry, 35,* 674–679.

Bugelski, B. R. (1962). Presentation time, total time, and mediation in paired-associate learning. *Journal of Experimental Psychology, 63,* 409–412.

Bulcock, J. W., Lee, W. F., & Luk, W. S. (1979). *The variance normalization method of ridge regression analysis.* Paper presented at the annual meeting of the American Educational Research Assoication, San Francisco.

Burrows, C. K., & Okey, J. R. (1975). *The effects of a mastery learning strategy on achievement.* Paper presented at the annual meeting of the American Educational Research Association, Washington, D.C. (ERIC Document Reproduction Service No. ED 109 240)

Buss, A. R. (1976). The myth of vanishing individual differences in Bloom's mastery learning. *Journal of Instructional Psychology, 3*(Special Edition, Summer), 4–14.

Buss, A. R., & Poley, W. (1976). *Individual differences: Traits and factors.* New York: Gardner.

Carroll, J. B. (1962a). The prediction of success in intensive foreign language training. In R. Glaser (Ed.), *Training research and education* (pp. 87–136). Pittsburgh: University of Pittsburgh Press.

Carroll, J. B. (1962b). Computer applications in the investigation of models in educational research. In A. G. Oettinger (Ed.), Proceedings of a Harvard symposium on digital computers and their applications. *Annals of the Computation Laboratory of Harvard University, 31,* 48–58.

Carroll, J. B. (1963a). A model of school learning. *Teachers College Record, 64,* 723–733.

Carroll, J. B. (1963b). Research on teaching foreign languages. In N. L. Gage (Ed.), *Handbook of research on teaching* (pp. 1060–1100). Skokie, Ill.: Rand McNally.

Carroll, J. B. (1963c). *Programmed self-instruction in Mandarin Chinese: Observations of student progress with an automated audiovisual instructional device.* Wellesley, Mass.: Language Testing Fund. (ERIC Document Reproduction Service No. ED 002 374)

Carroll, J. B. (1963d). *Programed instruction and student ability. Journal of Programed Instruction, 2*(4), 7–12.

Carroll, J. B. (1965). School learning over the long haul. In J. D. Krumboltz (Ed.), *Learning and the educational process* (pp. 249–269). Skokie, Ill.: Rand McNally.

Carroll, J. B. (1966). *A parametric study of language training in the Peace Corps.* Cambridge, Mass.: Laboratory for Research in Instruction, Harvard Graduate School of Education. (ERIC Document Reproduction Service No. ED 010 877)

Carroll, J. B. (1967). Foreign language proficiency levels attained by language majors near graduation from college. *Foreign Language Annals, 1,* 131–151.

Carroll, J. B. (1974a). Fitting a model of school learning to aptitude and achievement data over grade levels. In D. R. Green (Ed.), *The aptitude-achievement distinction* (pp. 53–78). Monterey, Calif.: CTB/McGraw-Hill.

Carroll, J. B. (1974b). The aptitude-achievement distinction: The case of foreign language aptitude and proficiency. In D. R. Green (Ed.), *The aptitude-achievement distinction* (pp. 289–303). Monterey, Calif.: CTB/McGraw-Hill.

Carroll, J. B. (1974c). Learning theory for the classroom teacher. In G. A. Jarvis (Ed.), *The challenge of communication* (pp. 113–149). Skokie, Ill.: National Textbook Co.

Carroll, J. B. (1975). *The teaching of French as a foreign language in eight countries.* Stockholm: Almqvist & Wiksell; New York: Wiley (Halsted).

Carroll, J. B. (1976). Comment on Buss's article. *Journal of Instructional Psychology, 3*(Special Edition, Summer), 20.

Carroll, J. B. (1981). Twenty-five years of research on foreign language aptitude. In K. C. Diller (Ed.), *Individual differences and universals in language learning aptitude* (pp. 83–118). Rowley, Mass.: Newbury House.

Carroll, J. B., & Burke, M. L. (1965). Parameters of paired-associate verbal learning: Length of list, meaningfulness, rate of presentation, and ability. *Journal of Experimental Psychology, 69,* 543–533.

Carroll, J. B., & Sapon, S. M. (1959). *Modern Language Aptitude Test.* New York: The Psychological Corporation.

Carroll, J. B., & Spearritt, D. (1967). *A study of a model of school learning* (Monograph No. 4). Cambridge, Mass.: Center for Research and Development in Educational Differences, Harvard University. (ERIC Document Reproduction Service No. ED 045 477)

Carver, R. P. (1970). A test of an hypothesized relationship between learning time and amount learned in school learning. *Journal of Educational Research, 64,* 57–58.

Centra, J. A., & Potter, D. A. (1980). School and teacher effects: An interrelational model. *Review of Educational Research, 50,* 273–291.

Chadwick, C. N. (1979). Why educational technology is failing (and what should be done to create success). *Educational Technology, 19*(1), 7–19.

Chant, V. G., & Luenberger, D. G. (1974). A mathematical theory of instruction: Instructor/learner interaction and instruction pacing. *Journal of Mathematical Psychology, 11,* 132–158.

Clifford, M. M. (1973). How learning and liking are related—A clue. *Journal of Educational Psychology, 64,* 183–186.

Colton, F. V. (1974). Effects of giving students data on task completion time in a college media course. *Audio-Visual Communication Review, 22,* 279–294.

Cooley, W. W., & Emrick, J. A. (1974). *A model of classroom differences which explains variation in classroom achievement.* Paper presented at the annual meeting of the American Educational Research Association, Chicago.

Cooley, W. W., & Leinhardt, G. (1975). *The application of a model for investigating classroom processes.* Pittsburgh: Learning Research and Development Center, University of Pittsburgh.

Cooley, W. W., & Lohnes, P. R. (1976). *Evaluation research in education.* New York: Irvington (Halsted).

Cotton, J. W. (1975). Theoretical perspectives for research on college teaching: A cognitive viewpoint. *Instructional Science, 4,* 59–98.

Cronbach, L. J. (1972). Book review of Block, J. E. (Ed.), *Mastery learning: Theory and practice. International Review of Education, 18,* 250–252.

Cronbach, L. J., & Snow, R. E. (1977). *Aptitudes and instructional methods: A handbook for research on interactions.* New York: Irvington.

De Cecco, J. P. (1968). *The psychology of learning and instruction: Educational psychology.* Englewood Cliffs, N.J.: Prentice-Hall.

Denham, C., & Lieberman, A. (Eds.). (1980). *Time to Learn.* Washington, D.C.: National Institute of Education.

Denton, J. J., & Seymour, J. A. G. (1978). The influence of unit pacing and mastery learning strategies on the acquisition of higher order intellectual skills. *Journal of Educational Research, 71,* 267–271.

Dorsel, T. N. (1978). Mastery learning approach to practicing athletic skills. *Perceptual & Motor Skills, 46,* 1243–1246.

Edelstein, W., & Hopf, D. (Eds.). (1973). *Bedingungen des Bildungsprozesses.* Stuttgart: Ernst Klett.

Eigler, G., Macke, G., Nenniger, P., Poelchau, H-W., & Straka, G. A. (1976). Mehrdimensionale Zielerreichung in Lehr-Lern-Prozessen. *Zeitschrift für Pädagogik, 22,* 181–197.

Feldhusen, J. F., Hynes, K., & Ames, C. A. (1976). Is a lack of instructional validity contributing to the decline of achievement test scores? *Educational Technology, 16*(7), 13–16.

Fisher, C. W., Marliave, R. S., & Filby, N. N. (1979). Improving teaching by increasing "academic learning time." *Educational Leadership, 37*, 52–54.

Fiske, E. B. (1980, March 30). New teaching method raises hopes in inner city. *New York Times.*

Flammer, A. (1973). Individuelle Differenzen im Lernen nach der "Mastery-Learning"-Strategie. *Zeitschrift für Experimentelle und Angewandte Psychologie, 20*, 529–546.

Flammer, A. (1975). *Individuelle Unterschiede im Lernen.* Weinheim: Beltz.

Fredrick, W. C. (1977). The use of classroom time in high schools above or below the median reading score. *Urban Education, 11*, 459–464.

Fredrick, W. C., & Walberg, H. J. (1980). Learning as a function of time. *Journal of Educational Research, 73*, 183–194.

Garner, W. T. (1978). The public economics of mastery learning. *Educational Technology, 18*(12), 12–17.

Geissler, E. M. (1974). A new way of looking at old ideas. *International Nursing Review, 21*, 169–171.

Gettinger, M., & White, M. A. (1979). Which is the stronger correlate of school learning? Time to learn or measured intelligence? *Journal of Educational Psychology, 71*, 405–412.

Glaser, R. (Ed.). (1962). *Training research and education.* Pittsburgh: University of Pittsburgh Press.

Grannis, J. C. (1978). Task engagement and the consistency of pedagogical controls: An ecological study of differently structured classroom settings. *Curriculum Inquiry, 8*, 3–36.

Guskey, T. R. (1980). Mastery learning: Applying the theorty. *Theory into Practice, 19*, 104–111.

Guthrie, J. T., & Tyler, S. J. (1978). Cognition and instruction of poor readers. *Journal of Reading Behavior, 10*, 57–78.

Hambleton, R. K. (1974). Testing and decision-making procedures for selected individualized instructional programs. *Review of Educational Reearch, 44*, 371–400.

Harnischfeger, A., & Wiley, D. C. (1976). The teaching-learning process in elementary schools: A synoptic view. *Curriculum Inquiry, 6*, 5–43.

Harnischfeger, A., & Wiley, D. E. (1978). Conceptual issues in models of school learning. *Curriculum Studies, 10*, 215–231.

Hefferlin, J. B. L. (1972). Intensive courses: An old idea whose time for testing has come. *Journal of Research and Development in Education, 6*(1), 83–98.

Hicklin, W. J. (1976). A model for mastery learning based on dynamic equilibrium theory. *Journal of Mathematical Psychology, 13*, 79–88.

Horton, L. (1979). Mastery learning: Sound in theory, but ... *Educational Leadership, 37*, 154–156.

Huckabay, L. M. (1978). Cognitive and affective consequences of formative evaluation in graduate nursing students. *Nursing Research, 27*, 190–194.

Huckabay, L. M., & Arndt, C. (1976). Effect of acquisition of knowledge on self-evaluation and the relationship of self-evaluation to perception of real and ideal self-concept. *Nursing Research, 25*, 244–251.

Husén, T. (1979). General theories in education: A twenty-five year perspective. *International Review of Education, 25*, 325–345.

Hyman, J. S., & Cohen, S. A. (1979). Learning for mastery: Ten conclusions after

15 years and 3,000 schools. *Educational Leadership, 37*, 104–109.

Hymel, G. M. (1974). *An investigation of John B. Carroll's model of school learning as a theoretical basis for the organizational structuring of schools* (Final Rep., NIE Project No. 3-1359). New Orleans: University of New Orleans.

Jakobovits, L. A. (1970). *Foreign language learning: A psycholinguistic analysis of the issues.* Rowley, Mass.: Newbury House.

James, A. (1975). An experimental comparison of conditions related to concept learning from written instruction. *Bulletin of the British Psychological Society, 28*, 238.

Keller, F. S. (1968). Goodbye, teacher. . . . *Journal of Applied Behavior Analysis, 1*, 79–89.

Kepler, K. B. (1980). BTES: Implications for preservice education of teachers In C. Denham & A. Lieberman (Eds.), *Time to learn* (pp. 139–157). Washington, D.C.: National Institute of Education.

Kibby, M. W. (1979). The effects of certain instructional conditions and response modes on initial word learning. *Reading Research Quarterly, 15*, 147–171.

Kiesling, H. (1978). Productivity of instructional time by mode of instruction for students at varying levels of reading skills. *Reading Research Quarterly, 13*, 554–582.

Kim, H. (1968). Learning rates, aptitudes, and achievements. Unpublished doctoral dissertation, University of Chicago.

Kretschmann, R., & Malburg, H. (1976). Generelle und differentielle Effekte dreier verschiedener Formen adaptiven Unterrichts. *Zeitschrift für Pädagogik, 22*, 889–900.

Ladas, H. S. (1980). A handbook of irreducible facts for teaching and learning. *Phi Delta Kappan, 61*, 606–607.

Latta, R. M., Dolphin, W. D., & Grabe, M. (1978). Individual differences model applied to instruction and evaluation of large college classes. *Journal of Educational Psychology, 70*, 960–970.

Lee, M. M., & McLean, J. E. (1979). A comparison of achievement and attitudes among three methods of teaching educational psychology. *Journal of Educational Research, 72*, 86–90.

Leinhardt, G. (1977a). Evaluating an adaptive education program: Implementation to replication. *Instructional Science, 6*, 223–257.

Leinhardt, G. (1977b). Program evaluation: An empirical study of individualized instruction. *American Educational Research Journal, 14*, 277–293.

Leinhardt, G. (1978). Applying a classroom process model to instructional evaluation. *Curriculm Inquiry, 8*, 155–176.

Leinhardt, G. (1980). Modeling and measuring educational treatment in evaluation. *Review of Educational Research, 50*, 393–420.

Lewis, L. A. (1970). A test of Carroll's model of school learning. Unpublished doctoral dissertation, Florida State University.

Lundgren, U. P. (1972). *Frame factors and the teaching process.* Stockholm: Almqvist & Wiksell.

Manasse, H. R., Jr., & Lasker, P. A. (1976). Some considerations regarding norm-referenced and criterion-referenced testing in pharmaceutical education. *American Journal of Pharmaceutical Education, 40*, 275–278.

Mentzer, D. S., & Scuglia, R. C. (1975). Teaching life science to student nurses: A modular approach. *American Biology Teacher, 37*, 358–360.

Meyen, E. L., & Lehr, D. H. (1980). Least restrictive environment: Instructional implications. *Focus on Exceptional Children, 12*(7), 1–8.

Miller, J. W., & Ellsworth, R. (1979). Mastery learning: The effects of time constraints and unit mastery requirements. *Educational Research Quarterly, 4*(4), 40–48.

Morris, E. K., Surber, C. F., & Bijou, S. M. (1978). Self-pacing versus instructor-pacing: Achievement, evaluations, and retention. *Journal of Educational Psychology, 70*, 224–230.

Morrison, H. C. (1926). *The practice of teaching in the secondary school.* Chicago: University of Chicago Press.

Mueller, D. J. (1976). Mastery learning: Partly boon, partly boondoggle. *Teachers College Record, 78*, 41–52.

Munck, I. M. E. (1979). *Model building in comparative education: Applications of the LISREL method to cross-national survey data* (IEA Monograph Series, No. 10). Stockholm: Almqvist & Wiksell.

Myers, D. A. (1974). Why open education died. *Journal of Research and Development in Education, 8*(1), 60–67.

Nance, D. W. (1976). Bloom's "mastery learning" in college math limits critical and essential coverage. *Journal of Instructional Psychology, 3* (Special Edition, Summer), 23–27.

Nieman, L. L. & Smith, W. F. (1978). Individualized instruction: Its effects upon achievement and interest in beginning college Spanish. *Modern Language Journal, 62*, 157–167.

O'Connor, P. D., Stuck, G. B., & Wyne, M. D. (1979). Effects of a short-term intervention resource-room program on task orientation and achievement. *Journal of Special Education, 13*, 375–385.

Packard, R. B. (1972). Models of instructional instruction: The search for a measure. *Educational Technology, 12*(8), 11–14.

Paradis, E., & Peterson, J. (1973). Concept of mastery learning applied to reading. *Journal of Research and Development in Education, 6*, Monograph, 166–173.

Peterson, P. L., & Walberg, H. J. (Eds.). (1979). *Research on teaching: Concepts, findings, and implications.* Berkeley, Calif.: McCutchan.

Pfaff, J. K., & Schmidt, W. H. (1974). *Mastery learning strategies: Application to the teaching of statistics.* Paper presented at the annual meeting of the American Educational Research Association, Chicago. (ERIC Document Reproduction Service No. ED 097 357)

Powell, B. S. (1976). *Intensive education: The impact of time on learning.* Newton, Mass.: Education Development Center.

Pratzner, F. C. (1972). Estimates of teaching-learning time. *Educational Technology, 12*(8), 58–62.

Rosenshine, B. V. (1979). Content, time, and direct instruction. in P. L. Peterson & H. J. Walberg (Eds.), *Research on teaching: Concepts, findings, and implications* (pp. 28–56). Berkeley, Calif.: McCutchan.

Rosenshine, B., & Berliner, D. C. (1978). Academic engaged time. *British Journal of Teacher Education, 4*, 3–16.

Rupley, W. H., & Longnion, B. L. (1978). Mastery learning: A viable alternative? *Reading Teacher, 32*, 380–383.

Sagiv, A. (1979). General growth model for evaluation of an individual's progress in learning. *Journal of Educational Psychology, 71*, 866–881.

Sanderson, H. W. (1976). Student attitudes and willingness to spend time in unit mastery learning. *Research in the Teaching of English*, *10*, 191–198.

Satterly, D. J., & Telfer, I. G. (1979). Cognitive style and advance organizers in learning and retention. *British Journal of Educational Psychology*, *49*, 169–178.

Sjogren, D. D. (1967). Achievement as a function of study time. *American Educational Research Journal*, *4*, 337–343.

Skager, R., Morehouse, K., Russock, R., & Schumacher, E. (1973). *Evaluation of the Los Angeles Alternative School: A report to the Board of Education of the Los Angeles Unified School District*. Los Angeles, Calif.: Center for the Study of Evaluation, University of California.

Smith, J. K., & Katims, M. (1977). Reading in the city: The Chicago Mastery Learning Reading Program. *Phi Delta Kappan*, *59*, 199–202.

Smith, N. M. (1979). Allocation of time and achievement in elementary social studies. *Journal of Educational Research*, *72*, 231–236.

Stuck, G. B. (1980). *Time-on-task and school achievement: Classroom intervention research*. Paper presented at the annual meeting of the American Educational Research Association, Boston.

Szilak, D. (1976). Strings: A critique of systematic education. *Harvard Educational Review*, *46*, 54–75.

Terrill, A. F., Berger, V., & Mulgrave, N. W. (1973). The application of a modified mastery approach to the teaching of graduate educational psychology. *Psychology in the Schools*, *10*, 253–258.

Thompson, S. B. (1980). Do individualized mastery and traditional instructional systems yield different course effects in college calculus? *American Eduational Research Journal*, *17*, 361–375.

Thurstone, L. L. (1930). The relation between learning time and length of task. *Psychological Review*, *37*, 44–58.

Torshen, K. P. (1977). *The mastery approach to competency-based education*. New York: Academic Press.

Trogdon, E. W. (1980). An exercise in mastery learning. *Phi Delta Kappan*, *61*, 389–391.

Walker, D. F., & Schaffarzick, J. (1974). Comparing curricula. *Review of Educational Research*, *44*, 83–111.

Wang, M. C. (1970). The use of the canonical correlation analysis in an investigation of pupil's rate of learning in school. *Journal of Educational Research*, *64*(1), 35–45.

Wang, M. C. (1979). Maximizing the effective use of school time by teachers and students. *Contemporary Educational Psychology*, *4*, 187–201.

Wang, M. C., & Lindvall, C. M. (1970). *An exploratory investigation of the Carroll model and the Bloom strategy for mastery learning*. Pittsburgh: Learning Research and Development Center, University of Pittsburgh. (ERIC Document Reproduction Service No. ED 054 983)

Wang, M. C., & Yeager, J. L. (1971). Evaluation under individualized instruction. *Elemenatary School Journal*, *71*, 448–452.

Washburne, C. W. (1922). Educational measurements as a key to individualizing instruction and promotions. *Journal of Educational Research*, *5*, 195–206.

Washburne, C. W., Vogel, M., & Gray, W. S. (1926). Results of practical experiments in fitting schools to individuals [Supplementary educational monograph]. *Journal of Educational Research*. Bloomington, Ill.: Public School Publishing Co.

Weiner, B. (1974). Motivational psychology and educational research. *Educational Psychologist, 11, 96–101.*

White, M. A., & Duker, J. (1973). Models of schooling and models of evaluation. *Teachers College Record, 74,* 293–307.

Wiley, D. E., & Harnischfeger, A. (1974). Explosion of a myth: Quantity of schooling and exposure to instruction, major educational vehicles. *Educational Researcher, 3*(4), 7–12.

Willerman, L., & Turner, R. G. (Eds.). (1979). *Readings about individual and group differences*. San Francisco: Freeman.

Wolf, V. C., & Quiring, J. (1971). Carroll's model applied to nursing education. *Nursing Outlook, 19,* 176–179.

Yeager, J. L., & Lindvall, C. M. (1976). An exploratory investigation of selected measures of rate of learning. *Journal of Experimental Education, 36*(2), 78–81.

3

A Model of School Learning

John B. Carroll
Harvard University*

EDITORS' INTRODUCTION

This chapter is the article that influenced every person writing for this volume. It is a classic paper in the field of educational psychology. Interestingly, it appeared in a journal issue that featured another seminal paper in educational psychology, "Course Improvement Through Evaluation," by Lee J. Cronbach. Two such enduring papers in one issue is a very unusual occurrence.

The evolution of the idea presented in this article is documented by Carroll in Chapter 2. Here the "idea" is presented. It would appear that in a 20-year history we have little reason to question Carroll's conclusion that "this conceptual model probably contains, at least at a superordinate level, every element required to account for an individual's success or failure in school learning (at least in the learning tasks to which the model applies). The explication and refinement of these factors and the exploration of their interactions constitute a major task of educational psychology."

This volume is, we hope, another step in the explication and refinement of our understanding of the variables and the model offered to us. The fun is really just beginning as researchers and practitioners recognize the heuristic value and practical utility of the model.

Reprinted from *Teachers College Record,* 64(8), 1963, 723–733, with permission.
*Professor Carroll is currently at the University of North Carolina at Chapel Hill.

The primary job of the educational psychologist is to develop and apply knowledge concerning why pupils succeed or fail in their learning at school, and to assist in the prevention and remediation of learning difficulties.

This job is inherently difficult because behavior is complex and has a multiplicity of causes. To deal with it, educational psychologists have evolved a number of concepts which they find useful in classifying the phenomena of behavior. Textbooks in the field are commonly organized around such concepts as maturation, individual differences, learning, thinking, motivation, and social development. These are useful categories, but because they overlap or refer to different levels of organization in the subject matter, it is difficult to build them into an integrated account of the process of school learning. What is needed is a schematic design or conceptual model of factors affecting success in school learning and of the way they interact. Such a model should use a very small number of simplifying concepts, conceptually independent of one another and referring to phenomena at the same level of discourse. It should suggest new and interesting research questions and aid in the solution of practical educational problems. With the aid of such a framework, the often conflicting results of different research studies might be seen to fall into a unified pattern.

Many such formulations, perhaps, are possible. A conceptual model will be presented here that seems to have the advantage of comprehensiveness combined with relative simplicity. The model is amenable to elaboration, but for our immediate purposes, we will leave aside any such elaborations.

SCOPE OF THE MODEL

We need first to define *learning task*. The learner's task of going from ignorance of some specified fact or concept to knowledge or understanding of it, or of proceeding from incapability of performing some specified act to capability of performing it, is a learning task. To call it a task does not necessarily imply that the learner must be aware *that* he is supposed to learn or be aware of *what* he is supposed to learn, although in most cases it happens that such awarenesses on the part of the learner are desirable.

Most, but not all, goals of the school can be expressed in the form of learning tasks or a series of such tasks. Teaching the child to read, for example, means to teach him to perform certain acts in response to written or printed language. Examples of other learning tasks taught in the schools can be multiplied at will: learning to spell all the words in common use, learning to perform certain operations with numbers, learning to explain or otherwise demonstrate an understanding of the subject matter of biology, learning to speak a foreign language, learning to perform in competitive sports, and learning to carry out certain responsibilities of a citizen. Some of these tasks are very broadly defined, such as learning to read printed English, but we can also consider narrowly defined tasks like mastering the content of Lesson 20 in a certain textbook of French, or even mastering a certain grammatical construction covered in that lesson. The model presented here is intended to apply equally well to all such tasks, no matter how broad or narrow. It is required, however, that the task can be unequivocally described and that means can be found for making a valid judgment as to when the learner has accomplished the learning task—that is, has achieved the learning goal which has been set for him.

It will be seen that as many as possible of the basic concepts in the model are defined so that they can be measured in terms of *time* in order to capitalize on the advantages of a scale with a meaningful zero point and equal units of measurement. An effort is made to provide for a mathematical description of the degree to which a learning task is achieved. Although the model applies only to one learning task at a time, it should be possible in principle to describe the pupil's success in learning a series of tasks (*e.g.,* all the work of the fifth grade) by summating the results of applying the model successively to each component task.

The model is admittedly oversimplified. The assumption that the work of the school can be broken down into a series of learning tasks can be called into question. In actual school practice, the various tasks to be learned are not necessarily treated as separate and distinct, and the process of teaching is often organized (whether rightly so or not) so that learnings will take place "incidentally" and in the course of other activities. Nevertheless, a conceptual model requires certain simplifying assumptions, and the assumption of discrete learning tasks is a useful one to make.

The model can be regarded as applying even to those educational goals ordinarily formulated in terms of "transfer"—that is, the ability to apply in a "new" situation something learned previously. The concept of the learning task is defined to include the attainment of that degree of competence which will make "transfer" essentially as automatic as demonstration of performance in the original setting. "Transfer," correctly viewed, is a term in a metalanguage which states the conditions under which particular learnings occur or manifest themselves. Thus, when we say that "learning which occurred in situation A transfers to situation B," we are really saying that "something learned in situation A also manifested itself in situation B, there being sufficient commonality between the two situations to elicit the learned performance in both."

The model is not intended to apply, however, to those goals of the school which do not lend themselves to being considered as learning tasks. Such, for example, are those goals having to do with attitudes and dispositions. Educating a child so that he has tolerance for persons of other races or creeds, respect for parental or legal authority, or attitudes of fair play, is thought to be largely a matter of emotional conditioning or of the acquisition of values and drives. Learning tasks may indeed be involved in the cognitive support of such attitudes (as where the child learns facts about different races or creeds), but the acquisition of attitudes is postulated to follow a different paradigm from that involved in learning tasks. Perhaps the distinctions made by Skinner (6) are of use in this connection: We could say that whereas learning tasks typically involve "operants," the attitudinal goals of education typically involve "respondents."

OVERVIEW OF THE MODEL

Briefly, our model says that the learner will succeed in learning a given task to the extent that he spend the amount of time that he *needs* to learn the task. The terms of this statement, however, require special definition, explication, and interpretation if the statement is to be properly understood.

First, it should be understood that "spending time" means *actually spending time on the act of learning.* "Time" is therefore not "elapsed time" but the time during which the person is oriented to the learning task and actively engaged in learning. In common parlance, it is the time during which he is "paying attention" and "trying to learn."

Second, there are certain factors which determine how much time the learner *spends* actively engaged in learning.

Third, there are certain factors which determine how much time a person *needs to spend* in order to learn the task. These factors may or may not be the same as, or associated with, those which influence how much time he spends in learning.

The major part of this article is devoted to a presentation of the factors conceived as determining the times needed or actually spent in the course of a learning task and the way in which these factors interact to result in various degrees of success in learning. Four of these factors are convenient intervening variables or constructs which may, in turn, be regarded as functions of still other factors or variables; one, however, is in principle a directly manipulable and measurable factor ("opportunity").

This model of school learning should not be confused with what is ordinarily called "learning theory," that is, with the exact scientific analysis of the essential conditions of learning and the development of systematic theory about this process. Rather, the model may be thought of as a description of the "economics" of the school learning process; it takes the fact of learning for granted.

The five factors or variables in the model will be presented under two headings: (1) determinants of time needed for learning, and (2) determinants of time spent in learning.

TIME NEEDED IN LEARNING

Aptitude

Suppose that a randomly selected group of children is taught a certain learning task by a teacher (or teaching device) with the best possible teaching techniques. Suppose further that each child is willing to stick attentively with the learning task for the number of minutes, hours, or days required for him to learn it to the specified criterion of success, and that each child is in fact given the opportunity to do this. Common experience, as well as abundant research evidence, suggests that the amounts of time needed by the children even under these ideal conditions will differ widely. Let us think, then, of the amount of time the pupil will need to learn the task under these conditions as the primary measure of a variable which we shall call his *aptitude for learning this task*. In ordinary parlance, learners who need only a small amount of time are said to have high aptitude; learners who need a large amount of time are said to have low aptitude. Some learners, it may be, will never learn even under these optimal conditions; we may say that these learners would need an indefinitely large (or an infinite) amount of time to learn the task.

It will be noted that this variable is measured in the opposite direction from the usual way of measuring aptitude—the shorter the time needed for learning, the higher the aptitude.

Furthermore, it will be noted that the measure of aptitude is specific to the task under consideration. Aptitude may be regarded as a function of numerous other variables. For one thing, it may depend upon the amount of prior learning which may be relevant to the task under consideration. A learner who has already progressed far towards the mastery of a task may not need much time to complete his learning. On the other hand, aptitude may also depend upon a series of traits or characteristics of the learner which enter into a wide variety of tasks; whether these traits can be accounted for solely on the basis of generalized prior learnings, or whether they reflect genetically determined individual characteristics, is of no immediate concern here. It may be useful, however, to conceive that a learner's estimated needed time, a_t, for learning a given task, t, may be written as a mathematical function of a series of basic aptitudes, symbolized with Greek letters and subscripts, minus the amount of time, s_t, saved by virtue of prior learnings relevant to the task. Thus:

$$a_t = f(\alpha_1, \alpha_2, \ldots, \alpha_n) - s_t$$

The exact form of this formula would vary for different tasks. Presumably, the basic aptitudes $\alpha_1, \alpha_2, \ldots, \alpha_n$ could be measured with considerable exactitude by appropriate tests.

Ability to Understand Instruction

We find it useful to postulate as a variable separate from those we consider under "aptitude" the ability to understand instruction, since this variable (in contrast to pure aptitude variables) is thought of as interacting with the method of instruction in a special and interesting way. The ability to understand instruction could be measured, one would suppose, as some combination of "general intelligence" and "verbal ability"; the former of these two would come into play in instructional situations where the learner is left to infer for himself the concepts and relationships inherent in the material to be learned, rather than having them carefully spelled out for him, while the latter would come into play whenever the instruction utilized language beyond the grasp of the learner. The way in which ability to understand instruction is postulated to interact with the type of instruction will be explained after we introduce a third variable affecting time needed for learning, the *quality of instruction*.

Quality of Instruction

One job of the teacher (or any person who prepares the materials of instruction) is to organize and present the task to be learned in such a way that the learner can learn it as rapidly and as efficiently as he is able. This means, first, that the learner must be told, in words that he can understand, what he is to learn and how he is to learn it. It means that the learner must be put into adequate sensory contact with the material to be learned (for example, one must insure that the learner will adequately see or hear the materials of instruction). It also means that the various aspects of the learning task must be presented in such an order and with such detail that, as far as possible, every step of the learning is adequately prepared for by a previous step. It may also mean that the instruction must be adapted for the special needs and characteristics of the learner, including his stage of learning. All these things may be summarized in what we call *quality of instruction*. This variable applies not only to the performance of a teacher but also to the characteristics of textbooks, workbooks, films, teaching-machine programs, etc.

   Now, if the quality of instruction is anything less than optimal, it is possible that the learner will need more time to learn the task than he would otherwise need. Some learners will be more handicapped by poor instruction than others. The extent of this handicap is conceived to be a function of the learner's *ability to understand instruction*. Learners with high ability in this respect will be able to figure out for themselves what the learning task is and how they can go about learning it; they will be able to overcome the difficulties presented by poor quality of instruction by perceiving concepts and relationships in the teaching materials which will not be grasped by those with lesser ability.

   For the purposes of this conceptual model, we shall say that the amount of time actually needed by a person to learn a given task satisfactorily is a function not only of aptitude (as defined previously), but also of the quality of instruction in so far as it is less than optimal. And the amount of additional time he will need is an inverse function of his ability to understand instruction.

We could, of course, apply Occam's razor and get rid of both of the two preceding variables by conceiving that a change in the quality of instruction causes an essential change in the learning task itself. In this case, we would deal only with learner's aptitude for learning a given task, subscripted with the quality of instruction attached to it. Such a modification of our model seems undesirable, however, for one would tend to lose sight of instructional quality as one of the important manipulable variables in educational psychology.

TIME SPENT IN LEARNING

Time Allowed for Learning ("Opportunity")

It may come as a surprise to some to be told that the schools may allow less than adequate time for learning any task, but second thought will make one realize that this is very often the case. It is partly a consequence of the very large amount of material that the schools are expected to teach; the available time must somehow be distributed among many things. And it is partly a consequence of the very great variation that exists in the amounts of time that children *need* for learning, even under a good quality of instruction, and particularly when the instructional quality is such that many children of lower ability to understand instruction require much more time than they might otherwise need.

The school responds to differences in learning rates (for that is what differences in aptitude are) in many ways. Sometimes the policy of the school is, in effect, to ignore these differences; a certain amount of time is provided for everybody to learn, and no more. (For example, at some military academies, study time is prescribed and scheduled uniformly for all cadets.) At the opposite extreme is the case where each student is allowed to proceed exactly at his own rate; private instruction in music or foreign languages and self-instruction by teaching machine or other means are approximations to this case. The middle position is occupied by learning situations in which there is some kind of "ability grouping": Pupils are assigned to different groups, classes, or curricula on the basis of estimated learning rates.

Even when there is some constraint upon the amount of time "officially" provided for learning, teachers and instructional programs vary in the amount of time they allow for learning. Some programs present material at such a rapid pace that most students are kept under continual pressure; only the apter students can keep up with this instruction, while the others fall back or out, sometimes never to get caught up. In other programs, the instruction is paced for the benefit of the slower student. The faster student is fortunate if the teacher takes appropriate steps to "enrich" his instructional content; but this will not always happen, and it is undoubtedly the case that many fast learners lose some of their motivation for learning when they feel that their time is being wasted or when they are not kept at the edge of challenge.

PERSEVERANCE

Obviously, failure to allow enough time for learning produces incomplete learning. If a person needs two hours to learn something and is allowed only one hour, and if we assume that learning proceeds linearly with time, the degree of learning is only 50 per cent. Probably one of the most aversive things which a school can do is not to allow sufficient time for a well-motivated child to master a given learning task before the next is taken up. Children meet such frustrations by indifference or the more extreme avoidance reactions and are, in any case, handicapped in undertaking the next task.

The Time the Learner Is Willing
to Spend in Learning ("Perseverance")

The term *perseverance* is used here, rather than persistence, because of the somewhat pejorative connotations of the latter. Nevertheless, the concept is similar to what Paul Brandwein describes in the following passage:

> The characteristics grouped under the Predisposing Factor ... include a spectrum of traits which the writer places under the head of *Persistence*. This is defined as consisting of three attitudes. (1) A marked willingness to spend time, beyond the ordinary schedule, in a given task (this includes the willingness to set one's own time schedules, to labor beyond a prescribed time, such as nine to five). (2) A willingness to withstand discomfort. This includes adjusting to shortened lunch hours, or no lunch hours, working without holidays, etc. It includes withstanding fatigue and strain and working even through minor illness, such as a cold or a headache. (3) A willingness to face failure. With this comes a realization that patient work may lead to successful termination of the task at hand (*1*, pp. 9–10).

But the variable of perseverance applies not only in the case of the "gifted student" and not only in the case of long durations of effort, but also to all other learners and also to learning tasks which require only short times for mastery. That is, in the general case, a learner who (in view of his aptitude, the quality of the instruction, and his ability to understand the instruction) needs a certain amount of time to learn a task may or may not be willing to persevere for that amount of time in trying to learn. It is not a matter of his predicting how long he will be willing to learn: we simply postulate that there is a certain time over and above which he will not continue active learning of a task, and this time may lie anywhere on the scale from zero to infinity. The learner may not be motivated to learn at all, or he may regard the task as something too difficult for him to learn; in either case, he may spend no time at all in trying to learn. He may start to learn and later become distracted or bored, or he may lose confidence in his ability. He may go far toward mastery and then overestimate his achievement, thus prematurely terminating his efforts to learn. He may, of course, be so highly motivated that he would be willing to spend more time than he needs in order to reach a specified criterion of mastery. Nevertheless, for the purposes of our conceptual model, it will be assumed that the learner will never actually spend more time than he needs to master the task as defined, that is, that he will stop learning as soon as he has mastered the learning task. (In this way we avoid, for the present, the necessity of incorporating a concept of "overlearning" in the model.)

This variable, which may be called *perseverance-in-learning-to-criterion*, is thus measured in terms of time, and if it is not sufficiently great to allow the learner to attain mastery, it operates in our conceptual model to reduce the degree of learning. Assume, as before, that learning proceeds as a linear function of time. Then if a child needs two hours to learn something, is allowed one hour, but will persevere only thirty minutes, the degree of learning is only 25 per cent. Perseverance-in-learning is measured only in terms of the amount of time the child is actively engaged in learning; a child who is actively engaged in learning for various periods totaling only thrity minutes during an hour is presumably not paying attention to learning for the other thirty minutes, and this time is not counted.

Perseverance-in-learning is itself a function of many other variables which will not be separately treated in this conceptual model. It is a function partly of what is ordinarily called "motivation" or desire to learn. But there are many reasons for desiring to learn a given thing: To please the teacher, to please one's parents or friends, to get good grades or other external rewards, to achieve self-confidence in one's learning ability, to feed one's self-esteem, to avoid disapproval—all these can operate *in place of* or *in addition to* any incentives for learning which may derive from the intrinsic interest or perceived utility of the thing being learned. And there are probably just as many reasons which one may adopt (consciously or unconsciously) for *not* learning: to avoid the responsibilities which learning brings, to avoid the exertion of learning, to behave consistently with one's image of oneself as a non-learner, or to avoid wasting time on learning tasks of no perceived importance.

Perseverance-in-learning may also be a function of what are ordinarily called emotional variables. One may desire to learn but be unable to endure frustrations caused by difficulties in the learning task or distractions from external circumstances. It may also interact with the quality of instruction; poor quality of instruction may reduce perseverance-in-learning even beyond the toll it takes in wasted minutes or even weeks.

THE COMPLETE MODEL

It will be noticed that the model involves five elements—three residing in the individual and two stemming from external conditions. Factors in the individual are (1) aptitude—the amount of time needed to learn the task under optimal instructional conditions, (2) ability to understand instruction, and (3) perseverance—the amount of time the learner is willing to engage actively in learning. Factors in external conditions are (4) opportunity—time allowed for learning, and (5) the quality of instruction—a measure of the degree to which instruction is presented so that it will not require additional time for mastery beyond that required in view of aptitude.

Three of the factors are expressed purely in terms of time. If ability to understand instruction corresponds to a combination of general and verbal intelligence, it can be assessed in relative terms by currently available measuring devices. The most elusive quantity in this model is that called *quality of instruction,* but both it and the ability to understand instruction are interconnected with temporally measurable variables in such a way that by appropriate experimental manipulations, they could eventually be indexed in terms of time. Temporarily, let us put quality of instruction on a scale from 0 (poor) to 1 (optimal), and ability to understand instruction on a standard score scale with mean $= 0$ and $\sigma = 1$.

The five factors can be worked into a tentative formula which expresses the degree of learning, for the ith individual and the tth task, as a function of the ratio of the amount of time the learner actually spends on the learning task to the total amount he needs. Thus:

$$Degree\ of\ learning\ =\ f\left(\frac{time\ actually\ spent}{time\ needed}\right)$$

The numerator of this fraction will be equal to the *smallest* of the following three quantities: (1) opportunity—the time allowed for learning, (2) perseverance—the amount of time the learner is willing to engage actively in learning, and (3) aptitude—the amount of time needed to learn, increased by whatever amount necessary in view of poor quality of instruction and lack of ability to understand less than optimal instruction. This last quantity (time needed to learn after adjustment for quality of instruction and ability to understand instruction) is also the denominator of the fraction. It is not necessary or worthwhile here, however, to pursue the detailed mathematical formulation, which has been given elsehwere (3).

As an illustration of the usefulness of this model in clarifying other educational concepts, let us see how it provides a framework for interpreting the notion of "underachievement" as criticized by Henry Dyer (*4*). While we are at it, let us also look at the notion of "overachievement." It is our contention that these terms are useful and salvageable if properly defined.

Underachievement and overachievement, like underweight and overweight, are ordinarily taken with reference to some norm or baseline of expectation. The underachiever does poorer than we expect him to, and the overachiever does better than we expect him to. The issue is this: Upon what do we base our expectation? The approved manner of doing this is to make predictions from those tests or other measurements which in fact yield the best predictions of success, and statistical theory tells us how to make best use of these predictors (*i.e.*, by making our predictions along a regression line). There is, however, a paradox here. Suppose our predictions were perfect. Then there would be no "underachievers" and no "overachievers." An unlikely eventuality to be sure! Nevertheless, our intuitive rejection of the case of perfect prediction lends credence to the following analysis of what we mean by "underachievement": Underachievement is a situation in which there is a discrepancy between actual achievement and that expected on the basis of a certain *kind* of evidence—evidence concerning the "capacity" or "aptitude" of the individual to achieve in a particular context. Such evidence is recognized as being quite distinct from evidence concerning other factors in achievement, *e.g.*, "motivation," "opportunity for learning," etc., and these latter factors would not figure in forming our expectations. Instead, we would hope to gather as much evidence as possible concerning the "capacity" or "aptitude" of the individual, defined as his learning rate when all other factors are optimal.

ACHIEVEMENT AND EXPECTANCY

With reference to the conceptual model presented earlier, our expectation of an individual's achievement in a given learning task would in the strictest sense be that which he would attain when he spends all the time he needs—that is, when the ratio of the time spent to the time needed is unity. Anything less than this is, to some degree, underachievement. From this point of view, *all* learners are underachievers unless they are superhuman beings in an ideal world. Perseverance sometimes flags; the quality of instruction is seldom optimal, and time allowed for learning is not always sufficient.

Let us, therefore, strike some sort of average for perseverance, instructional quality, and opportunity for learning. Our expectation of the degree of learning will be somewhat less than unity because, on the average, individuals will spend less time in learning than they need. And we may gauge underachievement and overachievement with reference to this expectation. In effect, this is what we do by the customary regression techniques based on aptitude measures, although in a less precise way than might be done if we were able to measure each of the components of achievement as stated by the model. In the framework of the model, however, underachievement is now seen to be a state of affairs which results whenever perseverance is less than some "reasonable value," whenever the quality of instruction is poor, whenever time allowed for learning has not been sufficient, or whenever some combination of these conditions has occurred. "Overachievement," contrariwise, may occur when there is an especially favorable combination of attendant events: high perseverance, instruction of high quality, or ample opportunity for learning.

We have a feeling about the relative amenability of different factors in achievement to manipulation or treatment: "Aptitude" is regarded as relatively resistant to change, whereas it is the hope of the psychologist that he can readily intervene to modify "perseverance," "quality of instruction," or "opportunity for learning." To some extent, this feeling is justified not only by logic but also by research findings—by the research on the apparent constancy of the IQ, on the effect of various instructional variables, etc. On the other hand, if aptitude is largely a matter of prior learnings, it may be more modifiable than we think, whereas, conversely, some kinds of clinical findings suggest that motivational characteristics of the individual may be much harder to change than one might think. These considerations, however, need not detract from the basic utility of the concepts of underachievement and overachievement. The concept of "underachievement" does not automatically imply the possibility of remediation any more than the concept of illness does. Some patients never get well, and some underachievers remain underachievers.

BABIES AND BATHWATER

Henry Dyer (*4*) has drawn attention to possible dangers in the concept of underachievement—for example, the dangers of making predictions from unreliable or invalid predictors, of assuming that ability is innate or fixed, of making unwarranted inferences from school marks, and of overlooking determinants of school performance which are external to the pupil. Nevertheless, in suggesting that we kill the notion of underachievement, it would seem that he wants to throw out the proverbial baby with the bathwater. The concepts of underachievement and of overachievement are meaningful from both a statistical and a clinical point of view, as shown by the many fruitful studies of "underachieving" groups of students (*e.g., 5*). Careful attention to the elements of the conceptual model presented here will afford a safeguard against misuse of the concepts: Aptitude must be estimated by relevant and reliable meaures (in actuality, all of them measures of past performance); the degree of learning must be accurately appraised, and the possible role of instructional variables must be considered. Above all, the variable which we have called *perseverance* must be validly assessed; the most direct evidence concerning it, our model would suggest, would come from observations of the amount of time the pupil actively engages in learning.

Before leaving this topic, let us consider another way in which the term "overachievement" is sometimes used. When a person is designated as an overachiever, it is often implied that his achievements derive more from his perseverance than from his aptitude or his intelligence. In terms of our model, this can occur when the learning task can be broken down into a series of subtasks of varying difficulty with difficulty roughly gauged in terms of average learning time. Because of his great perseverance, the overachiever masters to a criterion more of the *easy* tasks—tasks which are within the compass of his aptitude—than the student of average perseverance. While he may fail to learn some of the more difficult tasks, the net result may be a high score on an achievement test—a score considerably higher than predicted from aptitude measures. This concept of overachievement is distinctly different from the concept of overachievement suggested previously; responsible users of the term must clearly state which of these meanings they intend.

FUTURE RESEARCH

Our conceptual model could lead, it would seem, to almost endless possibilities for research. It should provoke renewed effort to develop measures of each of the basic variables included in the model. The measurement of *aptitudes* is a fairly well advanced art, although the exact ways in which these aptitudes are relevant to school learning tasks remain to be worked out. The same remark may be made about the measurement of *ability to understand instruction*. But measurements of *perseverance* and of *instructional quality* are practically nonexistent. It should be intriguing to attempt to provide a general way of measuring *opportunity to learn*, that is, the actual time available to individual students to learn in view of the pacing of instruction; for it is our hypothesis that variations in the pacing of instruction have remained largely unrecognized in pedagogical discussions.

Research is also needed on the interactions of the several variables in the model. Is the model correctly put together? To what extent are the variables interdependent? For example, how does instructional quality affect perseverance? In what way is the degree of learning a function of the ratio of the amount of time spent in learning to the amount of time needed? Are we correct in postulating an interaction between instructional quality and ability to understand instruction such that pupils low in the latter ability suffer most from poor instructional quality?

One of the most exciting possibilities suggested by the model is that of being able to state parameters for different types of learning by learners of varying characteristics under stated instructional conditions. Perhaps ultimately such parameters could be tied back to the data of pure learning theory. One of the bolder hypotheses implicit in the model is that the degree of learning, other things being equal, is a simple function of the amount of time during which the pupil engages actively in learning. Psychologists have paid little attention to this variable of pure time in human learning. A recent experiment by Bugelski (2) is one of the few to consider time factors in the field of paired-associate learning; and interestingly enough, it supports the hypothesis that more parsimonious descriptions of learning may be obtained by use of time as a variable rather than, say, number of trials.

What is important to emphasize is that this conceptual model probably contains, at least at a superordinate level, every element required to account for an individual's success or failure in school learning (at least in the learning tasks to which the model applies). The explication and refinement of these factors and the exploration of their interactions constitute a major task of educational psychology. Its other major task is to account for those types of school learning (*e.g.,* attitudinal and emotional conditioning) to which the present model is not intended to apply and for which a separate model might well be constructed.

REFERENCES

1. Brandwein, P. F. *The gifted student as future scientist*. New York: Harcourt Brace, 1955.
2. Bugelski, B. R. Presentation time, total time, and mediation in paired-associate learning. *J. exper. Psychol.*, 1962, *63*, 409–412.
3. Carroll, J. B. The prediction of success in intensive language training. In Glaser, R. (Ed.) *Training research and education*. Pittsburgh: Univer. Pittsburgh Press, 1962. pp. 87–136.
4. Dyer, H. S. A psychometrician views human ability. *Teach. Coll. Rec.*, 1960, *61*, 394–403.
5. Goldberg, Miriam, *et al*. A three-year experimental program at DeWitt Clinton High School to help bright underachievers. *High Points*, 1959, 41, 5–35.
6. Skinner, B. F. *Science and human behavior*. New York: Macmillan, 1953.

4

Learning for Mastery

Benjamin S. Bloom
*University of Chicago**

EDITORS' INTRODUCTION

In the mid-1960s, Benjamin Bloom and his colleagues were deeply involved in conceptualizing and developing practical procedures for school reform. Potent solutions to the problems of schooling as they perceived them were derived, in part, from Carroll's model of school learning. The result of this broadly conceived work was what we now know as mastery learning. One of Professor Bloom's first articles on "a learning strategy for mastery" was published in May 1968 and is reprinted here. In the years since that first publication, scores of articles, books, and curriculum materials have been generated from the extensive research on and the widespread practice of mastery learning. Thousands of classrooms in more than a dozen countries have been profoundly affected by the ideas articulated in this chapter. After almost two decades the article continues to be remarkably current. In spite of the major impact of mastery learning on American schools, the current spate of commisssion reports on school reform echo many of the points championed by Bloom in 1968. It would seem that school learning is still characterized by passivity on the part of learners, that curricula are textbook driven, and that schooling emphasizes competition among learners. Reformers are still calling for reorganization of instruction to allow more differentiation in the treatment of individual learners, for instruction that is squarely based on carefully chosen student-learning outcomes, and for continual and lifelong learning. It is noteworthy that in much of the literature on school reform, instructional time is a central theme for the conceptualization, development, and implementation of effective learning environments.

Reprinted from *Evaluation Comment, 1*(2), 1968, with permission.
*Mr. Bloom is currently professor of education at both the University of Chicago and Northwestern University.

Each teacher begins a new term (or course) with the expectation that about a third of his students will adequately learn what he has to teach. He expects about a third of his students to fail or to just "get by." Finally, he expects another third to learn a good deal of what he has to teach, but not enough to be regarded as "good students." This set of expectations, supported by school policies and practices in grading, becomes transmitted to the students through the grading procedures and through the methods and materials of instruction. The system creates a self-fulfilling prophecy such that the final sorting of students through the grading process becomes approximately equivalent to the original expectations.

This set of expectations, which fixes the academic goals of teachers and students, is the most wasteful and destructive aspect of the present educational system. It reduces the aspirations of both teachers and students; it reduces motivation for learning in students; and it systematically destroys the ego and self-concept of a sizable group of students who are legally required to attend school for 10 to 12 years under conditions which are frustrating and humiliating year after year. The cost of this system in reducing opportunities for further learning and in alienating youth from both school and society is so great that no society can tolerate it for long.

Most students (perhaps over 90 percent) can master what we have to teach them, and it is the task of instruction to find the means which will enable our students to master the subject under consideration. Our basic task is to determine what we mean by mastery of the subject and to search for the methods and materials which will enable the largest proportion of our students to attain such mastery.

In this paper we will consider one approach to learning for mastery and the underlying theoretical concepts, research findings, and techniques required. Basically, the problem of developing a strategy for mastery learning is one of determining how individual differences in learners can be related to the learning and teaching process.

BACKGROUND

Some societies can utilize only a small number of highly educated persons in the economy and can provide the economic support for only a small proportion of the students to complete secondary or higher education. Under such conditions much of the effort of the schools and the external examining system is to find ways of rejecting the majority of students at various points in the educational system and to discover the talented few who are to be given advanced educational opportunities. Such societies invest a great deal more in the the prediction and selection of talent than in the development of such talent.

The complexities of the skills required by the work force in the United States and in other highly developed nations means that we can no longer operate on the assumption that completion of secondary and advanced education is for the few. The increasing evidence, Schultz (1963) and Bowman (1966), that investment in the education of humans pays off at a greater rate than does capital investment suggests that we cannot return to an economy of scarcity of educational opportunity.

Whatever might have been the case previously, highly developed nations must seek to find ways to increase the proportion of the age group that can successfully complete both secondary and higher education. The problem is no longer one of finding the few who can succeed. The basic problem is to determine how the largest proportion of the age group can learn effectively those skills and subject matter regarded as essential for their own development in a complex society.

However, given another set of philosophic and psychological presuppositions, we may express our concern for the intellectual and personality consequences of lack of clear success in the learning tasks of the school. Increasingly, learning throughout life (continuing learning) will be necessary for the largest proportion of the work force. If school learning is regarded as frustrating and even impossible by a sizable proportion of students, then little can be done at later levels to kindle a genuine interest in further learning. School learning must be successful and rewarding as one basis for insuring that learning can continue throughout one's life as needed.

Even more important in modern society is the malaise about values. As the secular society becomes more and more central, the values remaining for the individual have to do with hedonism, interpersonal relations, self-development, and ideas. If the schools frustrate the students in the latter two areas, only the first two are available to the individual. Whatever the case may be for each of these values, the schools must strive to assure all students of successful learning experiences in the realm of ideas and self-development.

There is little question that the schools now do provide successful learning experiences for some students—perhaps as high as one third of the students. If the schools are to provide successful and satisfying learning experiences for at least 90 percent of the students, major changes must take place in the attitudes of students, teachers, and administrators; changes must also take place in teaching stragegies and in the role of evaluation.

THE NORMAL CURVE

We have for so long used the normal curve in grading students that we have come to believe in it. Our achievement measures are designed to detect differences among our learners, even if the differences are trivial in terms of the subject matter. We then distribute our grades in a normal fashion. In any group of students we expect to have some small percent receive A grades. We are surprised when the percentage differs greatly from about 10 percent. We are also prepared to fail an equal proportion of students. Quite frequently this failure is determined by the rank order of the students in the group rather than by their failure to grasp the essential ideas of the course. Thus, we have become accustomed to classify students into about five categories of level of performance and to assign grades in some relative fashion. It matters not that the failures of one year performed at about the same level as the C students of another year. Nor does it matter that the A students of one school do about as well as the F students of another school.

Having become "conditioned" to the normal distribution, we set grade policies in these terms and are horrified when some teacher attempts to recommend a very different distribution of grades. Administrators are constantly on the alert to control teachers who are "too easy" or "too hard" in their grading. A teacher whose grade distribution is normal will avoid difficulties with administrators. But even more important, we find ways of convincing students that they can only do C work or D work by our grading system and even by our system of quiz and progress testing. Finally, we proceed in our teaching as though only the minority of our students should be able to learn what we have to teach.

There is nothing sacred about the normal curve. It is the distribution most appropriate to chance and random activity. Education is a purposeful activity and we seek to have the students learn what we have to teach. If we are effective in our instruction, the distribution of achievement should be very different from the normal curve. In fact, we may even insist that our educational efforts have been *unsuccessful* to the extent to which our distribution of achievement approximates the normal distribution.

"Individual differences" in learners is a fact that can be demonstrated in many ways. That our students vary in many ways can never be forgotten. That these variations must be reflected in learning standards and achievement criteria is more a reflection of our policies and practices rather than the necessities of the case. Our basic task in education is to find strategies which will take individual differences into consideration but which will do so in such a way as to promote the fullest development of the individual.

THE VARIABLES FOR MASTERY LEARNING STRATEGIES

A learning stragegy for mastery may be derived from the work of Carroll (1963), supported by the ideas of Morrison (1926), Bruner (1966), Skinner (1954), Suppes (1966), Goodlad and Anderson (1959), and Glaser (1968). In presenting these ideas we will refer to some of the research findings which bear on them. However, our main concern here is with the major variables in a model of school learning and the ways in which these variables may be utilized in a strategy for mastery learning.

Put in its most brief form the model proposed by Carroll (1963) makes it clear that if the students are normally distributed with respect to *aptitude* for some subject (mathematics, science, literature, history, etc.) and all the students are provided with exactly the *same instruction* (same in terms of amount of instruction, quality of instruction, and time available for learning), the end result will be a normal distribution on an appropriate measure of achievement. Furthermore, the relationship between aptitude and achievement will be relatively high (correlations of + .70 or higher are to be expected if the aptitude and achievement measures are valid and reliable). Conversely, if the students are normally distributed with respect to aptitude, but the kind and quality of instruction and the amount of time available for learning are made appropriate to the characteristics and needs of *each* student, the majority of students may be expected to achieve mastery of the subject. And, the relationship between aptitude and achievement should approach zero. It is this basic set of ideas we wish to develop in the following.

1. Aptitude for Particular Kinds of Learning

We have come to recognize that individuals do differ in their aptitudes for particular kinds of learning and over the years we have developed a large number of aptitude tests to measure these differences. In study after study we have found that aptitude tests are relatively good predictors of achievement criteria (achievement tests or teacher judgments). Thus, a good set of mathematic aptitude tests given at the beginning of the year will correlate as high as + .70 with the mathematics achievement tests given at the end of the course in algebra, or some other mathematics subject.

The use of aptitude tests for predictive purposes and the high correlations between such tests and achievement criteria have led many of us to the view that high levels of achievement are possible only for the most able students. From this, it is an easy step to some notion of a causal connection between aptitude and achievement. The simplest notion of causality is that the students with high levels of aptitude can learn the complex ideas of the subject while the students with low levels of aptitude can learn only the simplest ideas of the subject.

Quite in contrast to this is Carroll's (1963) view that *aptitude is the amount of time required by the learner to attain mastery of a learning task*. Implicit in this formulation is the assumption that, given enough time, all students can conceivably attain mastery of a learning task. If Carroll is right, then learning mastery is theoretically available to all, if we can find the means for helping each student. It is this writer's belief that this formulation of Carroll's has the most fundamental implications for education.

One type of support for this view is to be found in the grade norms for many standardized achievement tests. These norms demonstrate that selected criterion scores achieved by the top students at one grade level are achieved by the majority of students at a later grade level. Further support is available in studies where students can learn at their own rate. These studies show that although most students eventually reach mastery on each learning task, some students achieve mastery much sooner than do other students (Glaser, 1968; Atkinson, 1967).

Can all students learn a subject equally well? That is, can all students master a learning task at a high level of complexity? As we study aptitude distributions in relation to student performance we have become convinced that there are differences between the extreme students and the remainder of the population. At the top of the aptitude distribution (1 percent to 5 percent) there are likely to be some students who have a special talent for the subject. Such students are able to learn and to use the subject with greater fluency than other students. The student with special aptitudes for music or foreign languages can learn these subjects in ways not available to most other students. Whether this is a matter of native endowment or the effect of previous training is not clear, although this must vary from subject to subject. It is likely that some individuals are born with sensory organs better attuned to sounds (music, language, etc.) than are others and that these constitutional characteristics give them special advantages in learning such subjects over others. For other subjects, special training, particular interests, etc. may develop these high level aptitudes.

At the other extreme of the aptitude distribution, we believe there are individuals with special disabilities for particular learning. The tone deaf individual will have great difficulty in learning music; the color blind individual will have special problems in learning art; the individual who thinks in concrete forms will have special problems in learning highly abstract conceptual systems such as philosophy. Again, we believe these may constitute less than 5 percent of the distribution, but this will vary with the subject and the aptitudes.

In between are approximately 90 percent of the individuals where we believe (as does Carroll) that aptitudes are predictive of rate of learning rather than the level (or complexity) of learning that is possible. Thus, we are expressing the view that, given sufficient time (and appropriate types of help), 95 percent of students (the top 5 percent + the next 90 percent) can learn a subject up to a high level of mastery. We are convinced that the grade of A as an index of mastery of a subject can, under appropriate conditions, be achieved by up to 95 percent of the students in a class.

It is assumed that it will take some students more effort, time, and help to achieve this level than it will other students, For some students the effort and help required may make it prohibitive. Thus, to learn high school algebra to a point of mastery may require several years for some students but only a fraction of a year for other students. Whether mastery learning is worth this great effort for the students who may take several years is highly questionable. One basic problem for a mastery learning strategy is to find ways of reducing the amount of time required for the slower students to a point where it is no longer a prohibitively long and difficult task for these less able students.

We do not believe that aptitude for particular learning tasks is completely stable. There is evidence (Bloom, 1964; Hunt, 1961) that the aptitude for particular learning tasks may be modified by appropriate environmental conditions or learning experiences in the school and the home. The major task of educational programs concerned with learning to learn and general education should be to produce positive changes in the students' basic aptitudes. It is likely that these aptitudes can be most markedly affected during the early years in the home and during the elementary years of school. Undoubtedly, however, some changes can take place at later points in the individual's career.

However, even if marked changes are not made in the individual's aptitudes, it is highly probable that more effective learning conditions can reduce the amount of time required to learn a subject to mastery for all students and especially for the students with lower aptitudes. It is this problem which must be directly attacked by strategies for mastery learning.

2. Quality of Instruction

Our schools have usually proceeded on the assumption that there is a standard classroom situation for all students. Typically, this has been expressed in the teacher-student ratio of 1-30 with group instruction as the central means of teaching. There is the expectation that each teacher will teach the subject in much the same way as other teachers. This standardization is further emphasized by textbook adoption which specifies the instructional material to be provided each class. Closely related to this is the extensive research over the past 50 years which seeks to find the one instructional method, material, or curriculum program that is best for all students.

Thus, over the years, we have fallen into the "educational trap" of specifying quality of instruction in terms of good and poor teachers, teaching, instructional materials, curriculum—all in terms of group results. We persist in asking such questions as: What is the best teacher for the group? What is the best method of instruction for the group? What is the best instructional material for the group?

One may start with the very different assumption that individual students may need very different types and qualities of instruction to achieve mastery. That is, the same content and objectives of instruction may be learned by different students as the result of very different types of instruction. Carroll (1963) defines the *quality of instruction in terms of the degree to which the presentation, explanantion, and ordering of elements of the task to be learned approach the optimum for a given learner.*

Much research is needed to determine how individual differences in learners can be related to variations in the quality of instruction. There is evidence that some students can learn quite well through independent learning efforts while others need highly structured teaching-learning situations (Congreve, 1965). It seems reasonable to expect that some students will need more concrete illustrations and explanations than will others; some students may need more examples to get an idea than do others; some students may need more approval and reinforcement than others; and some students may even need to have several repetitions of the explanation while others may be able to get it the first time.

We believe that if every student had a very good tutor, most of them would be able to learn a particular subject to a high degree. A good tutor attempts to find the qualities of instruction (and motivation) best suited to a given learner. And, there is some evidence (Dave, 1963) that middle-class parents do attempt to tutor their children when they believe that the quality of instruction in school does not enable their children to learn a particular subject. In an unpublished study, the writer found that one-third of the students in an algebra course in a middle-class school were receiving as much tutorial instruction in the home in algebra as they were receiving group instruction in the school. These students received relatively high grades for the algebra course. For these students, the relationship between their mathematics aptitude scores (at the beginning of the year) and their achievement in algebra at the end of the year was almost zero. In contrast, for the students who received no additional instruction other than the regular classroom instruction, the relationship between their mathematics aptitude scores and their algebra achievement scores was very high (+ .90). While this type of research needs to be replicated, it is evident in this small study that the home tutoring help was providing the quality of instruction needed by these students to learn the algebra—that is, the instruction was adapted to the needs of the individual learners.

The main point to be stressed is that the quality of instruction is to be considered in terms of its effects on individual learners rather than on random groups of learners. Hopefully, the research of the future may lead to the definition of the qualities and kinds of instruction needed by various *types* of learners. Such research may suggest more effective group instruction since it is unlikely that the schools will be able to provide instruction for each learner separately.

3. Ability to Understand Instruction

In most courses at the high school and college level there is a single teacher and a single set of instructional materials. If the student has facility in understanding the teacher's communications about the learning and the instructional material (usually a textbook), he has little difficulty in learning the subject. If he has difficulty in understanding the teacher's instruction and/or the instructional material, he is likely to have great difficulty in learning the subject. *The ability to understand instruction may be defined as*

*the ability of the learner to understand the nature of the task he is to learn
and the procedures he is to follow in the learning of the task.*

Here is a point at which the student's abilities interact with the instructional materials and the instructor's abilities in teaching. For the student in
our highly verbal schools it is likely that this ability to understand
instruction is primarily determined by verbal ability and reading comprehension. These two measures of language ability are significantly related to
achievement in the majority of subjects and they are highly related (+ .50
to + .60) to grade point averages at the high school or college level. What
this suggests is that verbal ability (independent of specific aptitudes for each
subject) determines some general ability to learn from teachers and
instructional materials.

While it is possible to alter an individual's verbal ability by appropriate
training, there are limits to the amount of change that can be produced.
Most change in verbal ability can be produced at the preschool and
elementary school levels with less and less change being likely as the student
gets older (Bloom 1964). Vocabulary and reading ability, however, may be
improved to some extent at all age levels, even though there is a diminishing
utility of this approach with increasing age. Improvements in verbal abilities
should result in improvements in the individual's ability to understand
instruction.

The greatest immediate payoff in dealing with the ability to understand
instruction is likely to come from modifications in instruction in order to
meet the needs of individual students. There is no doubt that some teachers
do attempt to modify their instruction to fit a given group of students.
Many teachers center their instruction at the middle group of their students,
others at the top or bottom group—these are, however, reflections of the
teacher's habits and attitudes. They are, by no means, determinants of what
it is *possible* for a teacher to do. Given help and various types of aids,
individual teachers can find ways of modifying their instruction to fit the
differing needs of their students.

Group study procedures should be available to students as they need it.
In our own experience we have found that small groups of students (two or
three students) meeting regularly to go over points of difficulty in the
learning process were most effective, especially when the students could
cooperate and help each other without any danger of giving each other
special advantages in a competitive situation. Where learning can be turned
into a cooperative process with everyone likely to gain from the process,
small group learning procedures can be very effective. Much depends on the
composition of the group and the opportunities it gives each person to
expose his difficulties and have them corrected without demeaning one
person and elevating another. In the group process, the more able students
have opportunities to strengthen their own learning in the process of helping
another person grasp the idea through alternative ways of explaining and
using the idea.

Tutorial help (one to one relations between teacher and learner) represents the most costly type of help and should be used only where alternative procedures are not effective. However, this type of help should be available to students as they need it, especially where individuals have particular difficulties that can't be corrected in other ways. The tutor, ideally, should be someone other than the teacher, since he should bring a fresh way of viewing the idea or the process. The tutor must be skillful in detecting the points of difficulty in the student's learning and should help him in such a way as to free the student from continued dependence on him.

Another approach to variations in the students' ability to understand instruction is to vary the instructional material.

Textbooks may vary in the clarity with which they explain a particular idea or process. The fact that one textbook has been adopted by the school or by the teacher does not necessarily mean that other textbooks cannot be used at particular points in the instruction when they would be helpful to a student who can't grasp the idea from the adopted textbook. The task here is to [be] able to determine where the individual student has difficulty in understanding the instructions and then provide alternative textbook explanations if they are more effective at that point.

Workbooks and programmed instruction units may be especially helpful for some students who cannot grasp the ideas or procedures in the textbook form. Some students need the drill and the specific tasks which workbooks can provide. Other students need the small steps and frequent reinforcement which programmed units can provide. Such materials may be used in the initial instruction or as students encounter specific difficulties in learning a particular unit or section of the course.

Audiovisual Methods and Academic Games. Some students may learn a particular idea best through concrete illustrations and vivid and clear explanations. It is likely that film strips and short motion pictures which can be used by individual students as needed may be very effective. Other students may need concrete material such as laboratory experiences, simple demonstrations, blocks and other relevant apparatus in order to comprehend an idea or task. Academic games, puzzles, and other interesting but not threatening devices may be useful. Here again, the point is that some ways of communicating and comprehending an idea, problem, or task may be especially effective for some students although others may not use or need such materials and methods. We need not place the highest priority for all on abstract and verbal ways of instruction.

With regard to instructional materials, the suggestion is not that particular materials be used by particular students throughout the course. It is that each type of material may serve as a means of helping individual students at selected points in the learning process—and that a particular student may use whatever variety of materials are found to be useful as he encounters difficulties in the learning.

Throughout the use of alternative methods of instruction and instructional material, the essential point to be borne in mind is that these are attempts to improve the *quality of instruction* in relation to the ability of each student to *understand the instruction*. As feedback methods inform the teachers of particular errors and difficulties the majority of students are having, it is to be expected that the regular group instruction could be modified so as to correct these difficulties. As particular students are helped individually, the goal should be not only to help the student over particular learning difficulties but also to enable him to become more independent in his learning and to help him identify the alternative ways by which he can comprehend new ideas. But, most important, the presence of a great variety of instructional materials and procedures should help both teachers and students to overcome feelings of defeatism and passivity about learning. If the student can't learn in one way, he should be reassured that alternatives are available to him. The teacher should come to recognize that it is the learning which is important and that instructional alternatives exist to enable all (or almost all) of the students to learn the subject to a high level.

4. Perseverance

Carroll defines *perseverance as the time the learner is willing to spend in learning.* If a student needs to spend a certain amount of time to master a particular task, and he spends less than this amount in active learning, he is not likely to learn the task to the level of mastery. Carroll attempts to differentiate between spending time on learning and the amount of time the student is actively engaged in learning.

Perseverance does appear to be related to attitudes toward and interest in learning. In the International Study of Educational Achievement (Husén, 1967), the relationship between the number of hours of homework per week reported by the student (a crude index of perseverance) and the number of years of further education desired by the student is + .25.

We do believe that students vary in the amount of perseverance they bring to a specific learning task. However, students appear to approach different learning tasks with different amounts of perseverance. The student who gives up quickly in his efforts to learn an academic subject may persevere an unusually long time in learning how to repair an automobile or in learning to play a musical instrument. It would appear to us that as a student finds the effort rewarding, he is likely to spend more time on a particular learning task. If, on the other hand, the student is frustrated in his learning, he must (in self-defense) reduce the amount of time he devotes to learning. While the frustration level of students may vary, we believe that all students must sooner or later give up a task if it is too painful for them.

While efforts may be made to increase the amount of perseverance in students, it is likely that manipulation of the instruction and learning materials may be more effective in helping students master a given learning task, in spite of their present level of perseverance. Frequency of reward and evidence of success in learning can increase the student's perseverance in a learning situation. As students attain mastery of a given task, they are likely to increase their perseverance for a related learning task.

In our own research we are finding that the demands for perseverance may be sharply reduced if students are provided with instructional resources most appropriate for them. Frequent feedback accompanied by specific help in instruction and material as needed can reduce the time (and perseverance) required. Improvement in the quality of instruction (or explanations and illustrations) may reduce the amount of perseverance necessary for a given learning task.

There seems to be little reason to make learning so difficult that only a small proportion of the students can persevere to mastery. Endurance and unusual perseverance may be appropriate for long-distance running— they are not great virtues in their own right. The emphasis should be on learning, not on vague ideas of discipline and endurance.

5.   Time Allowed for Learning

Throughout the world schools are organized to give group instruction with definite periods of time allocated for particular learning tasks. A course in history at the secondary level may be planned for an academic year of instruction, another course may be planned for a semester, while the amount of instructional time allocated for a subject like arithmetic at the 5th-grade level may be fixed. Whatever the amount of time allowed by the school and the curriculum for particular subjects or learning tasks, it is likely to be too much for some students and not enough for other students.

For Carroll, the time spent on learning is the key to mastery. His basic assumption is that aptitude determines the rate of learning and that most, if not all, students can achieve mastery if they devote the amount of time needed to the learning. This implies that the student must not only devote the amount of time he needs to the learning task but also that he be *allowed* enough time for the learning to take place.

There seems to be little doubt that students with high levels of aptitude are likely to be more efficient in their learning and to require less time for learning than students with lower levels of aptitude. Whether most students can be helped to become highly efficient learners in general is a problem for future research.

The amount of time students need for a particular kind of learning has not been studied directly. One indication of the time needed comes from studies of the amount of time students spend on homework. In our review of the amount of time spent by 13-year-old students on mathematics homework in the International Study of Educational Achievement (Husén, 1967), we find that if we omit the extreme 5 percent of the subjects, the ratio is roughly 6 to 1. That is, some students spend 6 times as much time on mathematics homework as do others. Other studies of use of time suggest that this is roughly the order of magnitude to be expected.

If instruction and student use of time become more effective, we believe that most students will need less time to learn the subject to mastery and that the ratio of time required for the slower and the faster learners may be reduced from about 6 to 1 to perhaps 3 to 1.

In general, we find a zero or a slightly negative relationship between final grades and amount of time spent on homework. In the International Study (Husén, 1967) the average correlation for twelve countries at the 13-year-old level is approximately –.05 between achievement test scores in mathematics and number of hours per week of homework in mathematics as reported by students. Thus, the amount of time spent on homework does not seem to be a very good predictor of achievement in the subject.

We are convinced that it is not the sheer amount of time spent in learning (either in school or out of school) that accounts for the level of learning. We believe that each student should be allowed the time he needs to learn a subject. And, the time he needs to learn the subject is likely to be affected by the student's aptitudes, his verbal ability, the quality of instruction he receives in class, and the quality of the help he receives outside of class. The task of a strategy for mastery learning is to find ways of altering the time individual students need for learning as well as to find ways of providing whatever time is needed by each student. Thus, a strategy for mastery learning must find some way of solving the instructional problems as well as the school organizational (including time) problems.

ONE STRATEGY FOR MASTERY LEARNING

There are many alternative strategies for mastery learning. Each strategy must find some way of dealing with individual differences in learners through some means of relating the instruction to the needs and characteristics of the learners. We believe that each strategy must include some way of dealing with the five variables discussed in the foregoing.

Were it not so costly in human resources, we believe that the provision of a good tutor for each student might be one ideal strategy. In any case, the tutor-student relationship is a useful model to consider when one attempts to work out the details of a less costly strategy. Also, the tutor strategy is not as farfetched as it may seem at first glance. In the preschool period most of the child's instruction is tutorial—usually provided by the mother. In many middle class homes the parents continue to provide tutorial help as needed by the child during much of his school career.

Other strategies include permitting students to go at their own pace, guiding students with respect to courses they should or should not take, and providing different tracks or streams for different groups of learners. The nongraded school (Goodlad and Anderson, 1959) is one attempt to provide an organizational structure that permits and encourages mastery learning.

A group of us at the University of Chicago have been doing research on the variables discussed in the previous pages. In addition, some of us have been attempting to develop a strategy of teaching and learning which will bring all (or almost all) students to a level of mastery in the learning of any subject. Our approach has been to supplement regular group instruction by using diagnostic procedures and alternative instructional methods and materials in such a way as to bring a large proportion of the students to a predetermined standard of achievement. In this approach, we have tried to bring most of the students to mastery levels of achievement within the regular term semester, or period of calendar time in which the course is usually taught. Undoubtedly, some students will spend more time than others in learning the subject, but if the majority of students reach mastery levels at the end of the time allocated for the subject, mastery will have affective as well as cognitive consequences.

We have had some successes and some dismal failures with this approach. We have been trying to learn from both the successes and the failures. In the near future we hope to have some of these ideas applied to a large number of classrooms in selected school systems. Initially, we have chosen to work with subjects which have few prerequisites (algebra, science, etc.) because we believe it is easier to secure mastery learning in a given time period in such courses. In contrast are subjects which are late in a long sequence of learning (6th grade reading, 8th grade arithmetic, advanced mathematics, etc.). For such subjects, it is unlikely that mastery learning can be attained within a term for a group of students who have had a long history of cumulative learning difficulties in the specific subject field.

In working on this strategy we have attempted to spell out some of the *preconditions* necessary, develop the *operating procedures* required, and evaluate some of the *outcomes* of the strategy.

Preconditions

If we are able to develop mastery learning in students, we must be able to recognize when students have achieved it. We must be able to define what we mean by mastery and we must be able to collect the necessary evidence to establish whether or not a student has achieved it.

The specification of the objectives and content of instruction is one necessary precondition for informing both teacher and students about the expectations. The translation of the specifications into evaluation procedures helps to further define what it is that the student should be able to do when he has completed the course. The evaluation procedures used to appraise the outcomes of instruction (summative evaluation) help the teacher and student know when the instruction has been effective.

Implicit in this way of defining the outcomes and preparing evaluation instruments is a distinction between the teaching-learning process and the evaluation process. At some point in time, the results of teaching and learning can be reflected in the evaluation of the students. But, these are *separate* processes. That is, teaching and learning are intended to prepare the student in an area of learning, while evaluation (summative) is intended to appraise the extent to which the student has developed in the desired ways. Both the teacher and the learner must have some understanding of what the achievement criteria are and both must be able to secure evidence of progress toward these criteria.

If the achievement criteria are primarily competitive, i.e., the student is to be judged in terms of his relative position in the group, then the student is likely to seek evidence on his standing in the group as he progresses through the learning tasks. We recognize that competition may be a spur to those students who view others in competitive terms, but we believe that much of learning and development may be destroyed by primary emphasis on competition.

Much more preferable in terms of intrinsic motivation for learning is the setting of standards of mastery and excellence apart from interstudent competition, followed by appropriate efforts to bring as many students up to this standard as possible. This suggests some notion of absolute standards and the use of grades or marks which will reflect these standards. Thus, it is conceivable that all students may achieve mastery and the grade of A. It is also possible in a particular year in a specific course for few or none of the students to attain mastery or grade of A.

While we would recommend the use of absolute standards carefully worked out for a subject, we recognize the difficulty of arriving at such standards. In some of our own work, we have made use of standards derived from previous experience with students in a particular course. In one course, students in 1966 were informed that the grades for 1966 would be based on *standards* arrived at in 1965. The grades of A, B, C, D, and F would be based on an examination which was parallel to that used in 1965 and the grades would be set at the same performance levels as those used in 1965. The students were informed that the proportion of students receiving each grade was to be determined by their performance levels rather than by their rank order in the group. Thus, the students were not competing with each other for grades; they were to be judged on the basis of levels of mastery used in 1965.

We do not believe this is the only way of arriving at achievement standards, but the point is that students must feel they are being judged in terms of level of performance rather than a normal curve or some other arbitrary and relative set of standards. We are not recommending national achievement standards. What is being recommended are realistic performance standards developed for each school or group, followed by instructional procedures which will enable the majority of students to attain these standards.

One result of this way of setting achievement standards was to enable the students to work with each other and to help each other without being concerned about giving special advantages (or disadvantages) to other students. Cooperation in learning rather than competition was a clear result from this method of setting achievement criteria.

In the work we have done, we attempted to have the teacher teach the course in much the same way as previously. That is, the particular materials and methods of instruction in the current year should be about the same as in previous years. Also, the time schedule during the course was about the same. The operating procedures discussed in the next section *supplemented* the regular instruction of the teacher. We have proceeded in this way because we believe a useful strategy for mastery learning should be widely applicable. If extensive training of teachers is necessary for a particular strategy, it is less likely that it will receive widespread use.

Operating Procedures

The operating procedures we have used are intended to provide detailed feedback to teachers and students and to provide specific supplementary instructional resources as needed. These procedures are devised to insure mastery of each learning unit in such a way as to reduce the time required while directly affecting both quality of instruction and the ability of the student to understand the instruction.

Formative Evaluation. One useful operating procedure is to break a course or subject into smaller units of learning. Such a learning unit may correspond to a chapter in a textbook, a well-defined content portion of a course, or a particular time unit of the course. We have tended to think of units as involving a week or two of learning activity.

Using some of the ideas of Gagné (1965) and Bloom (1956) we have attempted to analyze each unit into a number of elements ranging from specific terms or facts, more complex and abstract ideas such as concepts and principles, and relatively complex processes such as application of principles and analysis of complex theoretical statements. We believe, as does Gagné (1965) that these elements form a hierarchy of learning tasks.

We have then attempted to construct brief diagnostic-progress tests which can be used to determine whether or not the student has mastered the unit and what, if anything, the student must still do to master it. We have borrowed the term *Formative Evaluation* from Scriven (1967) to refer to these diagnostic-progress tests.

Frequent formative evaluation tests pace the learning of students and help motivate them to put forth the necessary effort at the appropriate time. The appropriate use of these tests helps to insure that each set of learning tasks is thoroughly mastered before subsequent learning tasks are started.

Each formative test is administered after the completion of the appropriate learning unit. While the frequency of these progress tests may vary throughout the course, it is likely that some portions of the course—especially the early sections of the course—may need more frequent formative tests than later portions. Where some of the learning units are basic and prerequisite for other units of the course, the tests should be frequent enough to insure thorough mastery of such learning material.

For those students who have thoroughly mastered the unit, the formative tests should reinforce the learning and assure the student that his present mode of learning and approach to study is adequate. Since he will have a number of such tests, the student who consistently demonstrates mastery should be able to reduce his anxiety about his course achievement.

For students who lack mastery of a particular unit, the formative tests should reveal the particular points of difficulty—the specific questions they answer incorrectly and the particular ideas, skills, and processes they still need to work on. It is most helpful when the diagnosis shows the elements in a learning hierarchy that the student still needs to learn. We have found that students respond best to the diagnostic results when they are referred to particular instructional materials or processes intended to help them correct their difficulties. The *diagnosis* should be accompanied by a very specific *prescription* if the students are to do anything about it.

Although we have limited evidence on this point, we believe that the formative tests should not be assigned grades or quality points. We have marked the tests to show *mastery* and *nonmastery*. The nonmastery is accompanied by detailed diagnosis and prescription of what is yet to be done before mastery is complete. We believe that the use of grades on repeated progress tests prepares students for the acceptance of less than mastery. To be graded C repeatedly, prepares the student to accept a C as his "fate" for the particular course, especially when the grades on progress tests are averaged in as part of the final grade. Under such conditions, there must come a point when it is impossible to do better than a particular grade in the course—and there is little value in striving to improve. Formative evaluation tests should be regarded as part of the learning process and should in no way be confused with the judgement of the capabilities of the student or used as a part of the grading process.

These formative tests may also provide feedback for the teacher since they can be used to identify particular points in the instruction that are in need of modification. The formative evaluation tests also can serve as a means of quality control in future cycles of the course. The performance of the students on each test may be compared with the norms for previous years to insure that students are doing as well or better. Such comparisons can also be used to insure that changes in instruction or materials are not producing more error and diffculty than was true in a previous cycle of the course.

Alternative Learning Resources. It is one thing to diagnose the specific learning difficulties the student has and to suggest the specific steps he should take to overcome these difficulties. It is quite another thing to get him to do anything about it. By itself, the frequent use of progress tests can improve the achievement of students to a small degree. If, in addition, the student can be motivated to expend further effort on correcting his errors on the progress tests, the gains in achievement can be very great.

We have found that students do attempt to work on their difficulties when they are given specific suggestions (usually on the formative evaluation results) as to what they need to do.

The best procedure we have found thus far is to have small groups of students (two or three) meet regularly for as much as an hour per week to review the results of their formative evaluation tests and to help each other overcome the difficulties identified on these tests.

We have offered tutorial help as students desired it, but so far students at the secondary or higher education level do not seek this type of help frequently.

Other types of learning resources we have prescribed for students include: (a) reread particular pages of the original instructional material; (b) read or study specific pages in alternative textbooks or other instructional materials; (c) use specific pages of workbooks or programmed texts; and (d) use selected audiovisual materials.

We suspect that no specific learning material or process is indispensable. The presence of a great variety of instructional materials and procedures and specific suggestions as to which ones the student might use help the student recognize that if he cannot learn in one way, alternatives are available to him. Perhaps further research will reveal the best match between individuals and alternative learning resources. At present, we do not have firm evidence on the relations between student characteristics and instructional materials and procedures.

Outcomes

What are the results of a strategy for mastery learning? So far we have limited evidence. The results to date, however, are very encouraging. We are in the process of securing more evidence on a variety of situations at the elementary, secondary, and higher education levels.

Cognitive Outcomes of a Mastery Strategy. In our work to date we have found some evidence of the effectiveness of a strategy for mastery learning. Our best results have been found in a course on test theory where we have been able to use parallel achievement tests for the course in 1965, 1966, and 1967. In 1965, before the strategy was used, approximately 20 percent of the students received the grade of A on the final examination. In 1966, after the strategy was employed, 80 percent of the students reached this same level of mastery on the parallel examination and were given the grade of A. The difference in the mean performance of the two groups represents about two standard deviations on the 1965 achievement test and is highly significant.

In 1967, using the same formative evaluation tests as used in 1966, it was possible to compare the 1966 and the 1967 results after each unit of learning. Thus, the formative evaluation tests became quality control measures. Where there were significant negative differences between the results on a particular test from 1966 to 1967, the instructor reviewed the specific learning difficulties and attempted to explain the ideas in a different way. The final results on the 1967 summative evaluation instrument, which was parallel to the final achievement tests in 1965 and 1966, were that 90 percent of the students achieved mastery and were given grades of A.

Similar studies are underway at different levels of education. We expect to have many failures and a few successes. But, the point to be made is not that a single strategy of mastery learning can be used mechanically to achieve a particular set of results. Rather, the problem is one of determining what procedures will prove effective in helping particular students learn the subject under consideration. It is hoped that each time a strategy is used, it will be studied to find where it is succeeding and where it is not. For which students is it effective and for which students is it not effective? Hopefully, the results in a particular year can take advantage of the experience accumulated over the previous years.

Affective Consequences of Mastery. We have for the past century conceived of mastery of a subject as being possible for only a minority of students. With this assumption we have adjusted our grading system so as to certify that only a small percent of students (no matter how carefully selected) are awarded a grade of A. If a group of students learns a subject in a superior way (as contrasted with a previous group of students) we still persist in awarding the A (or mastery) to only the top 10 or 15 percent of the students. We grudgingly recognize that the majority of students have "gotten by" by awarding them grades of D or C. Mastery and recognition of mastery under the present relative grading system is unattainable for the majority of students—but this is the result of the way in which we have "rigged" the educational system.

Mastery must be both a subjective recognition by the student of his competence and a public recognition by the school or society. The public recognition must be in the form of appropriate certification by the teacher or by the school. No matter how much the student has learned, if public recognition is denied him, he must come to believe that he is inadequate, rather than the system of grading or instruction. Subjectively, the student must gain feelings of control over ideas and skills. He must come to recognize that he "knows" and can do what the subject requires.

If the system of formative evaluation (diagnostic-progress tests) and the summative evaluation (achievement examinations) informs the student of his mastery of the subject, he will come to believe in his own mastery and competence. He may be informed by the grading system as well as by the discovery that he can adequately cope with the variety of tasks and problems in the evaluation instruments.

When the student has mastered a subject and when he receives both objective and subjective evidence of the mastery, there are profound changes in his view of himself and of the outer world.

Perhaps the clearest evidence of affective change is the interest the student develops for the subject he has mastered. He begins to "like" the subject and to desire more of it. To do well in a subject opens up further avenues for exploration of the subject. Conversely, to do poorly in a subject closes an area for further study. The student desires some control over his environment, and mastery of a subject gives him some feeling of control over a part of his environment. Interest in a subject is both a cause of mastery of the subject as well as a result of mastery. Motivation for further learning is one of the more important conseqiiences of mastery.

At a deeper level is the student's self-concept. Each person searches for positive recognition of his worth and he comes to view himself as adequate in those areas where he receives assurance of his competence or success. For a student to view himself in a positive way, he must be given many opportunities to be rewarded. Mastery and its public recognition provide the necessary reassurance and reinforcement to help the student view himself as adequate. It is the opinion of this writer that one of the more positive aids to mental health is frequent and objective indications of self-development. Mastery learning can be one of the more powerful sources of mental health. We are convinced that many of the neurotic symptons displayed by high school and college students are exacerbated by painful and frustrating experiences in school learning. If 90 percent of the students are given positive indications of adequacy in learning, one might expect such students to need less and less in the way of emotional therapy and psychological help. Contrariwise, frequent indications of failure and learning inadequacy must be accompanied by increased self-doubt on the part of the student and the search for reassurance and adequacy outside the school.

Finally, modern society requires continual learning throughout life. If the schools do not promote adequate learning and reassurance of progress, the student must come to reject learning—both in the school and later life. Mastery learning can give zest to school learning and can develop a lifelong interest in learning. It is this continual learning which should be the major goal of the educational system.

REFERENCES

Atkinson, R. C., Computerized instruction and the learning process. Technical Report No. 122, Stanford, California. Institute for Mathematical Studies in the Social Sciences, 1967.

Bloom, B. S., Stability and change in human characteristics. New York: John Wiley & Sons, 1964.

Bloom, B. S. (Ed.), Taxonomy of educational objectives: Handbook I, cognitive domain. New York: David McKay Company, 1956.

Bowman, M. J., The new economics of education. *International Journal of Educational Sciences*, 1966, 1:29–46.

Bruner, Jerome, Toward a theory of instruction. Cambridge, Massachusetts: Harvard University Press, 1966.

Carroll, John, A model of school learning. *Teachers College Record*, 1963, 64: 723–733.

Congreve, W. J., Independent learning. *North Central Association Quarterly*, 1965, 40: 222–228.

Dave, R. H., The identification and measurement of environmental process variables that are related to educational achievement. Unpublished doctoral dissertation, University of Chicago, 1963.

Gagné, Robert M., The conditions of learning. New York: Holt, Rinehart, & Winston, 1965.

Glaser, R., Adapting the elementary school curriculum to individual performance. *Proceedings* of the 1967 Invitational Conference on Testing Problems. Princeton, New Jersey: Educational Testing Service, 1968.

Goodlad, J. I. and Anderson, R. H., The nongraded elementary school. New York: Harcourt, Brace & World, 1959.

Hunt, J. McV., Intelligence and experience. New York: Ronald Press Co., 1961.

Husén, T. (Ed.), International study of educational achievement in mathematics: A comparison of twelve countries, Volumes I and II. New York: John Wiley & Sons, 1967.

Morrison, H. C., The practice of teaching in the secondary school. Chicago: University of Chicago Press, 1926.

Schultz, T. W., The economic value of education. New York: Columbia University Press, 1963.

Scriven, Michael, The methodology of evaluation. In Stake, R. (Ed.), *Perspectives on curriculum evaluation*. Chicago: Rand McNally & Co., 1967.

Skinner, B. F., The science of learning and the art of teaching. *Harvard Educational Review*, 1954, 24: 86–97.

Suppes, P., The uses of computers in education. *Scientific American*, 1966, 215: 206–221.

Part II

Instructional Time: Views from Three Disciplines

5

Time as the Terminus of Teaching: A Philosophical Perspective

Gary D Fenstermacher
Virginia Polytechnic Institute and State University

EDITORS' INTRODUCTION
Dr. Fenstermacher, a philosopher of education, has followed closely the course of reasearch on teaching. In this chapter he reminds us that philosophers distinguish between teaching as an activity inferred from student learning and teaching as an activity intended to bring about some learning. This distinction has important implications, and is elaborated on in this chapter.

The view of teaching that links it to the achievement of some learning outcomes, he believes, is an outgrowth of the behavioral-objectives movement and the societal press for teacher accountability for achievement. This view results in an overemphasis on the acquisition of basic skills and simple knowledge, since only in these areas does it seem possible to hold teachers responsible for specific learning outcomes. In the areas judged by Fenstermacher to be the more important areas of education, such as the building of character, the imparting of the norms of honesty and virtue, the understanding of one's emotions and feelings, teachers are not ordinarily held accountable. Consequently, teachers may not emphasize activities that are intended to foster such outcomes. When teaching is viewed as an activity intended (but not guaranteed) to foster learning, such important areas of the school curriculum can become more salient. Teachers, in this view, must try to foster achievement of these outcomes, but they are *not* responsible for student learning of these outcomes. Teaching and learning are viewed as distinctly separate concepts.

How do we know if teachers try to foster such outcomes? Engaged time in activities logically related to such outcomes, suggests Fenstermacher, is the measure of teacher trying. For example, student-engaged time in reading and discussing the concepts of *The Red Badge of Courage*, with emphasis on the concepts of cowardice and courage, or engaged time in viewing and discussing the television show *The Holocaust*, with emphasis on attitudes, feelings, and emotions, are ways of measuring teachers' attempts to foster these hard-to-measure outcomes. For Fenstermacher, engaged time in such activities is the terminus for teaching. He would not choose achievement of the intended outcomes as his sole criterion for successful teaching.

The concept of instructional time has played a major role in contemporary studies of teacher effectiveness. As a result of these recent studies, it is now believed that teachers can alter their instructional practices in order to increase the time during which students are engaged in academically relevant tasks.

By increasing the time spent on academic tasks, student achievement is thereby increased (Berliner, 1979; Rosenshine, 1976; Stallings, 1980). The findings of many of the time-on-task studies lend credence to the view that the classroom teacher is the producer of student learning, as it is the teacher who manages the learning environment so that student time-on-task is enhanced. I shall argue that it is an error to conceive of the teacher as the producer of student learning such that the teacher is held fully accountable for the student's achievement.

In the course of the argument, it will be claimed that the teacher can properly be held accountable only for *trying* to produce student achievement gains, *not* for actually producing such gains. If the argument is successful, it will demonstrate that one great value of the recent research on teacher effectiveness is that of offering us a sensible conception of the teacher making a legitimate effort to produce achievement gains. In other words, even though the research is typically conceived of as showing that the teacher is the causal agent of student learning, its greater value is found in a different conception: the teacher as one who tries (but may succeed or fail) to generate student achievement.

THE TASK AND ACHIEVEMENT SENSES OF TEACHING

If a teacher is conceived of as the causal agent of student learning, then it seems sensible to assert that if no learning occurs, no teaching took place. Why we would insist on this claim is something of a mystery, as not many of us are willing to make the same kind of claim in parallel cases. For example, we do not usually claim that if a parishioner fails to achieve salvation, the preacher has failed to preach. Nor do we generally argue that if a jury finds a defendant guilty, the lawyer failed to defend the accused.

Ryle's (1949) distinction between task and achievement words offers some insight into why we conceive of teaching in ways that lead us to make claims about it that we do not normally make about preaching or defending. Some words in the language may be thought of as task words, such as *searching*, *studying*, and *running* (in a race). The corresponding achievement words for these task words are *finding*, *mastering*, and *winning*, respectively. Other words in the language do not have separate terms to distinguish their task and achievement senses. These words are ambiguous with respect to task and achievement: that is, they carry both senses simultaneously. The term *selling* illustrates the task-achievement ambiguity. In its task sense, the clerk need only try to get the customer to purchase something before the clerk can be said to be selling. In its achievement sense, the customer must buy the product before the clerk can be said to be selling something to the customer.

Like *selling*, the term *teaching* exhibits task-achievement ambiguity (Green, 1971). In the task sense, one need only try to teach in order to be said to be teaching. In the achievement sense, teaching cannot occur unless someone is learning as a result of the teaching. If teaching can be regarded as either task or achievement, how shall we decide which it is? The first step in answering this question is to note that a *decision* is involved. One cannot simply presuppose that teaching is a task or an achievement, for to presuppose one or the other ignores the possibility that it may actually be otherwise. That is, because teaching may be either, it is necessary both to be clear about which sense is in effect, and to offer reasons why this sense is preferred over the other one. One searches the instructional-time research in vain looking for a discussion of which sense of teaching is preferred. Instead, it is presupposed in this literature that teaching is an achievement term—that the learner must learn what the teacher teaches before the teacher can be said to be teaching.

Inasmuch as the achievement sense of teaching is simply presupposed in the research literature, there are no reasons or grounds offered to defend this particular determination of the task-achievement ambiguity. What happens if we try to supply the grounds? Is it possible to come up with good reasons to support the achievement sense of teaching? I believe this last question must be answered in the negative. If we examine some of the recent history surrounding the last 15–20 years of instructional-time research, it becomes clear that the presupposition of the achievement sense is based on convenience and circumstance, not on logic or empirical evidence. It is worthwhile to review this history, in broad strokes, to see just how the presupposition of achievement took place.

THE SOCIOPOLITICAL CONTEXT
OF RESEARCH ON TEACHING

Teacher-effectiveness research, especially in the form of process–product studies, began in earnest at a time when the educational milieu was awash with the fervor of reform. Two distinct events of the mid-sixties era did much to shape the subsequent character of research on teaching. The first was increased federal support for educational research, impelled by President Johnson's conception of the Great Society. The second was a flourishing concern for accountability, which had as one of its most significant manifestations the move toward behavioral objectives. The clamor for behavioral objectives brought a level of specificity to educational goal statements unlike that ever experienced before. In the words of one of the more well-known proponents for behavioral objectives: "Meaningful instructional objectives must be stated in terms of student behavior, and they must specify the type of behavior a student will engage in (or be able to engage in) when he has satisfactorily achieved the objective" (Popham, 1973, p. 13).

Such precise specification of learning outcomes advantaged the statistically inclined researcher of the day, whose methods and data analysis techniques required criterion or dependent variables that were readily amenable to exact measurement. In speaking of the work he and his colleagues did on the Beginning Teacher Evaluation Study (BTES), Berliner (1979, p. 125) states that "in this conception of research on teaching, *the content area the student is working on must be specified precisely ...*" (emphasis added). The demand for specificity in learning outcomes, initiated by the press for accountability and furthered by the emphasis on behavioral objectives, served as sufficient justification for the researcher to state his or her criterion variables in as precise and measurable a form as possible. The exact specification of student outcomes enabled researchers to set off in search of those teacher behaviors that produced these outcomes. Once it had been determined that teacher behaviors would be linked with highly specified student outcomes, there was no longer any question of the sense in which the term *teaching* would be understood. It was simply presupposed that the term would be defined in its achievement, and not its task, sense.

This presupposition was further entrenched by the concentration of policy makers, social critics, and educational researchers on elementary schools. Those who were attentive to educational policy discussions in the late sixties and early seventies will recall the emphasis placed on early-childhood education. The guiding conception at the time was that if economically disadvantaged and culturally different learners were not given special assistance early in life, they might never catch up to the educationally well-nurtured children of the middle and upper classes. Projects Head Start and Follow-Through, as well as Parent and Child Centers, were among the major social action programs initiated to give the disadvantaged or different learner a better chance to compete with more economically advantaged peers. Much of this reform effort took place in elementary schools, where learning outcomes were couched in the form of "basic skills" and rudimentary knowledge. Given the basic character of these objectives, it must have seemed quite natural to specify them as precisely as possible. After all, these were young learners lacking the developmental capacity to confront sophisticated, high-level objectives. What could possibly be amiss in the desire to specify elementary objectives as precisely as possible? Moreover, such precision would be a boon to those who made policy and regulated the programs, for they were far away from the children, and the data sent to them would be valuable for deciding future courses of action.

Thus precise specification appeared to benefit everyone. Policy makers preferred it because it provided the kind of exact data needed to determine the success of their efforts. Program regulators preferred it because it enabled them to gauge the strengths and weaknesses of their programs. Researchers preferred it because it enabled them to employ the statistical devices that had become the tools of their craft. Amidst all this preference, scant attention was given to the fact that teaching was being interpreted exclusively in its achievement sense. Given these social and political circumstances, the presupposition of the achievement sense of teaching is far better understood as an upshot of the political economy of the time and the needs of the educational research community than as a logical, evidential requirement. In other words, the reasons for opting for the achievement sense of teaching are primarily ideological; reasoned analysis leads to a different conception. It is to that conception that I now turn.

ENGAGED TIME AS THE TASK OF TEACHING

Philosophers concerned with analyzing the concept of teaching have been careful to distinguish the generic meaning of the term from its variants. The question, 'What does *teaching* mean?' is different from the questions, 'What is good teaching?' and 'What is successful teaching?' The first question asks for the generic meaning of the term *teaching*. Answers to the second and third questions presuppose an answer to the first question; that is, it is necessary to grasp the meaning of *teaching* in its generic sense before coming to some understanding of what is meant by good teaching or successful teaching. The philosophical literature dealing with the concept of teaching shows a high degree of unanimity on treating the generic meaning of teaching in the task sense. Hirst (1973), for example, argues that teaching in its generic form requires only those activities that mark the intention of the teacher to instruct students in some subject: "Teaching is the label for those activities of a person, A, the intention of which is to bring about in another person, B, the intentional learning of x" (p. 172).

Note that for Hirst and many others who have undertaken to analyze the concept of teaching, the generic meaning of teaching is marked by the teacher's *intention* to bring about learning, not the actual bringing about of learning. As such, the generic meaning of teaching entails the task sense of the term. To intend to bring about the learning of X by person B is to *try* to do so; it is to set B's learning X as the task for the teacher. Until the advent of recent research on teaching, there was no reliable empirical standard or criterion for assessing the teacher's intention to impart X to B. However, certain concepts developed in the research on teaching literature offer a means for assessing the teacher's intention to impart content to learners. The concept of engaged time, the amount of time the student spends on academically relevant tasks, may be used as a standard or criterion for determining the degree to which teachers are realizing their intentions. Rather than hold the teacher accountable for actual gains in student learning (the success sense of teaching), we may choose instead to hold the teacher accountable for the amount of time the student is engaged on the assigned task. Holding the teacher accountable for engaged time rather than student achievement gain turns out to be highly consistent with the generic conception of teaching as a task.

A remarkable switch has just occurred. The argument began with the contention that researchers engaged in studies of teacher effectiveness have presupposed the achievement sense of teaching. Now it is claimed that the research itself provides the basis for adopting the task sense. How can this be? The answer is not very complex. It was shown that the primary reasons for adopting the achievement sense of the teacher were ideological—matters of political economy and research convenience. These ideological convictions did not prevent researchers from realizing findings that may be used to rethink the very presuppositions that impelled the research in the first place. The findings, and the conceptions that undergird them (conceptions contributed by the researchers), support the task sense of teaching, and may be used to illuminate and defend this sense. Why is the task sense preferable to the achievement sense of teaching? The answer to this question is critical, for it involves a thorough reconsideration of the concept of teaching typically presupposed by the research and policy communities. To make clear this reconsideration, it is necessary to return to the matter of specification of learning outcomes.

DIFFERENT FORMS OF LEARNING OUTCOMES

As already noted, the 1960s and 1970s were periods of demand for accountability. To meet this demand, learning outcomes were stated in what might be called 'high-specification' form. Objectives were stated in terms that permitted the measurement of changes in learner behaviors. High specification is most readily applied to certain kinds of outcomes, particularly those descriptive of basic skills and rudimentary knowledge. Other kinds of outcomes—those, for example, that are descriptive of understanding, emotional development, and traits of character—resist high specification. It is extremely difficult to state these "higher level" outcomes in high-specification form. They are low-specification outcomes, in that we are unable to specify them with much precision, at least with much measureable precision.

As the trend toward accountability gained momentum, the demand for high specification increased. The more successful we became at high specification, the more it seemed sensible to hold the teacher accountable for actual gains in student learning. I have already noted how this shift resulted in the eventual presupposition that teaching be understood exclusively in its achievement sense. As the achievement sense of teaching became the accepted standard, low-specification outcomes were either discarded (because they were too difficult to measure accurately), or they were converted into high-specification outcomes. In those cases where the outcomes were converted, it was assumed that converting low-specification outcomes to high-specification outcomes did not alter the meaning of the outcomes themelves. This assumption is erroneous. The nature of the error becomes obvious upon examination of the different forms of learning outcomes.

Skills and knowledge constitute but two kinds or forms of learning outcomes. Though there may be many different forms, only six need be considered here: (1) basic skills, (2) knowledge, (3) belief, (4) understanding, (5) feelings and emotions, and (6) traits of character. Most of the learning outcomes that appear in the literature of schooling can be subsumed under one of these six forms. For example, decoding and subtraction without regrouping fall under form 1, basic skills. Recognition of the chemical elements of pure water is a knowledge, or form 2, objective. Offering a correct explanation and justification for the decline of progressivism in American politics falls under form 4, understanding. Acting with due regard for the rights of racially different persons falls under form 6, traits of character. As the demand for outcome specification intensifies, so does the shift away from outcome forms at the end of the list above. The higher the specification sought, the more likely that objectives will take the form of basic skills and knowledge, as these forms of outcomes are most amenable to high specification. Thus the basic skills and knowledge forms are typically considered high-specification outcomes, while the remaining four forms are considered low-specification outcomes.

A strong shift toward high-specification outcomes has the effect of eliminating forms descriptive of understanding, feelings and emotions, and traits of character. The proponents of high specification have contended that low-specification outcomes need not be abandoned, they need only be restated as high-specification outcomes. Such restatement is a form of reductionism, wherein somewhat vague and abstract outcomes are reduced to their behavioral components so that they can be measured precisely. Wise (1979) refers to this process as "goal reduction," noting that as educational policies "are more and more centrally determined, abstract and salutary goals are reduced and trivialized, and only those goals which can be measured are implemented'' (p. 58). The cost is greater than trivialization, however. The grievous error in goal reduction is that it confuses the different forms of learning outcomes, in the naive belief that, for example, a character trait outcome can be respecified as a skill outcome and still possess all the features of the original character trait outcome. Not so.

Take the case of a plumber working on a new home. The plumber may solder pipe, locate valves, and install antihammer air cushions with great skill, yet be dishonest. This dishonesty takes the form of using thin-wall tubing where medium-wall tubing is required (thin-wall is cheaper than medium- or thick-wall), of using simple valves where stop-and-wastage valves are needed, and of saving on pipe by running it along exterior walls where it is subject to freezing. The plumber is, in short, skilled in the trade, but dishonest in its practice. Honesty is a trait of character, and is unlike soldering and pipe selecting, which are skills. There is simply no way to reduce the trait of honesty to a set of skills that can be learned, as one learns to solder or run pipe.

Yet this is the very thing the reductionists would have us do—restate the low-specification outcomes of honesty into some set of high-specification outcomes detailing the behaviors of honest persons. As Ryle (1975) and Passmore (1975) point out, traits of character cannot be taught by treating them as sets of component skills. Rather, traits of character are taught indirectly, by modeling or imitating those who already possess these traits. Were this not so, it would be possible to engender courage in others by telling them all about courage; but we already know that persons are not courageous because of how much they know and understand about courage. A coward may know a great deal about courage, just as the brave warrior may know almost nothing about it. Advocates of high specification are fond of pointing out that you cannot teach something unless you aim directly for it. One moral of this discussion of different forms of learning outcomes is that high-specification advocates would profit from taking their own advice: Teaching traits of character must be done by aiming for traits of character, not by converting them to skills or rudimentary knowledge, then aiming for these.

TIME AS THE TERMINUS FOR TEACHING

If the conversion of low-specification outcomes to high-specification outcomes is an error, how does a teacher attempt such important educational outcomes as the development of objectively reasonable beliefs (Green, 1971; Fenstermacher, 1979), understanding, aesthetic sensitivity (Hepburn, 1975), emotional development (Peters, 1975), and virtue (Ryle, 1975)? These outcomes are all low-specification forms of learning, and thus unsuited to precise description. The task seems impossible if teaching is defined exclusively in its achievement sense, for it is exceedingly difficult to hold the teacher accountable for the realization of outcomes that defy precise specification. If, on the other hand, the teacher is held accountable only for *trying* to achieve these outcomes, then the problem of outcome specification no longer rears its constraining head. It is, in short, the task sense of teaching that permits the teacher to engage in the pursuit of low-specification outcomes. Unfettered by the need to state student achievement gains in precise terms, the teacher is freed to seek those ends that mark the student as an educated person.

There has long been a difficulty associated with adopting the task sense of teaching: For what shall the teacher be held accountable, and how will we know whether the result is a success or a failure? It would seem that if the teacher is held only to trying, then one effort is as good as another; as such, there is no accountability and no standard of performance. Though an objection of this kind may, at some time in the past, have had merit, it is no longer a sound rebuttal to accepting the task sense of teaching. As already mentioned, extant research on teaching provides a standard of performance for appraising teaching in its task sense. That standard of performance is engaged time, the amount of time a student spends engaged at a learning task relative to the amount of time allocated for that task. The teacher is held responsible for the span of engagement, but not for the learning realized by the student so engaged. In this view, the teacher who allocates time to units involving low-specification outcomes is not required to realize specific, measurable gains with students. Indeed, if the teacher is so required, the interaction that occurs is far more likely to constitute indoctrination than reasoned instruction (for there is great risk in low-specification areas of demanding that the student accept the interpretation proffered by teachers or texts).

It is, of course, true that the use of engaged time as a criterion of teaching effectiveness offers no indication of the quality or worth of the time spent on learning activities. Yet this same point can be made about student achievement of high-specification outcomes. Here, too, there is no means within the body of research on instructional time to appraise the worth of teaching and learning activities. The question of worth is largely a curricular concern that has been almost ignored in research on teaching, and it is being largely ignored here as well. However, the matter of worth is not entirely shunted aside in this analysis. Any conception of teaching that permits full consideration of low-specification outcomes increases the probability that due consideration will be given to matters of quality and worth. By permitting the teacher to aim for such outcome forms as understanding, emotions and feelings, and traits of character, the argument advanced in this chapter offers new opportunities to deliberate on matters of quality and worth in education.

With the argument developed to this point, it is now possible to distinguish between standards of success for both the task and the achievement senses of the term *teaching*. The criterion of success in the task sense is student-engaged time; the criterion of success in the achievement sense is student mastery of the content taught. Differentiating the task sense and its success criterion (engaged time) from the achievement sense and its corresponding success criterion (mastery) permits far greater discrimination in the assignment of responsibility for learning outcomes. Opting for the task sense makes it possible to distinguish between a teacher's trying and succeeding at engagement, and the students' failing to achieve mastery. (Those familiar with recent research on teaching may find this contention so puzzling as to be counterintuitive, for there is a great temptation to posit an almost a priori relation between rate of engagement and degree of mastery. However, the relation between engagement and achievement is a contingent, empirical relation; the appearance of an a priori connection is due more to the fact that the outcomes studied to date are almost entirely of the high-specification variety. I believe that when low-specification outcomes are studied, the contingent connection between engagement and achievement will become obvious. Effective teachers seeking low-specification outcomes may succeed in eliciting high rates of engagement but modest levels of achievement gain.) Thus it is possible for a teacher to try to impart understanding, emotional range and sensitivity, and traits of character, and succeed at these goals even though students show little progress in acquiring the emotions, feelings, and traits the teacher seeks. Acceptance of this point allows us to distinguish teaching successes from learning successes, as well as teaching failures from learning failures.

If no such distinction is made, then the teacher has but three choices: (1) avoid low-specification forms of learning outcomes altogether; (2) convert low-specification outcomes to high-specification outcomes, an instance of goal reduction wherein the low-specification outcomes are actually vitiated; or (3) insist on so rigorous an interpretation of the outcomes as to engender indoctrination. No theory of what is educative of fellow human beings—at least none of which I am aware—justifies any of these choices, hence the need to distinguish between failures in teaching and failures in learning. In so doing, the teacher is free to pursue outcomes constitutive of education as a rational, aesthetic, and moral endeavor. The distinction between criteria of success for the task and achievement senses of teaching provokes another question: Is it justifiable to hold a teacher fully accountable for student mastery of high-specification outcomes, but relieve the teacher of accountability of student mastery of low-specification outcomes? I am uncertain of the correct answer. As must by now be obvious, I believe it is an error to hold teachers accountable for student acquisition of low-specification outcomes, though they may be held accountable for student engagement in activities leading to these outcomes. Is it also an error *not* to hold teachers accountable for student acquisition of high-specification outcomes?

Note what is being suggested here. Might there be a connection between forms of outcomes and degrees of accountability for achievement gains, such that the lower the outcome specification, the lower the degree of accountability? Were this connection to obtain, a teacher may be held accountable for student achievement gains in high-specification outcomes, while for low-specification outcomes, the teacher's accountability would be for the amount of student-engaged time. I am reluctant to accept such a connection between the task and achievement senses of teaching and degrees of accountability. The reason is simply that the failure of students to show achievement gains may as readily be attributed to their learning as it may be attributed to the teacher's teaching, regardless of the level of outcome specification. Time is thus the terminus of teaching, no matter what forms the outcomes take.

Future research on instructional time may profitably be devoted to studying the concept of engaged time in relation to the different forms of learning outcomes. This research began with the presupposition that teaching is to be understood exclusively in its achievement sense. The consequence of this presupposition, when linked to the climate of accountability so evident in the last two decades, has been a shift of our attention away from enduring educational purposes. That shift is leaving an impoverished legacy, devoid of the more profound educational ends—such as objectively reasonable belief, understanding, emotional sensitivity, enlightened feelings, and noble traits of character. It is ironic that the research program that, at first blush, seems to ignore, indeed negate, these hallmarks of civilized life actually contains the concepts and means for renewing our hope that teachers may once again pursue these outcomes in the classroom. But this time, there will be a standard to appraise the efficacy of their labors. Freed from the incessant, cacophonous call to produce gains in achievement, teachers may welcome the opportunity to be judged on a standard that permits them to explore a much broader range of educative activities. It would be a significant event if instructional-time researchers were to focus their studies of teaching in ways that aided and supported teachers in this exploration.

REFERENCES

Berliner, D. C. (1979). Tempus educare. In P. Peterson & H. Walberg (Eds.), *Research on teaching: Concepts, findings, and implications*. Berkeley, Calif.: McCutchan.

Fenstermacher, G. D (1979). A philosophical reconsideration of recent research on teacher effectiveness. In L. Shulman (Ed.), *Review of research in education* (Vol. 6). Itasca, Ill.: Peacock.

Green, T. F. (1971). *The activities of teaching*. New York: McGraw-Hill.

Hepburn, R. W. (1975). The arts and the education of feeling and emotion. In R. Dearden, P. Hirst, & R. Peters (Eds.), *Education and reason*. Boston: Routledge & Kegan Paul.

Hirst, P. H. (1973). What is teaching? In R. Peters (Ed.), *The philosophy of education*. New York: Oxford University Press.

Passmore, J. (1975). On teaching to be critical. In R. Dearden, P. Hirst, & R. Peters (Eds.), *Education and reason*. Boston: Routledge & Kegan Paul.

Peters, R. S. (1975). The education of the emotions. In R. Dearden, P. Hirst, & R. Peters (Eds.), *Education and reason*. Boston: Routledge & Kegan Paul.

Popham, W. J. (1973). *Criterion-referenced instruction*. Belmont, Calif.: Fearon Publishers.

Rosenshine, B. (1976). Classroom instruction. In N. Gage (Ed.), *The psychology of teaching methods: Part I of the seventy-fifth yearbook of the National Society for the Study of Education*. Chicago: National Society for the Study of Education.

Ryle, G. (1949). *The concept of mind*. New York: Barnes & Noble Books.

Ryle, G. (1975). Can virtue be taught? In R. Dearden, P. Hirst, & R. Peters (Eds.), *Education and reason*. Boston: Routledge & Kegan Paul.

Stallings, J. (December 1980). Allocated academic learning time revisited, or beyond time-on-task. *Educational Researcher, 9*(11), 11–16.

Wise, A. E. (1979). *Legislated learning*. Berkeley, Calif.: University of California Press.

6

A Sociological Perspective on School Time

Rebecca Barr and Robert Dreeben
University of Chicago

EDITORS' INTRODUCTION

Instead of dealing with individual time-on-task considerations, Rebecca Barr and Robert Dreeben ask how the conduct of students is affected by the instructional group in which they are placed, as well as by the class, track, school, and district within which they are expected to learn. They present in this chapter a sociological formulation of the various manifestations of time in school-system organization. At the district level, the meaning accorded to time pertains to questions of law and union contracts as well as to the length of school years and working days. At the school level, curriculum time allotments are made and school schedules developed. These decisions about time and content represent the resolution of competing claims over school resources. At the class level, teachers determine how available class time will be spent instructionally.

The authors argue that time available to students is affected by the teacher's time spent in supervision of instruction, the appropriateness of learning tasks in terms of their difficulty, and the amount of work assigned. The ratio of work accomplished to time available defines pace, a condition heavily influenced by the ability composition of instructional groups. The chapter ends with the message that a conceptualization of time as an accounting system, or a metric, devoid of meaning, is not appropriate. Time must have a referent, and that referent pertains to the different kinds of activities taking place at the various levels of school organization.

As a rule, sociologists have had very little time for time in their thinking about social organization. Ideas about social ecology, stratification, distance, and differentiation have been rendered more in metaphors about space than about time.

We are concerned in this chapter with the quality of time and its manifestations in the social organization of school districts and their parts. These considerations are very different from much, if not most, of the recent work on the nature of time as it pertains to schooling. That work is primarily concerned with the availability and use of time among individuals, and most of it deals with the question of the time individual students are engaged doing school tasks. In thinking about time from the perspective of social organization, one does not focus on the individual in the first instance but rather on collective units in their own terms. The collective units of school systems are nested—district, school, track, class, and instructional group—and each nested level has not only its own peculiar properties but also connections to other levels. What happens at the individual level—so frequently conceptualized as time-on-task—needs to be understood, at least in part, in the light of what happens at these other levels. Perhaps an example will make the point clear.

Harnischfeger and Wiley (1976, 1978), in two papers about how to think about school time, have argued the case that "the total amount of active learning time on a particular instructional topic is *the* most important determinant of the pupil's achievement on that topic" (1976, p. 13). Under this guiding principle, they determine how much time is actually available to each student by deducting time contingencies from a maximum total defined by the length of the school year and day. Examples of deducted time contingencies include those that arise at the district level from labor disputes, at the class level from the teacher's time priorities and class distractions, and at the individual level from the balance between absence and attendance. This scheme provides a method of estimating precisely how much time each student has available to pursue learning activities on a given topic. And with some additional elaboration, it also permits the identification of time spent under varying instructional arrangements such as grouping and supervision.

We must also note, however, that each element of school-system organization is introduced in this formulation to provide increasingly precise measurement of how much time each student has to engage in learning activities. If one's primary interest is to determine how individuals use time, then this is the right procedure. By contrast, if one's interest is in the social organization of time, this procedure does not yield the appropriate information. The fact is that many investigations of instructional and school effects on learning treat classroom and school characteristics as elements of individual student experience; and even though such characteristics *refer to* the social properties of classrooms and schools, they are not actually presented in a sociologically formulated way.

Consider another example. Summers and Wolfe (1977) show the effects of teacher experience, teacher preparation, and class size upon students' achievement in order to discover whether class-level properties influence individual learning. But in fact, the class-level properties are expressed at the individual level because all students in each class are assigned the experience, preparation, and size score characteristic of the class. What is actually measured, then, is the experience of individual students in classes with certain kinds of teachers and of certain size. No classroom-level phenomenon is thereby addressed in class-level terms. There is nothing wrong with this line of analysis. We must understand it, however, as showing the connection between individuals' experiences and their learning. It casts no light on the *character of the classroom* and its impact on learning viewed from an organizational perspective.

The question we will address here is the nature of time considerations at each level of school-system organization and the way in which these considerations are related to each other. Time, in our view, has different meanings and different manifestations in the various parts of school systems; accordingly, our comments here should be viewed as an exercise in the sociology of organizations in which the nature of time is the primary consideration. Only in a very subsidiary way are we interested in how much time individual students spend in their studies.

School systems are obviously complex and differentiated organizations, which means that both tasks and offices are divided up into jurisdictions with not only different responsibilities but also different segments of the system's overall resources to work with. We begin with the facts that the jurisdictions are hierarchically arranged and that time is one of the resources that becomes subject to organizational action at each level. It is also important to recognize that time considerations at each level do not necessarily pertain to individual learning. Accordingly, the settlement of district time issues is relevant to other district-level matters (although not only to them); the settlement of school time issues pertains to other school matters. The closer one comes organizationally to the conditions that bear directly on individual learning, the greater the relevance of time to learning.

School districts are constrained by state law to keep schools open a certain number of days each year. The law, then, puts a crude outside limit on the amount of time available for all system-wide activities—a condition that by itself has only remote implications for learning. School officials at the district level are charged with the responsibility of upholding state law. Setting the length of the school year, however, is not simply a question of law enforcement. More to the point, it is an element in the settlement of a labor contract with teachers (and other district personnel). More is at stake, however, than the length of the school year, for such contracts also include provisions that govern the length of the school day, the dates school will start and end, the duration and spacing of vacations, the inclusion of conference and in-service days, and the like. And although the length of class periods is not necessarily part of the master contract, the duration of class hours is usually set by the district.

Maximum time allotments for all instructional activities (as well as noninstructional ones) are established by the district administration. More than that, however, the division of the year into time segments, from vacation to vacation, has implications for the quality of time during the year. A school term that runs from mid-August until Christmas with only a Thanksgiving break contains a long stretch of unrelieved time, much of it spent in the heat. The instructional usefulness of the Thanksgiving-to-Christmas stretch might well differ in school years that begin in early September and those that begin in August. If school closes for the harvest in some rural communities, that changes the nature of things again. We really do not know very much about the spacing of time during school years, nor in the United States have we experimented with the six-day school week. One issue here is whether there are more or less comfortable and productive periods during the year and whether longer or shorter stretches between vacations (of varying lengths themselves) make for better or worse educational practice. The settlement of these time considerations, in short, involves the school system in its law enforcement capacity vis-à-vis the state; it also bears directly on the establishment of workable relationships with suppliers of labor and on the integration of the school system with households in local communities.

The time questions inherent in the formation of labor contracts are familiar; the school-household connection is less so. The times that schools open and close for the day influence when and whether parents can go to and leave from work. They affect the ways in which families arrange for the care of very young children and whether older ones must shift for themselves after school. A half school day for young children may mean that one parent cannot go to work at all. Odd school schedules such as staggered or double sessions wreak havoc on families. In effect, the timing of the daily school schedule has an important bearing on the division of labor within families and the participation of parents, not to mention older children who work after school, in the labor force. We denigrate these connections between schools and units of kinship by referring to the babysitting function of the schools. At issue, however, is the integration of schooling with family and work roles, and in the balance, community support for the school system. At the district level, then, the connection between time and individual learning is largely beside the point; other issues are far more salient.

Within a given set of yearly time constraints, the division of the school day into blocks of time opens unexplored questions. How long should class periods be? Should they be the same length for all subjects, at all levels of school? To be sure, pedagogical implications might be taken into account when total time allotments are fixed for the whole system. We suspect, though, that time decisions, particularly with respect to the spacing of vacations and determination of daily class periods, are made without knowledge of their implications—if any—for instruction and learning. Nevertheless, time breaks remain punctuation points during the school year, often setting limits on the range of teachers' planning and decisions about how much of what subject matters will be covered during each segment of the year.

With particular reference to secondary schools, district decisions about hiring and general time allotments are closely tied to decisions about the content of the curriculum. Secondary schools do not hire teachers in general but rather specialists in different curricular areas. Whom to hire, then, can only be determined after questions about the priority of curriculum content areas have been settled. These priority questions boil down to claims on time available over the school year. The state, for example, might mandate a course in American history and the state constitution; it may also set standards for the number of mathematics, English, science, and foreign language courses necessary to earn a diploma, standards also likely to be responsive to the expectations of colleges. But once these mandatory curricular minima are established, the more elective aspects of the secondary curriculum become established primarily at the school level.

Within district guidelines, time allotted to curricular activities is usually a matter of negotiation between school principals and teachers. At the school level, then, time becomes manifest in the form of curricular priorities and takes particular shape as the schedule, a formal statement expressed in fine-grained time units specifying how much time will be allotted to subject matters and to extracurricular pursuits. This is a very different kind of time determination from that made at the district level. In the latter case, time is an aspect of both general conditions of employment and of household integration; in the former case, it represents curricular priority.

In elementary schools, the details are somewhat different, but the main line of analysis is the same. Elementary schools are not departmentalized to nearly the same extent, and teachers are not as specialized by subject matter. Accordingly, time allotments for different subjects tend not to be as formalized, and teachers have considerable discretion in their own classes to determine how much time will be spent on the main curricular staples. School-level scheduling is more heavily focused on the distinction between the academic and the extracurricular. Nevertheless, as with secondary schools, time questions are expressed as curricular priorities.

The school schedule determines not only the time priorities of curricular elements but how much time students will be exposed to those different elements. The student's program, then, is a school-level phenomenon. It applies either to all students in a school, or to categories of them, usually distinguished in secondary schools by track. In elementary schools, which usually do not have tracks, all students experience the same curriculum save for those categories of them who receive special instruction for one reason or another. Accordingly, even though we can identify each student's individual program, which is an important thing to do when we think about individual learning and how it is influenced by instruction, that program is in actuality a curricular time schedule established at the school level to deal with school-wide questions of resources allocation.

We must keep in mind that the school schedule is not simply a document that pertains to time. In actuality, it reflects the resolution, perhaps stable, perhaps not, of many different priorities that manifest themselves in competing claims for both time and space. Time and space in any organization are forms of coinage; people deem it important to establish control over time and space because doing so enables them to accomplish the things they want. The schedule, then, is really a political document that acknowledges the resultant influences of administrative directives and the demands of teachers and parents expressing varying views about the welfare of the student body, of individual students, and of different types of students. The schedule embodies past decisions about how much ordinary instruction there will be, in which subjects, at which more or less desirable times, and in which more or less desirable places. It expresses how segregated or desegregated classes will be in response to higher-level administrative directives and delineates the integration of programs for the handicapped in regular and special classes. In sum, it is really a mistake to ask about the sociology of time at the school level, just as it is a mistake to ask about it at other levels, because time never stands by itself. The more appropriate question is how the competing claims on school resources, of which time and space are coins of the realm, get resolved.

Teachers, like school administrators, work within temporal constraints established by higher-level decisions in organizing social groups for instruction within the spatial confines of the classroom and the temporal constraints of the school day, week, and year. Later in the chapter, we consider how teachers treat the time they have available for instruction. Suffice it to say here that the consequences of their management of allocated time result in the time that children have available for productive work in the various curricular areas. At the individual level, students vary in the proportion of time they use for productive work. Obviously, the time made available through the instructional decisions and management of the teacher places a maximum limit on the time students can actually work.

What we have done here is to trace the allocation of time through the levels of school the system organization and show how it takes on different manifestations at district, school, class, and individual levels. We have seen that the treatment of time at one level becomes a time condition that influences productive processes at adjacent lower levels. Prior decisions about time limit but do not determine the allocation or use of time at the lower level. To this extent, then, decisions made about time at any level are not independent, but rather are influenced and constrained by preceding decisions. Accordingly, recommendations to alter time allocations in classrooms must consider how the time a teacher has avaialble has been established through school and district decisions.

We turn now to some time questions pertaining to the lower levels of school organization. At the individual level, the time spent by students pursuing instructional activities is a function of two sets of conditions: time made available by the school system, and such characteristics of individuals as aptitude, interest, and work skills which govern the translation of available time into productive time. We consider it important to keep these two components conceptually distinct. Whereas "making time available" to students is an organizational process, their "using time" is an individual one.

The time made available to students for productive work derives from three major sources. First, as decribed earlier, allocated class time is established by district- and school-level considerations. Then, at the class level, the teacher determines the available time in two ways: by scheduling and by managing instruction.

The nature of time scheduling problems differs at the elementary and secondary levels. In the latter, classroom time is allocated primarily by the school schedule to subjects. Subject-area teachers develop plans for the sequence of activities that occur during class periods such as review, presentation of new information, and seatwork. By contrast, in most elementary schools, time allocated to classroom teachers is relatively undifferentiated. Yet teachers do not have complete freedom in how they divide time among different instructional activities. Typically, suggestions for time allocations to reading, math, and other curricular areas are presented by the administration formally or informally, and teachers are expected to submit time schedules to the school principal. Nevertheless, teacher considerations do influence the share of time given to different curricular areas and the ordering of activities within the daily schedule.

Within scheduled curricular areas, teachers determine the particular activities to be undertaken and the social arrangements for instruction. For example, in reading, teachers establish the relative amount of time devoted to such activities as basal story reading, story discussion, and phonics. Further, the social arrangements of instruction, such as grouping, are part of the planning. Lower-aptitude students, for example, may be instructed in a different group from average- and high-aptitude students, and the teacher may provide more supervision for lower-ability students than for those of higher ability (or vice versa). Further, the order of instruction for groups may be fixed or may vary from day to day.

Time available for student work reflects not only scheduled time allotments but also teachers' management skills. Minimizing interruptions and intrusions, coping with discipline problems with minimal class disruption, planning to have needed materials at hand, and explaining assignments clearly so that students do not thrash about trying to figure what the task is are among the management activities that increase time for productive students use. Accordingly, two teachers who have similar amounts of scheduled time but who manage time differently will also differ in how much time their students actually have for productive work.

In thinking about making time available, one must bear in mind that we are talking about the social organization of instruction as it occurs in time and space. Time is simply a framework within which activities become organized. Quantity of time, then, always presumes further description in terms of social arrangements, activities, and the curricular content in question. We have identified three conditions, under the teacher's control, that influence both the quality of time and the implications for its use.

The first characterizes available time by how much the teacher supervises instruction. Existing evidence suggests that in the absence of a teacher, students use time less productively than when they are supervised. Further, during supervised activities, the fewer students there are per teacher, the better the student use of time. But it is clear that in supervising a class, there are trade-offs. For a teacher to offer thorough sueprvision in tutorial or small-group settings, there is the cost of having the remainder of the class working without direct supervision. This is so because a class is a collective entity.

The next two conditions pertain to the nature of assigned work. Time can be characterized by the appropriateness and the amount of work assigned. If the assigned task is too easy or too difficult, students will be less inclined to make good use of available time than if work is well matched to their abilities. Yet here again, the teacher is faced with a choice. The most appropriate matches between student capabilities and assigned tasks are possible through individualized instruction. Yet such instruction is difficult to supervise in the collective setting of classrooms. Alternatively, treating the class as an instructional unit or dividing it into groups creates aggregates that are diverse in aptitude. Accordingly, the assigned tasks will be too easy or too hard for some students.

The amount of work assigned will influence how much of the available time can be translated into productive time by students. Obviously, with too little work assigned, students will be unable to make productive use of some of the time because they will have nothing to do. Assigning more work may not only increase the proportion of time available to time used productively, but also increase the ratio of work to time, that is, the pace of instruction. Unlike supervision and task appropriateness, there are fewer constraints on the pace of instructional work. For example, it is fairly easy to assign 10 math problems instead of 5, or one story a day instead of one-half. Obviously, it is not possible to increase the work load indefinitely.

But the problems of pacing seem to be of a different order. Clearly, students will not work at a rapid pace over most of the school day. Indeed, there is evidence that not all daily minutes are equal in their potential productivity. For example, it is common practice for teachers in self-contained classes to schedule high-priority curricular activities during the early morning hours. The period preceding lunch and afternoon dismissal are viewed as poor in quality. Further, teachers have notions about how long different instructional activities should last, and some of these have become embodied in textbooks for the training of teachers and in district recommendations for scheduling. Finally, the sequence of scheduled activities in most self-contained classrooms reflects variations in types of activities. For example, a period of physical exertion often follows a period of intense mental work.

None of these phenomena can be accounted for on the basis of a view of time that assumes equal and qualitatively homogeneous units. Rather, notions of psychological time—time units characterized by the work capabilities and rhythms of children—are required. Teachers appear to plan sequences of class activities with such notions of time in mind; yet we have very little systematic knowledge about the limits of children's work capabilities and the manner of characterizing time that such limits imply.

We have tried in this chapter to develop several contentions. First, time never stands alone as an abstract entity. It always has a qualitative referent, such as an activity or a social arrangement. The quantitative measurement of time has little meaning without a corresponding qualitative characterization. Second, the nature of the qualitative characterization varies at different levels of school-system organization. That is to say, time questions manifest themselves in different ways at the district, school, class, group, and individual levels. Third, the settlement of time questions has many consequences at the various levels of organization; the direct consequences of their settlement in most cases has at best a remote connection with individual learning. Fourth, the closer in organizational terms that we come to the level of individuals, the greater the relevance of the amount and use of time to learning. Fifth, it is essential to distinguish the activities of teachers that determine the availability and quality of classroom and group time from the students' use of time and engagement in learning activities.

REFERENCES

Harnischfeger, A., & Wiley, D. E. (1976). The teaching-learning process in elementary schools: A synoptic view. *Curriculum Inquiry*, *6*, 5–43.

Harnischfeger, A., & Wiley, D. E. (1978). Conceptual issues in models of school learning. *Journal of Curriculum Studies*, *10*(3), 215–231.

Summers, A. A., & Wolfe, B. J. (1977). Do schools make a difference? *American Economic Review*, *67*(4), 639–652.

7

Economic Analysis of Time and School Learning

Byron W. Brown and Daniel H. Saks
Michigan State University*

EDITORS' INTRODUCTION

In this chapter, two eminent economists examine Carroll's model and then propose economic, rather than psychological, variables for thinking about instructional time. As economists, they are more interested in optimizing the use of time and in uncovering how and why teachers choose to spend time—their scarce resource. An emphasis on "choice" as a concept points out how teachers are key decision makers in the process of schooling. Economic terminology such as *taste* (the teacher's level of satisfaction with the class's level of learning) and *indifference curve* (the set of all possible outcomes for students that satisfy a teacher's taste) are used to describe teaching and learning.

Data from the Beginning Teacher Evaluation Study were used to give estimates of teachers' tastes and the indifference curves. The taste variable appeared to consist of two levels: teachers who tried to maximize student score variance, who were called by the authors "elitists"; and teachers who tried to minimize student score variation, who were called by the authors "levelers." Remarkably, based on the one data set, levelers appear to be more effective with high-ability students and elitists were more productive with low-ability students. This result was not expected and is difficult to interpret.

The authors conclude by acknowledging that the most important payoff of instructional-time research will be in teacher education, where teachers and administrators may learn to take into account the consequences of their decisions on one or another of the many time variables.

* The authors were both professors of economics at Michigan State University. Professor Saks currently is in the Department of Educational Leadership, Vanderbilt University. Their work on the economics of instructional time was supported, in part, by a grant from the Spencer Foundation.

For educational researchers, Carroll's "Model of School Learning" (1963) has achieved the status of a modern classic that few read but all know about. It is an educational psychologist's view of the way time usage determines classroom learning. As economists, we are also interested in the way that time determines school learning. While Carroll's work and our own have many areas of similarity and agreement, a comparison of the two approaches makes an instructive starting point for a discussion of how the economic analysis of time in school learning differs from the prevailing view of educational researchers.

This chapter begins with a friendly critique of the Carroll model and then goes on to develop with some rigor the essential elements of an economic model of school learning and shows how that model could be estimated from existing or potential data. The integration of theoretical and empirical perspectives in this area of research is crucial if the work is to do more than elucidate the obvious. Neither fancy thinking nor formal observation are required to establish the point that it takes longer to learn more. What we really want to know is how much longer it takes to learn how much more in what kinds of circumstances and, given that information, how the time in classrooms will be allocated.

AN ECONOMIST'S VIEW OF THE CARROLL MODEL

Carroll hypothesizes that the degree of learning for an individual on a particular task is "a function of the ratio of the amount of time the learner actually spends on the learning task to the total amount he needs" (p. 730). He develops a taxonomy of the conditions that affect the relationship between time and learning. These conditioning variables are (1) the learner's aptitude for the subject, (2) the learner's ability to understand instruction, (3) the learner's allocation of engaged time to the learning task, (4) the time available for the learner to allocate, and (5) the quality of instruction. The emphasis of the model is on the learning curve, or what economists call a production function, the mathematical description of the way that inputs to a production process generate output. In this case, the input is time and the output is learning.

Whereas Carroll as an educational psychologist is interested mainly in the determinants of the characteristics of the learning curve, economists tend to take those determinants as given and ask the question: What is the optimum use of the scarce resource called time in producing classroom learning? It is the optimization and choice aspect of the problem that distinguishes the approach of the economist from that of the educational psychologist. The relevant actors are seen to be decision makers struggling with the conflict between values and opportunities, trying to do the best they can given their circumstances.

To develop the distinction between goals and opportunities in this context, it may help to consider the graph in Figure 7.1. The curve $f(T)$ describes a possible relationship between learning and allocated time. All points along that curve are possibilities or opportunities associated with selection of alternate time allocations. The question of which point is best to pick along that curve depends on the goals and alternate opportunities of the decision maker. In the peculiar and unlikely case that the goal of the teacher was to maximize learning in the particular subject and there were no alternative valuable uses of time, then the optimal point would be at c, where learning is maximized for this subject. That is the point that Carroll and his successors have emphasized.

Consider, however, the case where the teacher must work with different students individually and they can be "engaged" only when both the teacher and the student are engaged. Furthermore, let us assume that there is not enough time for all the students to reach point c (perhaps because other things have to be learned as well). The teacher has to make a decision based on the teacher's goals for the individual students. If all students have the same curve and it is a straight line, then the teacher can maximize average learning by allocating the same time to each student. It is also possible to maximize the average but have some students be much closer to c and others much further away. The actual decision depends, then, on whether the teacher values the performance of each student equally. If student outcomes are not equally valued, then time must be allocated so that the *value* of the extra learning associated with an extra minute of time is the same for all students. If that is not the case, overall value or utility can

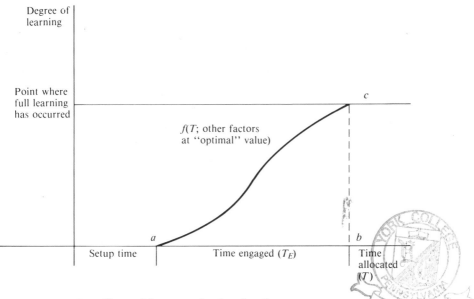

FIGURE 7.1 Carroll's model as a production function.

be increased by taking time away from producing the low-value student outcome and adding it to the high-value student outcome. Presumably there is some point where the added value for an extra minute on the high-outcome student begins to diminish relative to the loss of value from the student who loses time. Economists know this as the law of diminishing marginal utility.

The issue becomes even more complicated when the curve is not a straight line so that the extra or marginal learning is a function of where one is on the curve. But that is not all. The steepness of the curve (the marginal learning) should depend on a whole variety of factors. Carroll defines the steepness in terms of the height of the horizontal line through c. Time needed depends on aptitude, ability to understand instruction, and quality of instruction. To the extent that it costs something to adjust those variables, there is going to be an optimal level that may also (contrary to Carroll's implication) differ from the maximal level. For example, teachers have to allocate their scarce time in preparing alternate lessons. To the extent that student time is the only decision variable, the optimal allocation with varying and nonlinear learning curves is one in which the extra value of learning due of the extra unit of time is equal for all students. That point will probably be uncorrelated with c.

Although Carroll has emphasized several factors that adjust the learning curve, it is worth noting that analysis of variations in this curve is an appropriate framework for analyzing any factor that affects measured learning. Pace, style of instruction, grouping and classroom organization, sequencing of materials, and content (a matter inexplicably underrated in the educational research literature) could also affect time allocation and learning curves. Teacher, student, and community characteristics, previous learning, and numerous other items may all belong in the equation. Further, the curve assumes that engaged time is all the same, but student effort may differ although measured engagement might be the same. Because we cannot get inside the minds of students, it is simpler to think of factors that affect effort in a student who is not simply passive as affecting the learning curve.

Before turning to a more formal development of an economic model, we need to discuss one point of departure from Carroll's model. We have drawn $f(T)$ as if it were a logistic that begins at some point a after the origin. There are two issues here. First, to the extent that the time allocated but not engaged (which for expositional purposes we call setup time) is measurable and/or not in some way fixed, it is important to distinguish between allocated and engaged time. Otherwise, we have to use allocated time for empirical work. Second, the curve may not be a logistic. In fact, Carroll seems to imply a dichotomous function in which $f(T)$ moves along the horizontal axis from some point a, to some point b, and then jumps to point c. One either knows it or not. That may be appropriate for success or failure on small discrete tasks, but it is probably not so useful for more complex learning as measured by more complex tests. Perhaps one way to think about the problem is to measure along the vertical axis the probability of having learned the subject when one is thinking about a discrete task. That way, one would keep in mind the probably logistic nature of the $f(T)$ function even in the dichotomous case. One could also regard the $f(T)$ function as a smoothing of a step function that corresponded to a sequence of necessary learning subtasks.

Although we have emphasized how our view of the learning curve differs from Carroll's and how one could think about these issues in terms of optimization, not maximization, it is also worth noting that Carroll's approach in his original work is very much in the spirit of an economist's approach to the problem, because Carroll wants to "state parameters for different types of learning by learners of varying characteristics under stated instructional conditions" (p. 732).

AN ECONOMIC MODEL OF TIME ALLOCATION AND LEARNING

The economist's methods of optimization under a set of constraints can be used for a better understanding of the role of time in classroom learning. We present a model of classroom operation and management in which the teacher is the decision maker and time is an important scarce resource. The classroom itself is assumed to have many pupils who may have quite different abilities.

An important feature of the choice model is that it makes us think in some detail about the goals of teachers. By goals we mean those things that matter to the teacher, that if changed would alter the level of utility or satisfaction. In a general case these might include not only the learning levels of the students, but also the interest level of the students, the noise level in the class, and the approval of supervisors, peers, and parents.

Although all of these things affect teacher welfare at least some of the time, we have chosen to narrow the set of goals to include only the learning levels of the individual students in the class in some subject, say reading or math. Such a simplification not only makes the problem conceptually easier but reduces it to one that can be explored using available data. The teacher's problem is to maximize satisfaction, which depends on student learning levels subject to a series of constraints on what is possible. These constraints are of two kinds.

The first consists of the learning curves of the students, the underlying relation between the amount learned and the inputs to the learning process. The inputs that produce learning are many and varied, but we have chosen to focus on the amount of time the teacher devotes to instruction of the student. Typical learning curves for two students are shown in the upper left panel of Figure 7.2. The scores (measuring learning levels) of the students

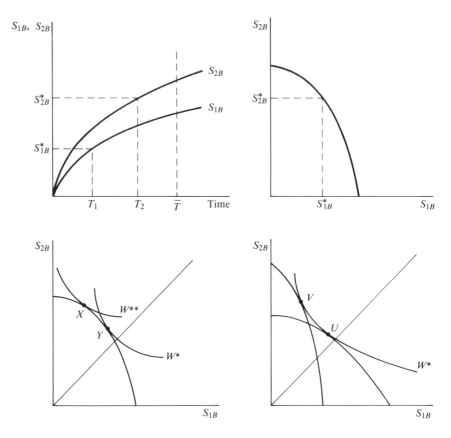

FIGURE 7.2   Illustrations of "levelers" and "elitists."

are placed on the vertical axis, while the time devoted to instruction for each appears on the horizontal axis. The second student, whose learning curve is labeled S_{2B}, is a more efficient learner than student 1, since her learning curve always lies above that of the latter. For any given amount of time devoted to them, the learning of the second student will be greater than that of the first.[1]

The second constraint on the problem is the fact that the time available for instruction is limited. If instruction were possible only by the tutorial method, a restrictive assumption we drop later, then time would be allocated to one student or the other. Depending on the time allocation chosen, a variety of outcomes is possible in terms of scores. If the total time to be allocated is $\overline{T}$ (see the upper left panel of Figure 7.2 again), then all of it can be allocated to student 1, or all to student 2, or some amount assigned to each. Each allocation will result in a different set of scores for the students. An allocation of T_1 to student 1 and T_2 to student 2, for example, would give learning levels of S_{1B}^* and S_{2B}^*, respectively. The entire array of possible outcomes is shown in the upper right panel of Figure 7.2 as the curved line. The axes measure the scores of the two students. All the points along the curved line, called a production possibilities curve by economists, are efficient from a production point of view. Points below and to the left of the curve ("inside" it) are inefficient because more learning could be obtained with the same time resources, $\overline{T}$. Points above and to the right of the curve are impossible to reach because the total time available is limited and fixed.

The problem for the teacher, then, is what point on the production possibilities curve to choose by allocating time to the students. Teacher preferences, as outlined above, provide the answer. If teacher satisfaction depends on the students' scores, we can describe those tastes with a set of indifference curves. An indifference curve, in economists' jargon, represents all the possible learning outcomes for the two students which give the teacher the same level of satisfaction. The indifference curve labeled W^* in the lower left panel of Figure 7.2 is one of an infinite number of such curves describing tastes of a particular teacher. Similarly shaped curves lying below and to the left of W^* (not shown) denote lower levels of satisfaction, whereas curves above and to the right describe outcomes giving greater satisfaction. (The curves are negatively sloped and convex to the origin to show that teachers are willing to substitute learning of one student for that of another, though not at a constant rate.) An optimizing teacher will seek the highest possible indifference curve, in this case W^*, by going to point Y. Another teacher with different preferences, favoring more learning for student 2, would choose point X and maximize utility along W^{**}.

We characterize teachers who choose points such as Y as "levelers," because they prefer outcomes where the students are more equal. The 45° line in the lower panels denotes perfect equality of outcomes across students. Teachers with tastes that result in points such as X we call "elitists," because they favor greater differences across students.

But the choices that teachers make reveal something about their opportunities as well as their preferences. Any particular set of outcomes is the result of the interaction of opportunities and preferences, and because both can vary across classrooms, great care must be exercised in evaluating the outcomes. To illustrate this very important point consider once again the lower left panel in Figure 7.2. Suppose that the chosen points, X and Y, really come from two classrooms in which the students have identical learning curves and time constraints (so the production possibilities curves are the same), but that the teachers' preferences differ. If the technologies are known to be the same, the different outcomes can result only from differing tastes. The teacher choosing X is more "elitist" than the one choosing Y.

But now consider the lower right panel. Again we have two outcomes, V and U, but here they result from two classes in which the student learning curves differ while the teachers have identical tastes. We would be wrong in concluding that the teacher of the class with outcome V has "elitist" tastes relative to the teacher of the class with outcome U. The larger difference between students in the former class results from the fact that the time input is relatively more productive with student 2.

If we cannot tell whether teachers favor more or less variance in outcomes simply by looking at the outcomes themselves, is there any way we can isolate the separate effects of preferences and the technology of instruction? In the next section we offer a simple model that allows us to do this. The model can be estimated using available data.

A MODEL OF CHOICE

By specifying functional forms for a teacher's utility function and the learning curves of the students we can estimate the tastes and production parameters. We choose for a teacher's utility function the single-parameter form[2]:

$$W = \frac{1}{\mu}S_{1B}^{\mu} + \frac{1}{\mu}S_{2B}^{\mu} \qquad (1)$$

where W is teacher satisfaction (unobserved) and S_{iB} is student i's ($i = 1, 2$) test score at the end (time B). The parameter μ specifies the value the teacher places on increasing the score of a student. If $\mu - 1 > 0$ (<0), an increase in the score for a high-scoring student adds more (less) to the teacher's satisfaction than the same gain for a low-scoring student. In the earlier terminology, a value of $\mu - 1 > 0$ means the teacher is an "elitist," and $\mu - 1 < 0$ means the teacher is a "leveler."

The learning curves for the students are[3]

$$S_{iB} = A_i T_i^{\alpha_i} \qquad (i = 1, 2) \qquad (2)$$

The parameters A_i and α_i are assumed to be positive, and α_i measures the percent change in score that a student can achieve from a 1% increase in time. The variable T_i represents the amount of tutoring time student i receives.[4]

We can let the α_i, which measure the student's learning efficiency, vary with the student's initial learning level (S_{iA}). It is an important question whether high- or low-scoring students have greater responses to the time input. Thus we let

$$\alpha_i = aS_{iA}^{b} \qquad (i = 1, 2) \qquad (3)$$

where a and b are parameters. If $b = 0$, then learning efficiency does not vary across students, and if $b > 0$ (<0) the higher- (lower-) scoring students have greater efficiency.

Finally, we have our time constraint

$$T_1 + T_2 = \overline{T} \tag{4}$$

where $\overline{T}$ is the total time available.[5]

The problem is to choose the time allocation to the students so as to maximize the teacher's satisfaction [equation (1)], subject to the constraints contained in equations (2)–(4).

An optimizing teacher will choose times, and therefore scores, such that[6]

$$\log(S_{2B}/S_{1B}) = \mu b \log(S_{1A}/S_{2A}) + \frac{1}{\mu}\log(T_2/T_1) \tag{5}$$

This relation holds whether group time (whole-class instruction) is included in the model or not. One way to look at equation (5) is to see it as a rule for choosing the amounts of time devoted to each student. The ratio of tutoring times between students 1 and 2 is related to the ratio of their desired scores. And this time ratio will depend on the ratio of their starting scores as well. This relationship permits us to identify and estimate two of the crucial parameters of the model, μ and b. Estimated values of μ will allow us to say whether teachers are elitists or levelers as the terms are defined above. And estimated values of b will indicate whether or not the learning curve parameters α_i vary across students, and if so, how. In short, this model will allow us to untangle the effects of teacher preferences and the technology of instruction, and to do it in one equation with quite minimal data requirements.

SOME ESTIMATES OF THE MODEL

The data required for the model are estimates of student learning in some subject in a classroom at two points in time and estimates of the amount of tutorial time each student receives in the intervening period. The Beginning Teacher Evaluation Study (BTES) (see Fisher et al., 1978) provides one set of data that can be used to estimate equation (5). The BTES tested students in 25 second-grade and 21 fifth-grade classes in both reading and mathematics at three different points during an academic year, and collected, as well, very detailed statistics on student and teacher time allocations in the classroom. The interested reader should see Denham and Lieberman (1980) for discussions of many aspects of BTES.

It is not the purpose of this chapter to report statistical results in detail, so we will only summarize the results of our estimation attempts here. We estimated the parameters of equation (5) for each of the 46 classes in both reading and math and for each of the two time periods covered in the BTES. This provided 184 estimates of each of the two parameters.

For the vast majority of the estimates of the taste parameters (μ), the standard error of the estimated coefficient was too large to permit us to state with certainty whether a teacher in a particular subject was a leveler or an elitist. For the grade two classes, 21 estimates of the taste parameter had small enough standard errors to say that 17 revealed leveler behavior and 4 elitist. In the grade five classes, there were only 11 reliable estimates of which 7 showed leveler tastes. The fact that most estimates of the taste parameter were not significant points out the very large amount of random behavior, as opposed to directed behavior, that takes place in classrooms.

Our estimates of the parameter (b/μ) were negative for 180 of the 184 cases. This result occurred despite the fact that the estimates of $1/\mu$ were almost exactly evenly divided with respect to sign, 90 negative, 94 positive. What this tells us is that the relative productivity of time for good versus poor students is almost perfectly predictable from even somewhat unreliable estimates of a teacher's preferences for score changes for those students. In almost every case leveler tastes, wanting more egalitarian outcomes, are associated with productivity states in which the teacher is more effective with the higher-achieving students. And conversely, teachers favoring a wider range of outcomes actually are more productive with the lower-scoring students. This is an unexpected result, and should be viewed with suspicion. It is, for example, an interpretation that relies heavily on many statistically unreliable estimates of tastes. Better information about how the productivity of time may vary with student ability might be obtained from a further analysis of the BTES or other data that would somehow control for variations in teacher preferences. This is clearly an important area for future research.

CONCLUSIONS

We have stressed the way time allocation in classrooms could be the focus of rational classroom decision making by teachers and we have tried to show how observations on time allocations are consistent with such a model. We are not so foolish as to believe that every minute of time spent by all the actors and groups in classrooms is the result of rational calculation. We are talking about average tendencies over relatively long periods. This naturally brings us to an appropriate concluding question about the sort of work described here. What is it supposed to achieve? Why do it?

It is not likely or, in our judgment, even desirable to think of this work as a precursor to the mechanization of time management in classrooms. The thought of a teacher, even with the aid of a computer, prescheduling every minute of the day is not only repugnant, it is also inefficient. Schools are not producing automobiles. In our view, the value of this work is in making teachers, students, and administrators aware that they are making choices, that the choices about time expenditures will affect the learning and achievement of students, and that the distribution of time will affect the distribution of outcomes in classes. Time is scarce and when, for instance, we impose some new curriculum, some new subject, or some new composition or grouping of students, we are affecting the outcome of schooling. Teachers and school policy makers should understand the general consequences of their decisions since they affect learning largely through affecting time allocation and the productivity of time allocations. It is in teacher training and in the evaluation of the consequences of policy changes that this type of work will have a payoff. Whether it can or should have a payoff in structuring lessons is more problematical.

NOTES

1. The same argument could be conducted in terms of the *changes* in the student's learning. In this case, the vertical axis would show the changes instead of the learning levels.
2. The function generalizes to any number of students in the class simply by addition of similar terms.
3. Again, we can have learning curves for any number of students in the class.
4. It is possible to include group as well as tutorial time and the results will be unchanged. The learning curve with group time would be $S_i = A_i T_i^{\alpha i} T_G^{\beta i}$, where T_G is the amount of group time and β_i is the percent change in learning for a 1% increase in group time.
5. If group time is considered, the constraint will be $T_1 + T_2 + T_G = \bar{T}$.
6. This relation will hold for a class of any size. In general, we need only substitute S_{iA}, S_{iB}, and T_i for the corresponding values of student 2. Thus for a class of n students we will have $n - 1$ relations like equation (5).

REFERENCES

Carroll, J. B. (1963). A model of school learning. *Teachers College Record, 64*(8), 723–733.
Denham, C., & Lieberman, A. (Eds.) (1980). *Time to learn.* Washington, D.C.: National Institute of Education.
Fisher, C. W., Filby, N. N., Marliave, R. S., Cahen, L. S., Dishaw, M. M., Moore, J. E., & Berliner, D. C. (1978). *Teaching behaviors, academic learning time, and student achievement. Final report of Phase III-B, Beginning Teacher Evaluation Study.* San Francisco: Far West Laboratory for Educational Research and Development.

Part III

Instructional Time: Contemporary Conceptions

8

Origins of Active
Learning Time

Annegret Harnischfeger and David E. Wiley
Northwestern University

EDITORS' INTRODUCTION

In this chapter, Annegret Harnischfeger and David Wiley build on the conceptual insights of the Carroll model to provide a framework delineating the social underpinnings of the teaching and learning process and linking them to pupil acquisition of learning. The core element in their view of the teaching-learning process is active learning time. The pursuits in which students accumulate active learning time are the mediators between school district, school, classroom, and teacher policy on the one hand, and student learning on the other. Chapter 6 further articulates the social organizational origins of these processes.

The concept of academic learning time—ALT—discussed elsewhere in this volume, is similar to the concept of active learning time put forth by these authors. This is not surprising since the concept of ALT was derived, in part, from earlier work on instructional time by Harnischfeger and Wiley.

As in Chapter 9, by Lorin Anderson, these authors adopt Carroll's distinction between different kinds of time: time needed and active learning time. One set of policies, activities, and behaviors is seen to affect the time a student needs to learn something, while another set is seen to affect active learning time. Many of the variables that increase or decrease the time needed, and that increase or decrease active learning time, are manipulable variables. Thus, by elaborating on the relations among many school and classroom factors, in terms of their influence on student pursuits, the authors show the potential usefulness of the model for influencing teaching and learning in schools.

In our first effort to link time to pupil achievement (Wiley, 1973), we used a crude indicator to measure student learning time, that is, quantity of schooling offered, measured in hours per year. The importance of that earlier work did not lie in its empirical part. The importance was the conceptual base: Quantity of schooling or learning time is a process, not a background variable. Of course, learning takes place in time. There is no learning without spending time to learn. In other terms, pupil achievement is determined by pupil learning pursuits. And these pupil pursuits are formed through teaching.

This insight was the beginning of our development of a model of the teaching-learning process. On our way, we were guided by Carroll's model of school learning (1962, 1963) as well as Bloom's work on time and learning (1974). Our first, primitive, theoretical work was published in 1974 (Wiley & Harnischfeger, 1974). Two years later, we had developed a more rounded and extensive conceptual framework (Harnischfeger & Wiley, 1976). This chapter builds on that earlier work with a focus on the determinants of active learning time.

Active learning time, time-on-task, or engaged learning time, and related terms such as academic learning time, opportunity to learn, and allocated learning time have, during the past eight years, become concepts that have redirected much of the earlier research of school and teaching effectiveness to focus on the teaching-learning process and its determinants: A pupil's time-on-task or active learning time determines his or her achievements. Thus, the question has become: How can we maximize students' active learning time? To help answer this question, we have continued the development of our conceptual work in a direction that allows us to focus on modifiable determinants of pupils' active learning times and, consequently, of their achievements.

In detailing the origins of active learning time, we considered still two other perspectives: resource allocation and loci of control. Our first attempt to use our model to trace the *resource flow* from the school district to the school, to the classroom, and to the individual pupil focused only on teacher-pupil interaction time, which relates to a teacher's grouping and individualization strategy (Harnischfeger & Wiley, 1980). This chapter unfolds all relevant aspects and relates them to active learning time and achievement. Our focus on modifiable determinants led us also to consider where the *control* of certain factors resides. This perspective allows us to turn research into policy-relevant research.

PUPIL PARTICIPATION IN THE LEARNING PROCESS

Experiences and activities of pupils play the central role in learning. The key idea that forms the core of our perspective is the commonplace and obvious notion that if pupils do not participate in the activities intended to educate them, they cannot learn:

All influences on pupil achievement must be mediated through a pupil's pursuits. No one can gain knowledge or take up new ways of thinking, believing, acting, or feeling except through seeing, looking and watching, hearing and listening, feeling and touching. These control what and how one learns. Less proximal influences, whether as general as the district curriculum and policy and the school organization or as idiosyncratic as a given teacher's education, personality, planning, and activities, directly control and condition these pursuits and not the student's ultimate achievement. The focus on this particular causal linkage is the central uniqueness of the model; most earlier studies, by contrast, have regarded teacher behaviors as directly, if mysteriously, influencing achievement. (Harnischfeger & Wiley, 1976)

This emphasis on active participation is not new. Twentieth-century psychology has been marked by a continually increasing emphasis on the activity of the learner. And this tendency has long been emphasized in education. Over 30 years ago Tyler (1949) wrote, "Learning takes place through the active behavior of the student; it is what *he* does that he learns, not what the teacher does" (p. 63).

The centrality of the pupil's participation in the learning process does not imply that it is sufficient to restrict one's attention to that participation only. All of the activities of educators—whether they be administrators, teachers, or supporting staff—are focused on creating and improving that participation. Thus, those activities must be scrutinized in terms of their relations to pupil participation and, via that participation, to achievement.

It is the character of these relationships that constitutes the commonality of view in the work of Carroll, Bloom, and Harnischfeger and Wiley:

The consensus of the three models is simply stated: Pupils' experiences, adequately plumbed by the amount of time spent actively learning, and pupils' characteristics, including their cognitive capabilities, are the sole proximal and distinctive determinants of achievement. Instruction influences active learning directly via the allocation and use of instructional time (opportunity) and indirectly via pupil motivation. (Harnischfeger & Wiley, 1978)

This consensus, which now forms the conceptual base for much practice-relevant research on school learning, has several distinct components:

- Pupils' participation and pupils' prior characteristics are the sole causes of achievement.
- Experience or participation is adequately summarized by a pupil's active learning times.
- Opportunity to learn and motivation are major determinants of participation.
- Opportunity is controlled by the allocation and use of available instructional time.
- Motivation and other factors that transform opportunity to active learning are strongly influenced by instruction.

Thus, the key concept is *active learning time*. Decisions and actions that enhance pupil participation by augmenting active learning time and that devote that time to specific achievement goals and objectives are the central levers for increasing achievement and apportioning it across subject areas. The formalized notion that active learning time is solely responsible for learning and that the amount of it needed to accomplish this learning is dependent on an individual's cognitive capabilities is due to Carroll (e.g., 1963).

CONCEPTIONS OF SCHOOL LEARNING: A SUMMARY

Education has been remarkable—in comparison to other research areas —for its lack of cumulative development. It is not often realized by the overly empirical educational research community that this is not an empirical problem but a symptom of the absence of cumulation of conceptual insights. In this section we attempt to remedy the situation by incorporating earlier insights directly into a base theoretical structure.

Carroll's Model of School Learning

Carroll (1962, 1963) was the first to develop a model of school learning in which time played the major role. In Carroll's model, achievement or the *degree of learning* has two direct determinants: *actual time needed for learning* and *time actually spent in learning*. We may summarize the impact of Carroll's two major variables in his functional equation:

$$\text{degree of learning} = f\frac{\text{time actually spent}}{\text{time actually needed}}$$

An important feature of Carroll's model is that these time variables are both defined in terms of the learner's active learning. That is, it is not the elapsed time actually or potentially taken by a learner to complete the task, but rather that part of such time which is actually spent "on the act of learning."

Carroll's original intent in formulating the model was to clarify the role that aptitude plays in school learning and achievement and to allow specification of the manner in which instruction affects that role. Thus, several key factors (see Figure 8.1) influence the time needed for learning and time spent in learning (participation). In turn, these are influenced by the learner—in the form of his or her abilities—and by the instructional process (actual teaching activities).

In Carroll's terms, the instructional process, as represented by teaching materials and activities, can only affect achievement in three ways.

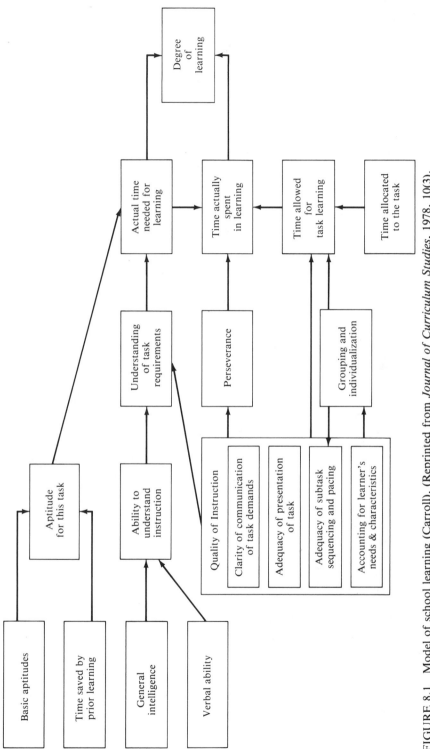

FIGURE 8.1 Model of school learning (Carroll). (Reprinted from *Journal of Curriculum Studies*, 1978, 10(3).

1. It may enhance understandings of the demands of learning tasks, that is, communicate what the learner is to do or to accomplish. This will reduce the *time needed for learning*.
2. It can make available and allocate times for specific learning activities or tasks. This apportions total instructional time among potential tasks and creates the framework within which pupils may actively learn.
3. It may improve task involvement, engagement, or attention, thus increasing perseverance. This will augment that portion of the time allowed for task learning which is actively devoted to such learning—thus creating *active learning time*.

Harnischfeger and Wiley's Model for the Teaching-Learning Process

It is against this fundamental structure that our more recent, theoretical work can be placed. This work accepts the basic structure of the Carroll model, focusing on and elaborating the origins of active learning time, primarily by means of an extensive analysis of the concept of learning opportunity or time allowed for learning. We start with the focal point of the theoretical framework, that is, that participation is controlled by (1) opportunity, and (2) task involvement.

Thus, the amounts and kind of learning time made available to pupils constitute the outer limits of their learning opportunities. Task involvement, summarized as perseverance by Carroll, converts a pupil's learning opportunity into active learning time.

The total degree of potential opportunity is a consequence of the lengths of the school day and year, modified by pupils' attendance. An actual teaching activity transforms a segment of the pupil's school attendance into an actual teaching-learning offering or pupil opportunity to learn. Pupils' actual learning experiences can be characterized by

1. the active learning that occurs during these opportunities,
2. their specific content or subject matter, and
3. the particular learning context within which they occur, that is, pupil grouping, staff supervision, set of instructional materials, and the consumption of other learning resources.

These pupil activities have thus exhausted (a) pupil opportunity (time) to learn and (b) the resources that were required to mount the teaching activity which occupied and transformed this opportunity.

The Organization of Learning Time. Pupils participate in a socially organized teaching-learning process. They are grouped into classes, courses, or subgroups, and these are the focus and the locus of teaching activities.

When we began to examine learning processes in detail, we were struck by a third feature of classroom reality namely, the cyclic or periodic character of classroom activities. A small number of distinct forms, such as seatwork or the reading group, recur with great regularity. They are the tiles that a teacher arranges into her instructional mosaic. Although they may be subtly rearranged or reshaped for a particular day's teaching, the basic types are the touchstones of the teaching-learning process and hold the key to both the content and the timing of learning. (Harnischfeger & Wiley, 1975)

These modules of teaching-learning activity form the context within which pupils may actively learn. And their active learning times within these modules are limited by the total instructional times allocated to them. In the teaching research literature it has become fashionable to term these *settings*.

Basically, a setting is a particular group of pupils—ranging in extent from the whole class to a specific individual—engaged in a common learning activity. Each pupil in the setting, at each particular time point between the beginning and ending of the activity session, is conceived to be either actively engaged in the current learning task or not. Thus, over the duration of the activity—say 30 minutes—the specific pupil may be engaged for only 15 minutes. The pupil's total active learning time—15 minutes—in this setting session is, therefore, also equivalent to a percent time-on-task of 50% (15/30 = 0.5).

Such a setting is thus an example of a learning task—in Carroll's sense of the term. It is also the vehicle that actualizes the pupil's learning experiences—in the sense used by Harnischfeger and Wiley. Thus, it can be characterized by

the amount of active learning it contains,
its content, subject matter, or goal,
the resources it consumes.

As such, it forms a critical link between the theoretical framework for school learning and a key focus for empirical study.

Productivity of Learning Settings. Clearly, the total active learning time for a particular pupil will be influenced by that pupil's characteristics; the resources, skills, and efforts devoted to the session; and the total time allocated. A large part of the search for improvements in the teaching-learning process has now begun to be focused on the "productivity" of settings, in terms of the rate of active learning or the percentage of active learning time associated with them. To accomplish this, two problems must be solved:

As particular sessions are unique and nonrepeatable, they must be characterized or categorized so that setting types can be created. Thus far, such categories have been based on group size and supervision—representing resource levels—subject matter, content, or type of goal; and features of the instructional methods used.

Active learning times or rates must be measured, aggregated, over the individuals attending particular sessions and, ultimately, over sessions within categories to assess the "productivity" of specific types of settings.

Once these issues are resolved, the "validity" of the resulting "productivity" index is still an open question. This validity depends on the inferences one wishes to make using the index. Currently, the inferences are intended to guide decisions about the organization and implementation of instruction to enhance pupil achievement. For this purpose, indices must be comparable across setting types, in the sense that characteristics of the setting sessions, empirically grouped together under distinct types, must be similar so that active learning rates are validly attributed to the "types" and are not by-products of other characteristics. Methodologically this could be accomplished in two distinct ways:

1. Via sampling plans for sessions within types that equalize distributions of other session characteristics across types;
2. Via statistical adjustment of rates of active learning for other setting characteristics so as to "purify" the comparisons of setting types.

Research on these issues, however, has not yet reached this refined stage. Therefore, available empirical estimates of setting "productivities" must be carefully evaluated for the representativeness and character of the aggregated sessions as well as the methods used to assess pupil engagement. Building on this theoretical fundament, we can begin to detail the determinants of active learning time.

ORIGINS OF ACTIVE LEARNING TIME

Teaching-learning policies influence and control the juxtapositioning of three entitites: pupils, content, and resources. And the resulting pursuits determine what a pupil learns via his or her active learning within them. These policies are formulated and implemented at a number of *loci of control*. The local community and state and federal governments make available resources and constrain and control their use. Local school boards have authority within particular pupil attendance areas and control the assignment of pupils to particular learning sites within federal and state guidelines and regulations. These boards also allocate resources to these sites via teaching and administrative assignments, expenditures for building and maintaining facilities, and the purchase and distribution of instructional materials, equipment, and teaching supplies. Finally, these boards promulgàte rules and procedures and set curricular policies and priorities, eventually constraining—although usually not dictating—the actual learning pursuits of particular pupils. Within the constraints of the resources available, local schools subdivide the pupils assigned to them into smaller units, usually classes. (In this context, a class is a collection of pupils with a common organizational identity, e.g., the high school class of 1982 or Mrs. Smith's current third grade class.) The schools also allocate teacher time commitments and other resources to pupils, and further articulate and specify the curriculum. These issues are much more fully discussed and explicated by Barr and Dreeben in Chapter 6.

Thus, at the locus of the class, a collection of pupils is joined by a teaching staff and other learning resources. This conjunction results in pupil pursuits, which on the one side, are formed by teaching activities, and on the other side, result in pupil learnings. Thus, we have defined the *teaching-learning process* to consist of teaching activities and pupil pursuits (Harnischfeger & Wiley, 1975). Consequently, in articulating this process, much of our earlier writing has concentrated on the parallel processes of teacher and pupil time use.

Our analysis of the teaching-learning process has thus focused on grouping and individualization of pupils, their supervision by teaching personnel, and the curricular content of the resulting pursuits. Thus, the central unfolding of the model up to this point has (a) imposed a tripartite structure on classroom activities—grouping, supervision, content; (b) noted that actual teaching segments or sessions can be exhaustively categorized by this structure; (c) exhibited the strict defining relations between the activities of the teaching personnel and the whole collection of pupil pursuits existing simultaneously; and (d) observed that the structure is actualized into process by the allocation of time, that is, by teaching personnel exhausting the time resources they have available, through participation in the structured collection of potential teaching activities. Once these individuals have actualized these teaching activity sessions by devoting specific times to them—that is, by giving them beginnings, endings, and durations—the actual learning pursuits of the class's pupils are strictly determined. And thus the times each pupil devotes to learning are actualized.

Empirical work and analysis based on this conception of the teaching-learning process have thus focused on grouping and individualization of pupils, their supervision by teaching personnel, and the curricular content of the resulting activities of pupils. Given this structure and this conception of process, three critical questions must be addressed:

1. How are teaching activities formed and actualized from resources and policies for pupils?
2. How do teaching activities control or condition the "productivity" of pupils' learning opportunities in terms of the amount of active learning within allocated time?
3. How do pupils' active learning times result in achievement?

We need answers to these questions in order to adequately assess schooling processes and to recognize or design features of those processes that are effective in improving learning and consequently achievement.

Thus, (1) if we know the ways that teaching activities are actually formed, constrained, and influenced by resources, school policies, and specific groups of pupils, we can gain insights into the allocation of our limited educational resources and form policies that are effective in creating the teaching activities we desire; (2) if we can assess the "productivity" of pupils' learning opportunities and relate them to the teaching activities that control them, we can choose those activities that have the most desirable consequences for pupils' learning; and (3) if we know how pupils' active learning and the time it occupies results in actual achievement, we can design our teaching activities to result in desired outcomes. We will attempt a structured response to these questions.

Teaching-Learning Process: Origins, Structure, and Consequences

Figure 8.2 gives a summative overview of the model. Pupils' opportunities to learn and the times they actually devote to learning (active learning times) are determined by actual teaching activities. However, depending on the capabilities that the pupils bring into a teaching-learning situation, their educative opportunities and experiences have different consequences for their achievements. These capabilities determine the amounts of time particular pupils need to learn specific tasks (actual learning time needed). Figure 8.2 explicitly attempts to

1. schematically outline some of the loci of control that produce the setting for the class-based teaching-learning process (community, board, school);
2. focus on several of the critical elements that form and make up that setting (teaching staff, class members);
3. schematically outline the roles of pupil characteristics, within a specific class (*n*), and a school's goals, resources, policies, and rules in the schooling process;
4. segment the teaching-activity component of the process into priorities and plans versus actual teaching activities; and
5. structure the process by which actual pupil learning experiences result in achievement by drawing on Carroll's dual concepts of *active learning time* and *actual time needed* for learning.

Teaching Priorities and Plans: Structure and Determinants

In order to analyze and comprehend the teaching activity component of the teaching-learning process, we distinguish *teaching priorities and plans* from *actual teaching activities*. Teaching priorities and plans incorporate the structure imposed on actual teaching activities by the characteristics of the pupils to be taught, the teaching materials and other nonhuman resources available, the curricula, the rules and policies of the school and district, and the planning skills of the teacher. These elements are thought to condition and constrain the actual plans and priorities that are eventually realized in

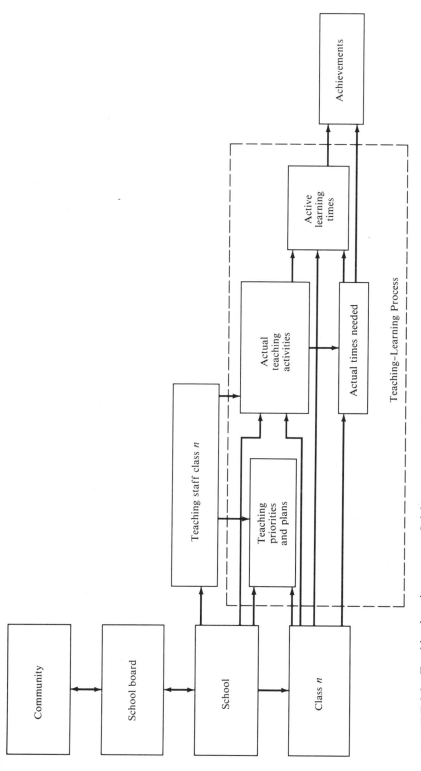

FIGURE 8.2 Teaching-learning process: Origins, structure, and consequences.

actual teaching (see Figure 8.3). We do not mean to imply that these "plans and priorities" are all consciously arrived at by the teacher. Textbook content and organization, teacher training experiences, recess timing, and even pupil abilities sometimes influence the structure of teaching activities without the conscious realization of the teacher.

We conceive of the planning part as having four main elements:

1. Grouping and supervisory strategies
2. Selection and organization of learning tasks (content, complexity, sequencing, pacing)
3. Setting of performance standards
4. Allocation of time to learning tasks (grouping, supervision, content)

Depending on the organization of the particular school different individuals will have responsibility for distinct parts of this process. Elementary schools with self-contained classrooms versus those that are partly departmentalized or that have specialist teachers exemplify such organizational differences.

Grouping and supervision are usually strongly conditioned by perceptions of pupils' cognitive capabilities and motivations, that is, by perceived difference in educative difficulties presented by particular pupils. Grouping, in turn, influences the selection and organization of particular learning tasks, via textbook and material selection, teaching plans, etc. Once tasks are selected, performance standards can be set—either explicitly or implicitly. Finally, with this structural background, timing priorities can be created or are implied.

Actual Teaching Activities: Structure and Determinants

Our conceptualization for actual or implemented teaching activities, as opposed to planned teaching activities, is organized around seven elements (see Figure 8.4). These elements are grouped roughly in four categories:

Management of Learning Tasks
1. Schedule maintenance and time management of task transition
2. Management of task-specific learning activities
3. Maintenance of performance standards for task completion

Actual Times Allowed for Learning Tasks
4. As a consequence of learning task management, planned time allocations are realized as actual times available for learning

Management of Pupil Learning Involvement
5. Surveillance and monitoring of pupil pursuits
6. Effectiveness and regularity of motivating interchanges with pupils

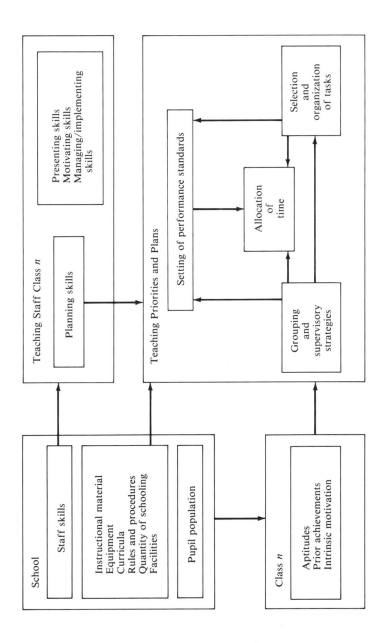

FIGURE 8.3 Teaching priorities and plans: Structure and determinants.

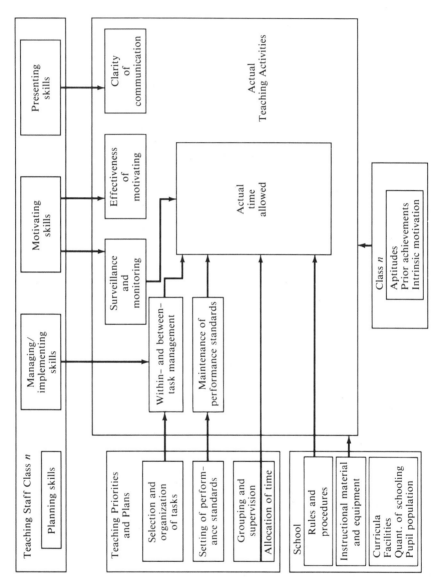

FIGURE 8.4 Actual teaching activities: Structure and determinants.

Communication about the Learning Tasks and Their Demands
7. Appropriateness and clarity of communications with pupils (including those in textbooks and materials)

The first three elements are determined by teaching plans and priorities as well as by the teaching staff's managing/implementing skills and the difficulties they face with pupils. More specifically, the selection and organization of tasks obviously condition their management, and the performance standards set affect the adequacy of their maintenance. These tasks managings and maintainings will, in turn, affect the fourth—actual time allowed for learning. Clearly, rules and procedures—such as recess timing—and the instructional materials and equipment will also affect these actual times.

In addition, there are characteristics of actual teaching activity that pervade the teaching process. These include (5) the staff's surveillance and monitoring of the pupils' activities—whether these are formally supervised or not, (6) their motivating interchanges with the pupils, and (7) the clarity of their specific communications to pupils. The prevalence and effectiveness of these characteristics are not generally influenced by the specific plans and priorities of the teaching staff, but are greatly influenced by the motivating and presenting skills possessed by that staff. Not all of these crucial characteristics are directly related to pupil activities. Their position in the model with respect to pupil pursuits is detailed below.

Pupil Pursuits: Structure and Determinants

If materials are adequate and if teachers possess and use good communication skills, that is, if they make clear the demands of their learning tasks and provide relevant information about them in a form and manner comprehensible to pupils, time needed to learn will be reduced for all pupils. If pupils are adequately motivated and monitored, the portions of their time actively devoted to learning will be generally increased. Thus, although the backgrounds of pupils do foster educative difficulties and some pupils are more greatly constrained than others in their prerequisite skills, knowledge, and motivations, both time needed and time actively spent in learning are impacted by the teaching process. One key origin of active learning is motivation. This concept refers to a personal characteristic that contributes to the willingness of an individual to persist in active learning ("perseverance" in Carroll's terms). Motivation is task specific, and as such, derives from characteristics that the learner brings to the task and from actions and practices that are used, by teaching personnel, to present and select tasks and to design and organize them.

If we are to adequately understand the actual total role played by active learning time in the learning process, we must refine and augment Carroll's basic conception. Carroll implicitly distinguishes between actually learning the task and understanding the requirements of the task. Quality of instruction, in his model, primarily influences the understanding of these requirements and—under ideal circumstances of totally effective teaching —results in task performance being solely a product of task-specific aptitude and active learning time. It is apparent that model development will profit from a more complete exposition of this concept.

As a step toward this end, it is obvious that to understand task requirements, the pupil must devote time. And this time is not explicitly accounted for in Carroll's formulation. Thus, we have divided the learning process in two: the understanding of task requirements and the actual task learning. In doing this, we have followed Carroll's lead in emphasizing *time needed* and *time actively spent* as sole direct determinants of cognitive outcomes. Thus, we have created such determinants for understanding of task requirements in addition to the original components determining degree of task learning or achievement. This formulation is represented in Figure 8.5.

This extension clarifies the role of teaching activities in the model: Surveillance and monitoring and specifically motivating teaching activities directly control time actively devoted to understanding task requirements as well as active task learning time. Clarity of communication directly affects only the time needed to understand the task requirements. Other components of actual teaching activity directly affect only actual time allowed, and via it the two types of active learning time.

It should be noted that a critical conceptual distinction within the theoretical framework for *active learning time* rests with its conceptual separateness—especially as it relates directly to task learning—from *time needed for learning*. The latter is a joint product of task-specific aptitude and (mostly communicative) aspects of teaching that are not directly related to active task learning. It is therefore critically important to distinguish aspects of teaching or the teaching-learning process that *reduce* time needed from those that *increase* active task learning time.

In order to make this distinction relevant to empirical work, special attention must be given to both concepts during the measurement process. If, for example, a teaching practice reduces time needed and does not change active learning, then if time allowed was adjusted by the teacher to time needed, percent time-on-task (active learning time divided by time allowed) would increase. Thus, depending on the teaching circumstance and strategy, differences in percent of time-on-task result either from reductions in time needed or from increases in active learning time.[1]

1. This issue was certainly not attended to in the Beginning Teacher Evaluation Study (Fisher *et al.*, 1978). There, instructional features linked to active learning time included: teacher diagnostic skills, clarity of directions, and feedback on the correctness of pupils responses. Surely these features increase percent time-on-task, because they reduce time needed and the teacher adjusts or tailors her time allocations to pupils' needs. On the other hand, findings that teachers with "academic goals" have greater pupil engagement could occur for either reason, and findings relating to the use of "praise" logically ought to reflect valid impacts on active learning.

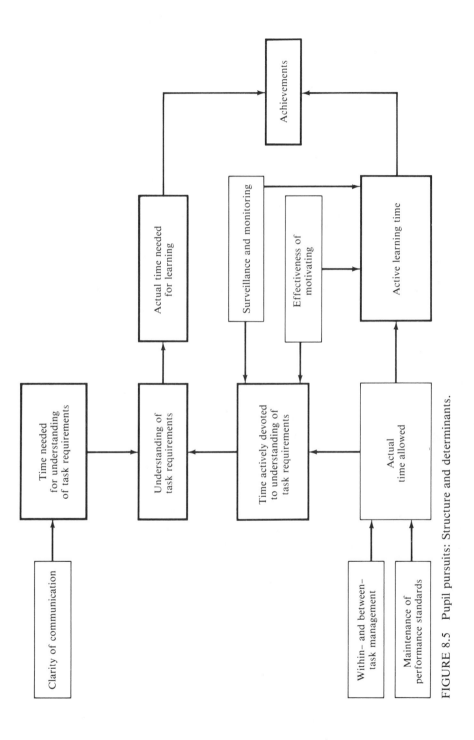

FIGURE 8.5 Pupil pursuits: Structure and determinants.

ACTIVE LEARNING TIME: DEFINITION AND ASSESSMENT

Key words and phrases that are typically used, especially in the empirical literature, to describe pupils' relations to the teaching-learning process include: on- or off-task, engaged or unengaged, attentive or inattentive, active or inactive. These terms are attempts to invoke the psychological precept that in order to learn, an individual needs to actively respond. Fundamentally, this notion is based on the conception that all learning consists of acquiring capacities to perform tasks. When learning is intentional, these capacities are often acquired by practicing and mastering those tasks, simplified versions of them, or parts of them (subtasks), which are usually then called "learning tasks." Such learning tasks, as any other tasks, must be "performed" and, therefore, activity of the learner—in some form—is mandatory. To paraphrase Tyler (1949), to learn to do, one must do.

Educationally, the matter is conceptually more difficult than when viewed in individual isolation. Unlike "subjects" participating in a short-term psychological learning task, pupils are engaged in many such tasks, which are strongly interrelated, have multiple objectives, and are sequenced over months and years. Thus, the relevance of the "activity" of the learner to the "task" becomes more difficult to fathom, at least in the abstract. Implicitly, most empirical researchers have chosen to define "the task" narrowly. That is, they have focused on the specifics of instructive communications and have asked whether the pupil was attending. Practically, this is less of a problem when pupils are learning specific, predefined content in a setting where they are being directly taught, that is, interacting with a teacher or an instructor. However, this solution is more problematic during times, stages, or phases of the learning process when the learners are on their own and the goals of the process are less specific. In both cases, there are conceptual difficulties in settling on "the task" in a context with multiple goals and demands, but they seem to be more often consensually resolvable in the former circumstance than in the latter.

Note that this problem is basically one of definition and not one of measurement. It is a matter of which criteria are to be used, given full information about the pupil's thought processes and perceptions, to decide whether or not these processes and perceptions are relevant to the task at hand. Clearly, one must be able to define and specify the "task at hand" before such criteria can be developed. This will be most difficult when tasks or classroom activities have multiple goals or when the goals are highly abstract. And these difficulties are compounded when teaching strategies permit or foster pupil autonomy and choice in attacking such goals. These circumstances are more common in secondary and post-secondary education than in elementary.

Empirically, only two procedures have been used to collect and assess information on the activity or engagement of learners in school settings:

1. Observations are taken of pupils in classrooms and judgments of their attentiveness to the instructor or of the task relevance of their behaviors are made.
2. Tape recordings or other stimuli are used to aid the later recall by pupils of their thought processes and perceptions during earlier periods of learning. The resulting recollections are then judged as to task relevance. This procedure has been termed "stimulated recall" (Bloom, 1953).

Thus far, research on pupils' engaged or active learning, which has focused on time conceptualizations, has only utilized observational methods. By far the most thoughtful historical review of the empirical educational research literature on learning engagement is Philip Jackson's (1968, chap. 3). He summarized the early literature on observations of student attention (e.g., Morrison, 1926) through the work of Bloom (1953) and his students in the early fifties and beyond to some significant linkages in the 1960s (Hudgins, 1967; Lahaderne, 1968). Taking Bloom's concept of stimulated recall as a touchstone, Jackson drew several conclusions of relevance here about the adequacy of observational measures of pupil attention:

1. Such measures are only gross indices of pupil engagement, lacking sensitivity to positive distinctions in the quality or degree of task involvement.
2. They are more adequate to detecting when pupils are completely off-task, but even with this focus, "faking" is possible.
3. Pupils are judged to be on-task less often when stimulated-recall methods are used than with observational procedures.
4. Observational measures are valid, at least minimally, in that pupils observed to be attending were better achieving when compared to pupils of similar ability who were not so judged.

Later studies by Bloom's students (Anderson, 1973; Arlin, 1973; Özcelik, 1973) and his own articulations (1974, 1976) shifted the form of measurement to a time perspective. First, they refined the observational measure of *attention* to an explicit definition based on the *proportion* of time pupils were judged to be attending. Second, they used this index to apportion the total instructional time to which the pupils were exposed into on-task and off-task categories. It was this shift from percent pupils on-task to percent time-on-task to total minutes or hours of time-on-task that empirically accommodated the earlier notions of pupil attention or engagement to Carroll's time-referenced model of school learning. And it is this definition of active learning time, assessed through classroom observations, that has been used in research during the past 10 years. But empirical studies aggregate their basic observational units in different ways depending on their intents. To inform judgments about the organization and implementation of teaching strategies, data have been aggregated over pupils and setting sessions. This aggregation has involved summating results for different days, and teachers, even across school districts and other organizational boundaries.

For studies linking active learning time to achievement, however, the manner of aggregation is completely different. First, because achievement test scores are typically available for individual pupils, aggregations have most often occurred over the instructional experiences of those individuals and not across more than one such individual. Second, because measured achievement is not usually narrowly enough defined or measured to be thought to result from a single learning session or even from a specific type of setting, active learning times (not rates) are aggregated over setting types to yield summary values for individuals.

Methodologically, to be minimally valid, studies of the relation of active learning time to achievement must meet several criteria:

1. The content and goals of the active learning that is summarized must bear, directly or indirectly, on the test content measured.
2. The time summaries must capture essentially all content-relevant instruction during the time period studied. This criterion could be met by sampling as well as by complete coverage. Also, as in all studies of school learning, problems will arise from learnings taking place out of class and out of school.
3. The time boundaries of the learning must be adequately marked on the achievement side as well as on the learning-time part. Most strictly, this criterion implies premeasurement as well as postmeasurement of achievement.
4. Somehow, either conceptually or analytically, the incompleteness of the content of the test used to measure achievement must be accounted. Such an accounting is currently very difficult because almost all available tests were not constructed for these purposes. Note that this criterion is not merely a matter of test-curriculum match because this concept is usually defined from the perspective of the test, not the curriculum. That is, tests are usually selected for their matches with content taught, but content taught is not used to construct matching tests.

From the conceptual background for active learning time sketched out above, it is clear that this concept is goal or content linked as well as time linked. It is also apparent that—in almost a trivial sense—both total instructional time and curricular content covered are prerequisites for pupil achievement. Thus, the empirical research literature now abounds with studies linking these concepts to tested achievement. Examples of the relations to content coverage or similar concepts include Dahlöff (1971), Husén (1967), and Walker and Schaffarzick (1974). The recent literature on total instructional or "allocated" time and achievement has also expanded (e.g., Wiley, 1976).

The mere fact of such relationships is not, however, a true *empirical* finding. Logically, if either "coverage" or "instructional time" is adequately defined, it *must* have a positive relation to amount learned. That is, if no time is spent, no learning is possible. On the other side, it is preposterous to allege, in a generalized sense, that pupils do not—sometimes—learn what they are taught. And because teaching always takes time and covers content, a positive relation is implied between both of these features of the learning process and achievement. Thus, a failure to find such a relation merely diagnoses methodological or procedural inadequacies, and a positive finding only reassures us that our data quality and analytic strategy are not totally inadequate.

Because active learning time is only a conceptual refinement of these concepts, albeit an extremely important one, the currently expanding set of findings of positive relations to achievement (e.g., Fisher et al., 1978; Stallings and Kaskowitz, 1974; Anderson, 1976; Özcelik, 1973; see also Chapter 14 in this volume) should be taken as great encouragement for this currently productive line of work, but not as a critical empirical foundation for the conceptual model.

IN ESSENCE . . .

There are only four ways to increase achievement. One is via a reduction in the time needed to learn. All of the others depend on increasing active learning time. These latter three routes consist of

increasing the total amount of time that is allocated to learning,
increasing the portion of that allocated time that is actually allowed for learning, and
increasing the amount of this allowed time that pupils actively devote to learning.

The last of these routes is solely influenced by a teacher's effectiveness in monitoring and maintaining pupil pursuits via surveillance and teaching interchanges with pupils, which motivate or coerce them to spend more of their time actively learning. Increasing the proportion of allocated time that is actually allowed or used for learning, on the other hand, is primarily achievable via managerial improvements, both intratask and intertask. Direct increases in allocated time are entirely the outcomes of procedural and curricular policies of districts and schools, together with their implementation through the teaching priorities and practices of those directly responsible for instruction.

Thus, we can now see some of the implications of the organizational structures and the loci of governance and policy control of education for the learning process. It becomes clear, for example, that the current social organization of American secondary education effectively removes from the individual teacher all responsibilities for and control of allocated time. This fact is solely a result of the course-unit/fixed-length class-period structure of the secondary curriculum. On the other hand, the standard self-contained American elementary classroom organization gives effective control of allocated time directly to the individual teacher. Understandings such as these become possible and their implications for learning feasibly analyzable only within the context of a comprehensive conceptual framework or "model."

Another example of the benefits of such a framework is in teacher evaluation. Conceptually, a valid scaffold for such evaluations is also dependent on a comprehensive and conceptually adequate understanding of the teaching-learning process. Only such an understanding would allow a meaningful and legitimate assignment of the varying educational responsibilities for learning. Which of these are the pupils', which are the teachers', and which are the institutions'? Clearly, in secondary schools we cannot hold the individual teacher responsible for the wise allocation of time over courses or subject matters. These are not under his or her control. Under the current social organization of elementary education in this country, however, we can hold the classroom teacher responsible and must do so.

Historically, educational research—at least that part of the enterprise that focused on enhancing teaching effectiveness or increasing achievement—has expended most of its resources on finding ways to reduce the amounts of time pupils need to learn. A major virtue of the new emphasis on learning time—active, allowed, engaged, or allocated—is that it opens to scrutiny and systematic analysis alternate paths for improving achievement. And a major goal of the model development and refinement that we report in this chapter is to allow and facilitate a meaningful evaluation of resource allocations to research on teaching and instruction. Have we overinvested in research that focuses on only a small number of the potential paths for the enhancement of the teaching-learning process? Can we not integrate the results of past research into a framework that will support wise policies for the improvement of education? Dare we hope for a conceptual organization that will lead to valid cost-benefit analysis of the educational process?

During the past 10 years, research on schooling has entered upon a promising road and the studies that have focused on the teaching-learning process have substantially furthered our knowledge and actually influenced educational practice. It now seems mandatory to focus research on how resources can most effectively be used to maximize pupils' active learning via concepts that are directly linked to active learning time. It has been our intent in this chapter to help those who design teaching-learning processes as well as researchers focus on such key concepts.

REFERENCES

Anderson, L. W. (1973). *Time and school learning*. Unpublished doctoral dissertation, University of Chicago.

Anderson, L. W, (1976). An empirical investigation of individual differences on time to learn. *Journal of Educational Psychology, 68*, 226–233.

Arlin, M. N. (1973). Learning rate and learning rate variance under Mastery Learning conditions. Unpublished doctoral dissertation, University of Chicago.

Bloom, B. S. (1953). Thought processes in lectures and discussions. *Journal of General Education, 7*, 160–169.

Bloom, B. S. (1974). Time and learning. *American Psychologist, 29*, 682–688.

Bloom, B. S. (1976). *Human characteristics and school learning*. New York: McGraw-Hill.

Carroll, J. B. (1962). The prediction of success on intensive foreign language training. In R. Glaser (Ed.), *Training research and education*. Pittsburgh: University of Pittsburgh Press.

Carroll, J. B. (1963). A model for school learning. *Teachers College Record, 64*, 723–733.

Dahlöff, U. (1971). *Ability grouping, content validity, and curriculum process analysis*. New York: Teachers College Press.

Fisher, C., Filby, N., Marliave, R., Cahen, L., Dishaw, M., Moore, J., & Berliner, D. (1978). *Teaching behaviors, academic learning time, and student achievement. A final report of Phase III-B of the Beginning Teacher Evaluation Study*. San Francisco: Far West Laboratory for Educational Research and Development.

Harnischfeger, A., & Wiley, D. E. (1975). Teaching-learning processes in elementary school: A synoptic view. *Studies of Educative Processes,* No. 9. Chicago: University of Chicago. Also as: Harnischfeger, A., & Wiley, D. E. (1976). The teaching-learning process in elementary schools: A synoptic view, *Curriculum Inquiry, 6*, 5–43; and in D. A. Erickson (Ed.) (1976). *Readings in educational research*: *Educational organization and administration* (pp. 195–236). American Educational Research Association. San Francisco: McCutchan.

Harnischfeger, A., & Wiley D. E. (1977). Conceptual issues in models of school learning. *Studies of Educative Processes,* No. 10. Chicago: ML-GROUP, CEMREL. Also as: Kernkonzepte des Schullernens, *Zeitschrift für Entwicklungspsychologie und Pädagogische Psychologie*, 1977, *IX*, 207–228.

Harnischfeger, A., & Wiley, D. E. (1978). Conceptual issues in models of school learning. *Journal of Curriculum Studies, 10*(3), 215–231.

Harnischfeger, A., & Wiley, D. E. (1980). Determinants of pupil opportunity. In R. Dreeben & J. A. Thomas (Eds.), *The analysis of educational productivity* (pp. 223–266). Cambridge, Mass.: Ballinger.

Hudgins, B. R. (1967). Attending and thinking in the classroom. *Psychology in the Schools, 4*(3), 211–216.

Husén, T. (Ed.). (1967). *International study of achievement in mathematics: A comparison of twelve countries* (Vols. I and II). New York: Wiley.

Jackson, P. W. (1968). *Life in classrooms*. New York: Holt, Rinehart and Winston.

Lahaderne, H. M. (1968). Attitudinal and intellectual correlates of attention: A study of four sixth grade classrooms. *Journal of Educational Psychology, 59*(5), 320–324.

Morrison, H. C. (1926). *The practice of teaching in the secondary school.* Chicago: University of Chicago Press.

Özcelik, D. A. (1973). Student involvement in the learning process. Unpublished doctoral dissertation, University of Chicago.

Stallings, J. A., & Kaskowitz, D. H. (1974). *Follow-through classroom observation evaluation, 1972-3.* Menlo Park, Calif.: SRI.

Tyler, R. W. (1949). *Basic principles of curriculum and instruction.* Chicago: University of Chicago Press.

Walker, D. R., & Schaffarzick, J. (1974). Comparing curricula. *Review of Educational Research, 44*, 83–111.

Wiley, D. E. (1973). Another hour, another day: Quantity of schooling, a potent path for policy. *Studies of Educative Processes*, No. 3, University of Chicago. Also in W. H. Sewell, R. M. Hauser, & D. L. Featherman (Eds.) (1976). *Schooling and achievement in American society* (pp. 225–265). New York: Seminar.

Wiley, D. E., & Harnischfeger, A. (1974). Explosion of a myth: Quantity of schooling and exposure to instruction, major educational vehicles. *Studies of Educative Processes*, No. 8, University of Chicago. Also in *Educational Researcher, 3*, 7–12.

9

Time and Timing

Lorin W. Anderson
University of South Carolina

EDITORS' INTRODUCTION

Professor Anderson notes that much of the research on time usage at the classroom level concentrates on the numerator (time spent) in Carroll's equation. Many research studies have focused on finding ways to increase the amount of time students spend, but relatively little research effort has examined ways to minimize the time needed for learning.

Anderson unravels the denominator in Carroll's model, which originally was made up of three interacting variables—aptitude, ability to understand instruction, and quality of instruction. He points out how five kinds of planning issues affect the denominator. His goal is to have us think about ways that the time needed by a student is lengthened or shortened by instructional practices. He identifies developmental timing as one issue and asks if we know *when* to teach some of the content and skills we want students to acquire. A second timing issue, entry-behavior timing, calls attention to the need to teach content that is matched to the student's characteristics, such as the student's ability. Entry-behavior timing also raises questions about the appropriateness of instruction for individual students. A third timing issue is called instantaneous timing. Here Anderson is concerned about "insight" and "peak learning experiences." Anderson focuses on the interrelationship of the task, the learner's characteristics, and the instruction that is offered. At certain moments this interrelationship results in a special intensity in the learning experience, leading to emotional responses and a dramatic reduction in the time needed to learn. The fourth timing factor Anderson considers is pace. Pacing, or the amount of content covered per unit of time, requires teachers to think through their speed of instruction. There is evidence that a common error in classroom teaching is to spend more time on some content areas than is needed by many of the students, particularly the better students in a class. Finally, Anderson interprets classroom management skills as timing skills, such as intervening at the right time with the right students. He shows how the Kounin management concepts such as "with-it-ness," momentum, and group alerting may be thought of as timing concepts.

The issues surrounding timing (and the denominator of the Carroll equation) are even more complex than those surrounding time spent (the numerator of

Carroll's equation). Thus, they are more likely to be overlooked in the search for ways to improve schools. Anderson argues that research on timing issues and the denominator of the Carroll equation have high potential for improving instructional design in the long run.

Virtually all major movements in education have identicable sources. With respect to what may be called the "time movement," that source, quite clearly, is John Carroll and, more specifically, his 1963 paper, "A Model of School Learning." In that paper Carroll suggested a direct, causal link between time and learning. Carroll's major proposition can be represented as follows:

$$\text{learning } = f \frac{\text{time spent}}{\text{time needed}}$$

In the 22 years that followed the publication of Carroll's paper, a vast number of research studies have been conducted that have explored the utility and limits of the time concept in schooling. An increasing number of reviews have attempted to integrate the knowledge in this area (see, e.g., Anderson, 1984; Denham & Lieberman, 1980; Frederick & Walberg, 1979; Lomax & Cooley, 1979; Rosenshine, 1979).

An examination of these reviews leads to an interesting observation concerning the relationship of this research to the original Carroll model. The bulk of the research has focused on the numerator of the learning equation, time spent. The two major time variables included in these studies, academically engaged time or time-on-task (which is closely akin to Carroll's notion of perseverance) and allocated time, are variables hypothesized by Carroll to influence the amount of time learners spend learning.

The emphasis on time spent also is illustrated by the nature of the conclusions and recommendations that follow from the time studies. Two of the most frequently cited conclusions from the Beginning Teacher Evaluation Study are that "the amount of time that teachers allocate to instruction in a particular curriculum content area is positively associated with student learning in that content area" (Fisher et al., 1980, p. 15) and "the proportion of allocated time that students are engaged is positively associated with learning" (Fisher et al., 1980, p. 16). Similarly, recommendations such as the following appear in the discussion sections of a large number of time-based studies. Berliner (1979) suggests that "many teachers can improve their effectiveness by ... reorganizing classroom practices to maximize teaching time and learning time" (p. 134). Borg (1980) echoes Berliner's sentiments when he writes, "We must now develop effective programs to give teachers both preservice and inservice training in skills and strategies that will increase the time students devote to relevant academic learning'' (p. 63). Both the conclusions and recommendations suggest that learning will be maximized to the extent that time spent in learning is maximized.

A reexamination of the Carroll model indicates there are two ways in which learning can be maximized. Consistent with the above conclusions and recommendations, one of these ways is to increase the numerator of the model, namely, increase time spent. A second way of maximizing learning, however, is to *minimize* the denominator of the model, that is, time needed to learn. Just as a direct relationship exists between learning and time spent, an inverse relationship exists between learning and time needed. Within the context of the previous discussion, the purpose of this chapter is to examine the extent to which a reemphasis on time needed to learn is necessary and/or potentially useful if a more complete understanding of the role of time in school learning is to be attained.

AN EXAMINATION OF TIME NEEDED TO LEARN

An examination of the denominator of the model, time needed to learn, must begin with the question, time needed to learn what? In response to this question, Carroll proposed the concept of learning task. Carroll defined learning task as "the learner's task of going from ignorance of some specified fact or concept to knowledge or understanding of it, or of processing from incapability of performing some specified act to capability of performing it" (p. 723). Carroll's definition is quite similar to that of Doyle (1979a), who defines a learning task as "(a) a goal and (b) a set of operations designed to achieve that goal" (p. 45). Thus, from Carroll's perspective we are talking about the *time needed to accomplish a specific task* or, from Doyle's perspective, the *time needed* to be involved in operations causally linked to the attainment of a specific goal.

According to Carroll there are three determinants of the amount of time learners need to accomplish a given learning task. These determinants are (1) the learner's aptitude for learning the task, (2) the quality of the instruction provided to the learner in an attempt to facilitate his or her task accomplishment, and (3) the ability of the learner to understand the instruction actually provided. Although Carroll suggests that the "amount of time actually needed by a person to learn a given task satisfactorily is a function not only of aptitude ... but also of the quality of instruction in so far as it is less than optimal" (p. 727), the relationship among the three determinants of time needed to learn is unclear.

Carroll hints at what may be termed an "interactive relationship" among these variables at at least two points in the paper. First, Carroll suggests that aptitudes are task specific. That is, different tasks require different aptitudes. Furthermore, the globalness or specificity of a task determines the globalness or specificity of the required aptitudes. For more global tasks these aptitudes also will be fairly global. If, for example, the task is learning to speak a foreign language, the appropriate aptitude may well be foreign language aptitude. Similarly, for more specific tasks, the aptitudes may resemble what Bloom (1976) calls specific cognitive entry behaviors or cognitive prerequisites. If, for example, the task is dividing a three-digit number by a two-digit number, the specific cognitive prerequisites may include a knowledge of division facts and an understanding of the basic division algorithm.

A second hint of an interactive relationship among the variables occurs when Carroll suggests the learner's ability to understand instruction "is thought of as interacting with the method of instruction in a special and interesting way" (p. 726). Whereas the former interaction may be referred to as the task-aptitude interaction, the latter may be termed the instruction-ability interaction.

These two hypothetical interactions imply that *aptitudes* are related to *what* is to be learned, while *ability to understand instruction* is related to *the way in which* the learning task is transmitted to the learner. If, then, learning with respect to a given task is to be optimal, the task must be appropriate for the learner's aptitudes and the instruction relative to that task must be appropriate to the learner's ability to understand the instruction. In simplest terms, if learning is to be optimal, the tasks must be presented at an optimal time and in an optimal way. Let us refer to the "optimal time" and "optimal way" as *timing*.

More formally, timing can be defined as the extent to which a learning task and the instruction relating to a learner's accomplishment of that task is appropriate for the current state of the learner. Within the context of this definition, then, the amount of time needed to accomplish a given task is a function of timing, the degree to which the task and the instruction relative to the task are optimal for the learner. In short, the better the timing, the shorter the amount of time needed to learn.

Several different conceptions of timing are possible. Five will be addressed in the subsequent sections: (1) developmental timing, (2) entry-behavior timing, (3) instantaneous timing, (4) timing as pacing, and (5) timing as managing.

DEVELOPMENTAL TIMING

Inherent in virtually all developmental theories is the fact that there are better and poorer times for learners to learn things. In his book, *Developmental Tasks and Education*, Havighurst (1972) states this point quite succinctly while coining the phrase "teachable moment."

> There may be critical periods in the development of the child—points or stages during which the organism is maximally receptive to particular stimuli. When

the body is ripe, the society requires, and the self is ready to achieve a certain task, the teachable moment has come. Efforts at teaching, which would have been largely wasted if they had [occurred] earlier, give gratifying results when they come at the teachable moment, when the task should be learned. For example, the best times to teach reading, the care of children, and adjustment to retirement from one's job can be discovered by studying human development, and finding out when conditions are most favorable for learning these tasks. (pp. 6–7)

In an interesting paper entitled "Prime Time for Education: Early Childhood or Adolescence?" Rohwer (1971), in part, supports Havighurst's position. Rohwer argues that many of the learning tasks currently included in school curricula are inappropriate, given the goal of education of assisting "the student to be adaptive with respect to extra-school tasks" (p. 325). If one considers more appropriate learning tasks such as learning to learn skills (which he views as most important), conceptual abilities, and perseverance, then the emphasis in formal education should be placed on adolescence rather than early childhood. In Rohwer's words, if such tasks form the focus of formal education the benefits will be greater for "children in the early adolescence age range than in the early childhood range" (p. 335). Rohwer concludes that "training in the use and acquisition of autonomous learning and thinking skills should be quite beneficial, *provided that such training is properly timed and sequenced* (p. 337).

From a developmental perspective, then, timing is essentially a question of, in Rohwer's terms, *what* to teach *when*. Translated into an educational framework, the problem of timing is one of designing curricula that are in line with the developmental capabilities of the learners—what should be taught when and how should the "whats" be sequenced.

ENTRY-BEHAVIOR TIMING

Entry-behavior timing can be thought of as timing *within* a particular developmental stage or phase. Entry-behavior timing is concerned with the extent to which specific learning tasks are appropriate for the specific knowledge, skills, and attitudes learners bring to the learning task. Perhaps one of the greatest advancements of the BTES studies (Fisher et al., 1980) over previous time research was the inclusion of the academic learning time concept. Although conceptually somewhat cloudy, it is clear that academic learning time includes an estimate of the appropriateness of the demands of the task for the knowledge and skills learners possess relative to those demands. Whether termed appropriate task difficulty or success rate, the concern for the selection of learning tasks that are appropriate for the present status of the learner became a critical aspect of the BTES research.

A similar concern for appropriate task difficulty and high success rate underlies the learning for mastery approach to instruction developed by Bloom (1968) and advanced by Block (1971, 1980). Within the learning for mastery approach, learning tasks are carefully sequenced. Learners are not permitted to progress to any task before having "mastered" the previous task(s). This "forced preparation" of learners for subsequent tasks increases the likelihood of the match between learner entry behaviors and task demands. Within the framework of this chapter, then, the learning for mastery approach to instruction enhances timing.

A slightly different approach to entry-behavior timing is that of Doyle (1979a, 1979b), whose approach emphasizes the instruction-ability interaction rather than the task-aptitude interaction. Doyle (1979b) contends that "dimensions of the setting or the activities that occupy classroom time influence outcomes indirectly by affecting the *efficiency* of task accomplishment" (p. 203) (emphasis mine). In support of this contention Doyle (1979a) offers the following empirical support.

> Davis and McKnight reported that high-ability junior high students actively resisted (that is, refused to cooperate with) an attempt to modify the level of information processing in a mathematics course. The modification consisted primarily of a shift from routine computational operations to an emphasis on the more difficult process of conceptualizing the underlying mathematical principles upon which the operations were based. Along similar lines, Wilson reported that teachers in an alternative high school were hampered in inquiry-teaching strategies because students would not readily cooperate until the ambiguity inherent in such procedures was reduced. (pp. 55–56)

It seems as though students with prior success on particular types of learning tasks or particular types of instructional methods experience difficulty adopting to deviations in tasks or methods. As a consequence, concerns for the timing of these changes are crucial.

If the BTES, learning for mastery, and Doyle perspectives are examined simultaneously, an interesting conclusion emerges. Timing is crucial if the task is to be accomplished. Timing can be enhanced by selecting tasks appropriate to the present state of the learner, by adequately preparing the learner for subsequent tasks, or by adequately orienting the learner to changes in instructional methods. (See Block, 1971, for a discussion of the importance of learner orientation.) If the disparity between the demands of the learning task and learner preparation relative to the task is too great, the learner will likely have great difficulty in accomplishing the task or even may refuse to attempt to learn the task.

Entry-behavior timing has both instructional design and teaching implications. Within a subject matter and age level, instruction should be planned as systematically and sequentially as possible. Concern for the interrelationship among the tasks, learners, and instruction should be considered. Care should be taken to ensure that learners accomplish each task before proceeding to the next. Instructional methods familiar to the learners and with which they likely have experienced some degrees of success in the past should be used. If changes are to be made, learners should be properly oriented to these changes before they are implemented.

INSTANTANEOUS TIMING

Instantaneous timing occurs when the learner, task, and instruction are in an optimal relationship to one another *at a given point in time*. Two examples of instantaneous timing are Wertheimer's (1945) "insight" and Bloom's (1981) "peak learning experience." Insight occurs when a solution to a problem, not readily apparent a moment earlier, becomes apparent to a learner as a result of his or her reorganization of the problem situation. In the context of this chapter, insight occurs when the task is appropriate to the learner, but the instruction demands that the learner restructure or reorganize the information given in order to accomplish the task (i.e., to solve the problem).

Bloom's (1981) modification of Maslow's (1959) concept of peak experiences into peak learning experiences also involves the interrelationship of learner, task, and instruction. Peak learning experiences occur when the experiences of the learner are so powerful that learning occurs instantaneously and recall of the learning after extensive periods of time is vivid. Peak learning experiences are emotionally laden and imbue students with a totally different *sense of time*. Bloom (1981), after a series of interviews, concluded that the "student's description of himself in relation to the situation suggests that he was so *involved* or *attentive* at the time that everything else receded in importance" (p. 194) (emphasis mine). In addition, students indicated to Bloom that the "time had passed 'so quickly' or (they) had not noticed the passage of time" (p. 194).

Both Wertheimer's "insight" and Bloom's "peak learning experiences" indicate that there are learner experiences created by, or at least related to, instruction that can reduce the amount of time needed to learn to virtually zero. In these cases, the amount of time a learner needs to spend in order to learn will be extremely short, largely because of the intensity of the time actually spent.

Instantaneous timing has implications for the way we teach. Rosenshine's (1979) "direct instruction" would likely not yield a great deal of insight or many peak learning experiences. Yet, as the research indicates, it does promote higher levels of academically engaged time. Perhaps nowhere is the conflict between optimizing learning by *increasing time spent* or *decreasing time needed* more clear than in the distinction between direct instruction and insight.

TIMING AS PACING

Pacing deals with the rapidity with which a set or series of learning tasks are presented to the learner. Research conducted by Barr (1974, 1975), Arlin and Westbury (1974), and Good, Grouws, and Beckerman (1978) suggests that pacing is related to learning. The major generalization of the pacing research is that greater amounts of learning occur if the pacing of learning is fairly rapid. Exceptions to this generalization occur if the pace is extremely rapid.

Barr's research further suggests that high-aptitude learners are hindered by pacing that is more appropriate for moderate- or low-aptitude students. Such hindering tends to produce what Arlin and Westbury term a "leveling effect," that is, a relatively homogeneous group of learners with depressed overall learning. The depression of overall learning is viewed somewhat relativistically by comparing the mean learning of a group of homogeneously paced learners with the mean learning of learners who are paced differentially, that is, allowed to proceed at difficulty paces. Barr's research supports Arlin and Westbury's and extends it somewhat to learners who are differentially paced within the same classroom by a single teacher.

In terms of the Carroll model, the pacing research—particularly that conducted by Barr—indicates that pace affects learning beyond that which can be predicted based on aptitude. Thus, appropriate pacing may, in fact, reduce the amount of time needed to learn required by a learner given his or her aptitude. Within the context of this chapter, pacing adds to Rohwer's concern for what should be taught when. A restatement of Rohwer's concern from a pacing perspective may well be, what should be taught when, *for how long*, and *how fast*. In this sense, pacing is timing.

TIMING AS MANAGING

The focus in this section, based primarily on the work of Kounin (1970), is on timing as an important factor influencing effective classroom management. Many of the variables identified by Kounin can be viewed within the context of timing. "With-it-ness" implies that the timing of the teacher's intervention into a potentially disruptive classroom situation is crucial. The teacher must intervene with the right student(s) at the right time. Momentum deals with the way in which the teacher maintains the pace of the lesson. Teachers with greater momentum are likely to have faster-paced lessons and, in view of the findings mentioned in the previous section, students with greater learning. Group alerting is another form of timing. Group alerting involves the timing of questions to students; timing that creates "suspense" in the classroom.

Timing as managing is related to time needed to learn in the following way. "Bad timing" from a classroom management perspective is likely to increase the amount of time needed to learn. The increase in time needed may be caused by a large proportion of time on disciplinary (rather than task-oriented) activities, large gaps of time between appropriate task-oriented activities, and/or time needed to reask or rephrase questions that were poorly timed.

TIMING REVISITED

The five types of timing mentioned in the previous sections all have the potential of reducing the amount of time learners need to learn. And, within the context of the Carroll model, such a reduction in time needed to learn would have a positive effect on the amount learned, even in those situations in which the amount of time spent learning remained constant.

Each type of timing impacts on the educational process at a somewhat different point or level. Four impact points or levels can be identified: (1) curriculum design, (2) instructional planning, (3) teaching, and (4) classroom management. The relationships, the types of timing, and these impact points or levels have been mentioned throughout and are summarized in Table 9.1. Table 9.1 also contains a brief restatement of the definition of each type of timing.

TABLE 9.1. Summary of Five Conceptualizations of Timing

Label	Definition	Implication for education
Developmental timing	Presenting learning tasks that are appropriate to the developmental stage or phase of the learner	Curriculum design
Entry-behavior timing	Presenting learning tasks that are appropriate to the specific knowledge, skills, and attitudes learners bring to the task	Instructional planning
Instantaneous timing	Presenting learning tasks at "just the right time" and *in a way* that elicits insight and/or a peak learning experience	Teaching
Timing as pacing	Presenting a set or series of learning tasks with a rapidity that is appropriate for the learner	Teaching
Timing as managing	Exhibiting teacher behaviors related to the management of learners at appropriate times	Classroom management

THE FUTURE OF TIME AND TIMING

A plea has been made in this chapter for an emphasis on timing and its correlate, time needed, for a full understanding of the impact of time on learning. Despite this plea it is likely that, at least in the immediate future, time spent rather than time needed will be emphasized in school learning research and practice. The likelihood of this continued emphasis on time spent can be explained in several ways.

Although Carroll called his model "a model of school learning," the adjective *school* seems to more appropriately describe the nature of the tasks encompassed by the model rather than the conditions under which learning in schools either occurs or fails to occur. As many sociologists (e.g., Barr & Dreeben, 1977; Cohen, 1972) point out, schools and classrooms are very complex settings. Given 30 learners in a given setting, entry-behavior timing and instantaneous timing are difficult to achieve. Given state-mandated core curricula, developmental timing likewise may be an impossibility for a certain percentage of the learners in a given classroom. Furthermore, while rapid pacing seems to be useful, in general, there is the problem of extremely rapid pacing identified by Barr (1974, 1975). This problem would likely be greater for more complex learning tasks (tasks involving analytical and evaluative skills, for example) than for less complex learning tasks (tasks primarily involving recall and recognition). Finally, managerial timing, while possible, is not within the behavioral repertoire of a good number of teachers.

Barr (1975) summarizes many of these issues when she writes, "Developing skill instruction for a group of about 30 six-year olds poses problems not encountered in planning instruction for the individual. Skill instruction requires sensitivity to learner responses and the adjustment of task demands according to those responses. Monitoring the responses of a large number of pupils is more difficult than if individuals are considered singly (as in tutorials)" (p. 494). If the word *timing* is substituted for the phrase *sensitivity to learner responses and the adjustment of task demands according to those responses*, the reason for a continued emphasis on time spent rather than an increased emphasis on time needed or timing seems clear.

To put it somewhat differently, time and timing may come out of two different perspectives. Whereas timing is a pyschological construct, time is an educational construct. Thus, while timing may help us to describe, time permits us to prescribe. The time movement arrived upon the educational scene just when educators where looking for prescriptions. And what a simple prescription to follow: Get students to spend more time learning.

Where will the continued emphasis on time spent rather than timing lead? Workshops on increasing academically engaged time abound. Research for Better Schools has produced an excellent set of training materials dealing with observing allocated time and student learning time and determining what instructional changes may be necessary to optimize either or both (see Research for Better Schools, 1981). Large numbers of school districts are considering what the time construct means to them and planning or making changes in their educational system based on these considerations (see Anderson, 1980, for a brief listing).

Further attention to time spent will quite certainly yield fruitful results, as the research suggests. Despite this increased fruitfulness, however, the thesis of this chapter remains clear. Better timing will reduce the amount of time students need in order to learn. Such a reduction in time needed will have quite positive effects on all learners, especially those who currently have difficulty spending ever-increasing amounts of time trying to learn.

REFERENCES

Anderson, L. W. (1980). Learning time and educational effectiveness. *NASSP Curriculum Report*, *10*(2).

Anderson, L. W. (1981). Instruction and time-on-task: A review with implications. *Journal of Curriculum Studies*, *13*(4), 289–303.

Anderson, L. W. (Ed.). (1984). *Time and school learning: Theory, research and practice*. London: Croom Helm.

Arlin, M., & Westbury, I. (1976). The leveling effect of teacher pacing on science content mastery. *Journal of Research in Science Teaching*, *13*l, 213–219.

Barr, R. (1974). Instructional pace differences and their effect on reading acquisition. *Reading Research Quarterly*, *9*, 526–554.

Barr, R. (1975). How children are taught to read: Grouping and pacing. *School Review*, *83*, 479–498.

Barr, R., & Dreeben, R. (1977). Classroom instruction. In L. S. Shulman (Ed.), *Review of Research in Education* (Vol. 5). Itasca, Ill.: Peacock.

Berliner, D. C. (1979). Tempus educare. In P. Peterson & H. Walberg (Eds.), *Research on teaching: Concepts, findings, and implications*. Berkeley, Calif.: McCutchan.

Block J. H. (Ed.). (1971). *Mastery learning: Theory and practice*. New York: Holt, Rinehart and Winston.

Block J. H. (1980). Success rate. In C. Denham & A. Lieberman (Eds.), *Time to learn*. Washington, D.C.: National Institute of Education.

Bloom, B. S. (1968). Learning for mastery. *Evaluation Comment*, *1*(2).

Bloom, B. S. (1976). *Human characteristics and school learning*. New York: McGraw-Hill.

Bloom, B. S. (1981). Peak learning experiences. In B. S. Bloom (Ed.), *All our children learning*. New York: McGraw-Hill.

Borg, W. R. (1980). Time and school learning. In C. Denham & A. Lieberman (Eds.), *Time to learn*. Washington, D.C.: National Institute of Education.

Carroll, J. B. (1963). A model of school learning. *Teachers College Record*, *64*, 723–733.

Cohen, E. G. (1972). Sociology and the classroom: Setting the conditions for teacher-student interaction. *Review of Educational Research*, *42*, 441–452.

Davis, R. B., & McKnight, C. (1976). Conceptual, heuristic, and S-algorithmic approaches in mathematics teaching. *Journal of Children's Mathematical Behavior, Supplement No. 1*, Summer, 271–286.

Denham, C., & Lieberman, A. (Eds.). (1980). *Time to learn*. Washington, D.C.: National Institute of Education.

Doyle, W. (1979a). Making managerial decisions in classrooms. In D. L. Duke (Ed.), *Classroom management*. The Seventy-eighth Yearbook of the National Society for the Study of Education. Chicago, Ill.: University of Chicago Press.

Doyle, W. (1979b). Classroom tasks and students' abilities. In P. Peterson & H. Walberg (Eds.), *Research on teaching: Concepts, findings, and implications*. Berkeley, Calif.: McCutchan.

Elkind, D. (1969). Piagetian and psychometric conceptions of intelligence. *Harvard Educational Review, 30*, 319–337.

Fisher, C. W., Berliner, D. C., Filby, N. N., Marliave, R., Cahen, L. S., & Dishaw, M. M. (1980). Teaching behaviors, academic learning time, and student achievement: An overview. In C. Denham & A. Lieberman (Eds.), *Time to learn*. Washington, D.C.: National Institute of Education.

Frederick, W., & Walberg, H. (1979). *Learning as a function of time*. Paper presented at the annual meeting of the American Educational Research Association, San Francisco.

Good, T., Grouws, D., & Beckerman, T. (1978). Curriculum pacing: Some empirical data in mathematics. *Journal of Curriculum Studies, 10*, 75–81.

Havighurst, R. (1972). *Developmental tasks and education*. New York: McKay.

Kounin, J. S. (1970). *Discipline and group-management in classrooms*. New York: Holt, Rinehart and Winston.

Lomax, R., & Cooley, W. (1979). *The student achievement–instructional time relationship*. Paper presented at the annual meeting of the American Educational Research Association, San Francisco.

Maslow, A. H. (1959). Cognition of being in the peak experiences. *Journal of Genetic Psychology, 94*, 43–66.

Research for Better Schools (1981). *Instructional improvement cycle for student engaged time*. Philadelphia, P.: Author.

Rohwer, W. D. (1971). Prime time for education: Early childhood or adolescence? *Harvard Educational Review, 41*, 316–341.

Rosenshine, B. V. (1979). Content, time, and direct instruction. In P. Peterson & H. Walberg (Eds.), *Research on teaching: Concepts, findings, and implications*. Berkeley, Calif.: McCutchan.

Wertheimer, M. (1945). *Productive thinking*. New York: Harper & Row.

Wilson, S. (1976). You can talk to teachers: Student-teacher relationships in an alternative high school. *Teachers College Record, 78*(1), 77–100.

10

Time Scales, Learning Events, and Productive Instruction

Nancy Karweit
The Johns Hopkins University

EDITORS' INTRODUCTION
Dr. Karweit addresses three issues related to instructional time. The first and least complex issue is duration. The policy implications of the effects of duration of learning time on student learning may not be as obvious as some have supposed. For example, Karweit points out that increases in student-engaged time of only 10 minutes a day in a curriculum area, such as mathematics, may require increases in duration of instructional time of about twice as much time. Given the already crowded school day, it is not very realistic to expect that much time to become free. Thus, Dr. Karweit warns against simplistic recommendations to increase achievement merely by increasing allocated time.

Decisions about the measurement of engaged time are often arbitrarily made and can cause considerable difficulty. One such problem is that equal time increments at the beginning, middle, and end of a lesson are not necessarily related to achievement in the same way. This and other problems of measurement severely hamper the interpretation of relations between time variables and achievement.

Dr. Karweit addresses a second issue, which she calls timing, concerned with the rate of learning over the course of instruction. She points out, as do Barr and Dreeben in Chapter 6, that the organization of time into a school year is a major decision with important effects. Interruptions in learning, whether within a lesson or over a summer, must be accounted for in models of school learning that hope to deal with issues of rate of learning. A model of learning rate is presented, in which the timing of instruction and its organization, the effort to learn by students, and efforts to teach by teachers are all included as variables.

The third problem to be addressed is related to the concept of pace. Dr. Karweit first distinguishes between hierarchical and nonhierarchical curricula, and then discusses the effects of pacing on students who know less or more than the teacher thinks they know. When teachers choose a pace for instruction that accurately reflects students knowledge and aptitude to learn, learning is efficient. When pacing decisions are not based on accurate asessment of students' knowledge and aptitude, learning efficiency of students suffers.

Karweit ends her discussion of issues of duration, rate, and pace with a discussion of time scales—the time it takes to teach a certain kind of curriculum to a desired level of achievement, given such factors as boredom, forgetting, holidays, and classroom interruptions. In this discussion, Dr. Karweit underscores the complexity and impact of decisions about the organization of time for teaching and learning.

Three issues have been of central concern throughout our work on instructional time and learning. First, we have sought to understand how specific *durations* of learning time are related to academic achievement growth. Second, we have explored how the *timing* or spacing of instruction in time affects achievement outcomes. Finally, we have addressed the issue of the manner in which the *pacing* of instruction in group-based classrooms affects the academic growth of students. These three topics—duration effects, timing effects, and pacing effects—are all preliminary to an understanding of how the use and organization of time in school affects learning. In this chapter, we describe our work in terms of the issues, duration, timing, and pacing. We then suggest how these issues as well as numerous other educational decisions about time use can be understood by consideration of the time scales of relevant learning events.

DURATION EFFECTS

Most work on instructional time has focused on determining the magnitude of the effect of specific durations of learning time on achievement. In this vein, our work has addressed two issues of consequence. The first issue for understanding duration effects concerns the conceptualization and measurement of instructional time as a variable. The second issue relates to the appropriate specification of the model linking time and learning.

Instructional Time as a Variable

Instructional time has been operationalized in numerous ways. Number of years of schooling completed, number of days in the school year, number of hours in each school day, minutes of time scheduled for instruction, and student attentiveness have all been used as indicators of instructional time. Studies using more proximate measures of student involvement with learning, such as engaged time, have produced more consistent, positive results of time on learning, although not universally. One incorrect interpretation of this tendency is that therefore the *only* important instructional time component to capture is academic engaged time. In a recent paper (Karweit & Slavin, 1981), we point out that although engaged time is the *appropriate* measure for assessing time effects on learning, other measures of instructional time are necessary in order to realistically *interpret* these effects of time on learning. For, without also measuring the amount of real time required to produce specific engagement times, making extrapolations about potential effects for time-on-task are fairy-tale exercises.

To make this point more explicit, we provide two concrete examples of the difficulties in extrapolation without consideration of the realistic constraints placed on the variables. In one study (Karweit & Slavin, 1981) of mathematics achievement and on-task time for third-grade students, we found that an increase of on-task time of one minute would increase posttest scores by a half point. Translating this result into metrics which are more readily understood, we predict that increasing engaged minutes from 37 minutes to 50 minutes daily would increase the posttest score from a raw score of 63 to 70, or a grade equivalent change from 3.4 to 3.8. This magnitude of change in the posttest is appreciable.

But, unless we consider the constraints that work against increasing engaged time by 13 minutes each day, it is difficult to know whether such optimistic predictions are warranted or not. In particular, we know that engaged time runs about 50–75% of the time allocated to instruction; therefore, classroom life would have to be altered significantly to garner such a gain in time-on-task. Greater efficiency in group management of the classroom and fewer classroom interruptions could possibly recover some of the lost minutes. Yet it is likely that the time allocated to instruction would have to be lengthened somewhat to produce appreciable gains in time-on-task. Such a time allocation change seems to be particularly problemmatic given the present congestion of the school schedule.

Another example of extrapolation without regard to realistic constraints was discussed in "A Reanalysis of the Effect of Quantity of Schooling on Achievement" (Karweit, 1976). In that paper, we replicated and extended earlier analyses reported by Wiley and Harnischfeger. They had documented quite sizable achievement effects for quantity of schooling, using a subset of the Equality of Educational Opportunity data. Using their same analytic procedures and variable definitions with other data from the Coleman survey and with new data sources, we did not find effects comparable to those reported by Wiley and Harnischfeger. However, in several analyses, the quantity-of-schooling component was large enough to be of practical as well as statistical significance. For instance, using the grade 12 data from the Equality of Educational

Opportunity data, we found that a one-unit change in the quantity-of-schooling variable, were it possible, would increase the verbal ability score by about half its standard deviation. But, as we argued in that paper, increasing quantity of schooling to the point of obtaining *detectable* achievement differences, much less differences of half a standard deviation, would be highly problematic. Using optimistic goals of increasing attendance from 93% to 95%, days of the school year from 179 to 180, and hours per day from 6.4 to 7, we find that the achievement effect of these increases would be quite minimal. This exercise points out the necessity for imposing realistic bounds for quantity-of-schooling variables in discussions of their potential impact.

The two examples above suggest the importance of considering the various *components* of instructional time and their sources. For assessing the relationship between time and learning, finely tuned proximal measures such as engaged time are appropriate. But, for understanding how and where changes in this engaged time may take place, the various time factors that contribute to engaged time have to be measured as well.

In general, an appreciation of the fact that time-on-task is the culmination of a complex chain of educational decisions would seem to be an important backdrop for discussions of instructional time and learning. For, although engagement with learning is a classroom event, it is influenced by numerous decisions outside the purview of the immediate actors, namely, the students and the teacher. Some of these decisions are well understood; others less so. Some of these allocation decisions can be manipulated by the teacher and students; others cannot. From the standpoint of effecting changes in the *use* of time, then, we will eventually need to understand in greater detail how decisions regarding allocation of time are actually made.

Our work on instructional time has also considered measurement issues faced in designing observational studies of on-task behavior (Karweit & Slavin, 1980). One such issue is how to balance the depth and breadth of coverage in a study. Phrased somewhat differently, there are always choices to be made in designing an observational study between the number of observations and the frequency of those observations. Given a specific budget for observer time, there are numerous ways to arrange the observational visits. For example, for one hour's worth of observer time, one could use any of the following combinations:

No. of teachers	No. of minutes	Total time
2	30	60
3	20	60
6	10	60

The choice among these alternatives is basically between observing enough classrooms to provide stable estimates for the effect of on-task time and scheduling enough time to ensure that the observed behavior is representative. If time-on-task is distributed fairly evenly throughout the day, then sampling intervals of time will provide accurate estimates of on-task rates. If time-on-task is not distributed uniformly, then the choice of sampling frame is of course important. We addressed this issue of the uniformity of on-task time using data from an observational study of 18 classrooms. In that study, we had observed students during their mathematics classes, a period of instruction of about one hour. We divided these periods of instruction into six 10-minute segments, and computed the time-on-task rate within each segment. We found that the estimates of the on-task rate differed quite substantially across the six intervals. Moreover, the differences were not consistent across the 18 classes. Some classes seemed to have lower on-task rates at the beginning and end, while others had their highest attentiveness during these same portions of the instructional period. We suggested that observations should include entire intervals of relevant teaching rather than samples of shorter segments.

Another decision that is routinely made in designing observation studies is the number of days of observational data that are to be collected. A common practice is to observe about 10 days. However, this practice seems not to have been based on systematic study. If sufficient information could be obtained in fewer days, for example 5 days instead of 10, it would be possible to observe roughly double the classrooms for the same observer cost. Also if the increased reliability accruing from observing more than 10 days strengthens the findings for time-on-task, studies should consider this fact in their design. We simulated different design decisions by manipulating a data set in which we had observed classrooms for 18 days (Karweit & Slavin, 1980). We pretended, via this data set, that we had designed three different studies, namely a study with (1) 5 days of observation, (2) 9 days of observation, and (3) 18 days of observation. We used the on-task time estimates from these three conditions as predictors in regressions of posttest on pretest score. We found that the estimates obtained for the on-task measures covering 18 days were appreciably larger than those for the 9- and 5-day simulations. In fact, although on-task behavior was a significant predictor at $p < .05$ level in the 18-day case, it was not significant in the 5-day case. This exercise suggested to us the need for more systematic investigation of the general issue of the number of days of observation required. Further, it suggested that observing for shorter periods of time, such as three or four days, may so drastically curtail the reliability of the on-task measure that the time effects will be inconsistently located.

Models of Time and Learning

One common assumption that seems to be shared throughout the literature on time and learning is that achievement outcomes will be related in a linear fashion to instructional time. This assumption implies that an increment in instructional time, at all places in the observed range, will produce the same learning effects. Put differently, the usual linear model implies that the learning rate is constant throughout the period of time under investigation. For understanding how learning is produced in classrooms, we have argued elsewhere (Karweit, 1978) that the learning rate is not constant and that it is important to consider these fluctuations in the learning rate. We think of classroom learning as the direct result of sustained interaction between students and teachers with subject matter. The lesson presented by the teacher has a beginning, a middle, and an end and comprises a sequential set of materials that must be gone through in a prescribed order. Learning at the beginning is critical for learning at the end; a student who misses the critical information at the start of the lesson is not going to understand the summary. This view of classroom lessons as connected discourse requiring continuing (although not continuous) student interaction suggests that variations in the learning rate are consequential. Further, it suggests that the time of the on and off periods of attention as well as the level of attention are important for the level of knoweldge attained.

This view that *timing* as well as the amount of time is important for learning suggests that the problem with the usual specification of learning as a linear function of time will not be addressed simply by addition of a nonlinear term to the model. For example,

$$ach_{t+1} = ach_t + time + time^2$$

would indeed allow for the possibility of threshold effects, and/or of warm-up effects or diminishing returns. But, as we suggest in the next section, our criticism of the specification of learning as a general linear model is more fundamental than the inclusion or exclusion of a squared term. Its major difficulty is that it cannot incorporate spacing, sequencing, and timing effects. To do so requires a quite different formulation of the *process* of learning than is implied by the use of an input-output formula. In particular, as we discuss in the next section, it requires some means of portraying the dynamics of the interaction among teachers, learners, and subject matter.

TIMING EFFECTS

If our view that learning is an interactive process has merit, then we need to develop some means to portray how interactions among teacher, learner, and subject matter do indeed produce learning. Such a view of learning as a dynamic process in time requires a substantially different representation than the usual input-output formulation. Indeed, it requires a representation that can incorporate effects of both timing and durations of time.

Such a representation requires a different formulation. Although such procedures are commonly used in other disciplines concerned with processes that vary through time, dynamic models have not been used frequently in education.

Our purpose in this chapter is not to present all the details of a dynamic model of teacher-learner-task interaction, because this is done elsewhere (Karweit, 1978; Karweit, 1980). Instead, we wish to present in sufficient detail only the motivation for developing such a model.

Learning is viewed as the result of a student and teacher paying attention to a learning task. The relevant parameters are the characteristics of teacher, learner, learning task, and pace of instruction. The teacher provides information at some rate to the learner, who absorbs some fraction of this imparted information. Learning occurs if there is a change in the quality or quantity of knowledge held by the learner. Learning is broadly construed to mean acquiring new skills, behaviors, or concepts. A necessary condition for learning to occur is that both teacher and student are involved in the learning task at appropriate times. If the teacher is presenting information and the student is daydreaming, the student will not learn. Or, if the student is paying attention, but the teacher is interrupted, the student will not learn. This model, then, views learning as the simultaneous application of teacher and student effort to a learning task.

The view assumes that the same amount of time spent in learning may have different results for different students, and for different learning tasks. Thus it explicity allows for the possibility that the results of time spent depend upon the nature of the material to be learned (primarily its difficulty and its degree of cumulativeness), the pace of instruction, and timing of teacher-student interaction.

A key feature of this dynamic model is that timing effects are of consequence for learning. The same duration of learning time may have quite different effects because some ways of organizing instructional time may be more efficient for learning than are others. The unit of time referenced may be hours, years, days, or seconds—that is, we may be referring to the temporal organization of the school day, the school year, the school week, or some particular learning unit. Regardless of the unit of time, an important decision (although not typically recognized) is how active and nonactive learning periods are to be arranged. The school year is based on a nine-month "on" cycle and three-month "off" cycle; however, other arrangements of "on" and "off" might be economically and educationally more efficient. By recognizing that any duration of learning time is composed of "on" and "off" periods and by allowing the organization of these on and off periods to affect achievement, the model extends the usual question—What is the effect of a certain amount of schooling? to What is the effect of organizing a specific amount of schooling in alternate ways?

This view sees learning as the product of teacher and student effort on a learning task. The effectiveness of the teacher and student in producing learning is influenced not only by how much time is spent, but by when and how it is spent. Thus, such a seemingly trivial episode as an interrruption can have, in this model, an important learning effect depending upon when it occurs. Fluctuations in student and teacher effectiveness are incorporated as well. Thus students can become bored or keenly interested in this model. Similarly, teachers can have good and bad instructional sessions. These myriad fluctuations in the learning rate are thus an important element of time use that can be incorporated into a model of the production of learning time.

In this model, learning is produced by joint teacher and student effort. Because both teacher and student have to be involved, we express an individual student's learning rate as a function of the teaching rate and the students' ability to learn at this rate. To indicate that variation in the learning rate (R), the teaching rate (K), and student ability factor (S) are possible, we use the subscript t. So, we define the learning rate R as the product of teaching rate, K_t, and student ability to learn at that rate, S_t.

$$R_t = K_t S_t$$

We know also that the amount of learning over time (L_t) must equal the initial amount of knowledge (L_0) plus whatever was learned in some time interval, say from 0 to t. What was learned in the interval 0 to t is a function of the learning rate. In a simple example, assume that a student learns facts in a history lesson at a constant rate of one fact per minute. At the end of 20 minutes, or in the interval 0 to 19, the student will have mastered 20 facts. When the learning rate is constant, we can define

$$L_t = L_0 + R \cdot t$$

However, we assume that the learning rate is not constant but varies over time. Over some small interval the learning rate may take on one value, then take on another value during another interval (see Figure 10.1).

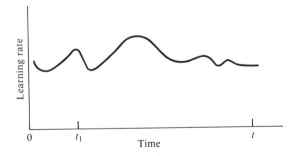

FIGURE 10.1   Variation of learning rate over time.

The amount of learning during the interval 0 to t, then, can be thought of as the sum of numerous products of learning rate during small increments of time, Δt. Or, we could express this variable rate by

$$L_t = L_0 + \sum_0^t R(t)\, \Delta t$$

If intervals Δt are allowed to become increasingly small, we can express total learning as

$$L_t = L_0 + \int_0^t R(t)\, dt \tag{1}$$

This formulation of learning, then, allows for variations in the learning rate. Moreover, since we have defined the learning rate to be a function of the teaching rate and student ability, we can rewrite equation (1) as

$$L_t = L_0 + \int_0^t K(t')S(t')\, dt \tag{2}$$

This rather simple formula therefore accomplishes two important things. One, it expresses learning as a function of simultaneous teacher and student effort. And two, it permits these efforts to vary in time. Thus it allows for the possibility of timing as well as time effects.

PACING EFFECTS

In addition to duration and timing effects another important factor of time use is the effect of pacing of instruction. In heterogeneous classrooms using whole-group instruction, probably one of the more important decisions made by the teacher is how to pace instruction. Conventional wisdom suggests that most teachers aim instruction at or below the class average. Few studies, with the exception of Dahlöff's work, however, have actually examined how teachers make pacing decisions or what pace is usually chosen. Very few studies have examined systematically the effect of variations in pace. Those that have do suggest that a relatively fast pace is more conducive to achievement than a more leisurely one (Good, Grouws, & Beckerman, 1978; Zahn, 1966).

We have argued elsewhere that one important element in determining the effect of pacing is the subject matter being presented (Karweit, 1978, 1980). In particular, because the degree of cumulativeness or hierarchy may condition the effect of pacing, it is useful to consider this factor more thoroughly.

Imagine that a teacher is presenting a lesson in decimals to a fourth-grade class composed of students of a variety of aptitudes and mathematical interests. Some students may already have been introduced to the concept, others may recognize decimals through dealings with money; still others may be totally unaware of the concept or of a concrete example of decimals. We will assume that the teacher is not thoroughly aware of the knowledge level of each student, and gears instruction toward those who have some idea about decimals, for example, those who know about money as an example.

If efficient use of time in classrooms is seen as time use in which learning rates are maximized, the strategy of teaching to the average knowledge level is more efficient for some students than it is for others. Furthermore, the efficiency is related not only to the rate of instruction, but to the degree of cumulativeness of the material.

Considering rate of instruction first, we see that when the student's level of knowledge is about where the teacher assumes it to be, the interaction between student and teacher is maximally efficient. That is, the learning rate is maximized. When the student knows *more* than the teacher expects and when the student knows *less* than the teacher expects, the learning rate of the student is diminished. Thus, efficient instruction, meaning instruction in which the learning rate is maximized, occurs for only those students whose knowledge level closely matches the teaching level. For those above or below the teaching level, the instruction is not optimally efficient.

The consequences of inefficient instruction will differ depending upon the nature of the learning task. In a nonstructured task, not learning one particular fact has little impact on whether one learns the next fact. For example, learning one French vocabulary word may not affect in any significant way learning of another French vocabulary word. But learning multiplication, for example, depends heavily upon mastery of addition. Thus, the cumulativeness of the learning task will be an important factor in understanding how the match between student learning rate and teacher teaching rate affects learning over time. Whether the student knows more or less than is expected is also an important element in how the cumulativeness of material affects learning. In Figure 10.2, we have graphically displayed student efficiency in learning as a function of the match with teacher teaching rate for two types of learning tasks.

For a very cumulative learning task we should find that student efficiency is drastically reduced both when the student knows less than what is expected and when the student knows more. Because what is presented at each step requires mastery of the previous step, the student who fails to grasp the previous step has his or her learning rate reduced greatly. Similarly, the student who already knew the material will have a reduced learning rate. Thus, cumulative learning tasks will be efficient only insofar as there is a good match between teaching and learning paces. In noncumulative learning tasks, the relationship between student efficiency and student-teacher matchedness is different. Efficiency of the student is not so drastically curtailed by knowing less than what is expected because at each

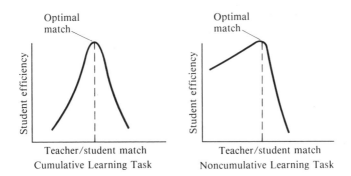

FIGURE 10.2 Student efficiency in learning as a function of the match with teacher teaching rate.

step the likelihood of learning the material is dependent solely on the student's ability to grasp that step and not on his or her knowledge of the accumulation of previously presented material. In less hierarchical lessons, the cumulative deficit of learning has less of an effect on acquisition of a new skill than it does in hierarchical subject matter.

We note that the efficiency in learning of the student who knows more than is expected is not affected by curriculum hierarchy in this model. These students are similarly disadvantaged in any case because their learning depends upon the teacher's presenting *new* material. In any event, they are coasting along waiting for the rest of the class to catch up to the level where "new" material for them is being presented.

The preceding discussion suggests that the effects of time will be different for different students within a classroom and that time effects will differ according to the nature of the curriculum. In particular, we speculate that students who achieve above the average for their class should show smaller effects of duration of instruction than students below the class average. This speculation is based on the view that students above the average do not need to spend the same amount of time to master a concept as do students at or below the class average. In an empirical test of this supposition, we divided a sample of 18 elementary school classes into those students "above" and "below" their class means and carried out regressions of posttest on pretest and engaged minutes (Karweit & Slavin, 1981). The effects for engaged time were larger for students at or below their class mean than they were for students above the class mean. Due to small sample size, the conclusions may properly be regarded as suggestive of differential effects in the predicted manner. Replication with other samples is an important next step. Also, as our discussion of the importance of curriculum suggests, these results may be more likely for hierarchical subject matter such as mathematics. Thus, care should be exercised in generalizing the effects found in studies of time and mathematics achievement to other less structured curricula.

TIME SCALES AND LEARNING EVENTS

We have proposed previously that any period of instructional time can be used in numerous ways, some being more productive for learning than others. We have suggested that the most important issue for future research into instructional-time effects is to understand how alternative arrangements of instructional time produce different learning consequences. That is, instead of examining the effect of specific durations of learning time, we could more profitably examine the effects of organizing learning time in alternative ways.

By the organization of instructional time, we refer primarily to pacing and timing aspects of time use. In order to consider other additional aspects of time use, we find it useful to incorporate the notion of time scales of learning events. We begin by describing what is meant by time scales and learning events and then provide illustrations of how knowledge of the time scale of learning events could be used to select educationally productive uses of instructional time.

We have assumed that a student does not have a uniform learning rate, but instead exhibits considerable variation reflecting interest or boredom in the subject or mode of presentation, appropriateness of the instruction, and other situational factors such as interruptions or distractions. One central feature of the dynamic model of classrooms presented earlier is its incorporation of these fluctuations into the learning rate. There are factors that increase the learning rate and factors that have a negative impact on learning rate. Collectively we have termed these factors learning events. Keen interest in a topic and match with teacher presentation rate should increase the learning rate. On the other hand, if the student knows less than or more than the teacher's expectations or if the student is bored, then the learning rate should be diminished. In order to examine how these factors will affect the learning rate we need to know their *time scale*, or time over which they are in effect. For example, we need to know how long a student can maintain a keen level of interest before fatigue or boredom sets in.

These learning events can all be characterized by how long they take to complete, or by their time scales. Some learning events are never completed, but these can be characterized by the time it takes to be nearly or 99% completed.

We are interested in time scales in learning so that we can decide what combinations of components of learning will maximally produce achievement. We have suggested a model of classroom dynamics that consists of factors involving learning each of which has an inherent, albeit unknown, time scale. We can list some of these factors:

t time to completion of teaching
t_D time to degradation of learning efficiency
t_B time to boredom

t_R time to recover from boredom
t_U average time of interruption
t_M mean time between interruptions
t_S time to recover from interruption

What we now emphasize is that the relative magnitudes of the various time scales should determine how we go about selecting educational strategies, and that decisions about packaging instruction in alternate ways should entail utilizing information about the time scales of these learning events.

Examples of Decision Making Using Time Scales

If, for example, a teacher wishes to attain a specific educational objective, knowledge about the time scale of these learning events for the particular learning task is required. Would it be better (i.e., more productive) to have one long time period of instruction with one break or two shorter periods with two shorter breaks interspersed? These two situations are depicted in Figure 10.3.

The important consideration that the teacher has to keep in mind in deciding whether to use two smaller breaks or one larger break (same total length) is the amount of time it takes to recover from a break in comparison to the amount of time it takes for the students to become bored. If the time to boredom (t_B) (see left side of Figure 10.4) is significantly longer than the recovery time from the break (t_R), then the best strategy would be to have very frequent breaks.

If the time to recover (t_R) is greater than time to boredom (right side of Figure 10.4), then it would be better to have few or no breaks in the instructional period.

We consider knowledge of these time scales of learning events to be crucial for making reasonable selections among alternate ways of allotting instructional time. The example just used pertained to a single teacher's choice in packaging instruction over a single instructional sequence. The importance of knowledge about time scales is not limited to such a micro-facet of the allocation issue, however. As another example, we consider

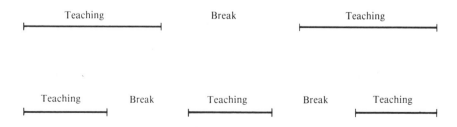

FIGURE 10.3   Alternate ways of organizing instruction and breaks.

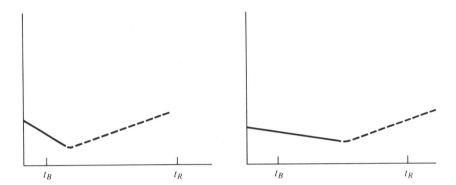

FIGURE 10.4 *Left*, time to boredom; *Right*, time to recovery.

alternative ways of packaging instructional days over the school year. Given that schools could run for only half their normal session, some possibilities are

1. Run school every school day for 90 normal school days (e.g., half the year).
2. Run school every other day for 90 days, spread out over the normal school year.
3. Run school every day for one-half the usual school day length.
4. Run school four consecutive school days, off the fifth, of normal school length for a school term of 144 days.

Suppose (quite unrealistically) that the only thing that had to be considered was the maximization of some learning objective. That is, we assume all options cost the same and are equally feasible. What option produces the most achievement? And, how could this be decided?

To assess the relative merits of options 1–4, we need to know the time scales of such learning events as forgetting, fatigue, boredom, and start-up and wind-down. If the time scale of "warming up" to school is of the order of a day (e.g., blue Mondays) then option 2 would be undesirable because most of the time would be spent in warming up and not in performing. If the characteristic time of "winding down" is four days, then option 4 would be desirable because it would eliminate Fridays. Option 3 might be attractive if time to forgetting were small, that is, if a constant stimulus to learning were required. Option 1 would be attractive only if this time to forgetting were extremely long. Otherwise, the amount of instruction retained would diminish appreciably over the long span of time completely out of school.

Although we have no data on the time scales of any of these learning events to make such judgments, it seems reasonable that option 1 would be the worst choice from the view of maximizing educational output, if for no other reason than learning requires frequent reinforcing. There is some evidence that achievement declines over the summer recess, suggesting that forgetting effects occur. Moreover, these effects are appreciably greater for children in disadvantaged home environments than for children who presumably receive greater learning stimulus during the out-of-school period. Unfortunately, option 1 may be the only viable political choice in face of the demands from teachers' unions, working parents, and forces of tradition.

Another example where knowledge of time scales should prove valuable is in decisions about what types of curricula can best be taught intensively. Most students study courses concurrently; for example, they spend their day studying math, social studies, English, and French. A few schools have abandoned the concurrent plan and instead teach a single subject at one time. A familiar example of such intensive education is the Berlitz approach to studying foreign language. Now the question arises whether intensive education is a more efficient way of packaging instruction, and if so, for what kinds of subject matter. The crucial consideration of time scales here is the time to boredom or fatigue versus the time to forgetting. Presumably the efficacy of this teaching approach is based on the assumption that minimizing the time to forgetting is very important. Whether the student's learning efficiency can be sustained for a given curriculum depends, however, upon the relative sizes of time to boredom and time to forgetting.

The notion of time scales is also useful in deciding the optimum size of classrooms for particular mixes of students. Assuming that the frequency of interruptions is positively related to class size, one would guess that for a fixed teacher/pupil ratio, it would be more productive to have smaller classes for students with long recovery times and larger classes for students with short recovery times.

We have described several examples in which a consideration of the time scale of the various learning events would provide a means for making a rational, educationally defensible choice. This same notion of time scales could be used to determine whether a school day of four hours or six hours might be optimum for instructional purposes, or whether a lunch break of one hour or one-half hour is a better scheduling of time. In all cases—whether the unit of time is days, seconds, hours, or years—we see that knowledge of the time scales can help determine the appropriate sequencing to maximize learning for a given duration of time.

These examples are suggestive of the variety of educational decisions that might be informed by attention to the time scales of episodes comprising a learning sequence. Some of the time scales are individual-curriculum dependent. Others, such as ones relating to interruptions, are more classroom-curriculum dependent and are likely to be time scales over which we have some control. By being able to identify and estimate the time scales of the uncontrollable factors, one can hope to improve the process of learning by appropriately setting the controllable ones.

DISCUSSION

The major point we have attempted to make in this chapter is the need to recast our questions concerning instructional time. Instead of asking, What is the effect of a specific duration of learning time? we should be asking, What is the effect of organizing learning time in specific ways? Thus, our work has been concerned not just with duration effects, but with effects of timing and pacing as well.

One general contribution we hope to have made here is the promotion of awareness of methodological tools that seem appropriate for conceptualizing learning as a process in time. In particular, we see the use of dynamic models as being very compatible with the present problem. The major difficulty in their use seems primarily to be their unfamiliarity. As an illustration of the usefulness of dynamic models for understanding classroom processes, we developed a simple yet powerful model that could incorporate duration, timing, and pacing effects. We stress that the model presented here was developed basically for didactic and illustrative purposes.

Despite its intent as a didactic device, the model as it stands incorporates several important ideas. A basic feature of the model is that all factors that determine the amount of learning can be expressed in terms of time. The difference between what the teacher expects and what the student knows can be expressed as the amount of time it takes to catch up. The degree of structure of the curriculum can be expressed in terms of the amount of time it takes for learning efficiency to be reduced. Transient effects such as interrruptions, boredom, fatigue, and keen interest can be expressed by the amount of time they take up and by the amount of time needed to recover from them. Consequently, the events and factors that affect learning can be expressed in the same metric—the amount of time required. Thus, knowledge of the time scales of various learning events is essential for developing realistic views of learning and for proposing how instructional time can be productively used.

REFERENCES

Good, T. L., & Beckerman, T. M. (1978). Time on task: A naturalistic study in sixth-grade classrooms. *Elementary School Journal*, 78, 193–201.

Good, T. L., Grouws, D. A., & Beckerman, T. M. (1978). Curriculum pacing: Some empirical data in mathematics. *Curriculum Studies*, 10(1), 75–81.

Hess, R. D., & Takanishi, R. (1973). *Teacher strategies and student engagement in low income area schools*. Research and Development Memorandum 105. Stanford: Stanford Center for Research and Development in Teaching. (ERIC Document Reproduction Service No. ED 087 768)

Karweit, N. L. (1976). A reanalysis of the effect of quantity of schooling on achievement. *Sociology of Education*, 49 (July), 235–246.

Karweit, N. L. (1978). *Organization of time in schools: Time scales and learning.* Paper presented at NIE Conference on Productivity, San Diego.

Karweit, N. L. (1980). Time in school. In *Research in sociology of education and socialization: An annual compilation of research.* (Greenwich, Conn.: JAI Press.)

Karweit, N., & Slavin, R. E. (1980). *Measuring time on task: Issues of timing, sampling, and definition.* Paper presented at the annual meeting of AERA, Boston.

Karweit, N., & Slavin, R. E. (1981). Measurement and modeling choices in studies of time and learning. *American Educational Research Journal, 18*(2), 157–171.

Kounin, J. S., & Doyle, P. H. (1977). Degree of continuity of a lesson's signal system and the task involvement of children. *Journal of Educational Psychology, 59*(5), 320–324.

Rosenshine, B. V. (1977). Review of teaching variables and student achievement. In G. Borich (ed.), *The appraisal of teaching: Concepts and process.* Reading, Mass.: Addison-Wesley.

Slavin, R. E. (1978). Separating incentives, feedback, and evaluation: Toward a more effective classroom system. *Educational Psychologist, 13*, 97–100.

Zahn, Karl G. (1966). Use of class time in eighth grade arithmetric. *Arithmetic Teacher, 13*, 113–120.

Part IV

Instructional Time: Classroom Research

11

What Are Students Doing When They Do All That Seatwork?

Linda M. Anderson
Michigan State University

EDITORS' INTRODUCTION

Dr. Anderson's chapter examines students' use of time spent in that frequently occurring classroom organizational structure one usually calls seatwork. The analysis goes well beyond earlier research on "time-on-task" by exploring aspects of students' thinking during seatwork activities and by focusing on "short-term" student outcomes. Dr. Anderson places her work at the juncture of two important lines of research: work on the role of student cognition in mediating instruction and work on the effects of teacher behavior on student learning. The chapter addresses the general question, What do teachers do that affects students' mediating processes and immediate behavioral responses that are necessary for students to learn from instructional episodes?

The chapter is based on extensive data collected on high- and low-achieving students in eight first-grade classrooms during reading instruction in seatwork settings. Seatwork activities of students are often heavily dependent upon commercially developed workbooks and, as a result, are often presented as a linear sequence of sessions each of which focuses on a single skill. In this context, students' perceptions of the goals of seatwork activities and the cognitive processes used to reach those goals are examined. It is reported that students often cannot identify the goal of an activity and, in some cases, may perceive the goal in terms of task completion (for its own sake) rather than in terms of understanding or development of a specific cognitive skill. This important observation has some obvious and some not-so-obvious implications for teaching and learning. Such misidentifications of the goals of seatwork activities are linked to the form of assignment, social setting, and characteristics of instruction that immediately produce the seatwork. The analysis provides insights into some of the mechanisms operating in seatwork settings to restrict or divert student learning from the instructor's expressed goals.

Anderson then expands her analysis by identifying potential relationships between task features (e.g., task difficulty) and the development of student definitions of success. This exploration of seatwork characteristics and their impact on how students make sense of work in seatwork settings provides an excellent example of how classroom research can provide insight into both theoretical and practical aspects of teaching and learning.

Recent studies of time in elementary classrooms are in agreement that a large portion of students' instructional time is spent in a format called *seatwork*. Seatwork usually includes tasks that require reading and writing that are performed without direct supervision by the teacher. Seatwork is often done in a social setting, although usually individual products resulting from independent efforts are desired. The Beginning Teacher Evaluation Study (BTES) demonstrated that students in elementary classrooms may spend up to 70% of their allocated instructional time with seatwork assignments (Fisher, Filby, Marliave, Cahen, Dishaw, Moore, & Berliner, 1978). Although this particular figure may seem surprising, the frequent use of such a format is sensible when one considers the demands on teachers to distribute their time across instructional groups and individuals. Using seatwork allows the teacher to focus on a small group or on individuals, presenting instruction or interacting about academic content, while other students are supposedly occupied. Thus, the evolution of this format can be related to teachers' desires to deal with students as individuals or in small groups where attention to an individual can be more sustained. Ostensibly, what students gain from doing seatwork is practice with skills in a different form from what has occurred in public interactions with the teacher.

However, the use of seatwork is not without problems, from the teacher's point of view, in that teachers must continue to monitor the work of seatwork students while they are teaching a small group or an individual. In fact, one prevalent management concern is how to keep seatwork students "on-task" so that they can benefit from doing seatwork and at the same time not interrupt an instructional group.

In spite of the prevalence of this format in elementary schools and the associated teacher concerns, little research has been done on the nature of seatwork and students' learning that results. When seatwork has been examined, researchers have usually focused on two superficial aspects of seatwork: the student's apparent attention to the work (as opposed to attention to something else in the room) and the student's success with the work (as measured by the proportion of correct answers). In the BTES, such measures suggested that teachers whose students achieved more were able to establish and maintain seatwork sessions in which students were usually on-task and had high levels of success (Fisher et al., 1978).

The purpose of this chapter is to suggest some additional questions that can be asked by teachers and researchers about what is going on when students are doing seatwork. The bulk of this chapter is speculative; the primary purpose is to present hypotheses and raise questions. The speculations are based on work by the author and colleagues in the Student Responses to Classroom Instruction Project[1] at Michigan State University. Therefore, this study is described briefly in order to provide a context for some of the examples that are given of students' seatwork performance. In the study, we paid close attention to how students did seatwork and to what we were calling "short-term" outcomes of instruction: various indicators that students are more or less likely to be learning from their seatwork. Thus, we looked at behavioral indications of attention and involvement, whether and how students sought help when they encountered difficulty while working, the success or correctness on daily seatwork assignments, and the students' reported understanding of how and why they were doing these assignments.

HISTORICAL CONTEXT

Two lines of conceptual and empirical work have led to the ideas discussed here. The first line is recent thinking about students' cognitive processing, students' mediation of instructional effects, and student perceptions of classroom events (Doyle, 1977, 1979a; Weinstein & Middlestadt, 1979; Winne & Marx, 1977). The major questions addressed by work in this tradition are, How do students think about what is going on in classrooms? and How does student thinking mediate classroom events to influence outcomes?

The second line of research, in contrast, has focused more on teachers and emphasized the question of teacher effectiveness: What do teachers do that affects students' learning in classrooms? Much of the research in this tradition has been described as process–product research (see reviews by Brophy, 1979; Good, 1979; Peterson & Walberg, 1979). This work focused primarily on teacher behavior and tried to relate it to student outcomes such as performance on achievement tests.

Within this second tradition of research, the BTES (Fisher et al., 1978) played an important role. Both methodologically and conceptually, one of the most important aspects of this study was its focus on "short-term" outcomes of instruction, in particular student-engaged time and student success on daily tasks. The BTES researchers then related the short-term outcomes to long-range achievement. Like the other process–product researchers, they also looked at teacher behaviors and attempted to link these to both short-term and long-term outcomes. Thus, from a very different perspective from that espoused by researchers in the first tradition, BTES researchers were also beginning to emphasize questions about what students do in classrooms and what is the role of short-term outcomes as mediators of long-term instructional effects.

However, the BTES design (with data collection in many classrooms) required that these short-term student variables be easy to measure quickly and reliably, so there were only behavioral indications of on- or off-task behavior, and rough estimates of success on seatwork. Thus, the overall conceptual design of the study allowed for consideration of students as mediators of instructional effects, but the particular measures used presented a limited view of such mediation. For example, no information was obtained about students' cognitions or about patterns of errors or misconceptions that would have been evident in a more intensive but smaller-scale examination of time use in classrooms.

Much current research in classrooms has followed the lead of the BTES researchers by combining the two traditional questions. That is, instead of separating the two questions, How do students think about what is going on in classrooms? and What do teachers do that affects student achievement? a new research question has emerged: What do teachers do that affects students' mediating processes and immediate behavioral responses that are necessary for students to learn from instructional episodes? However, through the use of different designs and methodologies, a greater variety of data sources are being utilized than was possible in BTES.

Thus, there is a relatively new research question that can be related historically to two distinct lines of inquiry as well as to the large BTES study with its focus on time use. This new way to frame the "big question" suggests alternatives for thinking about time issues that were not available to the first generation of instructional-time researchers (who tended to fall within the process–product tradition). This new focus allows researchers to look at the *quality* of time-on-task by examining student cognition and behavioral responses to determine what students are thinking and doing during their time-on-task. Teacher behavior can then be examined for its influences on the immediate and potentially mediating processes. Although the research-on-teaching community has not lost interest in the question of how teachers can influence long-range achievement growth, there has been growing recognition (e.g., see Brophy, 1979) that we can explain those relationships only by focusing on events closer in time to the instructional episodes. The work on the student-mediating paradigm by Doyle (1977) and others has suggested that the short-term events of greatest interest (and of greater explanatory value) may be students' cognitive states and responses and their associated influence on behavioral responses.

DESCRIPTION OF THE STUDENT RESPONSES TO CLASSROOM INSTRUCTION PROJECT

This work is one attempt to examine students' short-term outcomes and to determine how teacher, instructional, and setting characteristics may affect them. In designing the study, we were especially interested in young children who were learning how to read, and in students who might be considered at risk educationally because of socioeconomic factors. Therefore we selected eight first-grade classrooms in Title I schools in a middle-size urban school district.

Because of the scarcity of research on seatwork, we decided to focus much of our effort on observations of children doing seatwork, although the study was not limited to this. However, the seatwork data are emphasized in this chapter.

Sample

Eight first-grade classrooms in four Title I schools were observed during the 1980–1981 school year. All were self-contained classrooms taught by one teacher, although in some cases aides were present and delivered part of the instruction. Six of these classrooms had ability-based groups for reading instruction, with students doing independent seatwork when they were not with the teacher in the reading group. The other two classes had "individualized" programs, in which there were no formal reading groups. In these classes, the students spent most of their time either reading to themselves or doing reading seatwork, until it was their turn to talk individually with the teacher.

In each of the eight classes we observed four target students. Two of these were considered "potentially high achieving" students by the teacher at the beginning of the year, and two were viewed as "potentially low achieving." In most classes, there was one male and one female student in each of these categories.

Methodology

We observed each target student intensively on at least five occasions across the year, for an entire morning or an entire afternoon when reading instruction was the primary focus. Each observation produced detailed qualitative descriptions of the child's behavior, focusing especially on the primary short-term outcomes of interest: attention (or time-on-task), participation in group activities, initiative to seek help or clarify confusion, and success/correctness of daily assignments.

The observations were supplemented by informational conversations with students about their seatwork. In these conversations, we were especially interested in what students said about how and why they were doing their seatwork.

HYPOTHESES, SPECULATIONS, AND FUTURE DIRECTIONS FOR RESEARCH

Two major sets of issues have become important during this study of seatwork. One set concerns the nature of the work the children do, and the other concerns the nature of success or failure. In exploring both of these issues, questions are raised about how students are understanding what is going on with regard to seatwork and how teachers may influence that understanding.

The Nature of the Work Done during Seatwork

Descriptive Data. In these eight first-grade classes, from 30% to 60% of the students' allocated reading instructional time was spent doing some form of seatwork related to reading. In most of the classes there was a strong reliance on commercial workbooks and/or dittoes taken from commercial packages. In many cases, the workbooks, dittoes, and readers were all part of the same basal series.

Most of the reading seatwork from the commercial materials observed in this study emphasized discrete reading skills, with each page emphasizing a single skill. For example, every sentence on a page might include a word that has a soft *g* sound.

In all eight classes, at least part and sometimes all of the formal reading instruction consisted of moving in order through a reader and/or a reading workbook. That is, the sequence of the book was important, and one book was completed before another one was begun.

Within each class, certain forms of seatwork assignments became very familiar to the students and were used from two to five times a week. For example, there might always be a board exercise of the same form, in which students copied sentences with blanks and chose the correct word from several options. Similarly, certain forms of dittoes or workbook sheets were used many time, such as those requiring the students to read a sentence and then choose one of three pictures that illustrated the meaning of that sentence.

Two questions are raised about the nature of the work that affect how students use time when they are doing this work. The first question concerns how students perceive the goals or purposes of the seatwork, and the second concerns the nature of the cognitive processes that are actually used to do the work. These two points are parallel in some ways to Doyle's (1979a) definition of a classroom task: a goal and a series of steps necessary to achieve that goal.

Student Perceptions and Purposes of Seatwork

Our observations have suggested that the act of finishing work, progressing through a book, and therefore covering the content that is offered through the basal reader and the workbooks, may be as important or more important to the first graders than any specific content-related purposes of the assignment. Work is to be done as a predictable routine part of classroom life. The first-grade students do not behave as if or talk as if they spend much time reflecting on the specific purposes of the work. This has led us to ask these questions: To what extent do the students understand the content-related purposes of seatwork assignments and how do their understandings match the teachers' and curriculum writers' understandings? How do students' understandings of purposes of the work affect how they approach it? In particular, do students see finishing their assignment and progressing through the book for its own sake as more important than understanding and making sense of what they do, and if so, how is learning affected?

Overhearing students' comments first led us to question their understandings of purpose. For example, their comments to one another while doing work often focus on progress through a page, comments about who was working faster than someone else, and comments about how many pages were left to do. Students also made similar comments to themselves. In fact, one student was heard to say to himself, "I didn't understand that, but I got it finished."

The researchers' conversations with the students further convinced us that students' understanding of purpose may often be discrepant from the teachers' understanding. We asked students what they thought they were learning about or why they thought the teacher gave them a particular assignment to do. With a few exceptions, the students' answers do not reflect specific content-related purposes. They may say they are learning about reading or writing, or that they are just doing the work, but very seldom do they report that they are learning about the skill that is being highlighted in a particular assignment. This is in spite of the fact, as was noted before, that most of their seatwork is skill specific, and usually focuses on one skill at a time.

Certainly, one explanation for the students' failure to articulate specific content-related purposes may be developmental. Young children are not likely to engage spontaneously in content analysis or to ask probing questions about the purposes of various tasks. However, the prevalence of the pattern caused us to ask what else might be influential, and what teachers do that may affect the students' understanding of the purpose of the work.

In particular, the following are variables that seem potentially useful for describing teacher communications about the purposes of seatwork: (a) references in teacher explanation of assignments to specific content-related purposes, as compared to frequency of purely procedural statements; (b) frequency of reminders to look busy and finish up work, compared to frequency of comments about what is being accomplished or learned through the work; (c) frequency of statements from the teacher about ways to think about one's own thinking while performing seatwork, such as asking if items make sense, checking one's work for accuracy and meaningfulness, and identifying one's level of mastery or one's need for further practice on certain skills; and (d) frequency of feedback statements in which the correctness of answers is emphasized, as compared to feedback in which the processes by which the answers were acquired are emphasized.

It can be hypothesized that classrooms in which procedural explanations dominate, where little information is given to students about content-related purposes of seatwork, where very little emphasis is given to strategies for reflecting on one's thinking while working, and where feedback on seatwork is rapid and focuses on the form of answers rather than process, may be classrooms where students are less likely to recognize content-related purposes of seatwork.

Perceptions of the reasons for doing a task are likely to influence what one attends to while performing that task and how one monitors one's own progress. Therefore, in studying ways that students use time in seatwork, we believe it is important to ask how students understand the purposes of seatwork and how that affects their performance. It is equally important to ask how teachers' communications to students about their work may influence their understanding of purpose.

Cognitive Processes Used while Completing Seatwork

We have observed several occasions when we suspected that students had completed an assignment without really engaging in the skill or concept application that ostensibly was the purpose of the assignment. That is, the task that the student actually carried out was not what might be expected, given a surface analysis of the assignment out of the classroom context.

What causes this discrepancy between the expected and apparent cognitions? Our observations have suggested at least three factors that may help explain it: the form of the assignment, the social setting, and the instruction and explanation preceding the seatwork.

Form of Assignment. Many of the worksheets completed by the students require a choice of one of two or three alternatives. We have observed students marking the correct answer on the basis of luck, not being able to read the words to us. Students have sometimes told us that the length of the blank told them which answer was correct. A similar strategy reported by some students is to use the last remaining item for the last remaining question. We have observed students who encounter an unknown word while reading and they use the closest picture as a clue for reading that word. Much of the time, their answers make some sense, although they have incorrectly read the word. Such strategies often result in incorrect answers, of course, but not always. If teachers do not question students about processes used to obtain answers, they may assume that errors are due to "carelessness" or slight misunderstanding, when in fact any correct answers reflect luck and/or skills at analyzing the form rather than true competence in the skills that are supposedly being practiced through the assignment.

Social Setting. Seatwork, although it is essentially an individual activity, occurs in a social setting. Although we have not observed students who appear to be deliberately cheating with intentions to deceive the teacher, we have frequently seen students copying another's work, overhearing answers and then writing them down, or directly asking someone what to write. On such occasions, the teacher often checks the student's work quickly and gives the student credit for completing the assignment.

Instruction and Explanation.   Also we have observed occasions in which the teacher changes the nature of the task through the explanation that precedes it or through interaction with the student while it is being done. For example, we have observed students who go to the teacher when they have difficulty and the teacher simplifies the task so much that it is essentially changed. For example, one boy (a "low achiever") was observed with a workbook page that required him to identify pictures and write the beginning sounds. He did not do any items completely on his own, but asked the aide about each one. She would say the word, the boy would continue to stare at her, and then she would say the word very slowly and emphasize the beginning sound. Only when she did this could the child complete the item. However, the task was then very different for him: he had to remember the sound-letter association only, but he did not have to say the word and identify the sound before making that association.

In other cases, we have seen the teacher deliberately simplify the task by giving the answers before the students were required to complete the task. For example, one teacher wrote scrambled sentences on the board. The task, as she explained it, was to figure out the correct order (presumably by calling on one's knowledge of sentence structure and functions played by various words). Before releasing the students to do the work, she asked for volunteers to answer each one. During the seatwork time, students could ask her to repeat the answers. Thus, the task was changed into a memory and copying assignment for most of the children.

These ways of simplifying a task may be appropriate in some situations, but it is clear that they do change the nature of the task. The point for the study of how students use their time on seatwork tasks is that superficial analyses of curriculum materials do not predict what cognitive processes are actually utilized by a student in completing that task. High student engagement in a simplified task may not create the same kind of learning as student engagement on that task without simplification.

Achievement Differences.   Based on observational data, we concluded that strategies such as using pictures, using length of blank, seeking help from other students, seeking simplification from the teacher, and so on, were used by the lower-achieving students more than the higher-achieving students (Anderson, Brubaker, Alleman-Brooks, & Duffy, 1983). This suggests that higher achieving students and lower achieving students are doing seatwork tasks that differ not only in the rate at which various skills and concepts are encountered, but in terms of how closely the strategies used are related to the content to be learned. Lower-achieving students were more likely to use strategies that allowed them to "get by" without meaningful learning. We think that it is important to determine how teachers may influence development of such strategies by their instructional presentations and feedback as well as by their selection of seatwork assignments. We suspect that development of "getting by" strategies is most likely to occur when students are working on material that is too difficult for them, especially in a classroom where much emphasis is placed on getting work finished (Anderson et al., 1983).

The Nature of Success on Seatwork

Of course, the amount of "time-on-task" is not the only element of the concept of academic learning time. The level of success is also important, as was demonstrated by the BTES researchers. In the past, level of success was primarily measured by the percent of correct answers obtained by the students. Our recent work has suggested some additional aspects of success that should be considered when one is examining how students use their time on seatwork.

Certainly, it is important to recognize that correct answers may not reflect understanding of the content, as suggested by some of the examples in the preceding section. Other examples abound in such work as Erlwanger (1973), who demonstrated how students often apply arithmetic algorithms without understanding the mathematical concepts underlying them, and Holt (1964), who provided vivid anecdotes about students' misunderstandings while doing schoolwork.

Another aspect of success has become important to us: What constitutes success from the student's point of view? How do students' perspectives on success affect their cognitive processing and, thus, their use of time?

One's definition of success is related to one's perception of the purpose or the goal of the particular task. We have begun to ask when and how the idea that understanding and comprehension are desirable mental states becomes part of students' definition of successful performance. If, indeed, students are defining task purposes in terms of completing work and finishing papers, there may not be much room for the development of understanding of whether or not their work makes sense to them.

Developmental studies of metacognition (Brown, 1978) suggest that six- and seven-year-old children do not spontaneously identify why something does not make sense or monitor their own thinking in order to clarify an issue. However, it seems plausible to us that early classroom experiences may affect the later development of metacognitive strategies that can be applied to school tasks, and that may, over time, become automatic.

For example, subjective standards of success may determine how a student approaches a task and how he or she thinks while working through it. If, as we observed, the lower achievers are often placed in too difficult materials that are not completely comprehended by them, they may have fewer opportunities to learn to monitor whether tasks make sense to them. If the sense of comprehension or of "sense-making" is not regular or predictable, students may begin to define success in other terms, such as completing assignments, preventing teacher criticism by appearing to work hard, and thus appearing to be good students even when tasks are not meaningful.

Through the matching of seatwork difficulty to the ability level of the students, teachers may influence the extent to which students will expect school tasks to make sense and whether students begin to define success in terms of understanding and making sense of their work.

CONCLUSIONS

Questions have been raised about students' perceptions of goals and purposes of seatwork, their understandings of how to accomplish seatwork tasks, their subjective definitions of success on those tasks, and the ways in which these variables affect time use during seatwork.

When these questions are considered as directions for future research, some thorny methodological issues arise, in particular about how to describe students' understanding. For a variety of reasons, the usual problems with self-report data are exacerbated when one is working with children. However, methodological issues are not addressed here, although several persons have begun exploratory work along these lines (Good, 1981; Rohrkemper, 1981; Weinstein, 1981).

Instead, this chapter concludes with some implications for the ways we view teachers and the roles of researchers and teacher educators in helping teachers make sense of their tasks. It is personally important to me to end on this note, because I realize that a lot of the data described in the chapter suggest that teachers may contribute in many ways to a lack of meaning in seatwork assignments. However, I have not addressed at all the questions of *why* teachers run their classrooms the way they do, although teachers' actions are often very rational when one considers the demands that are made on those teachers. Reliance on commercial material, extensive use of seatwork, and the assignment of one task to many different students may be explained in terms of teachers' adaptive responses to the demands of their environment as they perceive them. They need to simplify the classroom situation in order to deal with it, and they need to obtain the cooperation of their students (Doyle, 1979b). Unless they can accomplish these tasks, they will not be able to do anything else. Therefore, I do not mean to portray teachers as thoughtlessly and deliberately depriving students of "meaningful" seatwork experiences. I think the solution to any problems that have been described here is to help teachers develop alternative ways to view classrooms and student on-task behavior.

Hypotheses were raised in this chapter about the relationships between teacher behaviors and student understandings about seatwork. If these hypotheses are supported, our teacher-education and research-dissemination efforts should be targeted to helping teachers think more about how students are using their time by considering the following topics, as well as to helping teachers develop strategies for carrying out instruction in classrooms that are full of students with varying needs.

First, an important topic for consideration by teacher educators and teachers is a strong grounding in cognitive development, in particular how children come to make sense of their world and try to simplify the information-processing demands of their world. Teachers could benefit from viewing the child as an information processor and theorist about the world, and relating this knowledge to the ways that students view classrooms and the demands made on them by teachers. For example, teachers could benefit from the knowledge about typical student perceptions and understandings about schoolwork, about ways that students view the process of learning and the role of ability, and about how students understand the causes of success in school. It strikes me that an important part of a teacher's education should be learning how to ask some of the same questions of students that researchers have begun to ask to determine student perceptions. Similarly, teachers can learn to observe some of the short-term responses that researchers are now focusing on. Some suggestions about this may be found in Anderson (1981).

Another topic that deserves consideration by teachers as they develop professionally is the relationship between the content they want to teach and the curriculum materials they use to support that instruction. As long as class sizes remain over five, teachers will continue to utilize commercial material out of necessity. The data in the Student Response Project do not at all suggest that this should not be done, but they do suggest that some teachers could use help to think about how they use that material, and to recognize that moving through the book and covering the content (by completing pages) is not the same as mastering the content.

Classroom management has long been a topic of concern to teachers and researchers, and much thinking about management is focused on ways to keep children "on-task." As noted earlier, management of students during seatwork is a special concern of many teachers. A large body of research has developed about the importance of accountability systems, clarity of rules, consistency of consequences, and so forth (e.g., see Emmer, Evertson, & Anderson, 1980). These sources emphasize ways that the teacher can establish and maintain a smooth flow of activities without disruptions. In short, much management research has studied ways that teachers can "keep the lid on," not an insignificant part of a teacher's responsibilities.

However, an additional and perhaps more important purpose of management can be the creation of opportunities for the teacher to check student understanding of those tasks that students spend time with, in addition to taking measures to insure high time-on-task. That is, an important objective of a teacher's management system should be the distribution of his or her time for the purpose of checking student understanding, not just checking papers for correct answers or monitoring the appearance of attention. It may be that maximizing student understanding and maximizing the appearance of time-on-task may lead to some trade-offs by the teacher between maximum student "busy-ness' and maximum student comprehension.

Thus, three aspects of teachers' knowledge about classrooms and students have been discussed: a view of students (as active information processors and mediators of instructional effects); a view of commerical materials (and how they can contribute or fail to contribute to student learning when used as seatwork); and a view of classroom management (in which checking for student understanding is a major goal). All three aspects of teachers' thinking affect how teachers view the way that time is to be used by students doing seatwork.

NOTE

1. The work described here was done in collaboration with Janet Alleman-Brooks, Nancy Brubaker, and Gerald Duffy, whose contributions are gratefully acknowledged. The study was funded by the National Institute of Education, NIE-G-80-0073. Details about methods and results may be found in the final report (Anderson et al., 1983).

REFERENCES

Anderson, L. (1981). Short-term student responses to classroom instruction. *Elementary School Journal, 82,* 97–108.

Anderson, L., Brubaker, N., Alleman-Brooks, J., & Duffy, G. (1983). *Student responses to classroom instruction: Final report, NIE-G-80—0073.* East Lansing, Mich.: The Institute for Research on Teaching, Michigan State University.

Brophy, J. (1979). Teacher behavior and its effects. *Journal of Educational Psychology, 71,* 733–750.

Brown, A. (1978). Knowing when, where, and how to remember: A problem of metacognition. In R. Glaser (Ed.), *Advances in instructional psychology.* Hillsdale, N.J.: Erlbaum.

Doyle, W. (1977). Paradigms for research on teacher effectiveness. In L. Shulman (Ed.), *Review of Research in Education* (Vol. 5). Itasca, Ill.: Peacock.

Doyle, W. (1979a). Classroom tasks and students' abilities. In P. Peterson and H. Walberg (Eds.), *Research on teaching.* Berkeley, Calif.: McCutchan.

Doyle, W. (1979b). Making managerial decisions in classrooms. In D. Duke (Ed.), *Classroom management. Yearbook of the National Society for the Study of Education, Part II.* Chicago: University of Chicago Press.

Emmer, E., Evertson, C., & Anderson, L. (1980). Effective classroom management at the beginning of the school year. *Elementary School Journal, 80,* 219–231.

Erlwanger, S. (1973). Benny's conception of rules and answers in IPI mathematics. *Journal of Children's Mathematical Behavior, 1*(2).

Fisher, C., Filby, N., Marliave, R., Cahen, L., Dishaw, M., Moore, J., & Berliner, D. (1978). *Teaching behaviors, academic learning time, and student achievement.* Final report of Phase III-B, Beginning Teacher Evaluation Study. San Francisco: Far West Laboratory for Educational Research and Development.

Good, T. L. (1979). Teacher effectiveness in the elementary school. *Journal of Teacher Education, 30,* 52–60.

Good, T. L. (1981, April). *Listening to students.* Paper presented at the annual meeting of the American Educational Research Association, Los Angeles.

Holt, J. (1964). *How children fail.* New York: Pitman.

Peterson, P., & Walberg, H. (Eds.) (1979) *Research on teaching.* Berkeley, Calif.: McCutchan.

Rohrkemper, M. (1981). *Classroom perspectives: A investigation of differential student perceptions of classroom events.* Unpublished doctoral dissertation. Michigan State University.

Weinstein, R. S. (1981, April). *Student perspectives on "achievement" in varied classroom environments.* Paper presented at the annual meeting of the American Educational Research Association, Los Angeles.

Weinstein, R. S., & Middlestadt, S. E. (1979). Student perceptions of teacher interactions with male high and low achievers. *Journal of Educational Psychology, 71,* 421–431.

Winne, P. H., & Marx, R. W. (1977). Reconceptualizing research on teaching. *Journal of Educational Psychology, 69,* 668–678.

12

Teacher Accessibility and Student Attention

Nikola N. Filby
*Far West Laboratory for Educational
Research and Development*

and

Leonard S. Cahen
Arizona State University

EDITORS' INTRODUCTION
Drs. Filby and Cahen explore the effects of classroom organization and teaching behaviors on student engagement. This chapter, like the preceding and following chapters in Part IV, focuses on a "short-term" student learning outcome and thereby probes the mechanisms by which teachers influence student achievement. In this chapter, the authors draw upon analysis of data from a large-scale process–product study and an innovative series of case studies to examine student attention as a function of classroom setting and the occurrence of specific teaching patterns. The analysis makes a very important distinction between the effects on student attention resulting from structural conditions (type of organizational arrangement in the classroom) and the effects of teacher behavior (amount of substantive instruction) enacted within a particular setting. Although the impacts of these two sources of effects on student attention are not easily separated empirically, Filby and Cahen identify a series of mechanisms that could account for the patterns in the correlation coefficients. The analysis presented in this chapter is especially interesting in that it complements and is complemented by important themes from other chapters in this volume. The effect of pacing, for example, is also considered by Barr and Dreeben (Chapter 6), and the differential effect of instructional behaviors in higher cognitive skills versus basic skills is discussed by Marliave and Filby (Chapter 13).

Numerous studies have confirmed that student attention is an important prerequisite for school learning (e.g., Chapter 1). This chapter presents several analyses of what teachers do to increase student attention. One set of analyses comes from the Beginning Teacher Evaluation Study (BTES) (Fisher, Filby, Marliave, Cahen, Dishaw, Moore, & Berliner, 1978); a second set comes from a later study of the effects of class size on instruction (Cahen, Filby, McCutcheon, & Kyle, 1983).

THE BEGINNING TEACHER EVALUATION STUDY (BTES)

One area of investigation in Phase III-B of the Beginning Teacher Evaluation Study was the relationship between teacher behavior in the classroom and student engagement. Information about data collection procedures and analyses can be found in Fisher et al. (1978) and in Filby and Cahen (1977, 1978). Student engagement, the term used for student attention, was defined as the percentage of instructional time during which the student appeared to be attending to an academic task.

Three interactive teaching functions were investigated in the BTES—presentation, monitoring, and feedback. During direct interaction with the student in the classroom, the teacher presents information to the student, checks to see what the student knows or has learned, and provides feedback to the students about how he or she is doing. Behaviors representing these three functions were measured through extensive direct observation in the classroom. The BTES observation system was a time-based, rotating-sample procedure. This classroom observation system recorded detailed information during the instructional day for individual target students. An event for each student was sampled about once every four minutes. Each event was coded along several dimensions. These dimensions included content of instruction, setting, student behavior (engagement and task difficulty), and the instructional behavior provided by teachers and other instructors.

The BTES sample included 139 students from 25 second-grade classes and 122 students from 21 fifth-grade classes. Classroom observation took place for a full day approximately once each week. The data reported are averages across about 15 days of observation between January and May.

The Interactive Teaching Behaviors

The interactive teaching behaviors that were observed are described in Table 12.1. Seven individual behaviors were coded. These behaviors represent aspects of the three interactive teaching functions. Notice that the behaviors can also be subdivided according to content. Some behaviors deal with substantive, academic content. Others deal with classroom procedure. For each of the seven behaviors, a description and an example are given in Table 12.1.

TABLE 12.1. Definitions and Examples of Interactive Teaching Behaviors

General function	Specific behavior	Description	Example
		SUBSTANTIVE BEHAVIORS	
Presentation	Explanation—need	The instructor explains academic content in response to a clear and immediate student need for help.	During a seatwork assignment on short vowels, the teacher notices that Sonia is having trouble, so he goes over the sounds with her.
	Explanation—planned	The instructor explains academic content but not in response to a specific or immediate student need. This often takes the form of a lecture.	The class comes to a section in the reading workbook on compound words. The teacher introduces this concept and puts some examples on the board.
Monitoring	Academic observation	The instructor looks at or listens to student academic responses, in order to see how the student is doing.	While Eric is doing seatwork, the teacher looks at his paper to make sure he understands what to do.
	Academic question	The instructor asks the student for a written or oral answer in order to observe and assess academic performance.	During group discussion, the teacher asks Mary to give the meaning of a word from that day's reading lesson.
Feedback	Academic feedback	The instructor tells the student whether his or her answer is right or wrong. Could involve giving the right answer. Does not involve explanation.	The teacher asks Johnny to read out loud to the class the answers to the arithmetic problems.
			In oral reading circle, Susan hears Jim reading out loud while she reads along silently.

(continued)

TABLE 12.1.   (Cont.)

General function	Specific behavior	Description	Example
		PROCEDURAL BEHAVIORS	
Presentation	Structure/ direct	The instructor states the goals of instruction or gives directions about the procedures and activities the student should carry out.	At the beginning of the math lesson, the teacher says, "Today we are going to work on 10s and 1s like we did yesterday. Turn to page 20."
Feedback	Task engagement feedback	The instructor acts to control inappropriate behavior or to praise appropriate behavior. The focus is on the student's actions rather than the correctness of his answers.	Billy is out of his seat and standing by the pencil sharpener. The teacher tells him to "hurry up and get back to work."

All instruction was coded as occurring in one of two general instructional settings—self-paced or other-paced. In self-paced settings the student works independently and determines the rate at which work gets done. The most frequent example of a self-paced setting is "seatwork." Seatwork may take place for a long period, with different students doing different tasks, while the teacher circulates around the room or provides help as needed. It is also possible during a group lesson for the teacher to let the students "finish the page on their own." In the latter case, the five minutes that students spend working problems individually would also be coded as self-paced. In other-paced settings, the student must interact with other students or must share the teacher's attention with other students. The pace of instruction is determined by the whole interactive unit and is beyond the control of the individual student. The most frequent example of an other-paced setting is a group lesson, where the teacher instructs two or more students at the same time. A group of students working together without the teacher would also be coded other-paced.

Table 12.2 provides descriptive statistics on the percentage of the time that an individual student receives different interactive teaching behaviors in each of the two settings. (More complete descriptive statistics, including class-level data, can be found in Filby and Fisher, 1977.) For instance, on the average, a student in grade two receives explanation based on need in a self-paced setting during 1.2% of his or her reading instruction. The sum of all behaviors with direct substantive academic content is shown in the rows labeled *Total substantive*. On the average, a second-grade student in this

TABLE 12.2. Frequency of Occurrence of Interactive Teaching Behaviors, by Setting [a]

Teaching behavior	Grade 2		Grade 5	
	Reading	Mathematics	Reading	Mathematics
SELF-PACED SETTINGS (SEATWORK)				
Explanation-need	1.2 (1.1)	2.2 (2.2)	0.4 (0.6)	1.5 (2.2)
Explanation-planned	0.1 (0.3)	0.2 (0.6)	0.0 (0.2)	0.0 (0.2)
Academic observation[b]	0.2 (0.4)	0.3 (0.8)	0.1 (0.2)	0.0 (0.2)
Academic question[b]	0.3 (0.5)	0.1 (0.3)	0.1 (0.2)	0.1 (0.5)
Academic feedback	3.4 (2.5)	2.4 (2.3)	1.2 (1.4)	1.1 (1.3)
Total substantive[c]	5.2 (3.3)	5.2 (4.1)	1.9 (1.7)	2.7 (2.8)
Structure/direct	0.4 (0.5)	0.4 (0.7)	0.1 (0.3)	0.1 (0.4)
Task engagement feedback	0.9 (1.2)	1.0 (1.6)	0.4 (0.8)	0.5 (0.8)
Total interaction	6.5	6.6	2.3	3.3
No teaching behavior	57.8	66.9	66.4	72.7
Total	64.3	73.5	68.7	76.0
OTHER-PACED SETTINGS (GROUP, INTERACTIVE)				
Explanation-need	0.3 (0.4)	0.9 (1.5)	0.3 (0.4)	1.1 (1.6)
Explanation-planned	1.9 (1.5)	3.3 (3.1)	2.1 (2.1)	4.5 (3.9)
Academic observation[b]	0.2 (0.4)	0.1 (0.3)	0.1 (0.2)	0.0 (0.0)
Academic question[b]	6.0 (3.2)	5.1 (4.8)	5.0 (3.2)	3.3 (3.9)
Academic feedback	13.0 (6.3)	4.9 (4.1)	12.1 (5.8)	6.1 (5.8)
Total substantive[c]	21.3 (8.2)	14.4 (9.7)	19.6 (7.6)	14.9 (10.6)
Structure/direct	4.5 (2.6)	3.6 (3.2)	3.5 (2.2)	2.5 (2.3)
Task engagement feedback	0.8 (1.5)	0.6 (1.0)	0.5 (0.7)	0.6 (1.0)
Total interaction	26.7	18.6	23.6	18.0
No teaching behavior	9.0	7.9	7.6	6.0
Total	35.7	26.5	31.2	24.0

[a] Entries are mean (standard deviation). All variables are expressed as *percentages* of student instructional time in reading or mathematics. Sample size is 139 students in grade 2 and 122 students in grade 5. Data came from the B–C period (January to May), with approximately 15 full days of observation per class.
[b] Partly because academic observation was so infrequent, academic observation and academic question were combined for analysis. The combined variable was labeled "academic monitoring."
[c] Total substantive includes explanation—need, explanation—planned, academic observation, academic question, and academic feedback.

sample receives substantive instruction in a self-paced setting during 5.2% of his or her reading time.

To put these percentages in perspective, overall statistics on percentage of time in each setting are also given. Students in both grades and both subject matter areas spend, on the average, at least 60% of their time in seatwork. There is more seatwork in grade five than in grade two. There is more seatwork in mathematics than in reading. (This same pattern was also reported in Phase II of the BTES. See McDonald and Elias, 1975.)

The amount of instruction received by a student during seatwork is very small, especially in grade five. Over half the time during reading and mathematics, students work on their own, with no instructional interaction.

Other-paced settings are, by definition, primarily interactive. Other-paced settings generally occur for less than one-third of the student's instructional time. During most, but not all, of this time some instructional interaction is occurring. Time with no immediate teaching behavior in a group setting would include such activities as having students put their names on their papers, having students briefly read some material or work a problem, or talking about nonacademic content during the reading or mathematics lesson.

Correlations with Engagement

Table 12.3 shows the correlation between each of the interactive teaching behaviors and student engagement. (A more detailed analysis and discussion of these relationships, including multiple regression analyses and scatter plots, can be found in Filby and Cahen, 1977, 1978.) In order to examine general effects, the percentage of time for each behavior was summed across the two instructional settings.

The results for the three interactive teaching functions and the individual behaviors can be summarized in a single parsimonious explanation of the data: More substantive academic interaction between teachers and students is associated with higher student engagement. As a

TABLE 12.3. Correlations of Interactive Teaching Behaviors with Percent Engaged[a]

General function	Specific behavior	Grade 2		Grade 5	
		Reading	Mathematics	Reading	Mathematics
Presentation	Explanation—need	04	−02	09	−15
	Explanation—planned	24	27	09	45
	Structure/direct	−03	20	−01	29
Monitoring	Academic monitoring	37	40	19	31
Feedback	Academic feedback	39	29	42	39
	Task engagement feedback	−22	−25	−43	−30
Total substantive interaction		48	42	43	46

[a] The entries in the table are the correlations obtained in the B–C period (January to May), with approximately 15 full days of observation per class. Total substantive is the sum of four behaviors: explanation—need, explanation—planned, academic monitoring, and academic feedback. Sample size is 139 students in grade 2 and 122 students in grade 5. Correlations reach significance at the .05 level when $r \geq .18$.

type of statistical summary, we computed the correlation between total substantive interaction and percent engaged. This correlation, for each grade level in reading and in mathematics, is shown at the bottom of Table 12.3. Total substantive interaction is the sum of four behaviors: explanation—need, explanation—planned, academic monitoring, and academic feedback. This particular combination was used because it was developed in the theoretical grouping of variables. Note both the size and consistency of the correlation. The strongest effect is at the general level—more interaction is associated with more engagement.

Teaching Behavior, Setting, and Engagement

From the descriptive statistics in Table 12.2, we know that most instructional interaction takes place in a group setting. From the correlations in Table 12.3, we know that the amount of instructional interaction is positively associated with student engagement rate. One way of integrating these two facts is to state that setting is related to engagement rate. Engagement rates are higher in a group setting than during independent seatwork. The more time a student spends in seatwork, the lower his or her overall engagement rate is likely to be. On the average, students in second grade had an engagement rate of 68% during seatwork and 84% during group work. In fifth grade, the average engagement rate was 71% during seatwork and 85% during group work. Engagement rate during seatwork was influenced, however, by the length of time students were in a seatwork setting. As the length of the seatwork period increased, average engagement rates decreased, perhaps as much as 10%.

This setting effect makes practical sense. Students are more likely to goof off when they are on their own, with only general supervision by the teacher, than they are when they are in a group with direct teacher attention. And, the longer they are left on their own, the more likely their attention is to wander.

The setting effect is only part, however, of a more general positive effect of academic interaction between instructor and student. The average correlation between total substantive interaction and engagement, as shown in Table 12.3, is about .45. The average correlation between percentage of time in group work and engagement is only about .31. "Total substantive interaction" is a better description of the desired condition than is "group work."

There are three reasons why instructional interaction shows a positive effect over and above setting. Two have to do with the fact that time in a group setting includes time when no instructional interaction is taking place, and during this time engagement is very low. As shown in Table 12.2, about one-quarter of the time during group work there is no immediate instructional behavior. But this percentage varies from one class to another. While substantive instructional interaction is taking place during group work, the level of engagement is very high. The range is from 95% engaged during substantive instructional behavior in grade five reading to 98% engaged during instructional behavior in the other three quadrants. While no instructional behavior is taking place in group work, the engagement rate drops to around 50%. (The range is from 48% to 53% across quadrants.) What happens during this time? For one thing, the teacher waits while the students put their names on their papers. Even while the students were writing their names they would be coded "not engaged." This would be labeled an "interim" task, and the students would be coded "not engaged—interim." Although they may be doing what they are supposed to do, the students are not learning math or reading while they write their names. Another type of not-engaged activity during group work is waiting. Some students wait while other students finish writing their names or finish working a problem. This reflects one of the disadvantages of other-paced settings—the students cannot go ahead at their own rates. In summary, engagement is high in group settings while instructional behavior is occurring and low in group settings when no immediate instructional behavior is occurring.

Naturally, the overall engagement rate in group settings is highly influenced by the amount of time when no instructional behavior is occurring. The percentage of other-paced setting time with no instructional behavior ranges from zero percent to over 70%. The impact of this difference is reflected in the correlations in Table 12.4. In all four quadrants there is a high correlation between the percent of other-paced time when instructional behavior is occurring and the engagement rate in other-paced settings.

Notice also in row two of Table 12.4 that there is a degree of transfer in the impact of instructional behavior in other-paced settings. The percentage of other-paced time with instructional behavior is related to engagement rates in seatwork. One interpretation is that a pacing effect is involved. If, during group lessons, most of the time is directly involved with substantive instruction this may contribute to a sense of purposefulness, whereas less substantive interaction may be associated with a sense of slow pacing and lack of real emphasis on academic learning. This general atmosphere may encourage off-task behavior during seatwork.

This effect of pacing on engagement in both other-paced and self-paced settings appears to be related to a finding reported by Anderson, Evertson, and Brophy (1979) in their study of organization and management techniques in first-grade reading groups. They found that reading achievement was strongly related to the time lapse between teacher and children reaching the reading group and the actual beginning of the lesson. They concluded that "once the last person (teacher or child) arrives in a reading group, the teacher should begin the lesson immediately. Any materials necessary for the lesson should be pre-arranged so that reading group time is not wasted

TABLE 12.4.   Correlations Between Instructional Behavior and Engagement Within and Across Settings[a]

Interaction variable	Engagement variable	Grade 2		Grade 5	
		Reading	Mathematics	Reading	Mathematics
Percent of other-paced time during which substantive interaction takes place	Engagement in other-paced settings	.54	.46	.56	.47
Percent of other-paced time during which substantive interaction takes place	Engagement in self-paced settings	.31	.03	.46	.11
Percent of self-paced time during which substantive interaction takes place	Engagement in self-paced settings	.18	.15	.18	−.14

[a] Sample size is 139 students in grade 2 and 122 studens in grade 5. A correlation $\geq .18$ is significant at the .05 level. Correlations are based on data from the B–C period (January to May). Substantive interaction is the sum of explanation—planned, explanation—need, academic monitoring, and academic feedback.

on organizational tasks." Pacing appears to relate to achievement, with student engagement rate as a mediating factor.

There is one final way in which teacher-student interaction influences engagement beyond the role of group settings. During seatwork, engagement rates are generally lower than in group settings, but engagement rates are higher during seatwork when students get more contact with the teacher.

During seatwork some teachers move around the room giving feedback and explanation; other teachers are busy doing other things. With a number of children to be covered, any one child cannot receive a lot of teacher attention; but in the classes we observed, some students received substantive instruction during as much as one-fourth of the time they were doing seatwork whereas other students never received individual attention during seatwork.

The correlations in Table 12.4 indicate that in three of the four quadrants the amount of substantive instruction a child received during seatwork was positively associated with student engagement in seatwork. This effect is even greater when one looks at only those classes with a high percentage of time in seatwork. As a group, these classes tend to have lower engagement rates and somewhat higher percentages of substantive instruction during seatwork. Within this group, the amount of substantive instruction in seatwork tends to be positively related to engagement. In grade two mathematics, classes with over 70% seatwork were divided into two groups. One group had substantive interaction during a relatively large percentage of seatwork time (an average of 11% per child); the other group had substantive instruction during only about 5% of seatwork time. The engagement rate during seatwork in the high-interaction classes averaged 71%. The engagement rate during seatwork in the low-interaction classes averaged 61%. In other words, if for some reason a large percentage of instructional time is spent in seatwork, it is important to monitor the students and provide academic feedback and explanation as often as possible.

THE CLASS-SIZE STUDY

These results on student attention were generally confirmed in a later study of class size (Cahen, Filby, McCutcheon, & Kyle, 1983). In this study the focus was on understanding the impact of class size on classroom processes. The study was carried out in four second-grade classes, two in urban California and two in rural Virginia. In all classes, class size was reduced by about one-third in January for the remainder of the school year. Extensive observation was carried out to document changes in instruction when class size was reduced. The teachers collaborated in the research and kept journals of their plans and their observations.

Based on the BTES results, we predicted that student attention would increase when class size was reduced. If time with the teacher is an important predictor of attention, it seemed logical that a smaller class size would allow more frequent contact and thus foster attention. The results supported this prediction.

Observation data on student attention were collected at the Virginia site. (Similar data collection was planned for the California site but could not be carried out due to last-minute schedule changes.) The procedure was basically the same as that used in the BTES but with a simplified set of coding categories. The results are shown in Table 12.5.

Student attention to academic tasks increased from 57% to 75%. This increase was accomplished through a reduction in both time spent waiting for help and time spent off-task. During seatwork, students received more frequent contact with the teacher. During reading groups, each student was able to have a turn more frequently.

Observation at the California site provided a number of incidents to confirm this general pattern. In the larger class, students were frequently lined up waiting to have papers checked, while the aide explained, "I can only check one paper at a time." In the smaller class, lines were shorter. The importance of the teacher's presence was also apparent. Student attention would drop off noticeably when the teacher moved to another part of the room. Even within a group, attention rates appeared to be negatively correlated with distance from the teacher; those in the outskirts of the group

TABLE 12.5. Attention Results in the Class Size Study (Virginia Site)[a]

Student behaviors	"Larger" class	"Smaller" class	Difference	Percent difference
Attention to academic task	57	75	18	32
Waiting for help	9	5	−4	−46
Off-task	12	8	−4	−34
No assignment— waiting	14	0	−14	100
Contact with teacher during seatwork	3	5	2	92

[a] Figures are percentages of observed time. Medians across observation days and across students were calculated for reading and for mathematics for each of the two classes. Percentages shown in the table are the medians of data averaged across reading and mathematics for the two classes.

were more likely to be inattentive. As the instructional group became smaller, each student could be drawn into the group lesson more effectively. Each student could have a turn more often, suggesting the impression of more rapid pacing, especially from the student's point of view. These observations were supported by the teachers' perception that lessons went more smoothly and that material could be covered more quickly.

DISCUSSION

In sum, the message from these data is that students are more attentive when they spend time in group lessons rather than independent work, especially when the lessons are fast-paced and group size is small enough to allow frequent student responses. Students are more attentive during seatwork when they have more frequent contact with an instructor.

If this conclusion is true, two new questions arise: (1) How does the teacher organize the classroom to provide frequent opportunities for substantive interaction; and (2) what form should this substantive interaction take?

The first question touches on one aspect of a basic teacher's dilemma (also discussed by Barr and Dreeben in Chapter 6 of this volume and elsewhere). A teacher can maximize instructional contact time by having whole-class instruction. However, this means that the same content must be taught to all students at the same time. If the class is heterogeneous in terms of skill levels or instructional needs, whole-class instruction may mean inappropriate instructional content for some students. In the BTES this issue of appropriateness was addressed by measuring the students' accuracy on class assignments. As discussed by Marliave and Filby, in Chapter 13, elementary school students learning basic skills tend to achieve more when they can carry out most classroom tasks accurately and successfully. In pursuit of appropriate instruction to meet individual needs, a teacher may establish groups in the classroom. Grouping immediately increases the complexity of the management task and is likely to decrease student attention. In other words, there is an apparent trade-off between student attention and task appropriateness as reflected in student success rate. We need to learn more about the relative importance of these two factors in different situations. We also need to learn more about how some teachers maintain high attention rates even in complex instructional settings (see Chapter 14).

The second question concerns what to do during instructional interaction. If these results are to be useful to teachers, some advice needs to be given about how best to fill interactive instructional time. Two general results from the BTES are relevent.

Academic feedback was particularly strongly and consistently related to student achievement as well as to student attention. Academic feedback included a variety of ways in which students learned whether an answer was right or wrong or heard the correct answer. Besides straightforward checking of written work, it included oral question-and-answer sessions and oral reading, where the student was reading along. The importance of feedback may then reflect, in part, the value of frequent student responses. This theme was touched on previously and will resurface in Chapter 13.

Instructional variables were more strongly related to achievement in conceptual areas such as reading comprehension or mathematics place value than in areas such as mathematics computation or word meaning. This relationship suggests the importance of high-quality instruction in selecting and presenting new concepts. Work in this area has been done by Duffy, Roehler, and Mason (1984) and Good and Grouws (1983), among others.

REFERENCES

Anderson, L., Evertson, C., & Brophy, J. (1979). An experimental study of teaching effectiveness in first-grade reading groups. *Elementary School Journal, 79,* 193–223.

Cahen, L., Filby, N., McCutcheon, G., & Kyle, D. (1983). *Class size and instruction: A field study.* New York: Longman.

Duffy, G., Roehler, L., & Mason, J. (Eds.) (1984) *Comprehension instruction: Perspectives and suggestions.* New York: Longman.

Filby, N., & Cahen, L. (1977, December). *Teaching behavior and academic learning time in the A–B period.* Technical note V-1b, Phase III-B Beginning Teacher

Evaluation Study. San Francisco: Far West Laboratory for Educational Research and Development.

Filby, N., & Cahen, L. (1978, February). *Teaching behavior and academic learning time in the B–C period.* Technical note V-2b, Phase III-B, Beginning Teacher Evaluation Study. San Francisco: Far West Laboratory for Educational Research and Development.

Filby, N., & Fisher, C. (1977, October). *Description of patterns of teaching behavior within and across classes during the B–C period.* Technical note IV-3b, Phase III-B, Beginning Teacher Evaluation Study. San Francisco: Far West Laboratory for Educational Research and Development. (ERIC Document Reproduction Service No. ED 156 641)

Fisher, C., Filby, N., Marliave, R., Cahen, L., Dishaw, M., Moore, J., & Berliner, D. (1978). *Teaching behaviors, academic learning time, and student achievement: A final report of Phase III-B of the Beginning Teacher Evaluation Study* Technical report V-1, Phase III-B, Beginning Teacher Evaluation Study. San Francisco: Far West Laboratory for Educational Research and Development. (ERIC Document Reproduction Service No. ED 183 525)

Good, T., & Grouws, D. (1983). *Active mathematics instruction.* New York: Longman.

McDonald, F., & Elias, P. (1975, November). *Beginning Teacher Evaluation Study: Phase II Final Report* (Vol. I, chap. 10). Princeton: Educational Testing Service.

13

Success Rate: A Measure of Task Appropriateness

Richard Marliave and Nikola N. Filby
*Far West Laboratory for
Educational Research and Development*

EDITORS' INTRODUCTION
Much of the research on which this volume is based has focused on the concept of time-on-task. This concept played a crucial role in "unpacking" the relationship between teacher behaviors and student achievement, in that it provided a measurable student outcome that was more proximal to instruction than the relatively distal achievement measures. Much new knowledge about and insight into the instructional process has resulted from this line of inquiry. However, one has sometimes been left with the question, time on which tasks? Surely the nature of the tasks on which students spend time is at least as important as the act of engagement itself. Any imbalance in emphasis on time spent as opposed to task characteristics was not suggested in the original Carroll model of school learning. This chapter deals directly with this issue. Marliave and Filby broaden the concept of time-on-task by using student success rate as an indication of task appropriateness. Following the BTES model, student success rate, engagement rate, and time allocated to criterion-relevant tasks are combined to form academic learning time. The chapter presents empirical findings on the relationship between student achievement and the three components of academic learning time. The authors make a strong case for the importance of student success rate in determining student learning and argue that relatively large amounts of high-success time are especially important for students with histories of low achievement.

Marliave and Filby discuss both cognitive and affective processes through which high-success time can be expected to influence student learning. The authors then turn to mechanisms and strategies that teachers may use to control or manipulate student high-success time in classroom settings. This wide-ranging chapter presents a clear view of the intricacy of the relationships among context variables, teaching behaviors, student classroom behaviors, and student perceptions in classroom learning situations, and provides a range of classroom examples that highlight the authors' points.

A considerable and growing body of research covering at least the last three decades (Block, 1971; Bloom, 1976; Fisher, Filby, Marliave, Cahen, Dishaw, Moore, & Berliner, 1978; Skinner, 1954, 1968) indicates that high success (or low error rate) during instructional tasks is crucial to the efficient acquisition of basic skills. This chapter presents a brief review of research on high success (low error rate) during instructional tasks in relationship to learning outcomes, with a discussion of alternative interpretations of the relationship. In addition, alternative strategies for controlling success during instructional tasks are considered.

THE CONCEPT OF HIGH SUCCESS

The concept of high success in this chapter is taken from the academic learning time (ALT) model of the Beginning Teacher Evaluation Study (Fisher et al., 1978). The ALT model describes ongoing student learning behaviors in terms of three basic variables: (1) task relevance to criterion or outcome, (2) student involvement in or attention to the task, and (3) the appropriateness of the task for the student as represented by the student's level of success on that task. This chapter considers the third of these variables, student success level, as a representation of task appropriateness.

High success in the ALT model represents student performance of an instructional task with no errors other than careless errors. In other words, the student commits either no errors or only errors that he or she would probably not repeat if given a second trial. Thus, the student has mastered the content, at least in terms of producing a correct response. However, this does not necessarily mean that the student can perform the instructional task quickly or easily. The ALT model classifies a student's task performance as high success even if it requires considerable concentration and effort, so long as the student responds correctly (excepting "careless" errors). Clearly, high-success instructional performance in this model does not require automaticity. Of course, automaticity is not excluded from high success. The student may perform the task quickly and even effortlessly, but this is not required in the ALT concept of high success.

It is important to distinguish the success levels of instructional tasks from the pacing of instruction. Instruction involving great proportions of high-success tasks might proceed at a slow or a rapid pacing. Increasingly rapid paces through a given set of instructional tasks may contribute to a reduced success level of student performance on individual tasks, if students commit more errors while trying to keep up the pace. However, it is also possible that tasks designed for high student success would result in more rapid pacing if students were thereby able to complete each task more quickly. Borphy (1979) and Harris (1979) make the distinction between success on instructional tasks (or task difficulty) and the pacing of instruction through a sequence of tasks, where high success may coincide with rapid pacing. Further, Becker (1977) points out that "Children enjoy the rapid pacing when circumstances allow them to be successful (using the Oregon Direct Instruction Model)" (p. 524).

RELATIONSHIP OF SUCCESS TO ACHIEVEMENT IN READING AND MATHEMATICS

The Beginning Teacher Evaluation Study research (Fisher et al., 1978) involved a field study conducted in 25 second-grade classes and 22 fifth-grade classes in several school districts, representing a range of socioeconomic groups in a large metropolitan area. Data were collected for six target students in each class over a five-week period from October to December (A–B period) and a 16-week period from January to May (B–C period). Achievement tests were administered before and after each period. Teachers kept daily records of allocated time throughout each period. Observers collected data on student engagement and success level (as well as verification data on allocated time) one day each week throughout each period.

The success data were collected in three categories: high, medium, and low. High success was coded when students exhibited no errors or only careless errors during an instructional task. Low success represented no correct student response to a task, or only the proportion of correct responses that one would expect by chance. Medium success covered the broad range of response accuracy between the high- and low-success categories. As one would expect, the low-success category occurred for only a very small proportion of instructional time, averaging less than 5%. Nevertheless, low success was an important negative predictor of student learning. High and medium success each accounted for about half of the remaining instructional time (50% for high success in grade two reading and mathematics; 46% for high success in grade five reading, 34% in grade five mathematics). Therefore, these two categories were essentially statistically redundant, so it was appropriate to analyze only one of the two categories. The positive effects found for high success indicate that the effects of medium success were negative (in relation to learning outcomes).

A summary of the achievement relationships of the ALT variables, including allocated time and engagement rate as well as high and low success, is presented in Table 13.1, for reading , and Table 13.2, for mathematics. A total of 52 regressions are summarized, where postachievement scores were regressed on preachievement scores and the four ALT variables. Regressions were run for subcategories of reading and mathematics achievement and total reading and mathematics achievement in grades two and five and over the two test intervals within each grade. Tables 13.1 and 13.2 indicate the number of significant effects ($p \leq .10$) for each ALT variable, the average residual variance accounted for by all four ALT variables

TABLE 13.1. Summary of Regressions
Combined Effects of ALT Variables
Regression of Postachievement on Preachievement in Reading, Allocated Time, Engagement Rate, High Success, and Low Success

Grade	Period	Total number of regressions	Number of significant effects ($p \leq .10$) positive + or negative −				Average residual variance, combined ALT variables[a]
			Allocated time	Engagement rate	High success	Low success	
Two (N = 127)	A–B Period (Oct. to Dec.)	4	2+	3+	2+	0	.07
Two (N = 139)	B–C Period (Jan. to May)	7	3+	2+	5+	2−	.12
Five (N = 122)	A–B Period (Oct. to Dec.)	4	0	1+	3+	0	.03
Five (N = 122)	B–C Period (Jan. to May)	4	1+	1+	0	3−	.13
Unique proportion of residual variance,[b] average of both grades, both periods, and all 19 regressions			.016	.013	.019	.009	.09

[a] Residual variance refers to the variance remaining in the postachievement measure after preachievement is "removed." This column reports the proportion of this residual variance that is accounted for by the set of ALT variables.

[b] This is the proportion of residual variance accounted for uniquely by the independent variable specified, averaged over all 19 regressions for grades two and five in the A–B and B–C periods.

TABLE 13.2.   Summary of Regressions
Combined Effects of ALT Variables
Regression of Postachievement on Preachievement in Mathematics, Allocated Time, Engagement Rate, High Success and Low Success

| Grade | Period | Total number of regressions | Number of significant effects ($p \leq .10$) positive + or negative − | | | | Average residual variance, combined ALT variables[a] |
			Allocated time	Engagement rate	High success	Low success	
Two (N = 127)	A–B Period (Oct. to Dec.)	7	1+/1−	1+	4+	1−	.04
Two (N = 139)	B–C Period (Jan. to May)	10	4+	0	5+	2−	.08
Five (N = 122)	A–B Period (Oct. to Dec.)	8	4+	2+	3+	4−	.09
Five (N = 122)	B–C Period (Jan. to May)	8	3+	2+	2+	6−	.11
Unique proportion of residual variance,[b] average of both grades, both periods, and all 33 regressions			.025	.003	.012	.015	.08

[a] Residual variance refers to the variance remaining in the postachievement measure after preachievement is "removed." This column reports the proportion of this residual variance that is accounted for by the set of ALT variables.

[b] This is the proportion residual variance accounted for uniquely by the independent variable specified, averaged over all 33 regressions for grades two and five in the A-B and B-C periods.

221

combined, and the unique proportion of residual variance accounted for by each ALT variable separately. Note that the sum of the separate unique proportions is less than the combined proportion. This is due to the fact that variance accounted for by two or more ALT variables mutually is excluded from the unique proportions.

Two aspects of the tables should be noted. First, with one exception, all of the significant effects for the ALT variables are consistent in sign. That is, the significant effects of allocated time, engagement rate, and high success are always positive whereas those for low success are always negative. Second, high success is at least equal to allocated time and engagement rate as a predictor of student learning outcomes. There are more significant effects for high success than for either allocated time or engagement rate at both grades two and five. In addition, high success accounts for more residual variance in achievement, on the average, than either allocated time or engagement rate. There are no significant effects for high success only during the B–C period in grade five reading. However, the counterpart to high success, low success, has significant negative effects in three out of the four regressions run for the grade five reading in the B–C period, whereas allocated time and engagement rate are signicant only in one regression each.

These results indicate that student success during instructional tasks is an ongoing learning behavior of equal or greater importance than that of time allocated to criterion-relevant tasks or student attention during those tasks. In addition, projection analyses indicate that the *practical effects* of high student success while engaged in criterion-relevant tasks can be of considerable importance. This is illustrated in Table 13.3, using examples from analysis of grade two reading instruction. This table displays total reading scores in October, student engaged time with a high success rate in reading over the period from October to December, and estimated total reading scores in December. The reading scores in December are estimated from linear regressions that use the actual test scores in October and December and the intervening engaged high-success time. The regression estimates the most likely December test score for a given combination of an October test score and intervening engaged time at high success rate. Total reading scores in October and December are shown both in terms of raw scores out of 100 items (percent of items correct) and in terms of percentile rank among students in the study. Student engaged time with a high success rate in reading (ALT) is shown both in terms of total time over the five-week intertest period and in terms of the corresponding average daily time (in minutes).

Table 13.3 shows that substantial increases in engaged high-success time are associated with important increases in achievement. Consider the student who started the period with a grade two reading score that was average (fiftieth percentile, see the top three rows). If this student experiences the average amount of high-success time (573 minutes total, or

TABLE 13.3.   Student Success and Achievement
Examples from Grade 2 Reading Based on the Beginning Teacher
Evaluation Study Results (October to December)[a]

Reading score in October		Student engaged time in reading with high success rate		Estimated reading score in December	
Raw score (out of 100)	Percentile	Total time over 5 weeks (minutes)	Average daily time (minutes)	Raw score (out of 100)	Percentile
36	50	100	4	37	39
36	50	573	23	43	50
36	50	1300	52	52	66
16	17	100	4	20	15
16	17	573	23	25	21
16	17	1300	52	35	36

[a] An average of 25 school days occurred between October and December. The December reading scores are estimated via linear regression. The values of all variables in this table are within the ranges actually obtained in the BTES sample. The average engaged time with high success rate in grade 2 reading for the October to December period was 573 minutes.

23 minutes per day in reading), then the student can be expected to show average reading achievement in December (fiftieth percentile again). Note also that the "average" student with "average" engaged high-success time does show considerable learning in terms of predicted raw scores, increasing from 36 to 43 items correct out of 100 in five weeks.

Table 13.3 also indicates that if this average student (in terms of October's test score) experienced only four minutes per day of engaged high-success time (100 minutes total for the intertest period), then he or she would be expected to show almost no change in raw score (36 out of 100 correct in October, 37 out of 100 in December) and would decline considerably in relative terms (fiftieth percentile in October, thirty-ninth percentile in December). However, if the same student experienced very large amounts of engaged high-success time, 52 minutes per day in this example, then he or she could be expected to answer almost 50% more items correctly on the December test than on the October test (36 out of 100 correct in October, 52 out of 100 correct in December). Furthermore, in this situation the student would show considerable improvement in reading achievement relative to the other students in the study (fiftieth percentile in October, sixty-sixth percentile in December). Additionally, the student who has lower achievement in October benefits as much or more from engaged high-success time than does the average student (see bottom three rows of Table 13.3). Finally, it should be noted that the range of 4–52 minutes per day of engaged high-success time in these examples is realistic, in that these values actually occurred in classes in this study.

Other Research

Considerable other research corroborates these findings on the importance of student high success during instruction in terms of learning outcomes. Two major theories of classroom learning with extensive practical application, mastery learning (Block, 1971; Bloom, 1976) and programmed learning (Skinner, 1954, 1968), emphasize the importance of attaining a high level of student success on one objective in a series before moving on to the next. Student success during instruction is a basic criterion of the ongoing effectiveness of that instruction under either mastery learning or programmed learning procedures.

Field studies including a wide range of common classroom settings have also supported the importance of high student success during instruction. Cooper (1952) reported that the highest level of task difficulty where the student produced no errors appeared to be the most appropriate for reading instruction at grades two through six. Crawford, King, Brophy and Evertson (1975) found that more effective teachers at grades two and three ask questions that students can answer correctly at least 75% of the time during oral recitation settings. This body of research provides ample evidence of the practical importance of student high success during reading instruction in the elementary grades.

Greater Importance at Lower Skill Levels

The Beginning Teacher Evaluation Study data (Fisher et al., 1978) indicate that high success during instruction is especially crucial to the learning rate of lower-achieving students. Tables 13.4 and 13.5 present data indicating how high-success instruction influences the learning rates of students at high, medium, or low initial achievement levels. The cell entries in Tables 13.4 and 13.5 for residual achievement may be loosely thought of as measures of learning rates. Each row represents an initial achievement level (top rows are high initial achievement, bottom rows are low). Each column represents a success rate during instruction over a seven-month period from October to May (low success is on the left and high success is on the right). Note at both grades two and five that the difference in learning rate (cell entries) due to changes in success during instruction (compare the left and right entries in each row) is greater for students with low initial achievement (the bottom row for each grade level). This same pattern—greater influence of success rate for low-ability students—was found by Barnett, Filby, and Bossert (1982).

Furthermore, note that the influence of success on learning is greater at grade two than at grade five. In fact, high achievers at grade five do not appear to benefit from increases in success during instruction. Apparently

TABLE 13.4. Conjoint Relationship of Preachievement in Reading (October Test and High Success (October to May) in Terms of Residual Achievement in Reading (May Test Score Residualized on October Test Score)[a]

Grade two ($N = 139$)		Low	Medium	High
	High	-13 ($n = 3$)	4 ($n = 22$)	0 ($n = 22$)
Preachievement (October)	Medium	-6 ($n = 13$)	-3 ($n = 19$)	5 ($n = 12$)
	Low	-10 ($n = 23$)	3 ($n = 19$)	37 ($n = 6$)
		Low	Medium	High
			High success rate[b]	

Grade five ($N = 122$)		Low	Medium	High
	High	2 ($n = 7$)	-3 ($n = 17$)	-1 ($n = 16$)
Preachievement (October)	Medium	3 ($n = 13$)	3 ($n = 24$)	11 ($n = 4$)
	Low	-5 ($n = 15$)	-2 ($n = 20$)	3 ($n = 6$)
		Low	Medium	High
			High success rate[b]	

[a] Cell entries are mean residual achievement for the October-to-May period and the number of students in the cell (n in parentheses). The standard deviation of residual achievement was 21.8 at grade two and 15.8 at grade five.

[b] Less than 40% high success rate was categorized as a low percentage (left column), while greater than or equal to 60% high success rate was categorized as a high percentage (right column).

the need for high success during instruction is related to developmental characteristics of the learner. One might hypothesize, on the basis of these data, that as the learner grows in maturity and intellectual skills it becomes possible for him or her to benefit from more challenging instructional tasks. However, the learner who is operating at a more rudimentary academic level appears to require very high levels of success during instruction,

TABLE 13.5. Conjoint Relationship of Preachievement in Mathematics (October Test) and High Success (October to .May) in Terms of Residual Achievement in Mathematics (May Test Score Residualized on October Test Score)[a]

Grade two (N = 139)

Preachievement (October)		Low	Medium	High
	High	−11 (n = 12)	−10 (n = 14)	3 (n = 21)
	Medium	4 (n = 10)	4 (n = 18)	12 (n = 15)
	Low	−7 (n = 24)	−8 (n = 12)	15 (n = 13)
		Low	Medium	High

High success rate[b]

Grade five (N = 122)

Preachievement (October)		Low	Medium	High
	High	0 (n = 10)	−2 (n = 16)	2 (n = 13)
	Medium	1 (n = 13)	−2 (n = 13)	3 (n = 14)
	Low	1 (n = 13)	−3 (n = 24)	8 (n = 6)
		Low	Medium	High

High success rate[b]

[a] Cell entries are mean residual achievement for the October-to-May period and the number of students in the cell (*n* in parentheses). The standard deviation of residual achievement was 23.5 at grade two and 17.4 at grade five.

[b] Less than 40% high-success rate was categorized as a low percentage (left column), while greater than or equal to 60% high-success rate was categorized as a high percentage (right column) in grade two. In grade five, cutoff percents were 20 and 45.

probably involving less direct challenge and more practice and review. Hence, high success appears to be most important in the basic-skill domains of *early* elementary grade instruction.

It should be noted that this interaction between high success and student preachievement levels, in terms of residual postachievement, tends to contradict the hypothesis that the effects of high success reflect student aptitude that is unmeasured by the preachievement test. Such an aptitude effect would not diminish at higher preachievement levels, nor would it disappear among high-achieving fifth-grade students. Hence, high success during instruction appears to be a *treatment*, the effects of which diminish as the student exceeds a fifth-grade level of reading proficiency. The high-success treatment is most powerful at the beginning level of academic skills (grades one and two).

PROCESSES UNDERLYING THE RELATION OF HIGH SUCCESS WITH LEARNING

Two areas of explanation for the relation of high-success instruction with learning will be discussed briefly here: cognitive processes and affective processes.

Cognitive Processes

The interaction described above, where high success during instruction is especially effective at the early elementary levels but appears to have no effect beyond the fifth-grade level of achievement, might be explained in terms of theories of cognitive development that posit important changes in cognitive processing over the elementary grade years (Bruner, 1964; Bruner, Goodnow, & Austin, 1956; Inhelder & Piaget, 1958). These theories describe the development of symbolic, abstract, verbal, and logical cognitive skills and abilities at age levels generally consistent with the achievement level at which high-success instruction was observed to no longer be effective in the data presented above (i.e., beyond grade five). This might suggest that the younger students need instructional tasks allowing them a high level of success because they lack the problem-solving skills necessary to deal with the abstract and symbolic requirements of more challenging tasks. That is, the younger student may be unable to learn efficiently when presented with tasks that he or she can not perform accurately during initial trials. At a later stage of development, with greater symbolic and logical skills, the student may be able to learn from prior errors, using the information of an inaccurate response to deduce what the desired response must be. The younger student, however, may learn most efficiently by a more gradual—perhaps inductive—process, where the accumulation of accurate responses on one set of tasks is required before the student understands that set of tasks well enough to move on to the next set.

This interpretation may be more valid for the more abstract and conceptual skills, such as decoding strategies and comprehension, than it is for skills that a child might learn through rote memory, as is possible with word recognition and spelling. The reduced value of high success during rote learning is indicated by Atkinson and Lorton (1969) in a study of computer-based rote spelling instruction among fourth- through sixth-grade students. It was found that the students learned spelling words more rapidly when they spent more time reviewing the words with which they had the most difficulty (least success). That is, they progressed more rapidly by reviewing what they did not already know. The spelling words were selected from a pool of words appropriate for fourth- through sixth-grade students, so that the frustration of an unreasonable task was avoided. Furthermore, the study was conducted with students at the transitional level of achievement, where high success during instruction is becoming less important (perhaps even unimportant among the sixth graders). Still, it is pertinent to compare this study, where high success reduced the rate of rote learning of spelling words, with the previously discussed data where high success was beneficial to overall rates of learning in reading, even at the fifth grade.

If rote learning can be effective at lower success levels, this is likely to be true only during the initial stages of instruction. Additional high-success practice may also be useful. If, as has been proposed by LaBerge and Samuels (1974) and Perfetti and Hogaboam (1975), automaticity in word recognition and in decoding skills is essential to the later development of comprehension skills, then it would never be sufficient to instruct only at the lower success levels for rote learning. High-success instruction would be required after the student had learned to respond accurately for a sufficient period of time to allow for the development of automaticity.

Affective Processes

Regardless of the effects of high-success instruction on cognitive processing, the relationship of high success and affective student response may account for the enhanced learning rates of early elementary students experiencing high success during instruction. There is evidence that elementary students who experience high success enjoy instruction more, have more positive self-concepts, and exhibit higher levels of attention and generally more appropriate classroom behavior than students with lower success rates. This would result in increases in attention levels during instruction, which would result in increased learning rates, particularly over longer periods of time.

Schotanus (1967) found that second-grade students, when allowed to choose, prefer to read material that is easy relative to their own reading abilities. Furthermore, this relationship was more pronounced among students with less positive attitudes toward reading, even though the students with less positive attitudes read as well as students with more positive attitudes. In other words, students like to read material with which they can feel successful.

Studies of students' self-concept also show the influence of success rate or accuracy. When asked to evaluate their own reading performance or that of their classmates, students focus primarily on observable classroom task performance, either oral reading or written work (Filby & Barnett, 1982a; Barnett, Filby, & Bossert, 1982). Doing the work correctly and reading aloud fluently are more salient and important to students than either reading-group membership or teacher feedback, although methods of giving feedback can influence the amount of information students have about accuracy rates, particularly public and comparable information (Bossert, 1979; Marliave, Dishaw, & Fisher, 1981). And low success or poor performance on classroom work are associated with lower self-ratings of reading ability, especially as students get older. Thus students who experience success have more positive beliefs about themselves as learners.

Positive self-concept and preference for success may account for the increased attention generally exhibited by elementary students when instruction is oriented toward high success. The Beginning Teacher Evaluation Study (Fisher et al., 1978) found high success during instruction to be positively associated with attention levels at both grades two and five, whereas low success was negatively associated with attention at both grades. Miller and Hess (1972) reported that fourth-grade students exhibited higher attention during computer-assigned instruction on tasks where they made 20% or fewer errors. Jorgenson, Klein, and Kumar (1977) found that third-through sixth-grade students showed generally more appropriate classroom behavior and motivation, in terms of a teacher-completed rating inventory, when reading instruction involved easier materials relative to the students' tested reading achievement levels.

Related studies involving college students suggest that the preference for relatively easier instructional tasks is related to anxiety evoked by the more difficult materials. O'Neil, Spielberger, and Hansen (1969), using computer-based mathematics tasks with college students, found that the more difficult tasks resulted in increased anxiety levels for all subjects. In addition, it was found that subjects with generally greater levels of anxiety made more errors on difficult tasks and fewer errors on easy tasks than did less anxious students. Crawford (1978), using programmed instruction in physiological psychology with college students, found that subjects with high achievement needs and low fear of failure performed better with more difficult instruction (40% errors rather than 7%), whereas subjects with low achievement needs and high fear of failure learned more with less difficult tasks.

The role of high success during instruction in producing more positive attitudes and higher levels of attention may be especially crucial to low-achieving students. These students may develop negative attitudes toward themselves as learners and toward school as a result of the unfavorable comparative situation in which they find themselves. Further, their lack of previous progress could be related to low levels of attention in some cases. In addition, their previous lack of success may cause academic instruction to be an anxiety-provoking event during which they experience fear of failure. Providing high-success experiences can lead to more positive affect and behavior.

THE CONTROL OF STUDENT
SUCCESS DURING INSTRUCTION

In this section we speculate about how teachers can control student success rate during instruction. Three issues are considered: (1) selection and sequencing of instructional objectives, (2) grouping of students for instruction, and (3) instructional procedures and activities.

Instructional Objectives

Clearly a major issue is the selection of material that is at an appropriate level of difficulty for the student. To illustrate with an extreme example, one would hardly try to teach algebra to a student who could not add or give a fifth-grade reading book to a student with a sight-word vocabulary of 50 words. The success-rate results suggest that an appropriate instructional level is one at which the student can respond completely accurately on at least half the tasks he or she is given.

The control of student success during instruction by identifying curriculum objectives appropriate for student success is represented by both the mastery learning (Block, 1971; Bloom, 1976) and programmed learning (Skinner, 1954, 1968) models of instruction. Each of these approaches depends heavily upon locating the student at a level within an organized sequence of objectives at which the student can readily attain a high level of success. The student may not initially experience high success during mastery or programmed instruction. However, high levels of student success will be attained rapidly and on a regular basis, because the student is placed at an appropriate objective level and is never allowed to proceed prematurely to an objective for which he or she is unprepared.

We know from a number of studies of classroom instruction and teacher planning that most teachers do not use an objective-based, mastery-oriented system. Instead they rely on textbooks, which often assume a "spiral" curriculum—practice a skill at intervals over a period of time and it will eventually click. That textbooks make this assumption can be inferred from the small number of practice items provided on any one skill at one point in time. Low achievers in particular are often cheated by this procedure. They encounter new concepts at a fast pace and seldom get to practice one thing until they can do it accurately or fluently. Teachers recognize this problem and talk hopefully of "exposure" that will eventually pay off. Or else they adapt the curriculum materials by rearranging them or supplementing them with practice pages from other sources.

One specific example from the area of reading deserves discussion. Students learning to read in school rarely have the opportunity to read the same passage more than once. Contrast this situation with that of a child at home. The child loves to hear the same story over and over, and to read it many times. In school, each story is typically read once. Opportunities to reread might be an important way to increase success rate. Samuels (1979) has experimented with repeated reading as an instructional procedure with remedial reading students. The central feature of this procedure is that a short, meaningful passage is read repeatedly until a satisfactory level of fluency is attained. Fluency is described in terms of accuracy and speed, with speed getting the greater emphasis during instruction. The underlying theory is that readers must attain automaticity before they can fully comprehend a passage, and they must comprehend before they can enjoy reading. Hence, repeated reading is used to attain speed, which leads to considerably greater comprehension, motivation, and pleasure. The value of repeated reading of text material in a regular classroom setting has also been demonstrated (Barnett & Filby, 1984). When low-ability first graders were given an opportunity to reread the stories in their preprimer, they gained in fluency and accuracy of oral reading. In addition to this kind of procedure, a number of materials lend themselves naturally to rereading, for instance, poems, songs, and plays.

The preceding discussion has emphasized the need for repeated practice on a given instructional objective so that mastery and fluency are obtained. The success-rate results suggest that this need exists in many classrooms for many students. It seems logical, however, that this practice could be overdone. Students need to move ahead through increasingly difficult material. Some research indicates that rapid pacing—moving through new concepts more quickly—is beneficial to learning (Barr, 1975). High achievers, in particular, can be held back if the amount of practice and pacing through objectives are geared to the needs of less bright classmates. But teachers may also underestimate what low-ability students can accomplish (Wang, 1981). This is an area where sensitive research is needed. How can teachers move ahead at a rapid pace while still maintaining adequate success rates?

Grouping

The preceding section discussed a difficult issue—how to place students at an appropriate instructional level and progress through the curriculum at a rate that allows maximum forward progress while maintaining high success rates. This issue is made even more complex by the fact that the teacher must accomplish this feat with 30 students simultaneously. The teacher must decide if the same material is appropriate for all students and if they can proceed at the same rate. If not, then the teacher must establish instructional subgroups. Thus, grouping and classroom organization become key mediators of success rate, attention, and learning (Barr & Dreeben, 1983; Filby, Barnett, & Bossert, 1983; Karweit, 1983).

It seems logical that grouping for instruction should increase the appropriateness of the instruction provided for students. The main reason teachers cite for using groups is to better meet individual needs. In particular, low achievers would be expected to have higher success rates under small-group instruction than under whole-class instruction. This pattern has been verified by Filby et al. (1983) and by Weinstein (1976). Low achievers in a whole-class setting may find themselves unable to read one-third of the words in their textbooks, whereas high achievers make only negligible errors. These differences are diminished, although not entirely eliminated, when students are placed in reading groups.

Such dramatic differences in success rate might constitute support for the use of instructional groups. Other factors, however, also need to be taken into account. Grouping introduces a more complex organizational structure that is more difficult to manage and may therefore lead to lower attention rates. Students in the low group may be particularly inattentive due to the social dynamics of the small reading group, as students pull each other off-task (Eder & Felmlee, 1984). Grouping may lead to lowered expectations, including slow-paced instruction, as discussed in the previous section. And grouping may detract from optimal instructional procedures and the use of coherent lesson sequences linking group presentation with independent practice. The influence of instructional procedures on success rate is discussed in the next section.

Instructional Procedures

Student success rate during instruction can also be influenced by the procedures and activities used to teach a particular skill to a particular group of children. One important area is that of providing directions to children about what they are to do. Observation in classrooms indicates that students spend over half their time working independently on written work (Fisher et al., 1978). To be successful in this independent work, students must understand both the substantive content and the format of what they are to do. For elementary school students, this understanding generally requires some direct instruction by the teacher. Direct instruction is especially important given the confusing nature of many workbooks and dittoes. The format changes from one page to the next and the directions may be more complicated than the task itself. In BTES, it was found that the more time students spent receiving directions from the teacher, the higher were their percentages of high-success performance. Whole-class instruction, as compared to using multiple small groups, may allow for more extensive and timely preparation for written work (Filby et al., 1983; Filby & Barnett, 1982b).

An additional aspect of instructional procedure was investigated in a small-scale experimental study of success rate (Marliave et al., 1981). In this study, the researchers taught reading to two small groups of second-grade students for an entire year and attempted to manipulate success rate in systematic ways. One manipulation involved different procedures for learning lists of spelling words. In the high-success condition, students copied the words; in the medium-success condition, they studied the words and then did practice dictation. The difference is in the type of activity students undertake. The results indicated that high success was more beneficial to learning but only when a further condition was also met. In one group, students copied the words more than three times in the high condition for every one that they wrote during the dictation practice. In the other group this same ratio was about two words to one. Greater learning took place for the group that copied the words more times. Apparently, the other group did not fully utilize the potential of the high-accuracy copying procedure for allowing rapid and numerous task responses during a constant period of time.

These recent results suggest the speculation that high-accuracy instruction obtains a positive effect on learning when it is used to facilitate a rapid pace of task responses. This type of instruction is to be distinguished from rapid pacing through curriculum objectives, in that the rapid pace of task responses during the high-accuracy copying treatments involved the same spelling objectives per unit of time as did the less rapid medium treatment. In fact, less rapid pacing through objectives may allow for more fast-response, high-success opportunities, as would be the case with rereading to increase reading fluency, discussed earlier. These new results suggest that slower pacing through objectives should be counterbalanced by increasing opportunities for rapid correct responding to maintain a sense of progress and accomplishment. It should also be noted that although high-accuracy conditions may enable students to produce more frequent task responses, increases in the rapidity of student response rates are not likely to result in increased accuracy of student responses.

In conclusion, we believe that these results on success rate indicate a direction for improvement in the instruction of many elementary school students, especially low achievers, that is, an increase in the provision of tasks providing high-success experiences. We acknowledge the need for further research to replicate and extend these results. Experimental studies are especially needed. These could eventually provide guidelines about desirable percentages of high success—how much is enough. Also, further work should look at the role of high success in learning tasks of different conceptual types and at different levels of initial difficulty for students of different ages. Finally, research is needed on alternative ways to increase success rate in the classroom and on the trade-offs that are involved. Optimal instructional levels, pacing through objectives, grouping, and instructional procedures all need to be considered. The role of high-success tasks in allowing more frequent responses should especially be considered.

REFERENCES

Atkinson, R. C., & Lorton, P., Jr., (1969). *Computer-based instruction in spelling: An investigation of optimal strategies for presenting instructional material.* Final Report, Project No. 8-1-026, Institute for Mathematical Studies in the Social Sciences, Stanford University, Stanford.

Barnett, B., & Filby, N. (1984, April). *Low-ability readers' exposure to instructional materials and oral reading performance.* Paper presented at the annual meeting of the American Educational Research Association, New Orleans.

Barnett, B., Filby, N., & Bossert, S. (1982). *Multiple instructional groups: A case study of an entire school.* Instructional Management Program, Far West Laboratory for Educational Research and Development, San Franciso.

Barr, R. (1975). How children are taught to read: Grouping and pacing. *School Review, 83,* 479–498.

Barr, R., & Dreeben, R. (1983). *How schools work.* Chicago: University of Chicago Press.

Becker, W. C. (1977). Teaching reading and language to the disadvantaged—What we have learned from field research. *Harvard Educational Review, 47,* 518–543.

Block, J. M. (1971). *Mastery learning: Theory and practice.* New York: Holt, Rinehart and Winston.

Bloom, B. S. (1976). *Human characteristics and school learning.* New York: McGraw-Hill.

Bossert, S. (1979). *Tasks and social relationships in classrooms.* New York: Cambridge University Press.

Brophy, J. E. (1979). Teacher behavior and its effects. *Journal of Educational Psychology, 71,* 733–750.

Bruner, J. S. (1964). The course of cognitive growth. *American Psychologist, 19,* 1–15.

Bruner, J. S., Goodnow, J. J., & Austin, G. A. (1956). *A study of thinking.* New York: Wiley.

Cooper, J. L. (1952). *The effect of adjustment of basal reading materials on reading achievement.* Unpublished doctoral dissertation, Boston University.

Crawford, J. W. (1978). Interactions of learner characteristics with the difficulty level of the instruction. *Journal of Educational Psychology, 70,* 523–531.

Crawford, J. W., King, C. E., Brophy, J. E., & Evertson, C. M. (1975, April). *Error rates and question difficulty related to elementary children's learning.* Paper presented at the annual meeting of the American Educational Research Association, Washington, D.C.

Eder, D., & Felmlee, D. (1984). The development of attention norms in ability groups. In P. Peterson, L. C. Wilkinson, & M. Hallinan (Eds.), *The social context of instruction: Group organization and group processes.* New York: Academic Press.

Filby, N., & Barnett, B. (1982a). Student perceptions of "better readers" in elementary classrooms. *Elementary School Journal, 82,* 435–449.

Filby, N., & Barnett, B. (December, 1982b). *Lesson plans and pacing for reading groups.* Paper presented at the annual meeting of the National Reading Conference, Clearwater Beach, Fla.

Filby, N., Barnett, B., & Bossert, S. (1983). *Grouping for reading instruction.* Instructional Management Program, Far West Laboratory for Educational

Research and Development, San Francisco.

Fisher, C., Filby, N., Marliave, R., Cahen, L., Dishaw, M., Moore, J., & Berliner, D. (1978). *Teaching behaviors, academic learning time, and student achievement*. Final report of Phase III-B, Beginning Teacher Evaluation Study. San Francisco: Far West Laboratory for Educational Research and Development. (ERIC Document Reproduction Service No. ED-183-525)

Harris, A. J. (1979). The effective teacher of reading, revisited. *The Reading Teacher, 33*, 135–140.

Inhelder, B., & Piaget, J. (1958). *The growth of logical thinking from childhood to adolescence*. New York: Basic Books.

Jorgenson, G. W. (1977). Relationship of classroom behavior to the accuracy of the match between material difficulty and student ability. *Journal of Educational Psychology, 69*, 24–32.

Jorgenson, G. W., Klein, N., & Kumar, V. K. (1977). Achievement and behavior correlates of matched levels of student ability and material difficulty. *Journal of Educational Research, 71*, 100–103.

Karweit, N. (1983). *Time-on-task: A research review*. Report No. 332, Center for Social Organization of Schools, Johns Hopkins University.

LaBerge, D., & Samuels, S. J. (1974). Toward a theory of automatic information processing in reading. *Cognitive Psychology, 6*, 293–323.

Marliave, R., Dishaw, M., & Fisher, C. (1981). *Studies on the effects of varying student accuracy rates during instruction*. Program on Teacher Development and Academic Learning Time, Far West Laboratory for Educational Research and Development, San Franciso.

Miller, R., & Hess, R. D. (1972). *The effect upon students' motivation of fit between student ability and the level of difficulty of CAI programs*. Research and Development Memorandum No. 84, Stanford Center for Research and Development in Teaching, Stanford.

O'Neil, H. F., Jr., Spielberger, C. D., & Hansen, D. N. (1969). Effects of state anxiety and task difficulty on computer-assisted learning. *Journal of Educational Psychology, 60*, 343–350.

Perfetti, C. A., & Hogaboam, T. (1975). The relationship between single word decoding and reading comprehension skill. *Journal of Educational Psychology, 67*, 461–469.

Samuels, S. J. (1979). The method of repeated reading. *The Reading Teacher, 32*, 403–408.

Schotanus, H. D. (1967). *The relationship between difficulty of reading material and attitude toward reading*. Technical Report No. 29, Wisonsin Research and Development Center for Cognitive Learning, Madison.

Skinner, B. F. (1954). The science of learning and the art of teaching. *Harvard Educational Review, 24*, 86–97.

Skinner, B. F. (1968). *The technology of teaching*. Englewood Cliffs, N.J.: Prentice-Hall.

Wang, M. (1981). Development and consequences of students' sense of personal control. In J. Levine & M. Wang (Eds.), *Teacher and student perceptions: Implications for learning*. Hillsdale, N.J.: Erlbaum.

Weinstein, R. (1976). Reading group membership in first grade: Teacher behaviors and pupil experience over time. *Journal of Educational Psychology, 68*(1), 103–116.

14

An Analysis of Program Design Implications for Teacher and Student Use of School Time

Margaret C. Wang
University of Pittsburgh

EDITORS' INTRODUCTION

This chapter describes a series of studies examining time use in the context of a specific instructional model—the Adaptive Learning Environments Model (ALEM). Five components make up the model: (1) prescriptive curriculum that is hierarchically formed, and supplementary open-ended learning activities; (2) management system; (3) family involvement; (4) multiage grouping and instructional teaming; and (5) staff development. Each of these characteristics is designed to (1) reduce the amount of time students need for learning; (2) increase the amount of time students have for learning, and/or (3) increase instructional (as opposed to managerial) activities of teachers and the engagement rates of students.

After presenting detailed descriptions of instructional processes and student activity in terms of time-based variables, Dr. Wang progresses systematically to explore the relationship between these variables and student-outcome variables. Evaluations of the ALEM showed that the program does result in high rates of student time-on-task, teacher-student interaction, and time spent on individual tasks. Dr. Wang provides a detailed analysis of time needed and time available for learning and traces the effects of these indices to student achievement. The analysis underscores the complexity of time-learning relationships.

The research reported herein was supported by the Learning Research and Development Center, supported in part as a research and development center by funds from the National Institute of Education (NIE), United States Department of Education. The opinions expressed do not necessarily reflect the position or policy of NIE, and no official endorsement should be inferred.

In the closing section of the chapter, an empirical analysis of teacher time use is presented. For continued productivity from the study of instructional time, the author calls for research on "time needed for learning," classroom management systems, and fine-grained microlevel studies of time use within specific classroom organizational structures.

The overall goal of this chapter is to discuss the design of, and selected findings from, a program of research aimed at providing a data base for the identification and analysis of ways in which school time is allocated and used by teachers and students to maximize learning for individual students. An underlying assumption is that the amount and effective use of school time can be increased through improvement of instructional design and program planning and implementation procedures. Specifically, the discussion in this chapter centers on three major topics. They are (1) the design of an educational program that includes features intended to reduce the amount of time needed by each student for learning while, at the same time, increasing the use of available school time by teachers and students for instruction and learning; (2) the major findings from a program of research designed to investigate the relations among program design, classroom processes, and students' academic achievement; and (3) the emerging questions and future research implications.

THE ADAPTIVE LEARNING ENVIRONMENTS MODEL

A major design objective of the Adaptive Learning Environments Model (ALEM) is to make optimal use of school resources, including student and teacher time, in order to provide the programming and classroom organizational supports required to maximize each student's learning through an adaptive instruction approach. Under the ALEM, effective use of school time is referred to as a reduction of the time needed by each student to learn and an increase in the time spent by each student on learning. School learning is seen as involving both "time needed" and "time spent" in a very dynamic way. The quantity and quality of time spent by students on learning generally are held to be the consequences of multiple factors. Among these factors are the amount of time to be spent on specific subject matter, based on state, local, and school requirements and the determination of teachers and other school personnel; teachers' competence in the management and provision of instruction; the design of the particular educational program or approach to be implemented (e.g., individualized or group-paced instruction); and each student's motivation and interest in the specific learning tasks. Thus, the contention is that different programs or instructional practices may not result in the same patterns of time use by teachers and students, and they can lead to quite different results.

The ALEM is an instructional program designed to provide experiences that accommodate the learning needs of individual students in regular classroom settings. Among the expected program outcomes are the provision of opportunities for students to acquire skills in academic subject areas through individually tailored and optimally paced progress plans, the development of students' competence in taking increased responsibility for managing their own learning behavior, and the fostering of a sense of social and cognitive competence and self-esteem. An underlying premise of the ALEM's design is that the teaching of basic skills need not be sacrificed to an emphasis on fostering students' involvement in making curricular choices and in planning and evaluating their own learning. Experience in implementation of the ALEM has shown that both sets of objectives can be achieved through systematic programming and close monitoring of program implemenation. As teachers become proficient in implementing the ALEM, they are expected to be able to spend greater amounts of time providing instruction than managing students (Wang, 1980; Wang & Walberg, 1983).

Essentially, the ALEM can be characterized as a product of the systematic integration of aspects of prescriptive instruction that have been shown to be effective in ensuring basic-skills mastery (Bloom, 1976; Glaser, 1977; Rosenshine, 1979) with aspects of informal education that are considered to be effective in generating attitudes and processes of inquiry, independence, and social cooperation (Johnson, Maruyama, Johnson, Nelson, & Skon, 1981; Marshall, 1981; Peterson, 1979; Wang & Stiles, 1976). Although basic-skills acquisition, as well as social and attitudinal growth, is emphasized in the design of the ALEM, this chapter focuses only on the relationships among program implementation, classroom processes, use of class time by teachers and students, and students' academic achievement.

Figure 14.1 is an illustration of a conceptual model of the hypothesized relationships among the implementation of critical dimensions of adaptive instruction programs, classroom processes, use of class time by teachers and students, and academic achievement. As suggested by the model, effective implementation of adaptive instruction programs in classroom settings requires the presence of two categories of critical dimensions: dimensions related to the provision of adaptive instruction, and dimensions related to classroom-level support for program implementation. It is hypothesized that inclusion of all these critical program dimensions results in classroom processes that (a) permit teachers to spend more time on instruction, (b) help students to make better use of their learning time, and (c) produce improved student achievement.

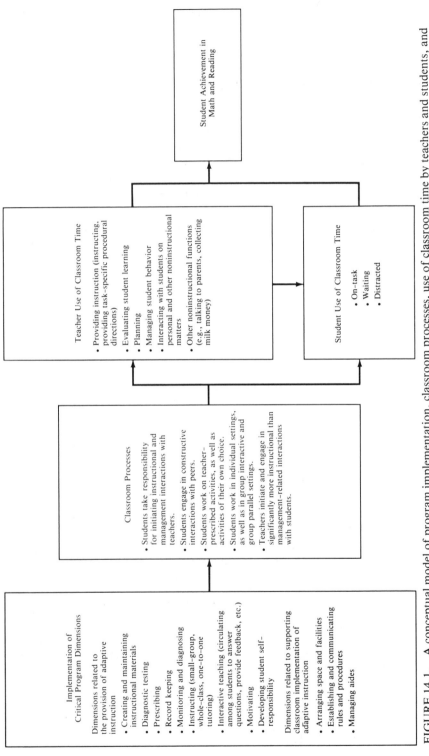

FIGURE 14.1. A conceptual model of program implementation, classroom processes, use of classroom time by teachers and students, and student achievement.

When the critical dimensions of adaptive instruction, as incorporated into the design of the ALEM, are in place, a unique classroom scenario emerges. Students are observed to work in virtually every area of the room at any given time, with the teacher working among them either on an individual basis or in small groups. Academic skills are taught directly, based on diagnostic test results, and each student is perceived by the teacher to be capable of learning. If individual learning problems occur, they are viewed not as the student's failure, but rather as a signal to the teacher to try other instructional alternatives. Because learning tasks are broken down into small steps, there are frequent opportunities for evaluation, so that many small successes can be recognized and acknowledged and momentary difficulties can be pinpointed before they become learning problems. Using a classroom management system known as the Self-Schedule System (Wang, 1974), students are taught to plan their own schedules, and they are expected to take responsibility for completing all their tasks, both teacher-assigned and student-selected, within the time limits jointly agreed upon with the teacher (e.g., one hour, half a day, one day, one week). Students are expected to be able to manage their school time effectively in order to complete all the tasks assigned by the teacher in the various prescriptive learning curricula as well as a number of exploratory learning activities of their own choosing.

It is hypothesized that, in such environments, major changes in classroom processes and student learning outcomes can be expected. A high rate of on-task behavior will be exhibited. The time needed by students to learn will be reduced, and the time teachers spend on instruction will increase. Finally, students will spend the time they need to learn, resulting in increased rates of basic-skills acquisition and, subsequently, higher achievement scores in math and reading.

SUMMARY OF MAJOR FINDINGS

In this section, major findings are summarized from selected studies included in a program of research that has been conducted in classrooms where the ALEM is implemented. Discussion of the findings focuses on ways in which the ALEM affected the amount of time students needed for learning, as well as the nature and patterns of time spent by teachers and students on instruction and learning.

Classroom Processes under the ALEM

A series of observation studies designed to document classroom processes under the ALEM was carried out over several years in a number of different school sites. Information was gathered on how teachers and students spent their time and on the nature and patterns of the classroom processes in classrooms where critical features of the ALEM were implemented (Wang, 1979; Wang & Brictson, 1973; Wang & Richardson, 1977; Wang & Stiles, 1976; Wang & Weisstein (1980).

The Student Behavior Observation Schedule (SBOS) (Wang, 1976), designed for systematic observations of students' classroom behaviors and instructional-learning processes, was used in all of the studies. The results of the observations are summarized in Table 14.1. As shown in the table, the absolute figures for any given classroom-process variable varied from study to study, but the overall pattern of results was quite consistent. The results show that student-teacher interactions under the program tended to be for instructional (median = 81%; range = 50% – 100%) rather than management (median = 18%; range = 0% – 33%) purposes. Students tended to interact with one another for constructive purposes most of the time (median = 100%; range = 86% – 100%), and there were very few discipline problems (overall, less than 2% disruptive interactions among students). The percentage of students' observed on-task time was relatively high (median = 82%; range = 70% – 94%), when compared to the statistics from other classroom-process studies (e.g., Fisher, Berliner, Filby, Marliave, Cahen, Dishaw & Moore, 1978). Contrary to the findings from studies of other individualized programs, students in the ALEM classrooms generally spent much less time waiting for teacher help (median = 6%; range = 1% – 16%). While "waiting for help" and "time-off-task" frequently have been cited as management problems for many individualized instruction programs (Bennett, 1976; McPartland & Epstein, 1975; Wang & Yeager, 1971), these behaviors did not seem to be problematic in the ALEM classrooms.

To summarize, results from a series of classroom observation studies conducted in a variety of ALEM classroom settings suggest the presence of classroom processes that are likely to have strong mediating effects on minimizing the time students need to learn and maximizing students' use of school time for learning. The most notable of such classroom-process outcomes are significantly more teacher-student interactions for instructional purposes (rather than management purposes) and high rates of on-task behavior.

An Investigation of Students' Use of School Time and the Effects of Their Learning

The study described in this section gathered detailed information on the patterns and manner in which individual students used their time in an ALEM classroom. Students were responsible on a daily basis for allocating and spending the time they needed to correctly complete all of their teacher-assigned and student-selected learning tasks (Wang, Kaufman, & Lesgold, 1982).

TABLE 14.1. Summary of Data on Classroom Processes Under the ALEM

Mean percentage of observed frequencies reported

Variable	Wang & Bricson 1973	Wang & Stiles 1976 (Experimental)		Wang & Richardson 1977						Wang & Weisstein 1980	Wang 1979				Median of means across studies
		Period 1	Period 2	Class S	Class D	Class E	Class G	Class L	Class J		Class A	Class B	Class C	Class D	
Manner in which activities were carried out															
On task	81	82	84	81	89	90	82	94	74	70	78	90	81	93	82
Waiting for teacher help	08	06	06	12	09	07	04	01	16	07	01	01	01	01	06
Distracted	13	10	10	07	01	03	14	03	10	24	20	08	18	05	10
Activity type															
Prescriptive	66	80	69	80	65	80	66	75	59	74	73	85	77	87	74
Exploratory	31	19	31	19	35	20	34	24	41	15	09	12	08	11	20
Other	02	01	00	00	00	00	00	00	00	11	18	03	15	02	01
Setting in which students worked															
Group interactive	09	08	04	07	15	08	16	08	21	19	17	22	15	15	16
Group parallel	15	03	03	00	00	04	00	03	00	03	39	44	31	49	03
Individual	76	87	93	92	85	88	84	87	79	78	44	33	53	36	82
Interactions with teachers initiated by															
Student	60	a	a	20	10	40	23	50	54	63	60	50	75	33	50
Teacher	40	a	a	40	20	20	31	50	31	18	40	50	25	66	32
Unknown	00	a	a	40	70	40	46	00	15	18	00	00	00	00	00
Purpose of interaction															
Instructional	50	90	71	87	100	83	92	100	93	64	80	80	66	75	81
Management	18	10	29	13	00	17	08	00	07	27	20	20	33	25	18
Other	32	00	00	00	00	00	00	00	00	09	00	00	00	00	00
Interactions with peers															
Constructive	96	a	a	100	100	100	100	100	94	96	86	100	100	100	100
Disruptive	04	a	a	00	00	00	00	00	06	04	14	00	00	00	00

[a] Information was not collected.

The setting for the study was the demonstration classroom of a university laboratory school. Forty-two students, ranging in age from five to eight years, were enrolled in this multiage, primary classroom. Detailed classroom data were collected through use of a computerized data management system (Wang & Fitzhugh, 1977). This system, known as the Classroom Information System (CIS), was used by teachers in the demonstration classroom to record their daily prescriptions of each student's assigned learning tasks and daily learning progress. Students used the CIS to obtain information about their assigned tasks and their learning choices. Among its other functions, the CIS provides a means of monitoring the assignment and correct completion of learning tasks, including the amount of time required to complete individual tasks.

Several indices were developed to document the amount of time students in the study needed to learn and the amount of time they actually spent on learning. The indices, which incorporated information on the patterns of students' learning progress (CIS), student achievement in the basic skills (Metropolitan Achievement Test), and selected classroom-process variables related to the manner in which time was spent by students (SBOS), are listed in Table 14.2.

Two categories of time-needed variables were indentified: rate of task completion (refers to the amount of time students needed to correctly complete teacher-prescribed learning tasks and/or student-selected exploratory tasks); and rate of mastery (refers to the amount of time students needed to master skills included in the ALEM's basic-skills curricula, based on diagnostic test results). In addition, Table 14.2 lists four indices that were identified to describe how students in the study spent their time. They include allocated time, time-on-task, waiting time, and distracted time. It should be pointed out here that the index of allocated time has unique implications in the context of the ALEM. Operating under the program's Self-Schedule System, students are responsible for determining the amount of time they will spend on given learning tasks. Therefore, not only does the allocated time for learning differ from student to student, but the actual amount of time allocated for given learning tasks is determined largely by each student, with teacher guidance as needed. Data on allocated time were based on the amount of time designated by each student for math tasks only. However, the measures of the other three time-spent variables (on-task, waiting, distracted) consisted of data from systematic time sampling of the classroom behaviors of students as they worked on various teacher-assigned and/or student-selected tasks. No specific time schedule is designated under the ALEM for working in particular subject areas, and students make decisions about the amount of allocated time and the designation of a specific time for working on a particular task. Therefore, in essence, these indices are general measures of the manner in which time is spent by students across a variety of tasks, including math tasks.

TABLE 14.2. Indices of the Time-Needed and Time-Spent Variables

Variables	Indices
Time needed: Amount of time students needed to learn	
Rate of task completion (T)	$\text{Rate } T_1 = \dfrac{\text{number of tasks completed correctly}}{\text{minutes spent completing the tasks}}$
	$\text{Rate } T_2 = \dfrac{\text{number of tasks completed correctly}}{\text{days in school}}$
	$\text{Rate } T_3 = \dfrac{\text{minutes spent completing the tasks}}{\text{number of tasks completed correctly}}$
Rate of mastery (M)	$\text{Rate } M_1 = \dfrac{\text{number of skills mastered}}{\text{minutes spent mastering the skills}}$
	$\text{Rate } M_2 = \dfrac{\text{number of skills mastered}}{\text{days in school}}$
	$\text{Rate } M_3 = \dfrac{\text{minutes spent mastering the skills}}{\text{number of skills mastered}}$
Time spent: Amount of time students spent on learning	
Allocated time	
Time students chose to spend working in a given subject area (e.g., math)	Total minutes spent in a given subject area per day
Time-on-task	Percentage of time students were observed to be on-task
Waiting time	Percentage of time students were observed to be waiting for teacher help
Distracted time	Percentage of time students were observed to be distracted or off-task

The data to be presented here are for 22 of the 42 children who were enrolled in the demonstration classroom during the 1979–1980 school year (two 5-year-olds, five 6-year-olds, nine 7-year-olds, and six 8-year-olds). These were children who were able to use the computerized data management system with high reliability. Students in this class were introduced to the use of computers after reaching a prerequisite level in the ALEM's beginning reading curriculum. The remaining 20 students were excluded from the study only because of the unavailability of computerized time-allocated and time-spent data. Except for computer usage, the two groups of students (those who were included in the time study and those who were not included) shared the same classroom resources and used the same program. No differences were found either in the task-completion rates or in the classroom-process measures for the two groups.

Although the limitations of the study's small and select sample are recognized, the results are presented here to illustrate the type of intensive studies and microlevel analyses that are needed to gain a better understanding of the relationship between time use and learning. The CIS and classroom-observation data were analyzed to determine the time needed by students for learning and the time spent on learning, as well as to investigate the relationship between both kinds of time and the students' learning processes and outcomes. Also analyzed were the relationship between the time students spent on their learning and the observed classroom processes and the relationship between student achievement and selected time-related measures.

Time Needed for Learning.   Table 14.3 summarizes the results of the analysis of the data on the time the students needed to correctly complete their assigned math tasks and the time they needed to master the skills included in the math curriculum. Students in the study averaged about 0.04 tasks per minute of time they has allocated for math each day (rate T_1). They correctly completed an average of 0.95 of the assigned tasks for each day they attended school (rate T_2), and the average time they needed to complete a math task correctly was about 28 minutes (rate T_3). In terms of their rate of mastery in the math curriculum, the data show that the students, on the average, mastered 0.01 skill in the allocated math time per minute (rate M_1). They mastered, on the average, 0.58 skills during each day they attended school (rate M_2), and they took an average of 89.61 minutes to master a skill (rate M_3).

Relationship between Time Needed Time Spent.   The results from a series of correlation analyses between the time-needed and time-spent measures and the resulting learning outcomes are reported in Table 14.4. Overall, the data suggest that although the total amount of time allocated for math learning did not seem to be significantly correlated with any of the time-

TABLE 14.3. Summary of Data on Time Needed[a] (*N*-22)

Variables	Mean	S.D.
Rate of task completion		
Rate $T_1 = \dfrac{\text{number of tasks completed correctly}}{\text{minutes spent completing the tasks}}$	0.04	0.01
Rate $T_2 = \dfrac{\text{number of tasks completed correctly}}{\text{days in school}}$	0.95	0.24
Rate $T_3 = \dfrac{\text{minutes spent completing the tasks}}{\text{number of tasks completed correctly}}$	28.02	7.32
Rate of learning		
Rate $M_1 = \dfrac{\text{number of skills mastered}}{\text{minutes spent mastering the skills}}$	0.01	0.05
Rate $M_2 = \dfrac{\text{number of skills mastered}}{\text{days in school}}$	0.58	0.24
Rate $M_3 = \dfrac{\text{minutes spent mastering the skills}}{\text{number of skills mastered}}$	89.61	37.30

[a] Data are reported on students' learning progress in the math curriculum from February through mid-June 1980.

needed measures, except for rate T_2 (the number of math tasks completed each day the students attended school), some interesting patterns of significant correlations were noted between the time-needed measures and the three measures associated with the manner in which the allocated time was spent (on-task, waiting, or distracted). Both the on-task and the distracted variables, for example, correlated significantly with rate measures that included in the indices the number of minutes spent completing the math tasks. Furthermore, significant negative correlations were found between the amount of time students needed to complete a task correctly (T_3) and students' observed on-task behavior, and between the amount of time students needed to master a skill and students' observed on-task behavior. This finding supports two of the study's hypotheses: The more frequently students are observed to be on-task, the less time that is needed to complete a task or achieve mastery of a skill; and the more distracted students are observed to be, the more time they need to complete a task or achieve mastery of a skill.

The time-needed measures also were found to be highly correlated with all of the learning-outcome measures (student achievement as measured by standardized achievement tests, the total number of tasks completed, and the total number of skills mastered), with only one exception—the correlation between rate T_1, the average number of minutes required to complete a task correctly, and scores on standardized achievement tests.

TABLE 14.4. Correlation Coefficients for the Time-Needed, Time-Spent, and Learning-Outcome Variables ($N = 22$)

Time needed	Time spent				Learning outcomes		
	Allocated minutes	% On-Task	% Waiting	% Distracted	Achievement level (percentile rank)	Total tasks completed	Total skills mastered
Rate of task completion							
Rate T_1 = $\dfrac{\text{number of task completed correctly}}{\text{minutes spent completing the tasks}}$	$-.23$	$.46^b$	$-.15$	$-.42^a$	$.29$	$.77^b$	$.59^b$
Rate T_2 = $\dfrac{\text{number of tasks completed correctly}}{\text{days in school}}$	$.42^a$	$.30$	$.05$	$.32$	$.65^b$	$.99^b$	$.82^b$
Rate T_3 = $\dfrac{\text{minutes spent completing the tasks}}{\text{number of tasks completed correctly}}$	$.16$	$.41^a$	$.20$	$.35^a$	$-.36^a$	$-.80^a$	$-.62^b$
Rate of mastery							
Rate M_1 = $\dfrac{\text{number of skills mastered}}{\text{minutes spent mastering the skills}}$	$-.09$	$.40^a$	$-.17$	$-.35^a$	$.52^b$	$.68^b$	$.87^b$
Rate M_2 = $\dfrac{\text{number of skills mastered}}{\text{days in school}}$	$.07$	$.25$	$.15$	$-.31$	$.55^b$	$.47^b$	$.58^b$
Rate M_3 = $\dfrac{\text{minutes spent mastering the skills}}{\text{number of skills mastered}}$	$.007$	$-.38^a$	$.11$	$.34^a$	$-.59^b$	$-.62^b$	$.86^b$

[a] $p < .05$.
[b] $p < .01$.

Thus, in general, the results of this study suggest that (a) allocated time did not seem to be related to student learning-outcome variables in any significant ways, (b) the amount of time students needed for learning was related to the manner in which they spent their learning time, and (c) the amount of time needed for learning was related to learning outcomes.

Relationship between Time Spent on Learning and Classroom Processes.
To further investigate the relationship between the manner in which learning time was spent and other classroom processes under the ALEM, the intercorrelations among all the classroom-process-related variables were examined. As reported in Table 14.5, the data suggest that the types of tasks and settings in which the students worked were highly related to observed on-task behavior. However, the nature and patterns of teacher interactions did not seem to be highly related to the manner in which students spent their learning time. It is interesting that, consistent with the findings in the effective classroom research literature, differences in on-task rates across varying types of instructional settings were noted. Students were more likely to be on-task when they worked in either group-interactive or group-parallel settings, whereas distractions were observed to be associated with students working in individual settings.

Some interesting patterns of interrelationship are suggested by the data on the nature of the learning tasks, the instructional setting, and the manner in which school time was spent. For example, a significant correlation was observed between individual settings and prescriptive tasks, suggesting that when students worked in individual settings, they tended to work on the tasks that were prescribed by teachers. However, the data also indicate that the time students spent working on prescriptive tasks was negatively associated with the observed on-task behavior. In addition, the data suggest that students were less likely to be distracted when they worked in group-interactive settings, and they tended to work on exploratory tasks of their own choosing in such settings. Although students tended to be more on-task when they worked in group-interactive settings, the management interactions between teachers and students occurred more often in such settings, particularly when students worked on exploratory tasks.

These findings, some of which seem to suggest a number of classroom-process patterns that are inconsistent with the study's hypotheses, pose several important instructional design questions for further study. Future investigations, for example, might focus on (a) why teachers interact more with students on management matters when they work on exploratory tasks, even though students appear to be more on-task in such situations and more distracted when working on prescriptive tasks; (b) whether or not teachers' management interactions with students lead to higher on-task rates, as the correlation between management interactions and exploratory learning tasks in the case of this study seem to suggest; and (c) whether or not the nature of the learning task dictates the type of interactions teachers

TABLE 14.5. Intercorrelations Among Classroom-Process Variables and Time-Spent Variables ($N = 22$ students)

Variables	Classroom-process variables					Types of activities on which students worked		Time-spent variables		
	Interactions between teachers and students		Settings in which learning activities occurred					Manner in which learning time was spent		
	Instructional	Management	Group interactive	Group parallel	Individual	Prescriptive tasks	Exploratory tasks	On-task	Waiting	Distracted
Types of interactions										
Instructional	1.00									
Management	−.10	1.00								
Settings										
Group interactive	−.13	.46[a]	1.00							
Group parallel	−.09	.35[a]	.14	1.00						
Individual	.15	−.53[b]	−.73[b]	−.77[b]	1.00					
Activity types										
Prescriptive tasks	.22	−.50[b]	−.60[b]	−.72[b]	.88[b]	1.00				
Exploratory tasks	−.29	.52[b]	.71[b]	.23	−.61[b]	−.73[b]	1.00			
Manner										
On-task	.10	.21	.43[b]	.41[a]	−.53[b]	−.43[a]	−.73[b]	1.00		
Waiting	−.12	−.16	−.23	−.19	.28	.25	−.21	−.19	1.00	
Distracted	−.06	−.16	−.35[a]	−.35[b]	.47[b]	.35	−.22	−.95[b]	−.13	1.00

[a] $p \leq .05$.
[b] $p \leq .01$.

have with students, that is, whether or not students require management-related attention when working on exploratory tasks and instruction-related interactions when working on prescriptive tasks.

Relationship between Student Achievement in Math and Selected Time-Related Measures. A series of multiple-correlation analyses was conducted using the students' end-of-year achievement test scores and selected sets of the time-related measures used in the study to investigate the extent to which student achievement was affected by variables associated with the time-needed and time-spent features included in the design of the ALEM. Table 14.6 provides a summary of the math results. The data suggest that the students' end-of-year achievement in math was significantly related to both the time needed to learn (the measures for the rate of task completion and the rate of mastery in basic skills) and the number of tasks and skills mastered in the total amount of time spent on-task. However, student achievement did not seem to be related to the manner in which time was spent by students. This finding is quite puzzling on the surface, particularly because it is inconsistent with findings from a number of widely cited studies (e.g., Bloom, 1974, 1976; Fisher et al., 1978; Good & Beckerman, 1978; Stallings & Kaskowitz, 1974). It may be speculated that the low correlation between student achievement and the manner in which students spent their learning time was the result of a number of factors, including the quality of the tasks on which students worked, the particular classroom-process patterns, and the consistent patterns of comparatively high on-task rates that were found in the ALEM classrooms (see Table 14.1). In the latter case, the low correlation may have resulted from the low variance in the on-task measures.

Finally, results from the last multiple R analysis summarized in Table 14.6 suggest that the students' end-of-year math achievement was significantly correlated with the amount of math work they completed each day, the progress they made in the math curriculum, the amount of time spent on-task, and the amount of time spent acquiring mastery of math skills. These results have two important implications: The time students spent completing their assigned tasks and learning what they were expected to learn in the math curriculum led to achievement in math; and the completion of prescribed math tasks and the progress made in the math curriculum also led to student achievement in math.

The types of information obtained from this study seem to have particularly important implications for further in-depth analyses of the linkage between the design of educational intervention programs and resulting classroom processes and outcomes. These kinds of analyses could greatly facilitate program refinement efforts such as the identification of workable patterns for maximizing the availability and use of school time for optimal learning and instruction. The intercorrelation patterns among the rate measures (indices of time needed for learning), the classroom-process

TABLE 14.6. Summary of Results of Multiple-Correlation Analyses of Standardized Achievement Test Scores in Math and Time-Needed, Time-Spent, and Other Achievement-Related Variables ($N = 22$ students)

Variables/Indices	Multiple R	R^2	r
Time needed	$.71^a$	.51	
Rate of task completion			
Rate $T_1 = \dfrac{\text{number of tasks completed correctly}}{\text{minutes spent completing the tasks}}$			.29
Rate $T_2 = \dfrac{\text{number of tasks completed correctly}}{\text{days in school}}$			$.65^a$
Rate $T_3 = \dfrac{\text{minutes spent completing the tasks}}{\text{number of tasks completed correctly}}$			$-.36$
Rate of mastery	$.69^a$	.48	
Rate $M_1 = \dfrac{\text{number of skills mastered}}{\text{minutes spent mastering the skills}}$			$.52^a$
Rate $M_2 = \dfrac{\text{number of skills mastered}}{\text{days in school}}$			$.55^a$
Rate $M_3 = \dfrac{\text{minutes spent mastering the skills}}{\text{number of skills mastered}}$			$-.59^a$
Time spent			
Manner in which time was spent	.34	.11	
On-task			.05
Waiting			.32
Distracted			$-.15$
Other achievement-related variables	$.78^a$	.62	
Total number of tasks completed			$.62^a$
Total number of skills mastered			$.72^a$
Total minutes spent completing tasks per day			$.72^b$
Total minutes spent mastering skills			$.51^b$

$^a p \le .01.$
$^b p \le .05.$

outcomes (indices of the patterns and manner in which students spent their school time), and the resulting learning outcomes have raised several critical instructional design questions.

One such question has to do with "pacing," a topic that has received increased attention in research on teaching (e.g., Arlin & Westbury, 1976; Barr, 1975; Dahlöff, 1971; Good, Grouws, & Beckerman, 1978). Too little emphasis has been placed, however, on providing information on the consequences of pacing for student achievement. Such information would be of great practical use to teachers in their instructional planning. Many of the difficulties teachers face in implementing instructional programs aimed at adapting to student differences are due to the lack of guidelines or baseline information on the time needed for learning. In order to adequately provide adaptive instruction, teachers need information on how fast a given rate of learning must be if it is to be challenging enough for a particular student, as well as information on "how slow is too slow." If the type of student rate-of-learning data reported for this study were collected with an adequate sample size over time, it could lead to the development of a much-needed normative data base for guiding instructional planning. For example, individual student rates of learning can serve as reference points or general guidelines for teachers as they make pacing decisions. Such normative data could be used to formulate statements such as, "All 7-year-olds who work in this particular unit take an average of 7 hours to master the skills in the unit, the range being 3 to 15 hours," and, "Students with end-of-year achievement scores at or above the eightieth percentile take an average of 4 hours to complete this unit, the range being 1 to 7 hours."

The rate data also can be analyzed from the diagnostic perspective. The data can be used to produce student histories of progress across different levels and in different subject areas. Individual students' learning trajectories can be calculated for the same types of skills (e.g., reading comprehension tasks, division tasks) over a period of time or for different subject areas. Individual students' rates of learning provide useful information for teachers as they make instructional decisions related to specific sets of learning tasks for individual students or groups of students. In addition, the student rate-of-learning data provide critical information for improving program design and program implementation. For example, a consistently slow rate of learning in a given instructional unit across settings (classrooms) may be a signal of a curriculum-related problem. Similary, a generally faster rate of learning for all students from a given class or in a specific area may indicate good implementation.

The kinds of data on classroom interaction patterns collected in this study also raise a number of further research questions. For example, although the close relationship between time-on-task and individual settings is suggested by these findings and those of others (e.g., Brophy, 1979; Rosenshine, 1980), in-depth analyses of this relationship are needed. Informal observations of classroom interactions and further examination of the observation procedures used in this study seem to suggest that the correlations between on-task behavior and instructional settings might only partly reflect the nature of the learning tasks and the settings in which students worked. The correlation results between students' on-task behaviors and group settings may be partly confounded by the way the observations were coded. For example, spontaneous conversations among students while working on individual art tasks in a parallel group setting were considered an on-task behavior as long as the students were not distracted from the task at hand, that is, as long as they continued their cutting or painting.

Another related issue has to do with the implications of findings from this type of correlation study for program development. The recent attention paid by practitioners and researchers to findings relating on-task behavior and instructional setting is a case in point. Results from correlation studies of time use and student learning have suggested, for example, that students' time-on-task can be increased by increasing the amount of time spent in group learning situations (e.g., Brophy, 1979; Rosenshine, 1980). However, there is little information from this type of analysis that can be (or should be) used to specify prescriptions for effective ways to reduce the amount of time students need to learn. Investigations of the nature of learning tasks and the functions of individual and group instruction in providing optimal learning conditions need to concentrate more on the complexities of the student and task/learning environment variables and the ways in which these variables can be manipulated to significantly reduce the amount of time students need to learn.

Intensive study of the distracted behavior of students working in individual settings is yet another area of research that could provide further insights on the relationship between time-on-task and instructional setting. For example, studies in this area could enhance current understanding of the nature and patterns of students' distracted behavior and the extent to which such behavior is system-imposed, teacher-specific, or task-specific. Similarly, studies focusing on the nature and pattern of teachers' feedback behavior and interactive decision making might provide insights on the relationship between teachers' interactions with students and reductions that occur in the amount of time needed by students for learning and/or increases in students' motivation to spend the time needed for learning.

An Investigation of Teacher-Time Use

Discussion in this section is based on findings from a descriptive study designed to investigate the patterns of teacher-time use in class-room learning environments where a major program design focus is to make instructional provisions for individual differences in students. The study was conducted in 28 classrooms where the ALEM was implemented as a mainstreaming program for mildly handicapped and academically gifted students during the 1981–1982 school year.

Teacher behaviors over an entire school day were recorded using the Teacher Behavior Record form (Wang, Strom, & Hechtman, 1981). Based on a preplanned, time-sampling system, whereby observers recorded their observations of teachers' classroom behavior at the end of every minute, a total of 11,806 one-minute observations (approximately 197 hours) of teachers' classroom activities were recorded across all the classrooms included in the study. The mean number of minutes of mean observation time for each of the 28 teachers was 199.3. The mean interobserver agreement was found to be 83.3%, with a range of 71.8%–88.4%. The intercoder agreement was 87.5%. The data were analyzed to examine the overall patterns of time use by teachers, as well as the extent to which teacher-time use differed according to the instructional grouping of students and students' academic achievement characteristics.

Overall Patterns of the Distribution of Teacher Time. Results from the examination of the percentages of time that teachers spent on various instructional and noninstructional functions are summarized in Figure 14.2.

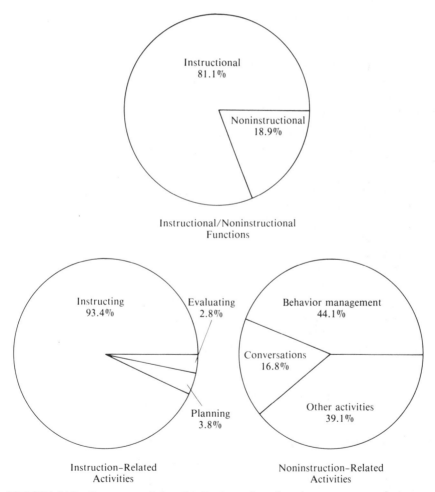

FIGURE 14.2 Summary of the distribution of teacher-time use among instructional and noninstructional functions. (*N* = 28 classrooms; the mean number of observation minutes per teacher was 199.3.)

As shown in the pie chart (at the top of the figure), the teachers were observed to spend approximately 81.1% of their time on instruction-related activities and 18.9% of their time on noninstruction-related activities. Of the time spent on instruction-related activities (the pie chart at the lower left of the figure), 93.4% was spent providing instruction to individual students in small-group or whole-class settings and giving task-specific, procedural directions (e.g., going over workbook directions, explaining how to get reference materials for specific learning tasks); 3.8% was spent on planning (e.g., prescribing learning task, keeping records); and 2.8% was spent on evaluating student work. Finally, 18.9% of the teachers' time was spent on noninstructional functions. Of this time, 44.1% was spent on behavior management, 16.8% on personal conversations with students, and 39.1% on other noninstruction-related activities.

Teacher-Time Use in Different Instructional Groupings. To investigate the extent to which the amounts of teacher time spent on different instructional functions varied according to the instructional grouping of students, the percentages of teacher time spent on various instruction-related and noninstruction-related tasks with individual students, in small-group instructional settings, and in whole-class instructional situations were examined. Results from the analysis are summarized in Table 14.7.

Some interesting differences in the patterns of time use are suggested by the data on the percentages of time that teachers spent on the various functions across the three instructional groupings. The ratios reported in Table 14.7 are based on 79.7% of the teachers' total class time. This is the total amount of time teachers spent with individual students, in small-group settings, and in whole-class situations for the six instruction-related and noninstruction-related functions listed in the table. A larger proportion of the teachers' time spent working in small-group settings was expended on instructing (78.1% versus 3.2% total time spent on the behavior-management function), compared to the distributions of teacher time in individual and whole-class groupings. In the latter whole-class situations, teachers were observed to spend more time on behavior-management functions (18.8%). As expected, teachers spent time checking work (4.7%), prescribing (2.8%), and conversing with students for personal reasons (3%) only when working with individual students.

Teacher-Time Use and Students' Academic Characteristics. A major interest in the analysis of teacher-time use under adaptive instruction programs is the extent to which teachers differentiate the nature and amount of instruction provided to students with varying academic learning needs. Results from an analysis of the amount and purpose of teacher

TABLE 14.7.   Percentages of Teacher-time Spent on Specific Functions During Interactions with Students in Different Instructional Groupings

Teacher function	Instructional grouping		
	Individual (76.56)	Small group (5.17)	Whole class (18.27)
Instructing	57.2	78.1	61.3
Giving task-specific procedural directions	29.4	18.7	19.9
Behavior management	3.1	3.2	18.8
Checking work	4.7	0	0
Prescribing	2.8	0	0
Conversations with students for personal reasons	3.0	0	0

time spent with students with different achievement characteristics are summarized in Table 14.8. As shown in the table, there was very little difference in the total percentages of teacher time (instructional and noninstructional) spent with general education, mainstreamed handicapped, and academically gifted students. On the average, teachers spent 3.6% of their time with each general education student, 3.5% with each handicapped student, and 3.4% with each academically gifted student.

Some variations were noted, however, in the time teachers spent performing specific instructional and noninstructional functions with the three different types of students. For example, the teachers seemed to spend only slightly different percentages of time instructing the three types of students (3.6% per general education student, 3.2% per handicapped student, 3.4% per academically gifted student). At the same time, when the per-student percentages of time spent on instructing were compared with the time spent giving task-specific procedural directions, major differences were noted. The teachers were observed to spend proportionately greater amounts of time giving task-specific procedural directions to the academically gifted students (5.7% per student), compared to the time spent instructing these same students (3.4% per student). By contrast, there was little difference between the time spent on instructing the general education and handicapped students and the time spent on giving task-specific procedural directions to these two groups of students (general education

TABLE 14.8.   Mean Percentages of Teacher-time Spent with Individual General Education, Handicapped, and Academically Gifted Students on Instructional and Noninstructional Functions

Teacher functions	Mean percentages of teacher time per student		
	General education students (N = 672)	Handicapped students (N = 77)	Academically gifted students (N = 35)
Instructional			
Instruction			
Instructing	3.6	3.2	3.4
Giving task-specific procedural directions	3.6	3.3	5.7
Planning	2.2	4.8	1.8
Evaluation	2.6	2.4	1.4
Noninstructional			
Behavior management	2.5	3.1	2.4
Conversations with students (for personal and other non-instructional purposes)	3.6	.8	4.4
Total per-student time across functions	3.6	3.5	3.4

students—3.6% on instructing, 3.6% on giving task-specific procedural directions; handicapped students—3.2% on instructing, 3.3% on giving task-specific procedural directions).

Differences also were noted in the patterns of teacher time spent with individual students for planning and evaluating their learning. Teachers tended to spend more time with the handicapped students (4.8% per student) on planning activities (e.g., prescribing tasks, keeping records) than with the academically gifted (1.8% per student) or general education students (2.2% per student). In addition, more time was spent evaluating the work of the general education and handicapped students (2.6% and 2.4% per student, respectively), compared to the amount of time spent evaluating the work of gifted students (1.4% per student).

Results from this study suggest several major findings. On the average, teachers in the ALEM classrooms spent comparatively large percentages of their time on instructional functions and considerably smaller percentages of time on noninstructional functions. Of the time spent on noninstructional purposes, less than half was for behavior management purposes. Furthermore, teachers' use of class time was found to be related to the nature of instructional groupings and to the achievement characteristics of individual students.

EMERGING QUESTIONS AND
DIRECTIONS FOR FUTURE RESEARCH

The studies described in this chapter were part of an ongoing program of research aimed at furthering understanding of the "basics" involved in the design of educational programs that are adaptive to student differences. A major emphasis of this work has been the development of programming strategies that effectively reduce the amount of time needed by individual students for learning, while increasing the amount of time teachers are able to spend on instructional functions and increasing the amount of time students actually spend on appropriate learning tasks.

The findings seem to be unique, when viewed against the rather low relationship between time use and student achievement that has been reported in several recent studies cited in a review article by Karweit (1983). It is hypothesized that the apparently stronger correlation between these two variables observed in the studies described in this chapter may be due to the fact that differential patterns of time use were adopted by teachers in the ALEM classrooms as they responded to the unique learning needs of individual students. In other words, incorporation of the time-use variables as an integral program design feature of adaptive instruction enabled teachers to actually manipulate these variables as an alternative strategy for adapting instruction to student differences and thereby varying the amount of time needed to learn and the amount of time spent on learning by individual students.

As has been pointed out by several investigators, time-on-task is an essential, but not a sufficient, condition for student achievement, and the nature and quality of teacher- and student-time use have much to do with the amount of learning that actually takes place (e.g., Anderson, 1976; Frederick, 1977; Karweit, 1983). The contention is that delineation of the differential effects of various practices on patterns of time use will be likely to yield an important data base that can be used to pinpoint those specific practices that lead to better use of school time for instructional and learning purposes. There is research evidence to suggest that the manner in which time is spent on learning makes a difference in the learning and instructional processes in school contexts, and that those processes have differential effects on student achievement. However, research in this area has yielded very little specific information that can be used to develop instructional interventions that are likely to effectively reduce the amount of time needed for learning or to develop classroom management systems that can facilitate teachers' and students' effective use of school time. Much further work is needed on these and related topics.

Two lines of research related to the general topic of time use and learning seem particularly promising: descriptive studies that incorporate much more fine-grained, microlevel analysis of time use (not only how it is spent, but its quality and relevance) and instructional experimentations that involve varying time-use patterns, learning tasks, and learning situations. There are at least two good reasons for pursuing both types of research at this point. The first has to do with the state of the art of research on time and schooling. The second is related to some of the current work in instructional design research. Recent advances, particularly research on subject-matter learning, are likely to contribute to further understanding of the quality of instruction. Such understanding has implications for the development of specific instructional interventions aimed at reducing the amount of time students need to learn. Progress in this area is suggested by the growing interest in cognitive-instructional research (on the cognitive processes involved in complex human behavior and in high levels of competence in major-skills areas) and in research on the nature and patterns of learning under various instructional conditions.

The identification of ways in which knowledge is used in different kinds of learning settings is another area of research with implications for the provision of effective instruction in basic-skills subject areas, such as reading and math, and more generic learning skills, such as problem solving and organizational and attending skills. Such research will provide a data base that is likely to broaden current understanding of what needs to be taught and the pedagogical issues related to how it can be taught more effectively. In addition, growing sophistication in the kinds of questions being asked in psychological and educational research, as well as improvements in techniques and methodologies, have resulted in greatly increased capabilities for studying and detailing the conditions under which school time is spent by teachers and students. These advances, coupled with the growing interest in improvement-oriented research related to classroom instruction and learning and effective management of learning, will undoubtedly facilitate the continued building of a knowledge base and the formulation of insights on the development of specific interventions that can be used by practitioners to maximize the allocation and effective use of time to improve student learning.

REFERENCES

Anderson, L. W. (1976). An empirical investigation of individual differences in time to learn. *Journal of Educational Psychology, 68*, 226–233.

Arlin, M., & Westbury, I. (1976). The leveling effect of teacher pacing on science content mastery. *Journal of Research in Science Teaching, 13*(3), 213–219.

Barr, R. (1975). How children are taught to read: Grouping and pacing. *School Review, 83*, 479–498.

Bennett, N. (1976). *Teaching styles and pupil progress.* Cambridge, Mass.: Harvard University Press.

Bloom, B. S. (1974). Time and learning. *American Psychologist, 29*, 682–688.

Bloom, B. S. (1976). *Human characteristics and school learning.* New York: McGraw-Hill.

Brophy, J. (1979). Teacher behavior and its effects. *Journal of Educational Psychology, 71*(6), 733–750.

Dahloff, U. (1971). *Ability grouping, content validity and curriculum process analysis.* New York: Teachers College Press.

Fisher, C. W., Berliner, D. C., Filby, N. N., Marliave, R., Cahen, L. S., Dishaw, M. N., & Moore, J. E. (1978). *Teaching and learning in the elementary school: A summary of the beginning teacher evaluation study* (Technical report VIII-1 *Beginning Teacher Evaluation Study*). San Francisco: Far West Laboratory for Educational Research and Development.

Frederick, W. C. (1977). The use of classroom time in high schools above or below the median reading score. *Urban Education, 11,* 459–464.

Glaser, R. (1977). *Adaptive education: Individual diversity and learning.* New York: Holt, Rinehart and Winston.

Good, T. L., & Beckerman, T. M. (1978). Time on task: A naturalistic study in sixth grade classrooms. *Elementary School Journal, 73,* 193–201.

Good, T. L., Grouws, D.A., & Beckerman, T. M. (1978). Curriculum pacing: Some empirical data in math. *Curriculum Studies, 1*(10), 1–7.

Johnson, D. W., Maruyama, G., Johnson, R., Nelson, D., & Skon, L. (1981). Effects of cooperative, competitive, and individualistic goal structures on achievement: A meta-analysis. *Psychological Bulletin, 89,* 47–62.

Karweit, N. (1983). *Time on task: A research review* (Research Report No. 322). Baltimore: Johns Hopkins University, Center for the Social Organization of Schools.

Marshall, H. H. (1981). Open classrooms: Has the term outlived its usefulness? *Review of Educational Research, 51,* 181–192.

McPartland, J., & Epstein, J. (1975). *The effects of open school organization on student outcomes* (Research Report No. 195). Baltimore: Johns Hopkins University, Center for the Social Organization of Schools.

Peterson, P. (1979). Direct instruction reconsidered. In P. Peterson and H. J. Walberg (Eds.), *Research on teaching: Concepts, findings, and implications* (pp. 28–56). Berkeley, Calif.: McCutchan.

Rosenshine, B. V. (1979). Content, time, and direct instruction. In P. Peterson & H. J. Walberg (Eds.), *Research on teaching: Concepts, findings, and implications* (pp. 11–27). Berkeley, Calif.: McCutchan.

Rosenshine, B. V. (1980). How time is spent in elementary classrooms. In C. Denham & A. Lieberman (Eds.), *Time to learn* (pp. 107–123). Washington, D.C.: National Institute of Education.

Stallings, J. A., & Kaskowitz, D. H. (1974). *Follow Through classroom evaluation 1972–73.* Menlo Park, Calif.: Stanford Research Institute.

Wang, M. C. (1974). *The rationale and design of the Self-Schedule System (LRDC Publication Series 1974/5).* Pittsburgh: University of Pittsburgh, Learning Research and Development Center.

Wang, M. C. (1976). The use of observational data for formative evaluation of an instructional model. *Instructional Science, 5,* 365–389.

Wang, M. C. (1979). Maximizing the effective use of school time by teachers and students. *Contemporary Educational Psychology, 4,* 187–201.

Wang, M. C. (1980). Adaptive instruction: Building on diversity. *Theory into Practice, 19*(2), 122–127.

Wang, M. C., & Brictson, P. (1973, February). *An observational investigation of classroom instructional-learning behaviors under two different classroom management systems.* Paper presented at the annual meeting of the American Educational Research Association, New Orleans.

Wang, M. C., & Fitzhugh, R. J. (1977). *Planning instruction and monitoring classroom processes with computer assistance* (LRDC Publications Series 1977/10). Pittsburgh: University of Pittsburgh, Learning Research and Development Center.

Wang, M. C., Kaufman, S. M., & Lesgold, S. B. (1982). *An investigation of the use of school time: Implications for optimizing student learning.* Pittsburgh: University of Pittsburgh, Learning Research and Development Center.

Wang, M. C., & Richardson, B. L. (1977, April). *The Self-Schedule System: Its effects on students' and teachers' classroom behaviors and attitudes.* Paper presented at the annual meeting of the American Educational Research Association, New York.

Wang, M. C., & Stiles, B. (1976). An investigation of children's concepts of self-responsibility for their school learning. *American Educational Research Journal, 13,* 159–179.

Wang, M. C., Strom, C. D., & Hechtman, J. (1981). *The Teacher Behavior Record Form.* Pittsburgh: University of Pittsburgh, Learning Research and Development Center.

Wang, M. C., & Walberg, H. J. (1983). Adaptive instruction and classroom time. *American Educational Research Journal, 20,* 601–626.

Wang, M. C., and Weisstein, W. J. (1980). Teacher expectations and student learning. In L. J. Fxans (Ed.), *Achievement motivation: Recent trends in theory and research* (pp. 417–444). New York: Plenum.

Wang, M. C., & Yeager, J. L. (1971). Evaluation under individualized instruction. *Elementary School Journal, 71,* 448–452.

15

Instructional Time: A Winged Chariot?

Gaea Leinhardt
University of Pittsburgh

EDITORS' INTRODUCTION
In this chapter, the use of instructional time in classroom research is traced in a
series of three major field studies. In an evaluation of the Individualized Science
Curriculum, allocations of time to various subject-matter areas were used to
account for variations in student achievement in mathematics, science, and
reading. In the Instructional Dimensions Study, a variety of time measures were
used to assess student opportunity to learn criterion material and to represent the
duration of instructional events. Of four process constructs, opportunity to learn
was most strongly related to student outcomes. In a third study, extensive
observation of individual students yielded even more sophisticated measures of
instructional process, many of which were time based. For some time-based
variables in the last study, as many as 30 hours of observation were required in
order to obtain stable estimates. The series of studies demonstrates several
important developmental trends in the use of time as a metric in the study of
classroom phenomena. Based partially upon this experience, Dr. Leinhardt
presents six basic findings from research on instructional time. The chapter
concludes with a call for research on use of instructional time from teachers'
points of view and for additional work on the "multiple" effects of time spent in
one content area on student acheivement in other content areas.

But at my back I always hear
Time's winged chariot hurrying near;
And yonder all before us lie
Deserts of vast eternity.
Andrew Marvell

It has been just a decade since I carried out my first piece of research using time as a variable. I think my development has been similar to that experienced by others in the field. Since then, my understanding of the construct has undergone considerable alteration. Initially, time spent was considered an excellent indicator for the quantity and quality of instruction that was needed by a student until a given concept or fact was learned (Anderson, 1973; Block, 1970; Bloom, 1974; Leinhardt, 1974; Welch & Bridgham, 1968), but this was true only for those studies in which the duration of the study was relatively short two to three months) and the instructional content scrupulously controlled. Timelike variables began to be discussed independently from the instructional content, and in some cases, claims were even made for the value of time passage in and of itself (Wiley, 1973; Wiley & Harnischfeger, 1974). Almost immediately, linkages were made between how time was spent—or at least what it was spent on— and its value as an educational construct (Fisher, Filby, Marliave, Cahen, Dishaw, Moore, & Berliner, 1978; Karweit, 1976, 1977, 1980; Marliave, 1980; Rosenshine, 1978; Stallings, 1980; Webb & Nerenz, 1980). The debate and criticism of time as a valuable tool in and of itself, although serious, never seemed to quite catch up with lawmakers and school officials who clung to the clarity and simplicity of instructional time as a meaningful indicator for instructional quality. Several researchers used time either as a multiple of process indicators or as a metric for valued classroom activities, which essentially bought them the analytic clarity and power of time, but not the vacuousness of time or task (Cooley & Leinhardt, 1975a, 1975b; Fisher et al., 1978, Harnischfeger & Wiley, 1977, 1978; Leinhardt, 1978). A decade after Bloom's article in the *American Psychologist* and two decades after Carroll's, we are in a position to try to understand what is useful about time and when it is a proxy for other things and turn from mindless debates on whether or not time matters. Of course it does, but we can do better than that!

In the next section, I have selected three of my own pieces of research to serve as illustrations (not exemplars) of how time can be viewed and used in research. Three studies are briefly reviewed and their major findings discussed. The chapter ends with some discussion of where we are and where we need to go. My objectives are to present an overview of the research and comment on what I think the future of this line of research holds.

SCIENCE STUDY

The Science Study was carried out in 1974 as part of the evaluation of the Learning Research and Development Center's (LRDC) Individualized Science Curriculum (IS) (Champagne & Klopfer, 1974; Leinhardt, 1974). In evaluating IS, we were faced with the difficulties of having a weak set of dependent measures and of having no point of comparison. There were at that time virtually no norms for success or failure in elementary science instruction (Leinhardt, 1977). In general, elementary school students in our area were not exposed to science education, so any child who was taught science was likely to look better on a test than a child who had no instruction in science at all. One serious concern, even in 1974, was whether or not time spent in science detracted from learning in the more basic areas of reading and math. We constructed a composite pretest and posttest battery and estimated time spent in science, mathematics, and reading instruction. The pretest consisted of the previous year's end-of-year Stanford Achievement Test (Madden, Gardner, Rudman, Karlsen, & Merwin, 1972) stanines in science, mathematics, and reading; the posttest consisted of the spring 1973 stanines. The modified allocated-time measures consisted of students' own punched-clock records in mathematics and reading and teacher logs of time spent in science. All of the time estimates were closer to allocated than engaged time estimates, but they were lower than strictly schedule-based allocations. The study was carried out in Oakleaf School, a demonstration school for LRDC, and included all 86 fourth and fifth graders enrolled. The results indicated that after pretest, the only other important predictor of test performance was time spent in science.

Table 15.1 shows descriptive statistics and results of a regression analysis of the time spent in subjects and achievement data. Notice that the zero-order correlation of time spent in science with outcomes is negligible, whereas the mathematics time is quite substantial. However, when the partial correlations are examined, science time emerges as an important predictor. The regression results are similar. There are several explanations for the phenomenon. Science time is not correlated with initial ability, whereas time spent in mathematics and reading is; science can be an even addition (across student abilities) to the knowledge base. Second, time spent in science reinforces reading comprehension by having action-based (follow the directions) short passages (two or three pages as a major component of instruction). Third, the science material is very well written, in fact, more precisely written than much reading material. There is also some limited amount of measuring and calculation that is required which reinforces math skills. The initial analysis consisted of correlations and partial correlations. By 1974, we knew that the initial ability of the student was the most powerful predictor of outcome and that many of one's favorite classroom-process variables, time among them, were confounded with initial ability.

TABLE 15.1.   Science Time Study: Combined 4th and 5th Grades ($N = 86$)

	Correlation matrix					
	Combined input	Science time	Math time	Reading time	Combined outcome	With input partialled out
Input						
Science time	− .05					.37
Math time	.36	.07				.07
Reading time	.09	.10	.62			− .03
Combined outcome	.90	.11	.35	.06		
Mean	17.99	1679.83	5405.97	1768.27	16.75	
S.D.	4.71	536.50	1534.00	801.53	5.07	

Outcome = $.89^a$PRE + $.16^a$ST + $.07$MT − $.08$RT. Adjusted mult R^2 = $.83^a$. ^{a}($p \le .05$)

We knew, therefore, that simple correlations with outcomes might be deceiving because one was really capturing only relationships between process and input. Hence, we examined partial correlations. The regression analysis has been added in an attempt to provide comparable results across the studies presented in this chapter.

This study points out the need for caution in interpreting studies of instructional time. As we strive to get schools and teachers to increase the engaged time spent by their students in academically fruitful activities, we must be careful about inappropriate increases or decreases in time allocated to specific subject areas. As allocated time in language arts creeps up from 60 to 120 minutes a day, time is taken away from substantive areas such as science and social studies, areas which undoubtedly have benefit for their own sake, but which may have unanticipated benefits for the so-called basics as well. Reading, after all, is studied in the elementary years, both as a content area and as a conduit for future information. Science and social studies represent the first use of that conduit.

INSTRUCTIONAL DIMENSIONS STUDY

The Instructional Dimensions Study (IDS) was designed by William Cooley and myself at the request of Congress and the National Institute of Education. It was carried out by Kirschner Associates and Education Turnkey (Kirschner Associates, 1977), primary implementors, although they have received little public acknowledgement. William Cooley and I wrote up the results. The following discussion comes largely from the report by Cooley and Leinhardt (1980). IDS differs from the Science Study in that instructional processes were directly measured. It was an attempt to unpack the "black box" of the classroom.

In 1975–1976, when IDS was being designed (Cooley & Leinhardt, 1975a, 1975b, process–product research was generally carried out by gathering large amounts of classroom data and correlating these measures with outcomes. Evaluation research often simply compared outcomes. IDS had some unique features: a basic theoretical model of classroom processes, direct measurement of instructional processes, carefully selected batteries of outcome measures, and a rather unique analysis system designed to partition explained variance.

The classroom-process model used by IDS is displayed in Figure 15.1 (Cooley & Leinhardt, 1975c; Cooley & Lohnes, 1976). The figure is a heuristic that sets up constructs with embedded variables. These constructs were believed to be both necessary and sufficient to explain the variation in student performance that occurred among classrooms after an extended period of instruction. One implication of the model is that students' criterion performance is a function of initial student performance and of specific classroom processes. The model leaves unspecified the relationships among the processes' relations that we are now—almost 10 years later—just beginning to understand. The classroom processes are represented by four constructs: opportunity, motivators, instructional events, and structure.

The opportunity construct represented the student's opportunity to learn what was tested in the criterion performance measures. The construct contained two key variables: the use of instructional time in classrooms and the similarity of the curriculum to the tests (overlap). The motivators construct included those aspects of the curriculum and in-class interpersonal behavior that were assumed to encourage learning. It was intentionally *not* a student attribute. Instructional events include the content, frequency, quality, and duration of instructional interactions. This was intended to be the "teaching" construct. Structure, the fourth construct, considered the level of organization of the curriculum, the specificity of the objectives, and the manner in which a student and a curriculum were matched. It was intended to be the "text" and methods construct.

In order to develop measures for the constructs, we first selected key variables from the literature and then identified the measurable features of each variable and designed measurement procedures that minimized classroom disruption and maximized precision. Measures within each construct were combined into variables, which were in turn combined into sets of variables representing the four constructs. One way of thinking about the constructs is to consider opportunity as a covariate that permits interpretation of the influence of the other constructs when time and content are held constant.

In designing IDS, we made a tactical decision about sampling. The sampling scheme emphasized the need to achieve variance in classroom processes rather than representativeness of current compensatory practices or geographic regions. We obtained variation in processes by using global descriptive information about the programs in use in a large number of school districts and then selecting classrooms from those districts. We were

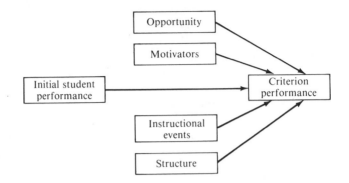

FIGURE 15.1 Model of classroom processes.

free to do this because IDS was only one part of the larger Compensatory Education Study and other parts of the study used systematic regional samplings.

The analysis that was used in IDS was commonality analysis. The results strongly suggested that the most important of the predictors in the model were pretest and opportunity to learn. Opportunity consisted of two variables: time and curriculum overlap. Time was estimated by attendance, allocation, and on-task rate as well as enrollment and transfers; overlap used both a teacher-based estimate and a curriculum analysis estimate. Pretest and opportunity to learn were the most powerful predictors of student growth in reading and math in the first grade. The commonality analysis permitted us to determine that for reading achievement, opportunity was the most important, while pretest and opportunity were of equal importance in math.

Of all the analyses, third-grade reading showed the highest correlation between pretest and posttest ($r = .86$), leaving the smallest amount of reliable variance for other predictors to explain. In spite of this, opportunity to learn was still important in predicting growth. Third-grade math also showed the importance of the opportunity construct. It was, in fact, the only construct that had a significant uniqueness for this sample. In summary, the most useful construct for explaining achievement gain was the opportunity that the children had to learn.

While time was a very important part of opportunity, curriculum content was another. Curriculum content made a major difference. Instructional techniques, both curricular and interpersonal, did not compensate for missing content. Children at these grades consistently performed better on tests if they had been exposed to both the *form* of the test items and the *content* covered by the test. Both what was taught and what was tested represented samplings from domains. Curriculum and test could clearly emphasize different content. The results of IDS showed that students were most likely to answer correctly if they had been taught the specific material covered by a test and if they had been frequently exposed to the test format.

In IDS, there were four basic instructional constructs. Of these four, opportunity was consistently the strongest predictor of achievement gains. However, within opportunity, the variable cluster that stood out was the one that assessed the degree to which the children in the classroom had an opportunity to learn what was tested by the end-of-year achievement test. One implication of this result is that evaluation studies that fail to include information on how time is used or on the degree to which the curriculum included what the achievement test measured are suffering from specification error. This error results in a danger of attributing instructional effectiveness or ineffectiveness to specific programs or ways of teaching when it is really a matter of the curriculum content being a good fit to the particular achievement test selected. A second implication more germane to the present discussion is that time itself is not the issue; it's what one is doing with the time.

The results of IDS pointed up most clearly the need to control the variation by classroom in time spent in academic areas and the content covered. Without control of these variables we were unlikely to find other important process variables. That does not mean that these other variables are not important, only that discovery of their importance is hampered. It is in this sense of adjustment that time becomes most critical in educational research. If we consider a situation in which time does not itself represent a major source of variation (for example, in France), the point becomes clearer.

READING INSTRUCTION IN CLASSROOMS
FOR THE LEARNING DISABLED

The third piece of research on which I want to report is a study of reading instruction in classrooms for the learning disabled carried out between 1977 and 1980 (Leinhardt, Zigmond, & Cooley, 1981). We set out to study the nature and extent of reading instruction in these classes and to assess its effects. The learning-disabled (L-D) study differed from the science study and IDS in that not only were process measures taken, but direct measures of students' learning behaviors were as well. The following description is taken in part from the published report (Leinhardt, Zigmond & Cooley, 1981).

We studied the reading lives of 105 students in elementary classrooms for the learning disabled. We took extensive detailed observations of students, teachers, and instructional material. The data were used to explore the plausibility of a causal model of the effects of reading behaviors and instruction on students' reading performance. The reading behaviors were scaled in a metric of time. In this study, one can see the final dissolution of time as a variable in itself and the transformation into time as a metric for behaviors as it was in the BTES studies (Fisher et al., 1978).

The results indicated that 72% of the variance in posttest reading scores was captured by a model that included pretest, three student reading behaviors, and instructional overlap; and that 59% of the variance in student time spent in reading was explained by a model that included pretest, teacher instructional behaviors, teacher affective behaviors and instructional pacing.

We wanted to study reading L-D classrooms for several reasons. First, the number of children classified as learning disabled had risen dramatically from 120,000 in 1968 to 1,281,395 in 1979. Second, the primary reason that elementary school children were diagnosed as learning disabled and assigned to special classrooms was that they exhibited relatively poor performance in reading. Third, within L-D classrooms, reading instruction was and is given considerable emphasis, and a wide variety of instructional practices and materials are tried. Finally, we wished to understand if these so-called learning-disabled children really needed and got qualitatively different instruction or if they appeared for the most part to simply need more of the same things other students needed. We sought to answer three major questions: (1) What is the nature of reading activities in L-D classes?, (2) What types of student activities lead to greatest improvement in reading test performance? and (3) What types of instructional situations generate these student activities?

Two basic assumptions about effective reading instruction guided our data collection and analysis activities. First, we assumed that what students learned was a function of what they did and that features of the curriculum and teacher behaviors influenced what students did rather than directly influencing what they learned. This represented a departure from the IDS study in which time was a variable and student behavior was not. We also assumed that beginning reading activities could be described by three broad categories: those *directly* related to the reading task in that they involved the student's responding to print; those that *indirectly* supported some aspect of reading, but were not reading (e.g., listening to the teacher or talking about a story); and finally, those activities that were so tangential to the acquisition of reading competence as to be nonreading (e.g., working with perceptual training boards or doing auditory discrimination tasks). The importance of this division was that *all three* activities went on during scheduled reading and were considered reading by the teachers.

Data on the classrooms, students, and teachers were obtained through several systems. Teachers were observed directly and interviewed. Students were observed directly and their work products and assignments monitored. We used a time-sampling procedure to observe both the teacher and the students (Leinhardt & Seewald, 1981). In addition, students were pretested and posttested and their prior test data were also recorded. For all analyses, the individual child was the unit of observation and analysis.

Teacher behaviors were coded and linked to the student(s) to whom they were directed. Thus, teacher behavior and time were treated as a distributed resource. Teachers' instructional and affective behaviors were coded. Instructional behaviors included model presentations, explanations, feedback, cuing, and monitoring. The separate measures were combined into a single estimate of the time that any individual child received teacher instruction each day. Affective behaviors included the number of reinforcers received by each child per day and the cognitive press exerted by the teacher toward a child. The core of the data collection, however, was clearly the child behaviors.

Figure 15.2 displays the schema used to organize the observations of student behavior. The system was designed to assess what students actually did during reading instruction. A detailed analysis of reading behaviors coupled with an assessment of the tasks presented to children during reading formed the bases of the observational system. The system was intended to be exhaustive, in that all of the students' time during observation would be accounted for. Students were coded as reading or not. If they were reading, the behaviors were classified further as direct or indirect. Direct reading behaviors included oral and silent reading of letters, words, sentences, and paragraphs. Indirect reading behaviors were those activities that were assumed to be related to reading but in which the student was not engaged in responses to print in the "normal" way. By normal, we meant going from print (as stimulus) to sound or silent reading (as response) as opposed, for example, to finding letters with a specific sound. The indirect reading behaviors included story discussion, circling pictures with a common phonetic element, and listening and writing (whether copying or spelling). The combined measures of reading included the amount of time per day a child was reading aloud, reading silently, or engaged in indirect reading behaviors. In this study we attempted to be extremely precise in our measurement of behaviors. Thus, although we had over 300 hours of data on each child, we only used measures at a level of aggregation that assured measurement stability over time, not simply observer agreement (Leinhardt & Seewald, 1981).

We observed the 105 students over a 20-week period, from December 1978 to May 1979. In each classroom, we randomly sampled 20 one-hour observation sessions in the morning and 10 in the afternoon. This considerable effort at extensive sampling was to assure adequate coverage and stability of the phenomena of interest (Cooley & Mao, 1981; Karweit & Slavin, 1980; Leinhardt & Seewald, 1981).

We estimated each student's classroom behaviors between pretest and posttest by weighting the samples. The weights were a function of the reciprocals of the sampling ratios; that is, if we observed a student for 20 morning hours and he or she was in school for a total of 320 morning hours, then the weight for the morning observations would be 320/20, or 16. Similarly, if a student was observed for 10 afternoon hours, and he or she was in school for 300 afternoon hours, the estimates for the afternoon strata would be weighted by 30. The weighted estimates were then scaled so that they approximated the minutes per day a child averaged in a particular activity. The complete sampling and weighting procedures are described in Cooley and Mao (1981).

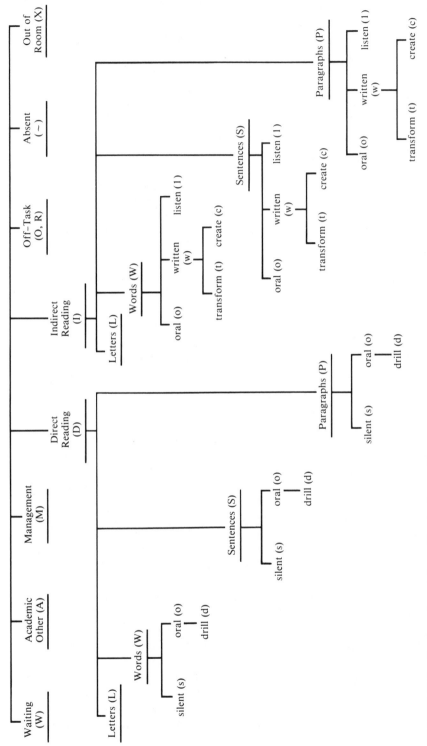

FIGURE 15.2 Student observation of beginning reading.

In conducting this study, we were trying to establish the connections between activities that students engaged in and student learning. We also wanted to explore how instructional features influence student activities. Essentially, the issue was the significance of time spent in specific activities on learning. These relationships were examined by a series of multiple regressions. The variables to be included in each regression were determined by a model for explaining reading achievement.

In Figure 15.3, the combined causal model of how the variables were assumed to be influencing each other in the classroom is summarized. Solid black lines indicate significant relationships that are time driven and in which the directionality of the arrow seems clear (e.g., pretest to posttest). Broken black lines indicate significant relationships in which we assume a causal directionality, but in which both variables were measured at approximately the same time (e.g., teacher instructional behaviors and time in reading activities). Dotted lines indicate relationships that we predicted would be significant but were not. In comparing this model to that used in IDS, one can see that although the elements are similar, the linkages are essentially quite new. Pre- and posttest are the same. *Opportunity* has been split into *overlap* and the metric for the student measures (student learning behaviors were absent in IDS); *motivators* has become *teacher affective behaviors; instructional events* was captured as *teacher behaviors*; and *structure* has become *pacing*. The regression helped us to build models that accounted for explicit within-predictor relationships.

Figure 15.3 can be read to show that posttest is dependent on student behaviors and instructional content; student learning behaviors are influenced by prior test performance and teacher behaviors. The regressions reported below the figure support the interpretation that posttest performance was significantly influenced by pretest, silent-reading time, and overlap, but not significantly influenced by oral reading or indirect activities. (Oral-reading time was significant when an oral reading test was used and no overlap estimate was included.) The results can be translated into a time language such that an average of one minute per day of additional silent-reading time could have increased posttest performance by one point. An increase of five minutes per day would have been equivalent to about one month (on a grade-equivalent scale) of additional reading achievement.

When we turn to those factors that increased time spent by students in both direct and indirect reading behaviors, total time in reading was expected to be influenced by what students knew in the beginning, what the teacher taught them, how the teacher encouraged or cajoled them, and how the instruction was paced. All but the last of these were verified. The regression suggested that an increase of one minute of teacher instruction per day had the potential of gaining a minute of student reading time and that each reinforcer also increases daily reading time. What was exciting about the results was that teachers could easily increase instructional time to several students at once. This brings out a point that we will discuss later,

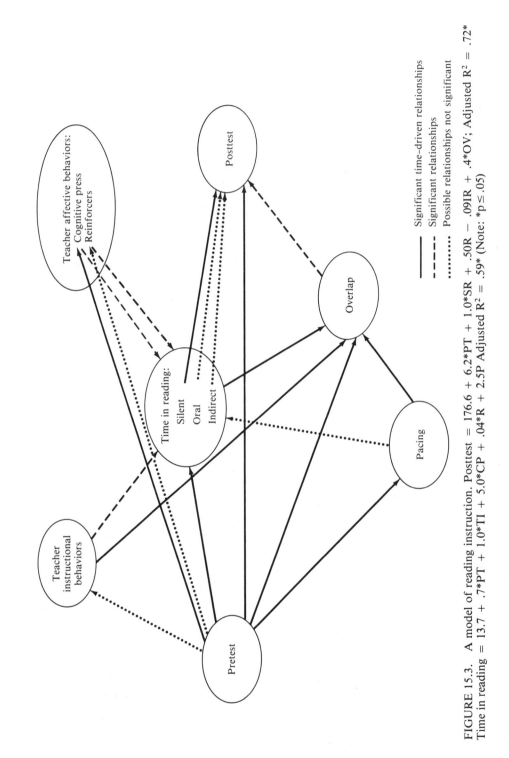

FIGURE 15.3. A model of reading instruction. Posttest $= 176.6 + 6.2*PT + 1.0*SR + .50R - .09IR + .4*OV$; Adjusted $R^2 = .72*$
Time in reading $= 13.7 + .7*PT + 1.0*TI + 5.0*CP + .04*R + 2.5P$ Adjusted $R^2 = .59*$ (Note: $*p \leq .05$)

namely, that time scales in a classroom are not easily equated, so students may get only four minutes of teacher time per day although the teacher is "teaching" almost all day.

The pacing result—that is, lack of a significant relationship—may be explained by the fact that these teachers tended to adjust the pacing to the level of student ability so that students of a given ability were not differentially "pushed" by longer or shorter assignments. Indeed, the strong zero-order relationship, .46, between pacing and pretest suggests this explanation, but its partial regression is not significantly different from zero. (Although this result is different from the results of Barr (1980) the model being tested is also different.)

It is important to note that in some cases combined sets of reading variables were used and in some cases single reading variables are used. For example, teacher effective support was aimed at increasing all of the students' reading activities, so the total reading time was the appropriate dependent variable. Posttest, however, was assumed to be influenced primarily by silent reading, somewhat by oral reading, and very little by indirect reading activities, so these were examined separately in their roles as explanatory variables. This distinction was made not merely for the purpose of conserving degrees of freedom, but because of the logic of the relationships.

We (Leinhardt, Zigmond, & Cooley) spent over two years studying the classrooms. Much of the information we obtained was captured by the specific variables and analyses. Much more, however, was also learned. In fact, after observing classrooms and teachers (some for more than 70 hours), we felt obliged to report what we had learned from both our more formal and less formal analyses. We felt that it was the informal analyses that grounded the formal and made it more than a collection of numbers. We reported two classes of findings from the study: those that dealt with the state of the art of research on effective classroom processes and those that dealt with the substantive import of our findings. To quote directly:

> After decades of effort, research on instructional domains has reached a point where classroom processes can be measured with reliability and validity. This is due to the improved strategies for sampling the instructional domain; precision with which observational measures can be crafted; incorporation of interpretable metrics into the observation system (namely time) and heuristic value of a causal scheme.
>
> Improved strategies for sampling included capturing more of the time than most previous work (30 hours) and randomly sampling the time of observation. Previous work has used as little as two hours and has intentionally waited until instruction "began" thus inflating estimates of instruction. In this study, the use of a schema to organize the observational measures dramatically improved the reliability of observers and eased final analysis. Using a unifying metric for the majority of measures improved analysis and interpretability as it has for other researchers in the area, notably the BTES work. Using a causal model has helped to clarify the paths through which variables may be operating.

Specifically, it is student behaviors during instruction that influence student learning while teacher behaviors influence student behaviors. (Leinhardt et al., 1981, pp. 356–357)

I have reviewed this study in some detail because it demonstrates not only the results, but the need for a rather meticulous methodology. As our understanding of the function of time has increased, we have been forced to be much more careful in the crafting of our measures and the explication of our theories.

WHAT HAVE WE LEARNED ABOUT TIME?

This set of three studies exemplifies both changing thinking and findings about instructional time. In the Science Study, we considered a modified estimate of allocated time to be useful in understanding student end-of-year performance. At that stage, time was simply a blocked competitive resource that needed justification. We made no effort to partition time in science into various student or teacher actions. Rather, we treated it as a homogeneous substance in which more of time meant more of the same. In IDS, somewhat more complex measures of time, attendance, and on-task rates were used to try to get at something more relevant for instruction than allocation. As we began to understand the importance of content covered, we tried to move toward notions of time spent in appropriate tasks. The L-D study carefully defined the instructional domain, heavily sampled it, and scaled it in terms of time.

Having reviewed this research, I would like to turn now to six basic findings that have emerged from the study of instructional time.

1. Time is most usefully thought of as metric, not a variable.
2. Time spent is overlapping and not mutually exclusive with one organism even when the focus is primarily on one type of activity.
3. Observations and interpretations must be at the same level. This is not the same as unit of analysis. The problem is illustrated by noting that children may spend four to ten minutes a day reading whereas teachers may spend two to four hours a day teaching reading.
4. Allocated time is not the upper bound for engaged time in some situations, but it is the upper bound for others.
5. Time-on-task is not the same as time on the right task.
6. To obtain a stable, generalizable estimate of students' time usage, there must be extensive sampling and extremely well defined variables.

Time is a metric, not a variable

The passage of time is, in itself, of no particular value to any research effort or any question. It is time as a metaphor or time as a metric that makes the concept useful in educational research. As a metaphor, it is useful to consider time as a scarce resource. It is finite for the consumer and sharply limited for the disperser across multiple receivers. As a metric, it is useful because it permits us to scale variables in a highly interpretable and additive way. However, caution is needed once behaviors or variables have been scaled in the metric of time. They appear to have an equivalence that may be false. One minute of teacher behavior in category Y is not the same as one minute of student behavior in category X. Issues of intensity and density need to be addressed. Time is often useful with respect to policy recommendations and notions of improvement and change. It is also the metric that gives us the greatest shock value. We seem to discover surprisingly small amounts of time spent in activities that we presume have high payoff for a variety of academic areas.

Time is overlapping and not mutually exclusive

Several behaviors go on at once for a given child or teacher. Two or more things can occur simultaneoulsy so that independent measurement of conceptually separate variables becomes difficult to interpret. In such situations, summation of time over different variables must be done with care and precision. We must know the boundaries within which we are summing. For example, consider a table that displays the following percentages: "80% of the time reading, 75% of the time in social contact, 65% of the time in contact with the instructional leader." When all these percentages are above 50, the interpretability gained by using time is lost. Caution is needed in deciding which element can be carved neatly away from which other element.

Observations and interpretations must be at the same level

Different actors in the same environment spend very different amounts of time in the same activity and, estimating one from the other is difficult. If we study the time use of a child and attach teacher behaviors to the child's time, we cannot estimate the teacher's use of time. Because a child receives less than a minute a day of cognitive instruction and about 15 minutes a day of instruction relevant in some way to reading, we cannot infer that the teacher wasn't working at teaching reading. Teacher time has to be estimated separately, and linkage may be a problem.

Allocated time may not be the upper bound for engaged time

Clearly, allocated time is pretty close to being the upper bound for mathematics instruction. Very little formal mathematics instruction goes on in any class other than math class. My concern with this notion of allocated time being the upper bound for engaged time stems from the Science Study described earlier. Remember, time spent in science influenced science, reading, and math achievement. This is not simply a matter of redefining allocation; it is a problem in understanding the total instructional day. We need to consider the total school day in order to address the question,

Should we allocate more reading time in order to get more engaged reading time, or should we permit allocated reading time to stay as it is? "Buying" more reading allocation will occur at the cost of social studies or science or music. However, time spent on social studies or science will also have a payoff in the area known as reading comprehension. The policy implications of this issue are clear, but not always acted on.

Time-on-task is not the same as time on the right task

This point is one that we certainly all understand, but it needs to be repeated frequently. Time-on-task is synonymous with engagement in relevant tasks only when the task content has been controlled for. Much of the time-on-task literature merely takes children being on-task during the time allocated to instructional area X with no regard to the content of the task they are performing. This notion fits very closely into the idea that time is a metric. In order for one to do a study of time that is meaningful, one must carry out a detailed analysis of the content of instruction. Simply taking a percentage of on-task behavior and multiplying it times allocation will not give an engagement rate that is useful, as we learned in IDS.

There is a need for extensive sampling and well-defined variables

The final point deals with methodology. In a generalizability study that was carried out as a part of the L-D study, we discovered that in order for estimates of student behavior to stabilize, we needed to have extensive sampling of those behaviors (Cooley & Mao, 1981; Lomax, 1982). Specially, 20 hours of observation time was needed as opposed to the two or three usually recommended. This large time sampling was not necessary for all variables, but it was necessary for many of the less frequently occurring ones. In addition to sampling concerns, adequate definition of behaviors is of crucial importance. As we get better at defining tasks, activities, and behaviors, our ability to connect them improves.

FUTURE

Having reviewed samples of the last decade's work, I would like now to turn to what we need to do in the future. One area that I think would be interesting to unravel is teacher time. We have done a fairly good job of understanding a student record, that is, taking a child, explaining how that child spends a day, and tagging on to it the amount of teacher time that the child has access to. But we have not looked at instructional time from the other end; that is, we have not tried to understand how teachers distribute their day in terms of time. I think that we need to understand teacher time if we are going to influence how teachers get children to spend time. Studies of teacher planning and teacher decision making are very relevant to this task.

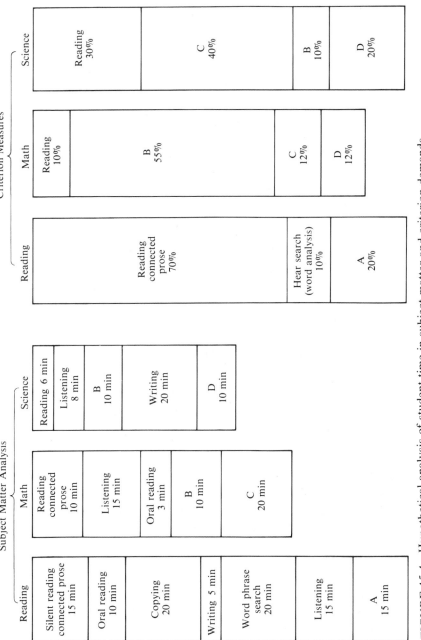

FIGURE 15.4 Hypothetical analysis of student time in subject matter and criterion demands.

280 / Instructional Tim6: Classroom Research

As we get more fine-grained estimates of what a teacher does as he or she goes through a lesson, we will be able to locate the places or slots where educational change can be introduced and anticipate the consequences of already suggested changes.

The second area that I think we ought to work on is the notion of multiple payoffs. Clearly, we begin to get payoffs in reading for time spent in drama or other content areas that involve contact with print, but are not called reading. Research on the multiple effects of instruction will require analysis of the entire school curriculum for the specific skills that are tested by the criterion measures. In the future, we need to analyze carefully the task components in a variety of subject-matter domains; science, reading, social studies, mathematics, and music would be my candidates. These analyses then need to be compared so that we can construct portraits of a student's day and map those on to the more complex aspects of student achievement. Figure 15.4 displays a simple version of what I have in mind. The point is to examine how various areas of instruction support each other in meaningful ways. Humanistic educators have long argued against back-to-basics, in part because of the enrichment value that is lost when the other subjects are deleted. But more may be lost. There may, in fact, be some specific "basic" skills being lost as well. For example, in my purely hypothetical case, silent reading of connected prose takes up 15 minutes in reading, 10 minutes in math, and 6 minutes in science. Oral reading takes up 10 minutes of reading and 3 minutes of math, and is negligible in science. Writing is done for 5 minutes of reading, but 20 minutes of science time. If we remember why we are supposed to study the "basics," perhaps it will be no surprise that children in subject-area classes spend time exercising these basic skills. In fact, in at least one school in Pittsburgh, there is no allocated reading time after third grade, in order to make way for expanded social studies, civics, and science classes. Mapping these activities and demonstrating their relationship to outcomes is a nontrivial task requiring many person-years of work. Simultaneously, we have to build more complex analyses of existing tests and to track areas of instruction where time is spent but never assessed.

Using time as an important link in our understanding of educational processes and their effects on learning is certainly something we need to continue to do; but it is critical that we move away from the simplistic slogans such as time-on-task and move toward carefully thought out pieces of research that incorporate time as a descriptor of activity.

REFERENCES

Anderson, L. W. (1973). *Time and school learning*. Unpublished doctoral dissertation, University of Chicago.
Anderson, L. W. (1980). *New directions for research on instruction and-*

time-on-task. Paper presented at the annual meeting of the American Educational Research Association, Boston.

Barr, R. (1980, April). *School, class, group and pace effects on learning*. Paper presented at the annual meeting of the American Educational Research Association, Boston.

Block, J. H. (1970). *The effects of various levels of performance on selected cognitive, affective, and time variables*. Unpublished doctoral dissertation, University of Chicago.

Bloom, B. (1974, September). Time and learning. *American Psychologist, 29* 682–688.

Champagne, A. B., & Klopfer, L. E. (1974). *An individualized elementary school science program*. (LRDC Publication 1974/10) University of Pittsburgh, Learning Research & Development Center.

Comprehensive Tests of Basic Skills. Monterey, Calif.: CTB/McGraw-Hill.

Cooley, W. W., & Leinhardt, G. (1975a). *Compensatory education study: Design for a study of the effectiveness of individualized instruction in the teaching of reading and mathematics*. University of Pittsburgh, Learning Research & Development Center.

Cooley, W. W., & Leinhardt, G. (1975b). *Design for the individualized instruction study: A study of the effectiveness of individualized instruction in the teaching of reading and mathematics in compensatory education programs*. University of Pittsburgh, Learning Research & Development Center.

Cooley, W. W., & Leinhardt, G. (1975c). *The application of a model for investigating classroom processes*. (LRDC Publication 1975/24) University of Pittsburgh, Learning Research & Development Center.

Cooley, W. W., & Leinhardt, G. (1980). The instructional dimensions study. *Educational Evaluation and Policy Analysis, 2*(1), 7–25.

Cooley, W. W., & Lohnes, P. R. (1976). *Evaluation research in education*. New York: Irvington Publishers.

Cooley, W. W., & Mao, B. J. (1981). The sample of classroom time observed. *Journal of Classroom Interaction, 17*(1), 31–36.

Fisher, C. W., Filby, N. N., Marliave, R., Cahen, L. S., Dishaw, M. M., Moore, J. E., & Berliner, D. C. (1978). *Teacher behaviors, academic learning time and student achievement: Final report of phase III-B, Beginning Teacher Evaluation Study*. San Francisco: Far West Laboratory for Educational Research and Development.

Harnischfeger, A., & Wiley, D. E. (1977, April). *Time allocations in fifth grade reading*. Paper presented at the annual meeting of the American Educational Research Association, New York.

Harnischfeger, A., & Wiley, D. E. (1978). *Teacher resource allocation: Consequences for pupils*. Chicago: ML-Group for Policy Studies in Education, CEMREL, Inc.

Karweit, N. (1976, July). A reanalysis of the effect of quantity of schooling on achievement. *Sociology of Education, 49*, 236–246.

Karweit, N. (1977). *The organization of time in schools: Time scales and learning*. Unpublished manuscript, Johns Hopkins University, Center for Social Organization of Schools, Baltimore.

Karweit, N. (1980). *Time-on-task: Issues of timing, sampling and definition*. Unpublished manuscript, Johns Hopkins University, Center for Social

Organization of Schools, Baltimore.

Karweit, N. L., & Slavin, R. E. (1980, April). *Measuring time on task: Issues of timing, sampling and definition.* Paper presented at the annual meeting of the American Educational Research Association, Boston.

Kirschner Associates, Inc. (1977). *Instructional dimensions study: Final report.* Washington, D.C.: Author.

Leinhardt, G. (1974). *An investigation of the effects of time.* University of Pittsburgh, Learning Research & Development Center.

Leinhardt, G. (1977). Outcomes of a strategy for program evaluation. *Science Education, 61*(1), 1–17.

Leinhardt, G. (1978, November). Opportunity to learn. In *Perspectives on the instructional dimensions study,* Washington, D.C.: National Institute of Education.

Leinhardt, G., & Seewald, A. M. (1981). Student-level observation of beginning reading. *Journal of Educational Measurement, 18*(3), 171–177.

Leinhardt, G., Zigmond, N., & Cooley, W. W. (1981). Reading instruction and its effects. *American Educational Research Journal, 18*(3), 343–361.

Lomax, R. G. (1982). An application of generalizability theory to observational research. *Journal of Experimental Education, 51*(1), 22–30.

Madden, R., Gardner, E. F., Rudman, H. C., Karlsen, B., & Merwin, J. C. (1972). *Stanford Achievement Test.* New York: Harcourt Brace Jovanovich.

Marliave, R. (1980, April). *Beyond engaged time: Approximations of task appropriateness in terms of ongoing student learning behaviors.* Paper presented at the annual meeting of the American Educational Research Association, Boston.

Rosenshine, B. V. (1978, March). *Academic engaged time, content covered, and direct instruction.* Paper presented at the annual meeting of the American Educational Research Association, Toronto.

Stallings, J. A. (1980, April). *Allocated academic learning time revisited, or beyond time on task.* Paper presented at the annual meeting of the American Educational Research Association, Boston.

Webb, N. L., & Nerenz, A. G. (1980, April). *The relationship of means of instruction and instructional time to reading skills outcome.* Paper presented at the annual meeting of the American Educational Research Association, Boston.

Welch, W. W., & Bridgham, R. C. (1968). Physics achievement gains as a function of teaching duration. *School Science and Mathematics, 68,* 449–455.

Wiley, D. E. (1973). *Another hour, another day: Quantity of schooling, a potent path for policy.* Studies of Educative Processes, Report No. 3, University of Chicago.

Wiley, D. E., & Harnischfeger, A. (1974). Explosion of a myth: Quantity of schooling and exposure to instruction, major educational vehicles. *Educational Researcher, 3*(4), 7–12.

16

Instructional Time and Staff Development: How Useful Is the Research on Time to Teachers?

Jane A. Stallings
Vanderbilt University

EDITORS' INTRODUCTION

Dr. Stallings points out how school time is divided into many subareas. She comments on the length of school day, the concept of academic learning time, and the effects of having students of different ability levels in a classroom on the use of time in that classroom. The studies on the last issue point out how gains in achievement can occur for low-ability students. Active or interactive teaching appears to be needed with low-ability students. Nonactive or noninteractive teaching exists when there is a reliance on workbooks, programmed instruction, written assignments, and silent reading or silent math exercises.

The instructional-time research has been integrated by Dr. Stallings into a staff development program that shows some similarity to Bloom's mastery model of instruction, a system described in Chapter 4. Data support the assertion that teachers can learn the skills required in such a program and that the students of those teachers learn more than do control groups of students. Some suggestions about the key variables in successful schools are offered. Thus, Dr. Stallings answers the question about the usefulness of instructional-time research that she poses in the title of this chapter. Her answer is that such research is very useful indeed.

What have we learned from the classroom research of the 1970s that can be useful to guide instructional practice in the 1980s? The most potentially useful variable to emerge from the past decade of research was time. However, Philip Jackson (1977) wisely noted:

> There has been a lot of talk about the importance of time in the determination of educational outcomes. ... Certainly, we should take a look at how time is being used or misused in our schools. It may indeed turn out to be the culprit that critics claim it is. As we test this possibility, however, we must keep in mind that time itself is valueless. It acquires value chiefly because it marks the expenditure of a precious commodity—human life ... let us not seize too quickly at remedies for our educational ailments that call for little more than adding days or hours to our present efforts. The real key lies in making better use of the time we already have. (p. 38)

Many educators are now convinced that if student time-on-task is increased, an increase in student achievement will follow. Although keeping students on-task may seem like a simplistic notion, it is a rather complex undertaking to make this construct useful in the classroom.

The issue of time and how it is spent has many dimensions that are sets and subsets of the total amount of time available. The first set within the total school day is the subject taught. Within the subjects taught are the activities that occur (i.e., making assignments, written work, silent reading, instructing, etc.). Within each activity is the focus of the teacher's attention (i.e., an individual student, a small group, the total group, etc.), and when the teacher is engaged with students, how does the teacher interact with those students? (See Figure 16.1)

The amount of time students actually spend on the academic tasks provided is determined in part by the appropriateness of the task, the activities selected for the class period, and the nature of the teacher's interactions with students. Do students have equal opportunities to interact with the teacher? Are the interactions supportive? The mix of activities and the time allotted for each activity should vary for different subjects and for different achievement levels of students. These various dimensions of time have been studied by numerous researchers.

HOW TIME IS SPENT

Length of School Day

The length of a school day in elementary school or the length of a class period in secondary schools defines the maximum amount of time available for instruction. Harnischfeger and Wiley (1978) found that the length of school days in the same district varied by 45 mintues for two second-grade classrooms. However, the variance of the actual time spent in class was only eight minutes. First-grade classrooms in the National Follow Through

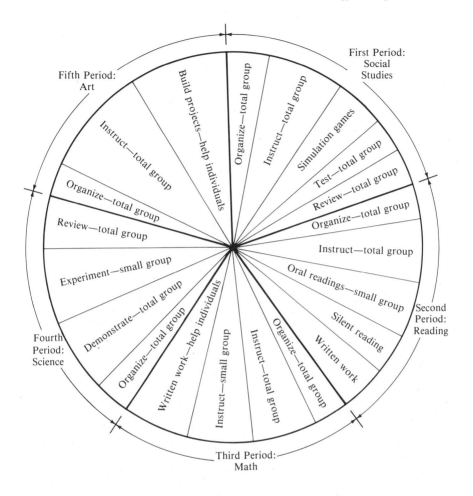

FIGURE 16.1   School day available time by periods and activities.

Observation Study (Stallings, 1975) varied as much as one hour and 30 minutes in length of school day; secondary class periods for remedial reading varied from 40 to 55 minutes (Stallings, Needels, & Stayrook, 1979). Findings from these studies indicate that mere length of the school day or the length of a class period in secondary schools was not related to student academic achievement. Clearly, student learning does depend on how the available time is used, not just on the amount of time available.

Academic Learning Time

Researchers at the Far West Laboratory for Educational Research and Development initiated the idea of academic learning time (ALT) in the Beginning Teacher Evaluation Study (BTES) (Fisher et al., 1978). ALT had four basic components. The first was the time available for academic work; the second was the students' time-on-task; the third was the error rate or the appropriateness of the work computed primarily from the errors students made in homework or seatwork; and the fourth was the relationship of the work being performed to the outcome measures that are used to assess performance.

Powell and Dishaw (1978), reporting data from the BTES, indicated that the actual time allocated to academic studies for second graders ranged from 62 minutes to 123 minutes per day, and for fifth graders from 49 to 105 minutes per day. The correlation of allocated learning time with achievement varied from one test to another in this study. However, in the Follow Through Observation Study (Stallings, 1975), time spent in mathematics, reading, and academic verbal interactions was related to achievement. Time spent working with textbooks (as opposed to time spent with puzzles, games, and toys) was related to achievement in reading and math. Time spent in small groups (as opposed to one-to-one instruction) was also associated with student academic gain. Conversely, time spent in more exploratory activities was positively related to scores on a nonverbal problem-solving test and to a lower student absence rate. Similar relationships were also found in a study of California third-grade Early Childhood Education classes (Stallings, Cory, Fairweather, & Needels, 1978).

It is of interest to know what percentage of time allocated to academic subjects is used by students to engage in academic work. Powell and Dishaw (1978), in the BTES study cited above, reported that the engaged time of second-grade students varied from 38 minutes to 98 minutes, and that of fifth-grade students varied from 49 to 105 minutes. Student-engaged time was positively associated with student achievement in all tests and at both grade levels. Summative findings reported by Berliner and Rosenshine (1977) suggest that the more academic learning time students accumulate, the higher their scores will be on criterion tests.

Achievement Levels and Academic Time

The variation in the amount of student-engaged time by achievement groups was reported by Evertson (1980). On the average, low-achieving junior high students were engaged 40% of the time in academic activities compared with 85% engaged time for high-achieving students. Low-achieving students experienced less variation in the activities that occurred during the class period and had more "dead time" (nothing happening) than did the more able students.

Even though high-achieving students are more inclined to be engaged in academic tasks, it is of considerable importance to allocate sufficient time and effort to working with low-achieving students who may not be so inclined. Stallings (1975) reported that low-achieving third graders in Follow Through prospered more from an increase in time spent in reading and math than did the higher-achieving students. *Caution*: For all students, there is a point at which more time does not produce more learning. Such curvilinear effects have been reported by Soar (1978).

Time Distributed across Activities

A study by Stallings, Cory, Fairweather, and Needels (1978) identified strategies for teaching basic reading skills in secondary schools. These included distributing time across activities, interactive instruction, and the focus of instruction. In classrooms where teachers were efficient in making assignments and allocating materials, there was more time available for instruction and students gained more in reading. It is important to start on time and continue until the closing bell rings. The distribution of time across several activities during the class period was also an effective strategy for keeping students on task. Effective teachers in three studies of secondary schools distributed time in the following ways:

Organization/Management Activities (15%)
Take roll
Make announcements
Make clear expectations for quality and quantity of work
Clarify behavioral expectations
Pass papers or books (out and in)

Interactive On-Task Activites (50%)
Review/discuss previous work
Inform/instruct (demonstrate/give examples)
Question/check for understanding
Reteach small group (if necessary)
Read aloud/develop concepts

Noninteractive On-Task Activities (35%)
Written work
Silent reading
Teacher monitoring/guiding

The percentage of time allocated to each of these activities varied across classrooms according to the achievement level of the students. Interestingly, an ample amount of oral reading was helpful for the low-achieving students, but was not so important for students achieving above the fourth-grade level (see Table 16.1). The oral reading was handled through lessons where vocabulary had been carefully developed, and where teachers helped students develop work concepts within a small-group setting of students with similar reading skills. Students who are operating at this level need to hear and say the words as well as read and write the words. These students can usually pronounce or sound out words but often do not understand words in the context of a story. Secondary students' comprehension scores

TABLE 16.1. Distribution of Time Across Activities in Four Ability Groups in Secondary Reading Classrooms[a]

	Group I[b] (X percent)	Group II (X percent)	Group III (X percent)	Group IV (X percent)
Interactive on-task activities				
Reading aloud	21	9	1	1
Instruction	16	11	17	10
Discussion	12	5	3	1
Drill and practice	4	4	4	2
Praise/support[c]	19	16	7	11
Corrective feedback[c]	20	16	4	12
Noninteractive on-task activities				
Classroom management	12	15	17	27
Reading silently	9	16	12	21
Written assignments	4	22	23	28
Off-task activites				
Social interactions	5	6	3	8
Students uninvolved	6	4	4	9

[a] These activities may occur simultaneously; therefore, the sum is greater than 100%
[b] Group I—low pretest/high gain. Group II—moderate pretest/moderate gain. Group III —high pretest/moderate gain. Group IV—No gain. X = group mean.
[c] This variable is reported as frequency of occurrence per 45-minute period.

are often lower than their vocabulary scores. Oral reading allows the teacher to hear the students' reading problems, ask clarifying questions, provide explanations to help students comprehend new words, and link the meaning to students' prior experience or knowledge.

Students who were in classrooms where slight or no gain was made spent more time than other students on written assignments (28%) and silent reading (21%). They had less instruction, discussion/review, and drill/practice. Some of these students were assigned to spend entire periods working in workbooks with very little instruction from the teacher. Such classrooms often registered more student misbehavior. Students with reading problems are likely to have shorter attention spans, and the opportunity to be involved in several activities during one class period seemed to help these students stay on-task.

STRATEGIES THAT HELP STUDENTS STAY ON-TASK

Students will be aided to stay on-task and misbehave less if the teacher's expectations regarding behavior and the quality and quantity of work to be accomplished are clear. The supportive and interactive nature of the instruction also affects the students' on-task behavior. Another important dimension is the appropriateness of the lesson for the achievement level of the student.

Clarity of First-Day Organization and Planning

Work by Carolyn Evertson and Ed Emmer (1980) focused upon an organization of 102 junior high school English and math classrooms. Several characteristics differentiated more and less effective teacher-managers. Classrooms where there was less student misbehavior and more student gain through the year had the following characteristics:

1. Teachers made rules, consequences, and procedures clear on the first day. They monitored the students and followed through with consequences for those who did not comply.
2. Teachers established a system of student responsibility and accountability for work on the first day.
3. Teachers were skillful in organizing several instructional activities.

Interactive Supportive Instruction

During the study of how teachers allocated time to various classroom activities, it became clear that teachers who were interactive in their teaching style had students who achieve more in reading. This interactive style included providing oral instruction for new work, discussing and reviewing students' work, providing drill and practice, asking questions, acknowledging correct responses, and supportively correcting wrong responses.

It was important that teachers try to include all students in classroom discussions and review sessions. The effective teachers did not call upon volunteers but rather called upon a particular student. When volunteers are solicited, the same people take part each day and many students may not be involved at all. When a student is called on by name, it is important that the question be at a level where the student is most likely to be successful. However, if the student gives an incorrect response, it is important that the instructor stay with that student and rephrase the question or give a clue so that the student can succeed and give a correct answer. A wrong answer can provide an opportunity for the teacher to clarify and reteach, if necessary. It is important in secondary remedial classrooms that wrong responses be handled in a supportive manner since research indicates these students do not thrive on demeaning experiences of failure.

This interactive type of instruction is important in the teaching of subjects other than remedial reading. Tom Good (1980) found that junior high school students learned more mathematics in classrooms where teachers were active in their instruction. These teachers made assignments and provided information in a clear manner. They asked students appropriate questions and provided immediate feedback to student responses. Unfortunately many teachers of general-math students are not active in their teaching style. In a study of math classes in 11 schools, Stallings and Robertson (1979) found that teachers more often told general-math students to do written workbook assignments in class and less often gave them instruction or review of seatwork than they did students in geometry or calculus classes. In classrooms where students are more involved, more achievement occurs. Students in general mathematics or prealgebra were off-task significantly more often than were students in algebra II, geometry, or calculus classes.

Eleven of the teachers in the study were observed in both lower- and advanced-math classes. When the observations of the teachers were compared, we found that the same teacher would be active with advanced classes and *not* active with the lower classes. These low-achieving students need instruction from teachers to stay on-task. Programmed workbooks will not help them learn the mathematical relationships necessary to cope in life. A teacher can see in students' faces whether or not they understand. A teacher can select another example from the students' background and explain it on the chalkboard. The most important finding in this research is that teachers need to actively teach. The advanced classes received active instruction and the less able students in general-science classes received workbook assignments. This is not effective instruction for low-achieving students. Relationships similar to those described in mathematics classes were found in general-science and physics classes.

Focus of Instruction

If teachers are interactive in their instructional style, to whom should they focus their instruction: individuals, small groups, or the total group? During the last decade considerable energy has been directed toward the development of individualized programs. Federal, state, and local funds have been spent to develop programmed reading, mathematics, and science books. All of these programmed materials were aimed at providing children with activities in which they could progress at their own rates. It was assumed that if students were working at their own pace through a series of sequential exercises, learning would occur—and it did for some students, but not for others. In general, there has been a great disillusionment with individualized instruction. Some students learn best when new information is presented to a small group of students who are operating at a similar pace (Stallings, 1975; Stallings, Needels, & Stayrook, 1979). Learning occurs when students read aloud, and hear others ask questions and respond. Hearing and speaking as well as reading and writing help students integrate and retain information. Individualized programs based almost totally on workbooks do not allow for this type of group learning.

At a conference sponsored by the National Institute of Education regarding instructional dimensions, 60 teachers discussed their experience with and attitudes toward individualized instruction. Teachers reported that in most individualized programs they felt relegated to being record keepers. Where workbooks were relied upon to provide instruction for students, teachers felt unable to integrate the students' learning (Amarel & Stallings, 1978). It appears that students need interactions with teachers. A teacher can develop concepts with a group and can change examples or illustrations to coincide with the group's background experience. If students do not understand, the teacher can find yet another example. Books or machines do not do that. Books or machines provide opportunities to practice and reinforce what teachers are teaching, but research suggests they are not sufficient to provide the instruction that students need (Stallings, 1975).

Curriculum and Instructional Strategy

Much of the research on student learning during the 1970s focused upon classroom instructional processes, that is, teaching processes rather than curriculum. Work by Carroll (1963) and Bloom (1974) provided models for planning instructional processes and curriculums that would insure student mastery. Hyman and Cohen (1979) suggest seven techniques that will increase participation and thereby insure mastery. The techniques are

1. Define instructional objectives behaviorally so that learner and teacher know exactly where they are, where they are going, and where they have been.
2. Modularize learning by cutting down the "bites" to small, self-contained "nibbles." Closure is the most potent of all positive-feedback techniques. The smaller the bite, the more immediate the closure.
3. Control the stimulus so we know exactly what the learner is responding to. That is a major problem in commercially published materials.
4. Go directly to the defined behavior—that is, direct reaching of the behavior or "attitude" sought rather than "building to it" or around it.
5. Check for understanding and provide immediate feedback to all learner responses. The more immediate the feedback, the more efficient the learning.
6. Set the level of instruction so that feedback is maximally positive. Success breeds success.
7. Reinforce by positive feedback the learner's critical response. The critical response is the one that responds to the appropriate stimulus defined precisely by the instructional objective.

HOW USEFUL IS THE TIME RESEARCH TO TEACHERS?

Experiments in Teacher Training

In an effort to make their research findings useful to teachers, several researchers (Anderson, Evertson, & Brophy, 1979; Crawford et al., 1978; Good & Grouws, 1979; Stallings, Needels, & Stayrook, 1979) translated their findings into in-service training. They conducted experiments with treatment and control teachers. All of these experiments reported teacher change and positive effects upon students.

Several of the studies mentioned in this chapter did not result in efforts to train teachers. Nevertheless, the findings have been reported in such specificity that teachers or teacher trainers can translate findings into practice. The Beginning Teacher Evaluation Study (Fisher et al., 1978) does present descriptions of how much time is spent in several activities: reading circle, seatwork, silent reading, games, transition, teacher presentation. Also reported is the percent of students involved, attendance of students, teacher's role, and student's role. These findings are being used by teachers and trainers of teachers.

A Model for Staff Development

The variables used in the Stallings et al. (1979) Teaching Basic Reading Skills in Secondary Schools study have considerable face validity, which makes the findings understandable to teachers and was an important factor in translating the findings into a staff development model called the Effective Time Training program.

Every staff development model includes a curriculum and a delivery system. *Curriculum* means the content and *delivery* means where, when, how, and number of participants. A good content with poor delivery, or vice versa, is not likely to be effective in bringing about change in teacher behavior.

The goal of the Teaching and Learning Institute's Staff Development Program is to help teachers learn to manage their classroom time effectively. The curriculum is based upon research findings. The delivery system is personalized instruction and interactive small-group problem solving. The content of the program is derived from research funded by the National Institute of Education. The delivery system was also developed with funds from that agency.*

Essentially our model could be called a Mastery Learning Staff Development Model. It has components similar to Bloom's mastery learning model (Bloom, 1974).

Pretest
Observe teachers
Assess what is needed from teacher observation profiles
Start where they are

Inform
Link theory, practice, and teacher experience
Provide practical examples from classroom situations

---

*The early research was carried out at SRI International in Menlo Park, California.

Organize and guide practice
Provide conceptual units of behaviors to change
Support and encourage behavior change
Assess and provide feedback
Help integrate into scheme

Posttest
Observe teachers
Provide feedback to teachers
Provide feedback to trainers

The key features are to state the objective of the staff development program; select or develop instruments that will measure the behavior of interest; observe and/or test teachers to see how they are implementing the instructional strategies before the intervention; provide the intervention; observe the teachers; and measure the behavior change.

Using that model in a quasi experiment (Stallings, Needels, & Stayrook, 1979), treatment teachers implemented 25 out of 31 variables by the end of the school year, and their students gained more in reading than did a control group of students.

HOW SCHOOL POLICY RELATES
TO EFFECTIVE USE OF TIME

During the past four years, in-service training has been provided to over 200 secondary teachers. The training program provided teachers with specific recomendations for using time more effectively. The sessions were very interactive and, in every group, the teachers reported school policy or principal leadership style that supported or discouraged their implementation of the program. Their primary concerns were with students' being absent, being tardy, and misbehaving. If the school policies on such matters were firm, clear, and consistent, teachers felt more able to implement the program. Teachers were also concerned about the number of interruptions during a class period. The loudspeaker, students' being called from class, or the late arriver—all of these stopped the smooth flow of instruction and took students off-task.

A study by Stallings and Mohlman (1981) examined these links between school policy, leadership style, teachers' and students' attitudes, and teachers' and students' behavior. The study was conducted in eight San Francisco Bay area high schools that had multiethnic student populations from low- to high-income families. The data were obtained from principal interviews, student and teacher questionnaires, and school and classroom observations. Scatterplots, correlations, and descriptive statistics were used to analyze the data. The major findings from this study were as follows:

In schools where policies and rules were clearer and more consistently enforced, there was higher teacher morale, fewer classroom intrusions, less litter and vandalism, a lower absence rate, less class misbehavior, and more time-on-task.

In schools where there were more administrative support services and fewer burdensome duties, there was higher teacher morale and less classroom misbehavior.

In schools where the principal was more collaborative and respectful, teachers had higher morale and students felt more friendliness.

In schools with more supportive principals, more teachers implemented the training program.

In schools where the policies and rules were clear and consistent, more teachers changed their classroom behavior as recommended.

In schools where the teachers implemented the Effective Use of Time Training program, students spent more time-on-task.

Findings regarding effective school policy and principal leadership style were similar for schools serving high-income and low-income students.

The research of Stallings and Mohlman (1981) primarily serves as a source for building hypotheses; however, two findings from this study have cost implications: (1) Student attendance rates were significantly better in schools where the principal provided a clear, consistent, collaboratively developed policy regarding student absence, cuts, and tardiness. It was also important that these policies were well communicated to parents, students, and teachers. (2) In schools with such policies, fewer dollars were spent on vandalism.

The primary source of school income is the average daily attendance of students. A source of cash outflow is school repair for vandalism. During a time of shrinking school budgets, these findings regarding school policy, student absence, and vandalism have important implications for school administration.

A SUCCESS STORY

The San Diego City Schools came under court order to improve the quality of education in 14 of their elementary and 5 of their secondary schools so that at least 50% of the students would perform at the fiftieth percentile within five years. This was a tall order because these schools' scores were between the thirtieth and thirty-eighth percentiles.

During the school year 1976–1977, the Elementary Basic Skills Task Force reviewed the Beginning Teacher Evaluation Study (BTES) and became interested in academic learning time and time-on-task. They also became more interested in the Follow Through Direct Instruction model (sponsored by the University of Oregon). Another interest was developed in classroom interruptions and intrusions via a study by Far West Laboratory and the Stallings Secondary Basic Skills study.

A fourth area of interest to the Task Force centered on the works of John Carroll and Benjamin Bloom. These works were examined during school year 1979–1980.

The San Diego program staff put together a staff development program with the components shown in Figure 16.2. They have used the various elements from much of the research of the 1970s to provide a valid instructional program.

To their credit, they used a training model that provided observation of the teachers before the intervention started, and systematic weekly feedback from site resource teachers. The sole responsibility of these resource teachers was to provide technical assistance to teachers trying to implement the quality program in reading and math.

At the end of the first year, some schools were above the requirements of the court orders. All others had made substantial gains. Specifically, in the fall of 1980, only 27.5% of the sixth-grade students were performing at or above the fiftieth percentile in reading. Ten months later, 37.8% of the sixth graders were performing at or above the fiftieth percentile. The gains in math were even more dramatic. In the fall, only 31% were performing at or above the fiftieth percentile. In spring, 48.8% were performing at that level. The credit must go to the comprehensive nature of the program that was established and the support it received from the superintendent's office, the school board, parents, principals, and teachers. A sign on many classroom doors is indicative of how serious they are about the program. It reads: "STOP! This means YOU! Achievement Goals Program in progress."

A DEVELOPING THEORY OF SCHOOLING

The nature of effective schooling has piqued the curiosity of researchers for many decades. In the last decade, we have studied schools in isolation, classrooms in isolation from schools, and students in isolation from class-rooms and schools. Findings regarding the percent of student time-on-task will not necessarily help a teacher do a better job. The teacher needs school policies that will support the good use of classroom time. The teacher also needs specific information about which students are off-task during which activities, so that adjustments can be made.

The charge of the 1980s is to study the whole school context, taking into consideration administration, teachers, and students, together. The results of this research, combined with the empirical findings generated during the

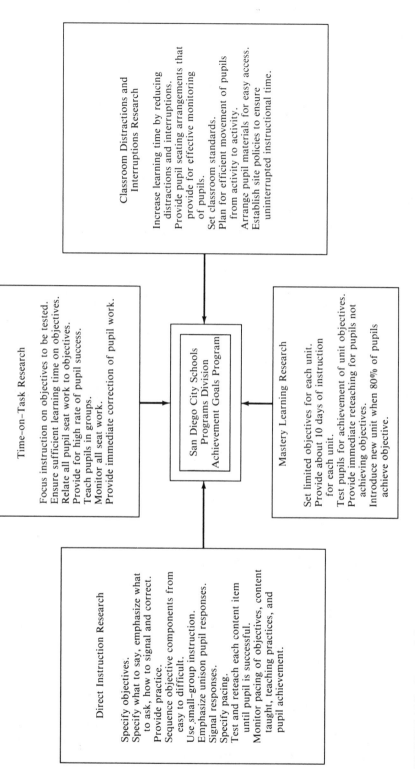

FIGURE 16.2   Research base of achievement goals program. (Reprinted with permission of the San Diego City Schools, September 1981.)

research in the 1970s, may enable us to generate a comprehensive and practical theory of effective schooling.

REFERENCES

Amarel, M., & Stallings, J. (1978). Individualized instruction. In *Perspectives on the Instructional Dimensions Study* (chap. 6). Washington, D.C.: National Institute of Education.

Anderson, L., Evertson, C., & Brophy, J. (1979). An experimental study of effective teaching in first-grade reading groups. *Elementary School Journal, 79,* 193–223.

Berliner, D. C., & Rosenshine, B. V. (1977). The acquisition of knowledge in the classroom. In R. C. Anderson, R. J. Spiro, & W. E. Montague (Eds.), *Schooling and the acquisition of knowledge.* Hillsdale, N.J.: Lawrence Erlbaum Associates.

Bloom, B. S. (1974, September). Time and learning. *American Psychologist, 29,* 682–688.

Carroll, J. B. (1963). A model of school learning. *Teachers College Record, 64*(8), 723–733.

Crawford, J., Gage, N. L., Corno, L., Stayrook, N., Mitman, A., Schunk, D., & Stallings, J. A. (1978). *An experiment on teacher effectiveness and parent-assisted instruction in the third grade* (Vol. I–III). Stanford: Center for Educational Research.

Evertson, C. (1980, April). *Differences in instructional activities in high and low achieving junior high classes.* Paper presented at the annual meeting of the American Educational Research Association, Boston.

Evertson, C., & Emmer, E. (1980). *Effective management at the beginning of the school year in junior high classes.* Austin: Research and Development Center for Teacher Education.

Fisher, C. W., Filby, N. N., Marliave, R. S., Cahen, L. S., Dishaw, M. M., Moore, J. E., & Berliner, D. C. (1978). *Teaching behaviors, academic learning time, and student achievement: Final report of Phase III-B, Beginning Teacher Evaluation Study.* San Francisco: Far West Laboratory for Educational Research and Development.

Good, T. L. (1980). *The Missouri mathematics effectiveness project.* Columbia, MO: School of Education, University of Missouri.

Good, T. L., & Grouws, D. A. (1979). The Missouri mathematics effectiveness project: An experimental study in fourth-grade classrooms. *Journal of Educational Psychology, 71,* 335–362.

Harnischfeger, A., & Wiley, D. (1978, March). *Conceptual and policy issues in elementary school teaching and learning.* Paper presented at the annual meeting of the American Educational Research Association, Toronto.

Hyman, J. S., & Cohen, S. A. (1979). Learning for mastery: Ten conclusions after 15 years and 3,000 schools. *Educational Leadership, 37*(2), 104–106.

Jackson, P. W. (1977). Looking into education's crystal ball. *Instructor, 87*(38), 38.

Powell, M., & Dishaw, M. M. (1978). *A realistic picture of reading instructional time.* Unpublished manuscript.

Soar, R. (1978, March). *Setting variables, classroom interaction, and multiple pupil outcomes*. Paper presented at the annual meeting of the American Educational Research Association, Toronto.

Stallings, J. (1975, December). Implementation and child effects of teaching practices in Follow Through classrooms. *Monographs of the Society for Research in Child Development*, *40*(7–8), 50–93.

Stallings, J. A., Cory, R., Fairweather, J., & Needels, M. (1978). *A study of basic reading skills taught in secondary schools*. Menlo Park, Calif.: SRI International.

Stallings, J., & Mohlman, G. (1981). *School policy, leadership style, teacher change, and student behavior in eight schools*. Final report to the National Institute of Education. Menlo Park, Calif.: SRI International.

Stallings, J., Needels, M., & Stayrook, N. (1979). *How to change the process of teaching basic reading skills in secondary schools*. Final report to the National Institute of Education. Menlo Park, Calif.: SRI International.

Stallings, J. A., & Robertson, A. (1979). *Factors influencing women's decisions to enroll in elective mathematics classes in high school*. Final report to the National Institute of Education. Menlo Park, Calif.: SRI International.

Part V

Instructional Time: Commentaries and Critiques

17

Time-off-Task at a
Time-on-Task Conference

Philip W. Jackson
University of Chicago

EDITORS' INTRODUCTION

Professor Jackson, a talented and respected critic of educational research, analyzes the conference by examining the closing lines of a Dylan Thomas poem that kept coming back to him as he sat and listened. Professor Jackson uses the analysis in describing his fear that the research on instructional time is rather close to being banal (see Chapter 18 for similar views). He sees little in the work that is new or that helps teachers improve life in classrooms. He sees the findings as commonsensical and, perhaps, as leading to a return to the efficiency notions of schooling that were so prominent in — and deleterious to — education during the first few decades of this century.

"Time held me green and dying/Though I sang in my chains like the sea." Those closing lines of Dylan Thomas's "Fern Hill" crossed my mind more than once as I sat listening to the speakers during the first day of the conference whose proceedings comprise the contents of this volume. Why the fragment of a poem I had not read in years should have occurred to me when it did, requires only common sense to understand. The theme of the conference and, consequently, the central concern of almost everyone there was *time*, *time* as a variable in the formulation of the teaching-learning process, *time* as a component in a model of how instruction should proceed. The *time* required for teaching and the *time* required for learning were thoughts uppermost in the mind of almost every participant. Small wonder, therefore, that attendance at such an event should trigger the remembrance of a line of poetry that contained the word *time*.

What was harder to figure out when it was happening was why those particular lines of poetry resonated as they did. For the fact is that the tag end of "Fern Hill" did pop in and out of consciousness whenever someone happened to mention the magic word *time*. Nor was it but one of many fragments dislodged from the storehouse of my memory by the events of the day.

On the contrary, once the refrain was sounded it was hard to shake off. It behaved like one of those catchy commercial jingles whose melody we continue humming to ourselves, whether we want to or not, long after the actual commercial has ceased to be heard. I realized at once, of course, that something more than hypnotic rhythm or melodic appeal was at the root of its tenacious hold on me. The trick was to fathom what that extra something might be.

Obviously, the passage from Thomas's poem was connected with my emerging reaction to the conference as a whole. But *how* was it connected? What was it seeking to say? I could not answer those questions immediately, nor do I believe I can do so now. Nonetheless, though much uncertainty remains, my grasp of the experience is now much better than it was at the start. Accordingly, I shall proceed to examine those two lines of poetry a bit more fully here, as a first step in bringing to light their bearing on my reaction to the proceedings of the conference. That much accomplished, I shall return to the questions that have just been asked.

This manner of reporting on my experience as a conference participant necessitates my paying scant attention to the details of individual presentations, even to the point of ignoring what are obvious whopping differences, not to mention a few sharp disagreements, among the views espoused by the various speakers. By overlooking such matters I do not intend to slight the importance of any of the papers presented that day. I trust, however, that whatever detailed observations and criticisms I might otherwise have made will be readily apparent to readers of the papers themselves. So too will be their obvious merits.

"Time held me green and dying/Though I sang in my chains like the sea." What meaning do those lines convey? The first thing to note is that they have something to do with a struggle, a struggle to escape from captivity. Next, it is obvious from the tense of the verbs that the struggle occurred in the past. The first-person pronouns tell us that the speaker himself, in all likelihood the poem's author, was the one who had been struggling. The word *green* makes it clear that the action took place when the speaker was relatively young.

So, at the start our brief exegesis yields an autobiographical portrayal of a young person in bondage, a mere child perhaps. The universality of the emotions evoked by such an image is worth noting. Among civilized people the world over, the mere thought of a child's being held captive, not to mention being kept in chains, is enough to arouse a mixture of rage, revulsion, and pity unmatched by nearly every other imagined form of cruelty and inhumanity. Heart-rending is the term usually reserved for such an effect.

When we turn to the question of the child's captor, we see at once that the evildoer is none other than time itself. Time holds green life in an embrace from which there is no escape. This, too, is a variant of an image deeply engraved in our collective consciousness. Time the villain, boney-fingered, wearing death's head, the grim reaper, the much-feared harvester of all living things—these and other portrayals of time as a despicable creature of one kind or another have become standard characters within our literary and artistic traditions.

But there is more to this image of a captive youth, held prisoner by monstrous time, than the emotions it evokes or the message it conveys about human mortality. To see what more there is we need remind ourselves of the obvious, which is that time is really not a person, no matter how cleverly an artist or poet or storyteller might dress the idea up. Not only is time not a person, it is not even a thing.

An answer to the question of time's ontological status, properly conceived, is a task for a physicist—or a philosopher perhaps—and need hardly detain us here. All we need note is that the struggle depicted in the lines of Thomas's poem is not between captor and captive in any ordinary sense. It is quite unlike the relationship between, say, humans and beasts or even between human prisoners and their equally human (though basically inhuman) guards. Rather it is a struggle between a living thing and something not living; indeed, something that is not even a thing. What is taking place, in other words, is a test of sorts between a person, on the one hand, and a fictionalized entity, an anthropomorphism, on the other.

The drama of human actors wrestling with abstract forces in human form is yet another artistic convention that has been around for a long time. In legend and in myth, humans have been depicted as engaged in battle with all sorts of nonmaterial combatants—time, death, sin, temptation, to mention but a few—each of them decked out in human disguise. Indeed, today's shoot-em-up western, with its saga of the good guys and the bad guys, is but a modern updating of that ancient dramaturgical format.

Finally, we need observe that the closing lines of Thomas's poem are not a lament. If anything, they come close to sounding jubilant. Though the hero of the story may remain captive in one sense, the final line reveals him to be the ultimate victor. What makes him so? His capacity for song. Despite his chains he is free to sing and in so doing escapes from captivity, figuratively speaking, on the wings of song. Thus, in the final analysis, youth succeeds in outwitting its captor. Through the device of art, the captive child eludes the bonds of time.

Having explicated what seem to me to be the central ideas embedded in the fragment of poetry that kept intruding into my thoughts during the conference, all that remains is to explain what those ideas have to do with my reaction to the conference as a whole. The explanation actually has two parts, only one of which need concern us here, that being the part specifically related to the substantive and methodological focus of the conference. The other part, which has to do with the contrast between the romantic imagination, as epitomized in Thomas's poem, and the dominant ideology of the educational research community in general, is too broad a topic to be treated in an essay such as this and is mentioned here only in passing.

The conference-specific part of the explanation begins with the acknowledgment of discomfort, a dominant motif—revealed in the phrases "held me," "dying," "chains"—of the lines we have been examining. Clearly, a part of me was not particularly happy with the goings-on of the conference. My silent recitation of what I remember of "Fern Hill" was but one way of expressing that unhappiness. Not only did the poem express what I was feeling in a general sense, it did so quite precisely. I identified with the character in the poem. Like him, I too was struggling with the abstract entity of time, in whose embrace my thoughts, quite literally, were being held captive. Prevented from singing in my chains like the sea (under the circumstances I dared not even hum!), I let Thomas's words do my vocalizing for me.

The source of my discomfort was twofold. First was the suspicion, which increased as the day wore on, that the investigation of time as an instructional variable is not nearly as promising a research endeavor as many of its advocates make it out to be. Second was my accompanying feeling of déjà vu, of witnessing something that has happened before. In this instance, that something was the rebirth of a perspective on schooling that I thought had gone out of fashion a long time ago (and for what seem to me to have been very good reasons). Each of these aspects of my reaction requires some elaboration.

At the risk of oversimplification, I would summarize as follows the reasoning behind much of the research discussed at the conference. The starting point is the observation that learning takes time. From there it is an easy step to the conclusion that the more time a person spends at a learning task, the more that person will learn (within broad limits, of course). But "time-spent-learning" is itself an ambiguous concept whose parameters, in real life at least, are not easily determined. We know, for example, that a first-grade boy can *seem* to be engaged in the act of learning something—as when we observe him sitting in a classroom—when, in fact, his thoughts are a million miles from the task at hand. Consequently, a more precise criterion of active engagement in learning is required; *ergo*, the notion of time-on-task, or as some researchers prefer, active learning time.

From these two premises—that learning takes time and that not all time allegedly devoted to learning is actually well spent—it is but a hop, skip, and jump to the practical suggestion that teachers and school administrators ought to be able to increase the learning of this or that school subject on the part of their students either by allocating a larger block of time to the subject in question or by seeing to it that the time already available is more productively spent (i.e., in a way that increases time-on-task). The search for ways of attaining the latter goal in particular provides the central focus of the applied side of the research endeavor.

The brevity of this overview of the guiding logic behind time-on-task research may create an erroneous expectation concerning the research derived from such simple-minded premises, namely that the research itself will be equally simple-minded or at best will succeed in merely proving the obvious. That need not be so by any means. Though the key ideas, as expressed here, do indeed come close to being banalities, there is nothing obvious about how those ideas work themselves out within the context of a classroom. Nor is there anything simple, much less simple-minded, about the answer to the question of how to improve educational practice within the framework of those indisputable observations about the nature of learning. For example, though it is little more than a truism to assert that all learners are inattentive from time to time, the question of *how* inattentive, when asked of the average student in today's classrooms, remains largely unknown. What little evidence does exist suggests that the problem of inattentiveness or, in the jargon of the day, time-off-task may be much greater than most educators suspect. Turning to the applied aspects of the research in question, it is easy enough to announce that time-on-task should be maximized, but it is quite another thing to develop ingenious ways for that to happen. Thus, within this overall program of inquiry there are both descriptive and prescriptive questions of considerable importance awaiting answers.

Yet, having acknowledged the legitimacy of the enterprise in intellectual terms, I must go on to say that I have grave doubts about its yielding very much in the way of genuine new insights into either the teaching or the learning process. I come to this conclusion because I fail to see where the basic set of ideas *leads to* in any important theoretical or conceptual sense. Of course researchers can and probably will continue to construct ever more elaborate "models" of the teaching-learning process. And time is bound to remain one of the important independent variables in such constructions. But most such "models" that I have seen to date do not even generate interesting hypotheses (i.e., ones that common sense would not itself suggest); much less do they point the way to useful and important knowledge. Quite frankly, the usual diagram of such a "model," with its neatly drawn boxes, its solid and dotted lines, and its pen-and-ink arrows pointing this way and that, makes me suspect that the person who drew it or directed it drawn not only cannot write but is suffering from a repressed desire to become an electrical engineer!

Time-on-task is an important concept, true enough. But most educators, though they may never have used the term itself, have known that for quite some time. Take John Locke as an instance. Almost 300 years ago he pointed out that "the great skill of a teacher is to get and keep the attention of his scholar; whilst he has that, he is sure to advance as fast as the learner's abilities will carry him; and without that, all his bustle and bother will be to little or no purpose." What I fail to see as yet are clear signs that the research in question will ultimately add very much to the wisdom of Locke's observation.

Alarming statistics that reveal how little time many of today's students spend at their tasks may serve the useful function of alerting educators to a problem that is presently being overlooked, that much I readily concede. But once the alert has been sounded, once we know that some youngsters receive as little as 18 minutes of instructional time per hour, or whatever the actual figure turns out to be, what does the researcher who made that startling announcement do for an encore?

Moreover, when we turn from empirical descriptions of inattentiveness to the question of what to do about such a state of affairs, the answers emanating from the research community to date are very small in number and strike me as being singulary lacking in inventiveness. For example, in one of the conference papers it was seriously proposed that pupils might be required to sharpen their pencils before class as a way of increasing engaged learning time. An additional suggestion was for the teacher to have paper passed out ahead of time. Now, really. I don't know how such advice strikes others, but I suspect most seasoned classroom teachers would find it highly amusing. I certainly do.

Added to my misgivings about what we might expect to come out of this line of research, either in the way of new knowledge about schooling in general or new ideas about how to make it better, was the disquieting feeling of déjà vu that has already been mentioned. On several occasions during the conference I felt as though I were witnessing the return of an outlook on education that had its heyday in this country around the time of World War I. That was when the thoughts of educational leaders about how to improve our schools were dominated by what the historian Thomas Callahan has aptly called "the cult of efficiency."

In his book on the subject Callahan describes in great detail the hold that visions of "scientific management" had upon the profession of educational administration at the time. The elimination of "waste" became an obsession of many administrators. Time and motion studies, a technique borrowed from industry, seemed to provide a surefire method of achieving that goal. The hero of the day was the efficiency engineer.

It is a very long way from such abandoned notions to today's studies of time-on-task, I grant, yet echoes of that earlier period can be heard, it seems to me, in contemporary talk about wasted time in classrooms and in today's insistence upon making every instructional minute count. There are great differences between the two perspectives, of course, but their similarities were great enough to start me thinking about that earlier time and wondering whether it might be possible to see history repeat itself. In my mind's eye I began to picture an army of efficiency experts descending once again upon America's classrooms. That thought led to the image of students squirming under such surveillance. The sound of clicking stopwatches was almost audible. Time, students! Time! Dylan Thomas's captive youth rose into view, straining at his bonds.

So much, then, for one set of reasons why the lines from "Fern Hill" stayed with me as they did during my attendance at the conference. There is an additional set of reasons, as I have said, but they comprise another story, for another time.

18

The Uses and Abuses
of Truisms

Denis C. Phillips
Stanford University

EDITORS' INTRODUCTION
Dr. Phillips, a valued critic of educational research, states his beliefs quite clearly. He points out that the basic arguments put forth in this book are so commonsensical as to be truisms. Some, Dr. Phillips goes on to suggest, are really trivial truisms and therefore quite useless.

(

THE "PLAIN MAN'S" VIEW

Let me set the stage by appealing to authority. To do this I cite two of the leading philosophers of the twentieth century. First, Bertrand Russell:

> The manner in which animals learn has been much studied in recent years, with a great deal of patient observation and experiment. Certain results have been obtained as regards the kinds of problems that have been investigated, but on general principles there is still much controversy. One may say broadly that all the animals that have been carefully observed have behaved so as to confirm the philosophy in which the observer believed before his observations began. Nay, more, they have all displayed the national characteristics of the observer. Animals studied by Americans rush about frantically, with an incredible display of hustle and pep, and at last achieve the desired result by chance. Animals observed by Germans sit still and think, and at last evolve the solution out of their inner consciousness. To the plain man, such as the present writer, this situation is discouraging. (Russell, 1960)

And second, Russell's one-time student, Ludwig Wittgenstein, who wrote at the end of his *Philosophical Investigations*:

> The confusion and barrenness of psychology is not to be explained by calling it a "young science"; its state is not comparable with that of physics for instance, in its beginnings.... For in psychology, there are experimental methods and *conceptual confusion....*
>
> The existence of the experimental method makes us think we have the means of solving the problems which trouble us; though problem and method pass one another by. (Wittgenstein, 1963)

Wittgenstein's point is one that psychologists and educational researchers have made themselves. Psychology and educational research are rich in method, but less rich in fruitful theory. They are replete with technical accomplishment, but rather barren with respect to fruitful results. To be sure, there are lots of findings, but are they findings that were worth finding?

Now it might be argued that the papers delivered at this present conference show that these remarks are completely unfounded—the papers did, in general, report findings that have tremendous potential to lead to improvement of teaching and learning in schools. On these grounds, the case runs, the research is worth continuing. I am not convinced on either score.

To convey my uneasiness, I ask you to adopt the role of Russell's "plain man." What would he have gleaned from the present conference? Here is my own tentative list of things that this worthy would have heard that researchers have recently established:

1. The more interruptions and distractions that creep into classrooms, the

less learning time there is available. Or, to put it "mathematically":

time allocated to a subject − time wasted or lost =
time available for learning the subject

2. Processes in the real world take time. Learning is a process. Learning takes time.
3. Students cannot learn what is not presented to them. (Students do not learn physics, or calculus, or how to read, by "osmosis" or solely by innate maturation.)
4. The more time that is spent actually learning a subject, the more that is learnt.
5. Less time is wasted in classrooms where teachers give clear instructions; children have trouble following unclear instructions.
6. What a student *does* will influence whether that student *learns*.
7. Children "goof off" less the more the teacher supervises them.
8. Students in small groups can have their attention maintained more successfuly than those in large groups.

There can be little doubt that Russell's plain man would find this situation "discouraging." What sort of research findings are these? All of them are patently obvious and some are "trivially true."

HAMLYN'S WORLD

David Hamlyn, the British philosopher who is editor of the journal *Mind*, has written several papers and a book on Piaget (Hamlyn, 1978). In the course of his critiques, Hamlyn suggested that his readers try to imagine a world where certain key ideas of Piaget's were *not* true—a world where children mastered abstract and complex tasks before concrete and simple ones, for example. Such a world would differ crazily from our own, and one gets the sense that many of Piaget's views are unsurprising and necessarily (if not trivially) true. It just does not make sense to suppose that the world could work in a way opposite to the general mode sketched by Piaget.[1]

One can take the same tack with the findings discussed at this conference. What sort of world would it be if children learned more the *less* time they spent on a subject? If achievement was *not* related to the time spent engaged on a topic? If processes in the real world did not take time to complete? If learning of a subject in class increased as more irrelevancies and interruptions crept into class time?

As with Hamlyn's points about Piaget, one gets the sense that these findings are almost necessarily (and perhaps even trivially) true. Other things being equal, the more time spent learning math, the more math that *has* to be known; and the more time spent deciding what makes certain poetry beautiful, the more that *has* to be known about beautiful poems. Indeed, it suddenly seems strange to dress these truisms up as "findings."

There are two important caveats to add here. First, the distinction must be drawn between truisms and the places where these apply or do not apply. Thus, while it may be a truism that distractions within a classroom lessen the time available for learning, it is *not* a truism that in my classroom or in your classroom there is an unexpectedly high degree of lost time. It is here that research on instructional time has potentially important payoffs, but where its significance has been misunderstood also. If there is a lot of wasted time in classrooms, and if this waste has gone undetected, then its "unmasking" is of great practical importance, for it may thereby be possible to increase academic learning time by a significant percentage. In its effects, this research is akin to the industrial "time and motion" studies of yesteryear. It is for this reason, I suspect, that Michael Scriven and others regard research on instructional time so favorably. However, it is also apparent that "industrial efficiency" research is not of itself *theoretically* or *conceptually* particulary significant. There is waste; waste is bad; waste ought to be detected and eliminated—well and good, but this does not establish that the concept of "waste" (or of "wasted time") is a key to understanding efficient industrial (or classroom) practice. Another way of putting this is that those doing "industrial efficiency" research ought to be pleased that they are eliminating waste and increasing efficiency, and they ought to rest content with this. They should not pretend that they have thereby done a deep piece of fundamental research or have uncovered some key concepts to further our theoretical understanding of the basic processes underlying the phenomena they have rendered more efficient.

The second caveat concerns the concept of "triviality," and it is worth a section to itself.

ON TRIVIALLY TRUE RESEARCH

Philosophically, there is a distinction to be drawn between truisms and statements that are trivially true; the latter are, in effect, a subgroup of the former. A truism is a statement the truth of which is self-evident or obvious (e.g., "It is not likely to rain on a hot, cloudless day"), whereas a trivially true statement is one that is true by virtue of the meaning of the terms involved (e.g., "All colored objects are colored," or "All bachelors are unmarried"). Thus, "learning is a process and takes time" is trivially true, for by definition a process involves the succession or passage of time; "it is easier to keep a small group of children working on a task than it is a large group" is a truism, for it is obviously true, but it is not true by virtue of the meanings of the terms involved.

Now truisms and statements that are trivially true are not thereby *trivial*. The terms *truism* and *trivially true* refer to the patentness of the truth of statements, whereas *trivial* refers to their degree of value or usefulness. The two do not automatically go together; many a statement the truth of which is far from obvious is of no practical use ("There is a boulder weighing 1,073 pounds exactly 20 miles north of Denver"), and many truisms are vitally important and even theoretically significant ("The sky is dark at night").[2]

Truisms uncovered by researchers, then, are not necessarily trivial. But on the other hand, truisms do not require research in order to be uncovered. Agencies would be wasting money if they awarded grants to researchers who wanted to determine if all bachelors in the United States were unmarried, or if the sky is dark at night, or if small groups are easier to control than large groups.

There is one further complexity. Some pieces of popular wisdom —some apparent truisms—turn out not to be true at all. Rousseau regarded it as a truism that Sophie was not an intellectual match for Emile, and folks for thousands of years regarded it as patently obvious that the earth was flat. There seems to be no easy way of distinguishing between real and apparent (or psuedo) truisms.

Although he does not want to be overconfident, it is the considered opinion of the present writer that the findings of much instructional time research are *genuine* truisms!

DISGUISING THE PROBLEMS

Truistic or not, research on instructional time seems to have important policy implications. First, it has revealed that there is often a great deal of wasted time and distraction in school classrooms. But, more fundamentally, this reasearch apparently can... "lead teachers and supervisors of teachers to examine classroom processes in ways that logically relate to student achievement. Without turning classes into authoritarian factories of learning, many teachers can improve their effectiveness by attending to these variables and reorganizing classroom practices to maximize teaching time and learning time—resources over which they have considerable personal control" (Berliner, 1979).

Just how helpful is this advice? It must be remembered that truisms will often *appear* to be helpful, because they are so patently true. To highlight (if not parody) the issue, consider a lonely bachelor who wants to have a family. "Oh, that's easy," runs the helpful advice, "if you want to stop being a bachelor, just get married." The *real* problem, of course, is how to go about doing this—what sort of spouse to seek, how to win her over, and so forth. These basic problems get disguised when the truism "all bachelors are unmarried" is trotted back dressed up in the form of advice.

A similar point can be made about classrooms. Children may not be learning in school, so the advice given is "increase engaged learning time."

This disguises the issue—*how* is engaged time to be increased? The answer does not lie totally with the truisms "reduce distractions" and "give clear directions to the students." An important part of the solution is in interesting the students, in motivating them, in sequencing the material so that it is readily learnable, and the like. And here the wheel has turned full circle, back to the traditional problems of classroom teaching! In 1868, in his *Essays on Educational Reformers*, R. H. Quick wrote: "The art of teaching Pestalozzi's system consists in analyzing the knowledge that the children should acquire about their surroundings, arranging it in a regular sequence, and bringing it to the children's consciousness gradually and in the way in which their minds will act upon it" (Quick, 1910 Edition).

Pestalozzi and others have given their opinions about how to do all this, but what is required is research. Instructional-time research, however, does not seem to have the potential to provide the answers, for it does not recognize—or, at least, grapple with—these real problems.

LIMITS OF MEASURING THE MEASURABLE

There is another way in which the key issues get disguised. In a survey of research on instructional time, Barak Rosenshine pointed out that "student-engaged time" was a "proxy" for "content convered" (Rosenshine, 1979), and similar points were made at the present conference. However, it is evident that over the years there has been a tendency towards reification. The humble proxy has become an entity worthy of study in its own right—and it has been examined by psychologists, sociologists, and economists, and a technology of measurement and testing has arisen. The words of the sociologist Stanislav Andreski contain an important caution here: "In truth, there is no reason whatsoever to presume that amenability to measurement must correspond to importance" (Andreski, 1972).

It is the thing that is proxied that should be researched, not the measurable proxy. Again, Andreski puts it well: "Those who refuse to deal with important and interesting problems simply because the relevant factors cannot be measured condemn the social sciences to sterility" (Andreski, 1972).

CONCLUSIONS

The point of this discussion has not been to make the old point that educational research merely establishes what common sense already knows. This is part of the story—and necessarily so. If common sense were always—or even often—wrong, our species would have perished.

But some things known by common sense are not known at all—for they are wrong. So, researchers will sometimes reach conclusions that the plain person already knew; but sometimes they will not, and the conclusions will come as a surprise. However, the key point is that sometimes researchers restate common sense in a way that makes plain people think either that something startling and profound has been uncovered, or that important mysteries have been explained. Unfortunately, perhaps, explanations involve more than the offering of disguised truisms.

Consider Dr. Spock. In one part of his *Baby and Child Care* (the most widely used and sold book in the English language after the Bible), he focuses on a phenomenon that all parents are aware of and puzzled about: Children about 24 months old became very obstreperous, very "countersuggestible," very temperamental, very "contrary," and argumentative. What explains this? Spock decides it is because they have reached the "two-year-old stage of development." This is truistic redescription that does *not* explain. And perhaps the sorts of redescriptions we heard at this conference—redescriptions in terms of "instructional time" and the like —really are not explanatory, either. In other words, there seem to be grounds for concern about our theories in education.

The criticism that has been presented here is harsh, so perhaps it is appropriate to end on a brighter note. Here is a passage taken from an irreproachable source; in the one sentence, there is both a remark that is close to being a truism and a thought that should comfort all recipients of negative feedback:

> Whoso loveth instruction loveth knowledge
> but
> he that hateth reproof is brutish.[3]

NOTES

1. This is not to imply that Hamlyn, and particularly the present author, do not have serious reservations about much of the Piagetian approach.

2. This statement has bearings for the theory of the expanding universe.

3. Proverbs 12:1.

REFERENCES

Andreski, S. (1972). *Social sciences as sorcery* (pp. 122–143). New York: St. Martin's Press.

Berliner, D. C. (1979). Tempus educare. In P. Peterson & H. Walberg (Eds.), *Research on teaching* (p. 134). Berkeley, Calif.: McCutchan.

Hamlyn, D. (1978). *Experience and the growth of understanding.* London: RKP.

Quick, R. H. (1910 Edition). *Essays on educational reformers* (p. 364). London: Longmans, Green, & Co.

Rosenshine, B. V. (1979). Content, time, and direct instruction. In P. Peterson & H.

Walberg (Eds.), *Research on teaching* (p. 30). Berkeley, Calif.: McCutchan.
Russell, B. (1960). *An outline of philosophy* (pp. 32–33). New York: Meridian.
Wittgenstein, L. (1963). *Philosophical investigations* (E. Anscombe, trans.) (p. 232). Oxford: Blackwell.

19

Rethinking Time

Michael Scriven
The University of Western Australia

EDITORS' INTRODUCTION

In this chapter, Dr. Scriven takes a broad view of the use of models and laws and their utility in education. This portion of the discussion provides an arena within which to examine the critiques contained in the various chapters included in this volume. Professor Scriven points out that fundamental laws or models, in spite of the fact that some are truistic in nature, provide a certain order in our thinking and thereby possess considerable utility. Providing information about the manipulability of variables rather than precision of prediction or the truistic nature of models is posited as a major criterion for models of educational attainment. From this point of view, Dr. Scriven challenges us to refine or reformulate Carroll's model of school learning in such a way that some of its alleged liabilities are overcome without losing any of its advantages. Scriven himself responds to the challenge by presenting a Model of Educational Progress. This model focuses explicitly on educational progress as "valued" learning, that is, a subset of all learning. In this way, Professor Scriven directly engages two issues that have permeated a number of chapters in this volume: How can a model be formulated that will provide clear guidance for the improvement of educational systems, and how can the quality of instruction be represented more elaborately and more explicitly in the model? Nine factors are presented to account for changes in educational achievement level. Responsibility of different agents—students, teachers, school, and school system—is briefly discussed for each of the factors. Professor Scriven's presentation of this model invites us to rethink the fundamental issues underlying the conduct and interpretation of much of the research presented in this volume. The attempt at explicit consideration of suitability, relevance, and importance of instructional activities in the model seems especially appropriate for conceptual and empirical work in this area.

INTRODUCTION

A case can be made that models—and laws—should be judged not by their content but by their effects. On this basis, Carroll's model of school learning (MSL) would certainly rate as a major contribution to educational psychology and, for that matter, to education. Nevertheless, there are a number of worrying features of its actual formulation and interpretation. One way to avoid merely negative criticism is to try for an alternative formulation of the relevant model/law/principle. Such an attempt, successful or not, will also provide a useful basis for some comments about several other issues that are currently pervasive in this field of research. For convenience of comparison, we here state the MSL in the form used by Lorin Anderson in Chapter 9:

$$\text{learning} = f \frac{\text{time spent}}{\text{time needed}}$$

where

$$\text{time needed} = \text{aptitude} \times \text{ability to comprehend instruction} \times \text{quality of instruction}$$

PRELIMINARY CONCERNS

The first problem is that the very heart of the formula, the element that has led to many of its most interesting effects, is fatally flawed. The key ratio, time spent over time needed, is obviously zero for all unattainable learning goals (e.g., adults trying to attain accentless foreign language pronunciation); yet learning along these dimensions—toward such a goal—can certainly take place, and an adequate formula should be able to say more about how it can take place than is possible when the key quantity is set to zero as soon as the goal is shown to be unobtainable. Scientific descriptions of goal-oriented processes should never be critically dependent on goal *achievement* since the function of goals is only to give direction to behavior; success or failure is a later event and can hardly be treated as influencing earlier ones. [The case for bringing goal achievement into *evaluation* is better, but in fact it can only figure in the rather limited question of determining *success*—and even then, to a rather limited extent—rather than determining merit, worth, or value—the usual evaluation task (Scriven, 1980).] Unfortunately, as will be explained, no obvious reformulation of MSL to handle this problem will work. So, the proposed replacement for MSL will have to avoid reference to this ratio, despite the cost.

There are, however, two grounds for concern about MSL that we can dismiss relatively quickly, if some references to early work can be excused in lieu of detailed recapitulation here. First, Carroll himself expresses some concern about the truistic nature of the MSL. But much of the content of the laws of physics—let alone those of economics—is truistic, even definitionally truistic; Hooke's law of elasticity, for example, claims to apply to a perfectly elastic substance, but there is no definition of such a substance except "one that obeys Hooke's law." The function of fundamental laws or models is mainly to provide some order in our thinking, in particular to give us a definition of normal behavior so that:

1 . We can more easily recognize abnormal behavior, which is what we should be spending most of our time explaining and correcting;
2 . This paradigm can in turn be explained, related to others, and in general fitted into the structure of knowledge.

Additionally:

3 . These basic models serve a mnemonic function because we are looking for ways in which to change some of the dependent variables they list, pointing the way to possible levers we can use in the intervention process.

None of the above functions is in the least impeded by the truistic nature of a basic law, indeed by its partially definitional character. It is for this reason that much of Phillips's criticism (Chapter 18) fails to be damaging. Historical explanations are readily available and useful despite the lack of interesting historical laws because they use commonplaces about human nature to provide their baselines and standard patterns (Scriven, 1959). In Chapter 17, Jackson, like Phillips, makes the mistake to which Lorin Anderson points, of ignoring the denominator of the MSL; it's hard to argue that there is no substantive content there. True, it hasn't been the primary focus of the research, but it would be absurd to suggest that there has been no serious discussion of aptitude, for example, or comprehensibility. Jackson's criticisms are disappointingly negative, since he could easily have asked himself how his own great knowledge of classroom process could lead to improvements in the MSL or its interpretation as a guide to pracitce. One could, of course, argue that he made a contribution in an unintended way, because his extensive soliloquy on a fragment of poetry is perhaps the clearest demonstration in the volume of the fact that time-off-task won't get the job done.

Ultimately one must remember that even if the MSL were simpler than it is—for example, if it said that learning is an unknown function of engaged time over aptitude—it might still lead to researchers generating thoughtful and provocative reanalyses of those concepts and/or of research data that had been misconceived. Such results, as in the Wiley and Harnischfeger studies frequently referred to at this conference, are of huge social importance in the way they affect our attitude to schools. Other consequences have included what appear to be large increases in the maximum expectable payoffs from teacher training, and the success of school reform efforts as in the San Diego intervention reported by Stallings in Chapter 16. In the light of this kind of evidence, criticisms that the MSL is trivial become trivial.

What we have to worry about is whether there have been erroneous interpretations that may lead to serious perversions of the schooling process. Here Jackson suggests we may be returning to what he sees as the "bad old days" of excessive concern with efficiency; to which it must be replied that excessive *lack* of concern with efficiency is also a bogey that frightens many parents, teachers, and students. And should.

This brings us to the second preliminary concern, the failure of the MSL to meet what is often put forward by naive scientists or philosophers of science as the Real Criterion of good scientific models/laws, namely their capacity to generate precise, confirmed, and nonintuitive (i.e., antecedently improbable) quantitative predictions. It is a truism that truistic laws will rarely generate precise or surprising predictions; but the value of the latter is little compared with the value of getting some order in our thought—and very few scientific laws of any note will in fact generate *precise* predicitions (Scriven, 1961). Of those that will, some are still mostly deductions from definitions; for example, the law that gives the period of a pendulum is derivable from purely *a priori* reasoning, plus one measurement.

Nevertheless, that some laws in physics and chemistry do generate quite good predictions of events about which we have no intuitions is a glory of the quantitative sciences; that few if any in the social sciences will do so is not a sign of immaturity but of the much greater complexity and familiarity of their subject matter. The rough predictions are part of common sense; and the exact ones are impossible. In fact, it is only when very few variables and very simple laws are at work in very simple environments, as in some problems in astronomy, that it is possible to generate precise predictions. The moment we have to deal with half a dozen independent variables, even if simple connections between them apply (which in the social sciences we can often show to be false by trial and error), we are reduced to approximative methods and lots of luck. This is true in astronomy—as the history of the three-body problem makes clear—and so strongly true in the social sciences that the quest for exact general laws is absurd. What we can hope for is illumination of general principles that help to organize our thoughts and actions, and deciding when we have one of these is very much a judgment call, not at all like the Popperian ideal of finding a strictly falsifiable yet universally true generalization. But the existence of that allowable sloppiness does not justify unlimited imprecision or conceptual error.

FUNDAMENTAL CONCERNS

The concerns that have to be addressed more seriously center on the *limited-control implications* of truistic, tautological, or semicircular fundamental laws and the *extent of permissible reconceptualization* of the concepts they incorporate. Centuries of discussion have failed to produce noncircular definitions of several key terms in Newton's laws of motion, so we can hardly argue that circularity is fatal. But it does have a cost; it does cut into the value of the law for the third function listed above, the function of guiding interventions. For if the meaning of many of the concepts involved is heavily involved with the meaning of others, the whole notion of independent manipulation becomes elusive. In Newton's third law, for example, where the notion of reaction is definitionally connected with the notion of action, one is unable to suggest or even conceive ways to affect the one independently of changing the other. Consequently, that law—unlike the second—has little value as a guide to intervention. It is best conceived as one of the structural definitions of a *system* of laws and application rules which has *holistic* informativeness. The question must therefore be raised as to exactly what the MSL and the associated definitions of its key concepts *do* contain in the way of information about manipulation of variables.

The fact that appears to confound this line of criticism is, of course, that a number of major changes in the training and evaluating of teachers, to take just one of many possible examples, have resulted from taking this model seriously. But that may be the result of inspiration, of serendipity if you like, rather than deduction; and it may be important for us to realize that, in order not to slide into other conclusions that are also suggested (to some) but in fact not supported by the MSL.

The second question concerns the extent to which the model is *misleading* or unnecessarily confusing in its associated definitions of key concepts: aptitude, quality of instruction, and so on. It is perfectly possible for those formulating the laws of thermodynamics to redefine temperature in order to preserve the simplicity of the laws, as has been done on at least three and arguably four occasions in the history of that subject. It is also possible to redefine the concept in order to avoid confusions that arise in describing the results of new experiments or analyses, even if that means one must reformulate the laws. But the *balance* of cost in terms of confusion must always be considered, and may be too great to justify change. This proved to be the case when the proposed use of "negative temperatures on the absolute scale" for certain aberrant system configurations was classified as a quasi-metaphorical use, not taken to warrant the abandonment or reformulation of the third law (according to which it is not possible to reach absolute zero, a claim that would be taken, prima facie, to exclude getting to negative temperatures absolute).

The net effect of these two difficulties is to raise serious problems about the exact meaning of the MSL; one cannot easily tell what it is reminding you of that is really a matter of definition, what it is redefining, and what, if anything, it is adding in the way of an empirical claim.[1]

Now, it would be possible to consider each of these worries in considerable detail on their own merit. But in the end, one would rightly

---

[1]This lack of clarity seemed to be at the root of a good deal of the disagreement that occurred at this conference, despite the many years with which those present had worked on the MSL. It is the main reason why it seemed, upon reflection, more useful to do the reaction/review chapter in this way rather than picking up a dozen or so individually interesting points for comment, as I did at Northwestern for the actual event.

still be willing to put up with many such deficiencies if the MSL is the best we can do. Its values, like those of the gas laws, transcend its faults—until a model can be proposed that avoids these problems and is equally good in other respects. Moreover, it is clear that the complaints just voiced are very much a matter of degree, and hence particularly hard to convert into a definitive case for rejection. Clearly, the more constructive approach is to see if we can spring from the MSL to something cleaner. The new product may only be a reformulation or a refinement, or it may be rather more than that, but whatever it is, if it represents progress at all, it is only possible because of the work that went before it. At worst, it may be a useful exercise for the reader to test her or his understanding of the MSL by looking critically at this proposed alternative.

A MODEL OF EDUCATIONAL PROGRESS

Some comments will be made in the course of introducing the Model of Educational Progress (MEP) to justify the changes from the MSL. In the first place, MEP is explicitly a model of *educational progress*, not of *learning*, because *education* has an evaluative connotation that *learning* (in this sense) lacks; one can learn a string of nonsense syllables, but doing so does not constitute education in the usual sense, let alone educational progress (extraordinary contexts apart).

This honorific aspect of learning has in fact been the focus of the MSL, as can be seen by the references in it to *quality* of instruction where the effort to avoid "empty learning" emerges. We are simply making it explicit. This is a normative model, not just a descriptive model, and it has to be a normative model if it is to provide us with clear guidance toward improvement rather than mere change.

In fact, if we are to use this model as a guide to education and in particular to teaching and classroom management, it is important to look at every element in the model and select its definition in accord with an overall concern with valuable learning, not just learning. (We could in fact have called it a Model of Valuable Learning, MVL, instead of the Model of (Educational Progress, MEP.) Education or valuable learning was not very well defined in the papers at this conference; sometimes it was said to refer to behavior changes, sometimes to knowledge changes, sometimes, but not consistently, to more than that. Let us be clear that it must be taken to refer to the acquisition of not only useful or otherwise valuable knowledge but of sound values, habits, skills, attitudes, styles of thinking or acting, and conceptual or perceptual schemes. Where *learning* is used below, it is a shorthand for the worthwhile elements of this collection. People who want to study changes in these elements without deciding or arguing for their merit are doing process research, but not research on educational improvement. "Learning gains" are not educational gains until they are shown to be so; increased teaching efficiency is not increased teaching effectiveness until the results are shown to be beneficial as well as substantial. Teachers are not in the least necessary for either learning or education, a point implicitly or explicitly denied on several occasions in this volume, and in fact no external human agency is required besides the learner, because experience and computers and books do the job very well, often much better than the available teachers.

Education, then, is acquired (and lost or destroyed) via a process that occurs in school and outside it, in a way that the MEP represents as covarying with nine factors. Conventionally, this is represented rather imprecisely by saying that education is a monotonically increasing function of these factors. The formula is presented first, followed by the definitions of those terms that are used in a way that is clearly different from the usage of many at the conference (the rest are not defined). It should be noted that the order of the terms in the formula is important for two reasons. First, in several cases, the definition of a term used later refers to the definition of an earlier term. Second, the terms are arranged in groups so that adjacent terms characterize or are the responsibility of different agents—the student, the school or school system, and the teacher. These groups of controllable factors overlap, in a way that is fairly obvious but that will be set out after the definitions.

If E_t stands for educational achievement level at time t:

$$E_t = E_0 + F \text{ (aptitude, motivation, time scheduled,}$$
$$\text{time logged, time engaged, relevance, importance,}$$
$$\text{suitability, presentation)}$$

DEFINITIONS

Aptitude

Aptitude is here defined as the product of two factors: first, the average rate of acquisition of useful learning from optimally presented experiences or materials of a certain type; second, the eventual level of achievement along that dimension. It is not defined as time to mastery or to criterion, contrary to the procedure in MSL, because of the following dilemma. *Either* one defines mastery—for example, of the piano—at a level that essentially no one except Mozart achieves, in which case no one except Mozart has any aptitude for the piano, which is absurd; *or* one defines it at a level achieved by many industrious learners. In the latter case, the late-blooming genius who took the average time to get to mastery level and then accelerated to become the best the world has ever seen—without special efforts such as much longer hours of practice than others at this level—cannot be said to have any special aptitude, which is equally absurd. Given the effect of maturation on athletic skills, we are increasingly finding that real aptitude only emerges long after reasonable mastery levels were reached in a normal time, so the MSL definition is increasingly inappropriate in the physical education area.[1]

Efforts by the Bloom school to suggest that aptitude is best thought of as entry-level achievement are equally inappropriate, as Carroll stresses (see Chapters 2, 3, 4, and 9). Entry achievement is intuitively only additive to later achievement, not multiplicative of it, and none of the research refutes this view. Aptitude is by its nature multiplicative; it is easy to find skills, such as the acquisition of new foreign languages, where aptitude keeps the gap open forever, long past the time when the advantage of an early start with one extra language runs out for most people. Aptitude will work something like a multiplier—the term is here used loosely, simply to contrast with addition—in the short run, but it seems implausible to suggest that someone coming into the piano class with a short head start on the other pupils will *either* maintain that edge indefinitely (which would often be the case if it were what we normally call an aptitude), *or* that that person will *always* lose it, which would be the case if there were no such thing as an aptitude. So the MEP puts both early-start and aptitude factors in, but in different roles. [Further discussion of the aptitude/performance distinction will be found in the aptitude/achievement anthology to which Carroll refers (Scriven, 1974).]

Finally, it will be noted that the notion of ability to comprehend instruction is built into the suggested concept of aptitude. This seems to be in accord with our normal usage, and when combined with the notions of suitability of instructional materials and presentation by teacher, defined below, it seems possible that we unpack the MSL factor of "ability to comprehend instruction" in a way that is more useful as a guide to practice.

Motivation

Motivation is the willingness to spend time *and effort* on education, not *liking* or *interest* or—in any direct sense—valuing, but simply *commitment* or perhaps merely *acceptance* of the necessity for the learning. Motivation can, of course, be facilitated by liking or respecting the instructional goals, or the instructor, or the process or the materials, and that's one way to get the job done. Notice that this definition leaves open *which*, learning or education, evokes the motivation. Many students who have high motivation to learn about, say, automobiles (or philosophy, or art), never evince any lengthy learning efforts at this or any other kind of learning, simply because no one ever tries to present the material in a way that will convert their motivation into a learning effort. Hence, the behavioral identification of motivation with freely chosen learning time will lead to some serious misdiagnoses.

---

[1] It will be clear upon reflection that an analogous dilemma can be constructed to show that one cannot avoid the problem of pervasive zero values for the ratio of time spent to time needed.

Time Types

The following list of time types includes one distinction that needs to be made, but was not consistently made or not made at all, in other contributions. It resolves the ambiguity in the commonly used term *allocated time* by distinguishing between scheduled time (preallocated time) and logged time (actually allocated).

Scheduled Time.   Scheduled time is the period planned or allotted by the system or by the individual teacher for teaching the particular skill (etc.), the "paper time" or "curriculum time" or "lesson plan" time. Much of the reanalysis work on the Coleman data has used scheduled time since it is the only version available.

Logged Time.   Logged time is the time that the teacher or, better, the observer would mark down as having been "spent" on teaching that skill, by contrast with, for example, roll call and "lining them up for the corridor" time in secondary school, though the latter will get lumped into the scheduled time "for the subject." Logged time will often vary markedly from scheduled time for a second kind of reason, the kind of unexpected reason that spoils many of the best-laid plans, most obviously in primary school. Logged time is, however, *engageable* time. (Alternative terms, sometimes encountered, that seemed more ambiguous than *scheduled time*, if the distinction presented here between scheduled time and logged time was to be maintained, were *nominal time, official time, opportunity*—which is content related—and *instructional time.*)

Engaged time.   Engaged time is not yet operationally defined, by a long way. In fact, we may be in danger of breeding a group of subjects whose major achievement is learning how to daydream while looking attentive. Engaged time is simply a theoretical construct for which we have a few good indicators, especially negative ones (the "off-task" indicators). Stimulated recall probably offers the best hope of realistic estimates on the positive side, apart from some activities that require full-time concentration in order to survive, such as intensive one-on-one argumentation, video games, and some programmed texts. Until we get more results from the stimulated-recall people, we may need to be very cautious when extending our conclusions beyond data based on studies of these special types of activity. The idea that we have shown that "engaged time is 50–75% of the scheduled time" is distinctly optimistic, though it strikes many people as bad enough news as it stands. But worse news is to come, for engagement is all too often with trivia, and in estimating educational progress we must certainly try to deal with that problem.

We now come to a set of factors that incorporate, among other things, the MEP equivalent of the notion of "quality of instruction" in

MSL. The MSL treatment seems not to break out the crucial difference between content quality and presentational quality. There are also uses of "instructional quality" by Carroll in this volume that suggest a very inappropriate meaning, for example, "instructional quality should be adjusted to meet the needs of students of lesser aptitude" (see chapter 2). It would seem to be better to say that the level of difficulty of the materials should be lowered (which would *increase* what is referred to here as suitability), or the presentation of them should be *improved*—but neither would be reduced.

Relevance

None of the factors listed so far ensures that what is being learned will contribute anything to education in the dimension under consideration, the dimension that often will be appropriately tested at the end of the period under consideration. There was very little discussion of this problem at the conference, but it may be more serious than any other in getting students to a reasonable level of education. How much of what is being learned is really going to take the students a step along the road to education? There are two parts of this issue. First, there is the problem of what is to count as relevant; this requires doing a needs assessment. Second, there is the problem of determining, perhaps even measuring, what is actually taught in terms of the categories of materials that the needs assessment shows are relevant. Traditionally this is done via an intermediary construct, the curriculum. It is indeed easier for a curriculum unit than an individual teacher to do a needs assessment, but even when the curriculum has been justified, there remains the question of the relevance of the instruction to the curriculum *and* and the problem of what to do about the significant part of actual teaching that is unrelated to the curriculum but important for education. One might as well bypass the curriculum in doing serious studies of the classroom, because it only introduces an extra step. The prospect here can be daunting, but we have to get a start because the rest of the classroom-management business can all too easily become a house built on sand.

Fortunately, exactitude will not be important for the next 20 years while we try to cope with the consequences of approximate figures. The time-on-task researchers are not by nature denizens of curriculum territory; but they may have to crosss the Rubicon that separates them from it, in order to achieve a comprehensive model of educational progress.

Importance

Relevance is not enough. There is another time-dependent issue, the economics of opportunity cost in the choice of topics or subskills. In other words, given a scheduled time of N hours per annum, and given a needs assessment, the choice of topics will always be severely limited and relevance is a far from adequate guide to selection. Educational progress could be doubled (tripled? increased tenfold?) by one choice of a shopping basket of relevant topics compared to another. Reviewing a comprehensive K–10 social studies curriculum recently, I doubt if I could have found three lines in the two or three hundred pages of goals and objectives that could have been rejected as irrelevant; yet the curriculum is a very weak one because it is entirely toothless—it avoids all controversial issues, all training in the tough skills of value analysis and conflict resolution, all unpleasant facts about the effects of local prejudices (e.g., the slaughter of indigenes) and the frequently moronic behavior of generals and civilian leaders under stress. Hence it simply does not equip the citizen with the crucial relevant facts and skills; in fact, it grossly miseducates them by omitting these components.

So importance is crucial. We could amalgamate the two concepts, since importance is the supervenient one, but there are two reasons not to do so. First, relevance can be determined to a first approximation and/or in a way that is of interest to the school system, when the curriculum clearly refers to important needs of the students, by simply doing content analysis of class coverage against curriculum content. Thus, for certain legitimate purposes, it is independently and quickly accessible. Second, the *distributional* considerations involved in the market-basket issue are conceptually separate from the *matching* considerations that control the study of relevance, and hence the methodology of the two issues is different. See, for example, the discussion of apportioning by Scriven (1978).

Suitability

However good and important the message, it—or some of it—will be over the heads of some and redundant for others. Matching the levels is a crucial part of ensuring educational progress, and it depends on suitability, and on presentation, the next factor in the list. *Suitability* refers to the materials or content and *presentation* refers to the way they are put forward. The two factors are separated in this list because the responsible agent is often different and because they can in any case be changed independently. Of course, in the context of group instruction, a number of desiderata are involved and may conflict; so the decision as to what is suitable will depend on whether one has "elitist" or "leveler" values,[1] to use the language of our economist colleagues (see Chapter 7). The most obvious of all the variables that fall under suitability is difficulty level; others would include the use of audio imagery for materials for blind, nondeaf students—and, in general, the matching of modes in the materials to the learning style of the group when something distinctive is known about it. The work on the importance of "high success rates on somewhat challenging tasks" in the BTES study

---

[1] The terminology was unfortunate; one might as well use the term *Marxist* to refer to economists who think that labor costs are the largest part of most consumer product costs.

has provided us with at least a useful hypothesis and perhaps a first approximation to a suitability index—for lower grades/abilities at least. (Programmed texts may yet stage a return as the best way to maximize learning for a wide range of student ability.) Materials are crystallized teaching, so their suitability is closely related to good presentation, our next concern.

Presentation

Presentation is the way in which the teacher, or the text, or both in combination, arrange materials of a given content and suitability so as to maximize their educational impact. We have amassed a wide repertoire of options here, and it is worth recapitulating some of it to emphasize the nontriviality of the specific issues in training teachers or in teachers' own choice options. Current favorites include: pacing, spacing, timing, sequencing, and alerting; the use of lively examples from current student interests or multimedia; the use of group work versus independent study; ability grouping versus social or random grouping; use of the staircase mastery approach versus the slope-traversing approach; discipline and classroom noise control; time spent on teaching meta-skills such as learning to learn or learning to evaluate your own work; the varying of the nature of the task; extent of monitoring and feedback (and its type—process feedback versus outcome feedback); the use of student questions and the amount of questioning by the teacher; eye contact and physical contact; the addition of cues to material that is too hard for the group; the use of advance organizers and review periods. Most of these provide ways to extend the range of levels at which materials are "suitable," so this is not a wholly independent factor from the preceding one. Most of these are also ways in which *teacher* time, spent *outside* the classroom, can pay of inside it—as more education for the student. There is also a significant issue about the gains from *student* time spent outside the classroom—homework, field trips, project research, television, traveling, working at a job, free reading, and talking.

The suggestion in Carroll and in Bloom that reduction in the variability of the achievements is desirable is not a plausible criterion for suitable instruction or good presentation—except for tasks on which postmastery performance has negligible value and mastery is almost universally attainable, as in tying shoelaces. So we do not include it here.

The recurrent worry about "black box" or "input-output" (i.e., macro) models by contrast with "dynamic" (micro) models relates to this and the previous factor, each of which are themselves complex functions of many other factors. Many of the comments about black-box models are based on methodological prejudices that lack any general justification. Nothing at all can be said against either kind of model, except by reference to a particular question. Some questions require a micro-model and others do not; and since a micro-model is not only much harder to come by, but also much harder to use because one needs enormously greater data input to feed it, we often have to settle for less if we are to get anything done. Evaluation often can be done with only a macro-model; explanation often requires a micro-model; but neither generalization is exceptionless. In any case, virtually all the steps we can make towards a micro-model are going to fit into the presentation or the suitability factors.

MANIPULABILITY

The factors in the MEP are arranged so that allocation of responsibility and location of manipulable variables are grouped as follows. (Note that responsibility extends well beyond manipulability *within the period under consideration*; parents who fail to take the now-available precautions against brain damage in children due to parental alcohol/drug intake are, of course, responsible for their lack of aptitude which is now irreversible and hence not manipulable. But, in the long run, that kind of lack of aptitude in the population is controllable by educating parents and possibly by laws.)

The crucial point about the logic of responsibility is that it obeys no conservation laws; it is not lessened by sharing. The fact that parents are responsible for motivating children does not make the schools less responsible. They are *also* fully responsible because, as we know, they can motivate children even when the parents won't cooperate; it's much harder but it's still possible (in most cases) and hence if it isn't done, the school is at fault. So are the parents. Since it is harder without parental help, the *blame* for failure is less; but the responsibility is still complete. People often oversimplify the connection between culpability/praiseworthiness and responsibility, thinking that they must covary continuously; but responsibility is best thought of as an on/off switch, a necessary condition for the other, but not a predictor of its amount.

Student, Parent, and Prior-School Responsibilities
  Manipulable variables:
    Entry-level education
    Aptitude
    Motivation
    Engaged time

The first factor is not under the control of any still-available educational levers short of a time machine, but the second is not quite immutable. For example, aptitude is affected by nutrition and maturation and might one day be affected by electroneural stimulation.

Responsibility for the first and second must of course be laid at the door of parents, previous schools, society, and the individual student. The motivation and engaged-time paramenters here are major intermediate variables, for whose condition responsibility is shared by all actors—the student, parents, peers, teachers, authors, and principals.

School Responsibilities
Manipulable variables:
Motivation
Time scheduled
Relevance of materials available, curriculum content, etc.
Importance of materials available, curriculum content, etc.
Suitability of materials available, curriculum content, etc.
Presentation, time logged, time engaged (these are categorized under school responsibilities because the school selects, supervises, and socializes its teachers)

Teacher Responsibilities
Manipulable variables:
Motivation
Time scheduled (the teacher partially controls this in primary school, and always has some of the responsibility through participation in the union or association negotiations over the length of the school year/day)
Relevance (when the teacher controls the content, e.g., tertiary education)
Importance (when the teacher controls this factor)
Suitability (when the teacher controls this factor)
Presentation (the heaviest of the teacher's responsibilities)
Time logged (the teacher's selection of tasks)
Time engaged (like motivation, an intermediate variable for which responsibility is shared)

CONCLUSIONS

In the hidden value system of that very abstract entity, the school, the most important outcomes may be reduced stress and increased income, hence less teacher turnover, campus crime, truancy, and vandalism. Those are a long way from the maximization of valuable learning, as far as face validity is concerned; but they may not be too far away in terms of concurrent validity. The school with a good sense of mission, and good management, has the kind of morale that helps learning, as well as helping with the social indicators—as Chapter 16 confirms. It should help in the development of such schools if a conceptualization of the components of education that makes good sense to teachers and administrators can be provided as a theoretical/practical basis for planning. It seemed to me that the efforts at this conference took us several steps nearer that goal.

REFERENCES

Scriven, M. (1959). Truisms as the grounds for historical explanation. In P. L. Gardiner (Ed.), *Theories of history* (pp. 443–475). Glencoe, Ill.: Free Press.

Scriven, M. (1961). The key property of physical laws—inaccuracy. In H. Feigl & G. Maxwell (Eds.), *Current issues in the philosophy of science* (pp. 91–101). New York: Holt, Rinehart and Winston.

Scriven, M. (1974). The logic of the aptitude/achievement distinction. In D. R. Green (Ed.), *The aptitude-achievement distinction* (pp. 326–335). Monterey, Calif.: CTB/McGraw-Hill.

Scriven, M. (1978, December). The apportionment problem. *Evaluation News.*

Scriven, M. (1980). *The logic of evaluation.* Inverness, Calif.: Edgepress.

20

One More Time

David C. Berliner
University of Arizona

and

Charles W. Fisher
Far West Laboratory for Educational Research and Development

EDITORS' INTRODUCTION

In this final chapter, the editors draw upon the previous chapters and other work to provide responses to six questions about the utility of research on instructional time. Is research on instructional time trivial? Can we use the results of research on instructional time to improve schools? Does research on instructional time suggest changes in school and classroom organizational patterns? Does research on instructional time have implications for teacher evaluation? How does research on instructional time relate to current concerns about classroom discipline and efficiency? Does research on instructional time have implications for educational research in general?

Research on instructional time has become an active and sustained pursuit of the educational research community during the past 20 years. The contents of professional and popular journals, as well as the programs of local and national conferences, reflect the extensive conceptual and empirical effort devoted to instructional-time issues. However, the meaning of this work, the assumptions made by research workers, the potential policy implications, and the translation of research findings into practical instructional programs have generated sharp differences of opinions. Since much of the rhetoric (if not the reality) of the current thrust for educational reform is based either directly or tangentially on research on instructional-time and effective instruction, it seems appropriate to examine further several of the issues that seem to characterize the relationship between research on instructional-time and classroom practice.

Our remarks are presented in response to a series of six questions. Some of the questions are raised by the previous chapters in this book, others are raised by the many current public concerns about education.

In our opinion, the single most important of the questions raised about instructional-time research was asked in Chapter 18 by Denis C. Phillips. Because his questions about the nature of this research are so basic, his questions must be addressed before other issues are explored. Thus, we begin this discussion with the following question.

IS RESEARCH ON INSTRUCTIONAL TIME TRIVIAL?

Phillips first points out how the findings of research on instructional time appear to be "obvious." To him they represent the kind of findings that any plain person would take as ordinary knowledge about the world. This is the kind of argument that has plagued social science research in general, and educational research in particular. Gage and Berliner (1975) provide an interesting exercise that is relevant to this issue. They point out that

> In his influential book on teacher education, Conant (1963) characterized educational psychology as largely making use of commonsense generalizations about human nature. These are "for the most part highly limited and unsystematized generalizations, which are the stock in trade of everyday life for all sane people." Thus, in Conant's [and Phillips's] view, educational research can offer only the obvious.
>
> To better understand Conant's [and Phillips's] concern, it may be helpful to present a few of these generalizations with some interpretive comments.
>
> 1. More intelligent children tend to receive less social acceptance from their peers in the classroom; that is, children high in IQ or scholastic achievement very often rank low in popularity. (*This is easy to understand because, as is well known, children resent the greater success, higher grades, and teacher acceptance of the more able children.*)

2. If a group of students is given a considerable amount of instruction and practice in developing a skill, those students will become more alike in that skill. (*Certainly, if a group of persons is subjected to a uniform experience, their homogeneity on dimensions relevant to this experience will become greater.*)

3. The only way to insure "transfer" (i.e., to insure that training received in one situation will prove helpful in another) is to increase the similarity, or the number of so-called identical elements, between the learning situation and the situation in which you want the learning applied. (*There is no such thing as "general transfer." Schooling should be made as much like real life as possible.*)

4. If you want to teach a man how to fire a gun, give him practice in firing a gun. (*"Practice makes perfect" has long been recognized as the basic rule in teaching most skills.*)

5. If a student is going to be tested on the materials presented in a lecture, he ought to take notes if his memory is bad; if he has a good memory, paying attention is all that is needed to learn the material well. (*If a person's memory is bad, he certainly ought to be writing everything down before he forgets it. If his memory is good, trying to keep notes will interfere with his learning, so just paying attention is probably sufficient.*)

6. When a child is first taught to read, providing a picture of the word to be mastered will aid her in tying the word to what it signifies. (*How else can one begin to learn words except through the knowledge that* car *stands for* ?)

7. It is important to keep the organization of any written material in some logical order; otherwise, the reader's comprehension of the material will suffer. (*Obviously, material that is well organized is easier to learn.*) ...

These commonsense generalizations are typical of what is being criticized when men like Conant [or Phillips] say that much of what is offered in educational psychology is obvious. Since these principles or findings are obvious, why do educational research workers put so much effort into finding and testing them? And why should such common sense notions be taught to prospective teachers? These would be legitimate questions except for one noteworthy fact about the seven generalizations presented above: *Every one of these statements is either in need of elaborate qualification or is in exact opposition to what actually has been found by educational psychologists.*

1. Gronlund (1959, p. 191) concluded from his review of a number of studies that "as a group, gifted pupils are distinctly superior in terms of social acceptance by their peers" (p. 191). This relationship held for achievement as well; the students most accepted by their peers had significantly higher scholastic averages than those least accepted.

2. From a review of pertinent studies, Anastasi (1958, p. 211) generalized that "individual differences usually increase with practice." This result held for skills as varied as learning vocabulary, canceling letters in a page of type, substituting digits for symbols, and finding hidden words. Variability among persons increased from trial to trial.

3. Despite popular belief to the contrary, research evidence suggests that teaching the principle underlying two tasks helps students transfer their skill

in one task to the other. "The high transfer value of principles has a long history. .... The major concepts and principles in a subject field show greater positive transfer to later tasks than does specific information" (Klausmeier & Davis, 1969, p. 1489). The principle can be highly theoretical and need *not* closely copy the form of the task in the real world.

4. While studying the task of training airmen in aerial gunnery, Gagne (1962) found that practice in firing at moving targets resulted in no significant gain in the measured proficiency of the gunners during one to ten missions. Even when the practice was accompanied by immediate information on the accuracy of the shot, improvement was negligible. Rather, the major improvement in this kind of performance came as a result of informing the learners of the correct procedures to be used in finding the range of their targets. Practice, by itself, is not always the best way to learn a complex skill.

5. In a series of studies, Berliner (1971) measured how much college students learned from lecture instruction. He also measured the short-term memory ability of the students with a test of ability to recall random series of letters. The students who were low in this kind of measured memory ability and who only paid attention during the lecture did as well as or better than students who took notes. Among students who were high in memory ability, those who took notes did far better than those who merely paid attention. Taking notes during the lecture hampered the students with poor memory ability but not those with better memory ability.

6. The extensive use of pictures to help the young student begin reading has been questioned in a series of studies by Samuels (1970). In one of his studies,

> two groups of randomly assigned kindergarten children learned to read four words (*boy, bed, man, car*) either with a picture or without a picture. ... The task for the subjects in both conditions was to learn the appropriate oral response associated with the printed stimulus. ... Each learning trial was followed by a test trial. On the test trials only the printed stimulus was on the card.
>
> ... On the test trials when pictures were not presented as prompts, the no-picture group gave significantly more correct responses" (Samuels, 1970, p. 398).

Further work led Samuels to conclude that, for the better readers the presentation of pictures neither helped nor hindered learning, while "among the poorer readers, the presence of pictures interfered with learning sight vocabulary" (p. 399).

7. Programmed instructional texts are often considered to provide the best organization of written instructional materials. Yet the research on organization has severely questioned the value of organization, or whether we know what good organization is, or how to measure its effects. Schramm (1964) reviewed the experiments on the immediate and delayed effect of logical ordering as against random ordering of programmed instructional materials. Of five studies of this type, three showed no difference, and one showed an immediate, but not a delayed, advantage for the ordered sequence. Only one of the five studies found a clear advantage for the

ordered sequence. Also, research on listening to disordered discourse (with randomly shifted paragraphs) shows no damaging effects on the listener's comprehension (Thompson, 1967). ...

As Lazarsfeld (1949) commented after a similar discussion: "If we had mentioned the actual results of the investigation first, the reader would have labeled these 'obvious' also. Obviously something is wrong with the entire argument of 'obviousness.'" Many of the generalizations about human behavior that laymen are ready to endorse turn out to be either simply untrue or insufficiently qualified. Almost any flat statement, delivered with conviction and without ifs, ands, or buts, will strike us as not only unquestionable but also obvious. This effect occurs especially in such areas as human behavior and education, where everyone has great familiarity (Gage and Berliner, 1975. p. 15–20).

Phillips argues about obviousness in a way that is unfair. Like so much in educational research, hindsight makes very obvious what we could not see clearly before.

A second part of Phillips's concern is with the truistic character of time studies. Perhaps, as with the "obvious" issue, Phillips uses the wrong criteria. Instead of concern for truisms and even trivial truisms, one should be concerned about the usefulness of concepts for conceptualizing school processes and for changing schooling. Against these criteria we think instructional time research is defensible, whether it appears trivial to Phillips or not.

It is important to note, however, that Phillips's position is supported by others. For example, Karweit (1984) finds instructional-time research to be of limited value at the policy level, and Rossmiller (1982) finds research on instructional time to be of little import for school administrators. It is interesting that Karweit acknowledges that about 10% of the variation in school achievement is attributable to different kinds of time variables; and that Rossmiller sometimes finds, for low-ability children in particular, that over 70% of their variance in achievement in reading can be attributed to time-on-task variables. Those individuals who found time variables to be of little concern apparently see nothing inherently useful about a policy variable so powerful that it can account for between 10% and 70% of the variation in student achievement scores. In fact, it appears that after initial ability is accounted for, no other educational variable is as useful in explaining differences in student achievement. Yet time variables are considered trivial by some individuals. This strikes us as odd!

The characteristics of schooling amenable to policy decisions by legislators, school boards, school administrators, etc., are such things as money, curriculum materials, personnel, computer terminals, building architecture, and organizational structure. When one such policy-relevant variable is seen to be as potent as instructional time is, it serves an extremely useful function for thinking about all the other policy variables. Decisions about personnel, money, or building architecture can all be analyzed for their effects on time usage. Such policy decisions can then be made, we think, more intelligently than if instructional-time issues are not considered. Truth, even patently obvious truth about relationships between time variables and achievement, is not the only test of a theory or a set of findings. Usefulness seems to be even more important.

But the policy level is only one level of analysis. We also want to see if these plain truths have usefulness at the classroom level. Certainly, it is evident to all that attention, time-on-task, or some similar term is a necessary and possibly even a sufficient condition for some kinds of learning. Does it follow that teachers regularly control for and monitor this variable? We think not. Teachers are not used to thinking of time as a metric or as an accounting system for many school activities, though to anyone who thinks about it, that is patently true and obvious. Moreover, we think that it is possible to study teachers who have consistently high rates of on-task behavior, say 90% and learn from them their "secrets" of classroom management. Thus, we need not end up, as Phillips asserts, by issuing such uninteresting statements as "keep attention levels, high"! We might end up saying very useful statements such as, "By monitoring the behavior of Mr. Plainperson, who has students that regularly evidence high levels of attention, we notice that high levels of student success are built into the curriculum experiences, that high levels of academic feedback are present, and that structuring statements occur at high rates per hour." These may, indeed, turn out to be truisms, but we think not. In fact, we believe that they are the components of what passes for expertise in pedagogy, and that such knowledge can serve as useful guides for the training of teachers.

Phillips noted that some of the in-class time variables were considered to be "proxies" for achievement on tests. Phillips goes on to properly point out that many scientists measure the measurable, leaving out of their purview events that are less easily measurable. He implies that some of these proxies for achievement are of that type. One such concept was studied extensively by Fisher and Berliner (Fisher, Berliner, Filby, Marliave, Cahen, & Dishaw, 1980; and Fisher, Filby, Marliave, Cahen, Dishaw, Moore, & Berliner, 1978). We called it ALT—academic learning time. We defined ALT as engaged time with curricular materials or activities that yielded a high level of success and that were related to outcomes that were valued. The differences in accrual of this kind of time, ALT, predicted a student's achievement test scores. The time-based measure of ALT was, therefore, seen as a kind of proxy for the less frequently seen and more distal achievement test score. Now it could be that concern for measuring ALT is mere measurement for the sake of it. On the other hand, it could also be that ALT is one of the first objectively measurable indexes of quality instruction. If Phillips's plain person walked into a classroom and found children engaged in what they were doing and succeeding at it, and perceived that what they were doing was related logically to the outcomes of instruction that were considered important, then it is likely that the plain person would be satisfied with instruction in that classroom. We think such a classroom would be described as high in quality. But could that plain person articulate the bases for such judgments? And would such a plain person attempt to objectify the measurement of such judgments, so certain types of research can take place? We think not. It would be the very rare plain person who could describe indicators of quality instruction in a clear and useful manner. To try to measure such complex but sensible variables strikes us as a most worthy scientific endeavor. It is not mere measurement for the sake of it.

In answer, then, to the questions posed by Phillips, about whether the findings of instructional-time research are obvious, yield only simple truths, and may even be trivial, we assert the following: Though some findings appear obvious, they are usually obvious only with hindsight; though some findings appear to be truisms, they can have enormously positive effects on schooling; and finally, we believe that no research that genuinely informs policy and also provides sensible indicators of quality in classroom instruction should be considered trivial.

CAN WE USE THE RESULTS OF RESEARCH ON INSTRUCTIONAL TIME TO IMPROVE SCHOOLS?

The answer to this question must be a resounding *yes*. There have been, and are likely to be, widespread attempts to influence day-to-day educational practice using research-based interventions. Much of this activity has focused on the observation, analysis, and interpretation of instructional-time variables. School improvement efforts incorporating instructional-time components have ranged from small-scale, relatively informal interventions (Muir, 1980; Noli, 1980), through well-controlled training studies (Good & Grouws, 1979), to systematic district-wide improvement efforts, as reported by Stallings in Chapter 16. The research on instructional time has heavily influenced large-scale development of staff development materials such as teacher guidebooks on the organization and management of instruction (Emmer, Evertson, Clement, Sanford, & Worsham, 1984; Evertson, Emmer, Sanford, Clement, & Worsham, 1984), comprehensive staff development materials on effective teaching (Rauth, Biles, Billups, & Veitch, 1983; Biles, Billups, & Veitch, undated), and a series of videotapes on effective instruction (Sparks & Sparks, 1984), among many others. Results from research on instructional time are definitely being used in efforts to improve schools.

The impact that instructional-time data and procedures will have depends not only on the utility of the information itself, but on the implementation and training strategies employed. The results of research on instructional time have several characteristics that should support school change. First, the results of the research are firmly grounded in the observable classroom phenomena with which teachers deal on a day-to-day basis. Second, many of the concepts have high face validity and are easily communicated to teachers and principals. Third, many improvement efforts focus on providing feedback to individual teachers about their actual performance and the performance of their students. Fourth, this feedback is perceived to be valuable by many teachers because it can be given in the context of a powerful accounting system. Teachers deal with time allocation, duration, and timing decisions as part of their everyday work. To have feedback on the results of their decisions, framed in understandable terms, is highly valued. Fifth, the provision of feedback to teachers (and students) promotes a spirit of inquiry in the classroom. Such inquiry on the part of teachers signals concern about quality instruction.

These comments are relevant to the influence of findings from research on instructional time on the quality of instruction. A note of caution is suggested for those who would forego serious attempts to improve the quality of instruction and instead manipulate only the quantity of instruction. Although increases in the length of the school day or the number of school days per year have often been suggested in recent proposals for school improvment, we believe that increases in the amount of instructional time without substantial efforts to improve the quality of instruction are likely to be disappointing. The primary reasons for our pessimism stem from the fact that increases in quantity of time alone will fail to provide useful feedback to teachers, to provide student-learning tasks that are more relevant to outcome measures, or to enhance in any way the skills and knowledge of teachers.

DOES RESEARCH ON INSTRUCTIONAL TIME SUGGEST CHANGES IN SCHOOL AND CLASSROOM ORGANIZATIONAL PATTERNS?

One of the advantages of the research on instructional time is that it encourages us to examine the tasks that students work on in schools very carefully. It is difficult to treat time-on-task data seriously without asking, time on *what* task? Some concepts, such as academic learning time (Fisher et al., 1980), go beyond time-on-task by incorporating an index of task relevance in their definition. Since the content knowledge that students are expected to acquire in school is embedded in the tasks they perform, the quality of the tasks will determine, to a large extent, what, how much, and in what order student learning occurs.

Beyond the qualities of the tasks themselves, the organization of tasks and students in schools affects student learning. The importance of classroom organization is illustrated in findings from instructional-time studies.

For example, student engagement rates are reported to be higher in seat-work settings than in recitation settings (Fisher et al., 1978; McDonald & Elias, 1976; Stallings & Kaskowitz, 1974). Thus, the amount of engaged time accumulated by students can be manipulated by increasing or decreasing the proportion of instructional time during which students work in recitation settings. Other things being equal, engagement rates could be maximized by providing large amounts of recitation. However, recitation settings require a common task for all students, and in all likelihood, the common task will be more appropriate for some students but less appropriate for others. Since seatwork allows students to work on different tasks, it follows that seatwork settings allow a better distribution of task appropriateness than do recitation settings. Because learning is a function of both student engagement and task appropriateness, and recitation tends to yield higher engagement whereas seatwork yields higher task appropriateness, it is not obvious which combination of seatwork and recitation will yield the greatest learning. Although this example has focused on common organizational arrangements such as seatwork and recitation, it should be clear that each organizational arrangement will have both advantages and disadvantages for fostering student learning. This point has been developed by both Marliave and Filby, in Chapter 13, and Filby and Cahen in Chapter 12. Given that organizational arrangements in the classroom influence student learning time, access to feedback, and the pacing of tasks, among other things, it is important to design instructional sequences to capitalize on the inherent characteristics of specific organizational arrangements. The work of Linda Anderson, reported in Chapter 11, attends to this issue by conducting research within one setting (in this case, seatwork). From this line of research on instructional time, we might expect that teachers would differentiate their instructional strategy depending upon the task and the organizational setting in which the task is to be worked on.

A second point regarding the organization of instruction concerns the choice of an organizing principle. In the discussion to this point, it has been assumed that instruction has been organized by setting up time periods within the day and that tasks are worked on by students within those time periods. This kind of organization usually implies that groups of students are taught for fixed time periods and, as a result, individual differences among students give rise to relatively large differences in student performance. It follows that, even over relatively short sequences of instruction, student achievement levels before and after instruction will be highly correlated.

In a growing number of schools, organization is based upon a fundamentally different rationale. In these classes and schools, organization is based upon tasks and, to the extent possible, time is allowed to vary with individual differences. This pattern was first described by Bloom (see Chapter 4) and has been extensively developed, tested, and implemented by Bloom and his colleagues. The organization of instruction on task characteristics rather than on time periods should have important consequences for the distribution of instructional time variables and, therefore, for student learning. The effect of organization of instruction on task appropriateness should be especially pronounced.

DOES RESEARCH ON INSTRUCTIONAL TIME HAVE IMPLICATIONS FOR TEACHER EVALUATION?

There is a growing interest in many states in the use of teacher-evaluation systems, both to identify master teachers and to identify inadequate teachers. In many states, there is concern about providing ample rewards for the former and retraining or counseling for the latter. The recent surge of concern about teacher evaluation builds on some basic premises: First, excellent as well as inadequate teachers exist; second, procedures exist to reliably identify these teachers; and third, deficiencies in teaching skills can be remediated through special in-service training programs.

A recent examination of teacher-evaluation programs (Wise, Darling-Hammond, McLaughlin, & Bernstein, 1984) reveals that some exemplary programs exist. Some of the exemplary programs use instruments for assessing teacher performance based on findings from research on teaching. Some use systems based on views of instruction derived from educational authorities, such as Madeline Hunter (1984). Some of the exemplary systems are run by the unions; some include community groups in the process. Student achievement is seen in many of the exemplary programs as a less important indicator of effective and ineffective teaching than are observable in-class teaching processes.

Conspicuous among the variables that underlie many classroom-based observational evaluation systems is the concept of time-on-task. Virtually all evaluators of teachers acknowledge the importance of this variable, though measurement techniques may vary. As noted by Barr and Dreeben in Chapter 6, no matter what level of schooling one is interested in, time is the coin of the realm. As seen by Wang (Chapter 14) and by Leinhardt (Chapter 15), classroom studies of teaching completed as part of educational program evaluations would be inadequate without concern for time-on-task and related time-based variables. Time, in its different manifestations (time-on-task, total time spent in a curriculum area, opportunity to learn, pace, success rate, etc.), is almost always seen by evaluators as a scarce resource. Therefore, the allocation of these different time-based measures usually is included in any systematic evaluation of classroom teaching. As Fenstermacher noted in Chapter 5, because time can be considered the terminus of teaching, it plays a prominent role in the evaluation of teachers and teaching.

Recent pilot work by Berliner has shown that a set of time-based measures derived from the Beginning Teacher Evaluation Study (Fisher et al., 1980), predicts classroom achievement on standardized tests quite well. The time variables were used to identify classrooms at risk, that is, classrooms predicted to perform relatively low on the California Achievement Test. Included in the set of variables were time allocated to a curriculum area, engaged time in a curriculum area, transition time, time lost due to interruptions, and time spent in high-success pursuits. These variables, entered as predictors in regression equations, almost always accounted for a substantial percent of variance in residualized achievement-test scores on standardized tests in grades two through six. Because of the empirical relationship of these variables with outcome measures of this type, such variables can, with a reasonable degree of accuracy, predict which classrooms will do well and which classrooms will do poorly on standardized tests. Evaluation systems that use time-based variables are soon likely to be developed to the point where they can reliably identify classrooms that are more or less "at risk," at least in terms of standardized test scores. Such evaluation systems, though now apparently feasible from a technical standpoint, are likely to meet resistance due to social and political considerations. The evaluation systems probably will not fail because of inadequate choice of variables for prediction of achievement.

HOW DOES RESEARCH ON INSTRUCTIONAL TIME RELATE TO CURRENT CONCERNS ABOUT CLASSROOM DISCIPLINE AND EFFICIENCY?

Research on instructional time has provided, among other things, concrete descriptions of how individual students spend time during school. Although the choice of categories used to depict student behavior varies among studies, few studies fail to include some version of time-on-task. Many other categories of student activity are included in studies of instructional time, but for some reason, time-on-task seems to have surprisingly high saliency for many researchers and research readers. Why is this so? When research studies find wide variation in student time-on-task, there is too often a tendency to conclude that low time-on-task is caused by discipline problems. There are those who say that if only students had more discipline, then more learning would occur in schools. This attribution certainly reflects our long-standing concern over control and authority in schools. It also tends to locate responsibility for low attention or low time-on-task solely with the student. There are times when such an attribution would seem to be justified. However, the same data could allow other interpretations. In many cases, low time-on-task may signal that the task is inappropriate for the student in question, or that the task conditions are in some way inappropriate. When tasks are inappropriate in some way for students, student misbehavior is often a by-product. In such situations, low time-on-task and student behavior that could be labeled a discipline problem are likely to occur together. However, attending to the discipline of students is unlikely to be a productive strategy for increasing learning of the intended skills, since "discipline," in this case, is the symptom rather than the disease itself. The research on instructional time provides an opportunity to examine the responses of students to different instructional tasks and task conditions. From this point of view, we believe that the research has great potential for reducing some discipline problems by influencing the development of higher-quality instruction.

Research on instructional time has been criticized for its focus on efficiency of instructional systems. The use of time as a common metric for instructional variables invites comparisons among variables. Time variables also can be easily transformed into rate variables and thereby encourage value judgments regarding more and less efficient instructional configurations. Certainly, there is great potential for misinterpretation when qualitatively different variables are measured in the same metric. There is also the danger that efficiency may become an end in itself rather than being one dimension on which to judge the relative merit of alternative instructional procedures and sequences. In spite of these potential dangers, identification and development of relatively efficient procedures for the attainment of valid instructional goals appears to us to warrant continued pursuit. The issue may not be the pursuit of efficiency, but rather the manner in which efficiency is pursued.

Given that information is available about time-on-task for a particular classroom, efficiency could be increased by two sets of actions. One could proceed to maximize the time-on-task or to minimize the time-off-task. Quite different learning environments would be likely to result, depending upon whether the major focus was on increasing the time-on-task or on decreasing the time-off-task. A consistent and pronounced focus on the latter could lead to a somewhat repressive learning environment. In cases of practical interest, the appropriate strategy is likely to involve a balanced approach wherein actions are taken to increase time-on-task and decrease time-off-task.

DOES RESEARCH ON INSTRUCTIONAL TIME HAVE IMPLICATIONS FOR EDUCATIONAL RESEARCH IN GENERAL?

There are three areas where research on instructional time is particularly instructive to all educational researchers. These areas have to do with the duration of treatments, the distinction between nominal and effective stimuli, and improvement in the specification of variables for research in education.

E. L. Thorndike launched modern learning theory with a description of his laws of learning. One of these, the law of practice, emphasized the positive effect of duration on learning. Few people, before or after Thorndike, ever believed otherwise. Contemporary educational research, concerned as it is with time-based variables, provides continuing evidence about the importance of the law of practice and reminds us of the importance of duration when comparing the effects of different treatments. If time is not held constant across treatments, then the possibility of some misinterpretation of findings is very high. For example, when comparing computer-assisted instruction with other instructional systems, or when comparing alternative programs of bilingual education, the research is simply inadequate unless descriptions of the treatments include measurement of instructional time. We are concerned that many educational researchers underestimate dramatically the sheer amount of time needed to produce changes in student behavior. Thus, we believe that instructional-time data are needed both to compare the effects of different treatments and to evaluate the validity of the treatments themselves. Just as the research community has learned to do an analysis of statistical power before choosing a specific sample size needed to declare a difference of a certain given magnitude to be statistically significant, so do we also need to estimate the duration of the treatment needed to produce changes that are of practical significance. Unless duration is taken seriously in designing treatments and in interpreting data from treatment comparisons in educational experiments, the potential for reaching faulty conclusions about the effects of educational treatments is quite high.

But duration alone describes only the nominal stimulus. The real educational treatment is what is actually attended to and processed by the student—the effective stimulus. Time-on-task or engaged time is a crude indicator of the internal processing of information by a student. Educational research that concerns itself with nominal treatments, and ignores differences in engaged time across treatments, is in danger of ascribing effects to the wrong factors. For example, we have seen research studies that appeared to be unconcerned about whether classrooms used to pilot new curricula showed large differences in attending rates. What we have seen is research comparing teachers whose classes have low attending rates during regular instruction to classes using high-quality television shows or exciting computer software. Attribution of instructional effects to characteristics of the innovative materials or medium is impossible when large differences in the effective stimulus exist between treatments. We may mistakenly attribute effects of the effective-stimulus-situation treatment to the nominal treatment.

Finally, we note how research on instructional time has helped in specifying educational variables with more precision. We have moved from a productive but quite molar concern about the duration of events, to a set of concerns about student attending behavior, to an even more complex variable comprised of allocated time, student attention, and student success rate. The variables used in research on instructional time get more complex and more precise as this research continues.

SUMMARY

The many perspectives on instructional time that have beem presented in this volume have influenced our thinking about a number of issues. We reiterate, for the last time, our beliefs. We believe that research on instructional time need not necessarily be trivial either in conception or in implications, despite Professor Phillips's analysis. And we can only agree with Professor Scriven, that Professor Jackson might have felt more positive if he had been on-task for more of the meetings he attended. We have argued that research on instructional time can be used to modify instructional practices, and thereby improve schools. The research also has been shown to relate to concerns about teacher evaluation, classroom discipline, and school efficiency. Finally, we note that research on instructional time informs all researchers by influencing the design of educational studies. In our opinion, Professor Carroll can be justly proud of what he has wrought.

REFERENCES

Anastasi, A. (1958). *Differential psychology*. New York: Macmillan.

Berliner, D. C. (1971). *Aptitude-treatment interactions in two studies of learning from lecture instruction*. Paper presented at the meeting of the American Educational Research Association, New York.

Biles, B., Billups, L., & Veitch, S. (undated). *Training and resource manual* (Vol. 1). Educational Research and Dissemination Program. New York: American Federation of Teachers.

Conant, J. B. (1963). *The education of American teachers*. New York: McGraw-Hill.

Emmer, E. T., Evertson, C. M., Sanford, J. P., Clement, B. S., & Worsham, M. E. (1984). *Classroom management for secondary teachers*. Englewood Cliffs, N.J.: Prentice-Hall.

Evertson, C. M., Emmer, E. T., Clement, B. S., Sanford, J. P., & Worsham, M. E. (1984) *Classroom management for elementary teachers*. Englewood Cliffs, N.J.: Prentice-Hall.

Fisher, C. W., Berliner, D. C., Filby, N. N., Marliave, R. S., Cahen, L. S., & Dishaw, M. M. (1980). Teaching behaviors, academic learning time and student achievement: An overview. In C. Denham and A. Lieberman (Eds.), *Time to learn*. Washington, D.C.: Department of Education, National Institute of Education.

Fisher, C. W., Filby, N. N., Marliave, R. S., Cahen, L. S., Dishaw, M. M., Moore, J., & Berliner, D. C. (1978) *Teaching behaviors, academic learning time and student achievement: Final report of Phase III-B, Beginning Teacher*

Evaluation Study. San Francisco: Far West Laboratory for Educational Research and Development.

Gage, N. L., & Berliner, D. C. (1975). *Educational psychology* (1st ed.). Chicago: Rand-McNally.

Gagne, R. M. (1962). Military training and principles of learning. *American Psychologist, 17*, 83–91.

Good, T. L., & Grouws, D. H. (1979). The Missouri Mathematics Effectiveness Project: An experimental study in fourth grade classrooms. *Journal of Educational Psychology, 71*, 335–362.

Gronlund, N. E. (1959). *Sociometry in the classroom*. New York: Harper & Row.

Hunter, M. (1984). Knowing, teaching, and supervising. In P. H. Hosford (Ed.), *Using what we know about teaching*. Alexandria, Va.: Association for Supervision and Curriculum Development.

Karweit, N. L. (1984, January). *Time-on-task: A research review*. Research Report No. 332. Baltimore, Md.: The Johns Hopkins University, Center for Social Organization of Schools.

Klausmeier, H. J., & Davis, J. K. (1969). Transfer of learning. In R. L. Ebel (Ed.), *Encyclopedia of educational research* (4th ed.). London: Macmillan.

Lazarsfeld, P. F. (1949). The American soldier—an expository review. *Public Opinion Quarterly, 13*, 377–404.

McDonald, F. J., & Elias, P. (1976). *Executive summary report: Beginning Teacher Evaluation Study, Phase II*. Princeton, N.J.: Educational Testing Service.

Muir, R. (1980). A teacher implements instructional changes using the BTES framework. In C. Denham & A. Lieberman (Eds.), *Time to Learn*. Washington, D.C.: National Institute of Education.

Noli, P. (1980). A principal implements BTES. In C. Denham & A. Lieberman (Eds.), *Time to Learn*. Washington, D.C.: National Institute of Education.

Rauth, M., Biles, B., Billups, L., & Veitch, S. (1983). American Federation of Teachers: Educational Research and Dissemination Program Final Report: AFL-CIO. Educational issues department.

Rossmiller, R. A. (1982, September). *Managing school resources to improve student achievement*. Paper presented at the state superintendent conference for district administrators, Madison, Wis.

Samuels, S. J. (1970). Effects of pictures on learning to read, comprehension and attitudes. *Review of Educational Research, 40*, 397–407.

Schramm, W. (1964). Research on programmed instruction: An annotated bibliography (OE Contract No. 34034). Washington, D.C.: U.S. Office of Education.

Sparks, G. M., & Sparks, D. (1984). *Effective teaching for higher achievement*. (Workbook and two videotapes.) Alexandria, Va.: Association for Supervision and Curriculum Development.

Stallings, J., & Kaskowitz, D. (1974). *Follow through classroom observations evaluations, 1972–1973*. Menlo Park, Calif.: Stanford Research Institute.

Thompson, W. N. (1967) *Quantitative research in public address and communication*. New York: Random House.

Wise, A., Darling-Hammond, L., McLaughlin, M. W., & Bernstein, H. T. (1984, June). *Teacher evaluation: A study of effective practices*. Final report on Contract # NIE-400-82-007. Washington, D.C.: National Institute of Education.

Index

BARBARA LARRIVEE, *Effective Teaching for Successful Mainstreaming*

GRETA MORINE-DERSHIMER, *Talking, Listening, and Learning in Elementary Classrooms*

FORTHCOMING

DEE ANN SPENCER, *Contemporary Women Teachers: Balancing School and Home*